THE PERFORMANCE OF INTERNATIONAL COURTS AND TRIBUNALS

International courts and tribunals now operate globally and in several world regions, playing significant roles in international law and global governance. However, these courts vary significantly in terms of their practices, procedures, and the outcomes they produce. Why do some international courts perform better than others? Which factors affect the outcomes of these courts and tribunals? *The Performance of International Courts and Tribunals* is an interdisciplinary study featuring approaches, methods, and scholarship from law and political science, which proposes the concept of performance to describe the processes and outcomes of international courts. It develops a framework for evaluating and explaining performance by offering a broad comparative analysis of international courts, covering several world regions and the areas of trade, investment, human rights, and criminal law, and offers interdisciplinary accounts to explain how and why international court performance varies.

THERESA SQUATRITO is Assistant Professor/Lecturer in the Department of Politics at the University of Liverpool.

ORAN R. YOUNG is Professor Emeritus at the Bren School of Environmental Science and Management, University of California, Santa Barbara.

ANDREAS FOLLESDAL is Professor of Philosophy at the University of Oslo.

GEIR ULFSTEIN is Professor of Law at the University of Oslo.

STUDIES ON INTERNATIONAL COURTS AND TRIBUNALS

General Editors

Andreas Follesdal, University of Oslo
Geir Ulfstein, University of Oslo

Studies on International Courts and Tribunals contains theoretical and interdisciplinary scholarship on legal aspects as well as the legitimacy and effectiveness of international courts and tribunals.

Other Books in the Series:

Mads Andenas and Eirik Bjorge (eds.) *A Farewell to Fragmentation: Reassertion and Convergence in International Law*

Cecilia M. Bailliet and Nobuo Hayashi (eds.) *The Legitimacy of International Criminal Tribunals*

Amrei Müller with Hege Elisabeth Kjos (eds.) *Judicial Dialogue and Human Rights*

Harlan Grant Cohen and Andreas Follesdal (eds.) *Legitimacy and International Courts*

Robert Howse and Geir Ulfstein (eds.) *The Legitimacy of International Trade Courts and Tribunals*

THE PERFORMANCE OF INTERNATIONAL COURTS AND TRIBUNALS

Edited by

THERESA SQUATRITO

University of Liverpool

ORAN R. YOUNG

University of California, Santa Barbara

ANDREAS FOLLESDAL

University of Oslo

GEIR ULFSTEIN

University of Oslo

CAMBRIDGE
UNIVERSITY PRESS

CAMBRIDGE
UNIVERSITY PRESS

University Printing House, Cambridge CB2 8BS, United Kingdom

One Liberty Plaza, 20th Floor, New York, NY 10006, USA

477 Williamstown Road, Port Melbourne, VIC 3207, Australia

314–321, 3rd Floor, Plot 3, Splendor Forum, Jasola District Centre, New Delhi – 110025, India

79 Anson Road, #06–04/06, Singapore 079906

Cambridge University Press is part of the University of Cambridge.

It furthers the University's mission by disseminating knowledge in the pursuit of education, learning, and research at the highest international levels of excellence.

www.cambridge.org
Information on this title: www.cambridge.org/9781108425698
DOI: 10.1017/9781108348768

First published 2018

Printed in the United Kingdom by Clays, St Ives plc

A catalogue record for this publication is available from the British Library.

Library of Congress Cataloging-in-Publication Data
Names: Squatrito, Theresa, editor. | Young, Oran R., editor. | Føllesdal, Andreas, editor. | Ulfstein, Geir, 1951– editor.
Title: The performance of international courts and tribunals / edited by Theresa Squatrito, University of Liverpool; Oran Young, University of California, Santa Barbara; Andreas Føllesdal, University of Oslo; Geir Ulfstein, University of Oslo.
Description: Cambridge [UK] ; New York, NY : Cambrdige University Press, 2018. | Series: Studies on international courts and tribunals
Identifiers: LCCN 2017051170 | ISBN 9781108425698
Subjects: LCSH: International courts.
Classification: LCC KZ6250 .P45 2018 | DDC 341.5/5–dc23
LC record available at https://lccn.loc.gov/2017051170

ISBN 978-1-108-42569-8 Hardback

CONTENTS

FIGURES

TABLES

MAPS

CONTRIBUTORS

STEINAR ANDRESEN is a political scientist from the University of Oslo, currently working as a research professor at the Fridtjof Nansen Institute in Norway where he has also been a research director. He has been a professor at the Department of Political Science, University of Oslo, and an adjunct professor at the PluriCourts Centre. He has been affiliated with a number of international research institutions including Princeton University and the Brookings Institution. He has published extensively internationally, including nine books, and has been a guest editor of several international journals. Most of his publications are on international environmental governance.

DANIEL BEHN is a Postdoctoral Research Fellow in International Dispute Settlement at the PluriCourts Centre, Faculty of Law, University of Oslo. His previous working experience includes legal practice in international arbitration and legal consultancy positions for institutions such as the World Bank. He is an associate editor for the *Journal of World Investment and Trade* and a member of Executive Council of the Yale Policy Sciences Society.

COSETTE D. CREAMER is the Benjamin E. Lippincott Chair in Political Economy and Assistant Professor in the Department of Political Science and Law School at the University of Minnesota. She holds a JD from Harvard Law School and a PhD from the Department of Government, Harvard University.

NICOLE DE SILVA is Assistant Professor of Political Science at Concordia University in Montreal. She was previously the IKEA Research Fellow in International Relations at the University of Oxford. Her research broadly focuses on international organizations and international law in regional and global governance. She is currently examining the politics of international courts, particularly in the areas of human rights and international criminal justice. Her research on how international courts promote compliance with international law received the International Studies Association's Lawrence Finkelstein Award, and her study of African states' opposition to the International Criminal Court received the British International Studies Association's *African Affairs* Prize and the International Studies Association's Stephen C. Poe Award.

JEFFREY L. DUNOFF is Laura H. Carnell Professor at Temple University Beasley School of Law. His research and writing focus on public international law, international courts, international organizations, international regulatory regimes, including international trade law, and interdisciplinary approaches to international law. His publications include *Interdisciplinary Perspectives on International Law and International Relations: The State of the Art* (coedited with Mark A. Pollack, Cambridge, 2012), and *Ruling the World?, Constitutionalism, International Law, and Global Governance* (coedited with Joel P. Trachtman, Cambridge, 2009). He is currently working with Mark Pollack on an interdisciplinary research project on international judicial practices.

BENJAMIN FAUDE is Senior Research Fellow in the Global Governance Department at the WZB Berlin Social Science Center. His research focuses on the implications of institutional overlap on global governance. After visiting scholarships at the University of California at Berkeley and the Vrije Universiteit, Brussels, he joined the WZB in 2011, coming from the University of Bamberg, where he held a grant from the DFG Training Group on "Markets and Social Systems in Europe" and earned a doctorate (*summa cum laude*). Faude has published his research in various international journals such as *The Review of International Organizations*, *Global Governance*, and *Global Environmental Politics*. Recently, he published his first book *Von Konkurrenz zu Arbeitsteilung: Komplexität und Dynamik im Zusammenspiel internationaler Institutionen* [From Competition to Division of Labor: Complexity and Dynamics in the Interplay of International Institutions]. Faude has taught at the University of Bamberg, at Free University Berlin, and at Charles University in Prague.

ANDREAS FOLLESDAL is Professor of Political Philosophy in the Faculty of Law at the University of Oslo. He is a codirector of the

PluriCourts Centre. He publishes in the field of political philosophy, mainly on issues of international political theory, globalization/ Europeanization, human rights, and socially responsible investing.

CHIARA GIORGETTI is Associate Professor of Law at Richmond Law School. She teaches and writes in the areas of public international law, international arbitration, international dispute resolution, and state failure and fragility. Her scholarship has appeared in the *American Journal of International Law*, the *Colombia Journal of Transnational Law*, and the *University of Pennsylvania Journal of International Law*. Professor Giorgetti is a member of the Executive Council and Executive Committee of the American Society of International Law. She is a codirector of Studies of the American Branch of the International Law Association, a member of the board of the International Law Students Association, and a Vice-Chair of the Academic Council of the Institute for Transnational Arbitration. Prior to joining the Richmond Law faculty in 2012, Professor Giorgetti practiced international arbitration in Washington, DC, and Geneva, Switzerland, and worked extensively with the United Nations in New York and Somalia. Professor Giorgetti clerked at the International Court of Justice in The Hague. She holds an LLM and JSD from Yale Law School, an MSc from the London School of Economics, and a Law Degree (Laurea) from Bologna University.

NOBUO HAYASHI specializes in the law of armed conflict, international criminal law, and public international law. His most significant works cover military necessity, threat of force, and the law and ethics of nuclear weapons. He has over seventeen years of experience performing advanced research, advising international prosecutors, authoring court submissions, teaching at universities, and publishing scholarly articles in the aforementioned areas as well as other related fields. Major positions he has held include: Senior Legal Advisor, International Law and Policy Institute; Visiting Lecturer, UN Interregional Crime and Justice Research Institute; Researcher, PluriCourts, Faculty of Law, University of Oslo; Visiting Professor, International University of Japan; Researcher, Peace Research Institute Oslo; Legal Advisor, Norwegian Centre for Human Rights; Legal Officer, Prosecutions Division, Office of the Prosecutor (OTP); International Criminal Tribunal for the Former Yugoslavia (ICTY); and Associate Legal Officer, ICTY OTP Legal Advisory Section.

HYERAN JO is Associate Professor of Political Science at Texas A&M University. She is the author of *Compliant Rebels: Rebel Groups and International Law in World Politics* (Cambridge, 2015). Her other works appeared in *International Organization, British Journal of Political Science, Journal of Conflict Resolution*, as well as in several edited volumes. She studies international institutions and international law, focusing on the role of international involvement in conflict zones around the world.

MARK A. POLLACK is Professor of Political Science and Law, Jean Monnet Chair, and Director of Global Studies at Temple University, where he conducts research on international law and international relations and on the European Union. He has published widely on these subjects, including most recently *Interdisciplinary Perspectives on International Law and International Relations: The State of the Art* (coedited with Jeffrey L. Dunoff, Cambridge, 2013), and *Who Supports International Law, and Why? The United States, the European Union, and the International Legal Order*, a special issue of the *International Journal of Constitutional Law* (Vol. 13, No. 4, 2015). He is currently working on a project, with Jeffrey L. Dunoff, on international judicial practices.

MITCHELL RADTKE is a Visiting Assistant Professor at St. Olaf College. His research interests include international conflict, autocratic decision-making, economic sanctions, and international intervention. His dissertation focused on the effect of cronyism and nepotism on autocracies' conflict behavior. He has recently published in *International Studies Quarterly*.

DINAH SHELTON is the Manatt/Ahn Professor Emeritus at the George Washington University Law School. She served as a member of the Inter-American Human Rights Commission (2010–2014) and in 2010 she was president of the Commission. Professor Shelton is the author of three prize-winning books, *Protecting Human Rights in the Americas* (coauthored with Thomas Buergenthal), *Remedies in International Human Rights Law*, and the three-volume *Encyclopedia of Genocide and Crimes against Humanity*. She has also authored other articles and books on international law, human rights law, and international environmental law. Professor Shelton is a member of the board of editors of the American Journal of International Law. She has served as a legal consultant to international organizations and is on the board of numerous human rights and environmental organizations. In 2006, Professor Shelton was awarded the Elisabeth Haub Prize for Environmental Law and, in 2013, she received the Goler Butcher Prize in Human Rights. She was conferred the degree of doctor *honoris causa* at the University of Stockholm in 2012 and the Pazmany Peter Catholic University of Budapest in 2014.

BETH A. SIMMONS is Andrea Mitchell University Professor of Law, Political Science and Business Ethics at the University of Pennsylvania. She received her PhD from Harvard University in the Department of Government, and she researchers and teaches international relations, international law, and international political economy. She has held positions at Duke University, the University of California at Berkeley, and Harvard University. Her current areas of research include improving international human rights, the effects of rankings systems on state policy choices, and the thickening of international borders despite globalization. Two of her most prominent prize-winning books are *Who Adjusts? Domestic Sources of Foreign Economic Policy During the Interwar Years* (2004) and *Mobilizing for Human Rights: International Law in Domestic Politics* (2009). She has been elected to the National Academy of Sciences, the American Academy of Arts and Sciences, and the American Philosophical Society.

THERESA SQUATRITO is Assistant Professor/Lecturer in Politics and International Relations in the Department of Politics at the University of Liverpool. She was previously a postdoctoral research fellow at the PluriCourts Centre at the University of Oslo and with the Transdemos Program at Stockholm University. She has a PhD in political science from the University of Washington, Seattle. Her research focuses on international institutions, including international law, international organizations, and international courts. She is a coauthor of *The Opening Up of International Organizations: Transnational Access in Global Governance*. Her research has appeared in several internationally recognized journals, including *International Organization*, *The Review of International Organizations*, and *The Review of International Studies*.

ANTON STREZHNEV is a PhD Candidate in the Department of Government at Harvard University. His research focuses on the political economy of law and the governance of international trade and investment with an emphasis on investor-state dispute resolution.

GEIR ULFSTEIN is Professor of International Law at the Department of Public and International Law, University of Oslo and a codirector of PluriCourts Centre at the University of Oslo. He has published in different areas of international law, including the law of the sea, international environmental law, international human rights, and international institutional law.

ORAN R. YOUNG is Professor Emeritus in the Bren School of Environmental Science and Management at the University of California (Santa Barbara). His theoretical work deals with the role of social institutions as steering mechanisms developed to solve a variety of societal problems and to guide societies toward the achievement of desired outcomes. He is closely associated with the rise of the concept of governance as a social function in contrast to government as an assemblage of organizations that often play important roles in fulfilling needs for governance. His applied work deals with issues of governance pertaining to the oceans, atmospheric issues including climate change, and the polar regions.

ACKNOWLEDGMENTS

This volume emerged from a stimulating exchange maintained over several workshops. We thank participants at two workshops on the effectiveness and performance of international courts and tribunals, at Harvard University and Temple University, for the insightful comments. In addition to the contributors of this book, participants included Karen Alter, Bill Burke White, Xinyuan Dai, Meg deGuzman, Larry Helfer, Jaya Ramji-Nogales, Ruth Mackenzie, Kathryn Sikkink, Jonas Tallberg, Joel Trachtman, and Erik Voeten. We thank the Weatherhead Center for International Affairs at Harvard and the Law School at Temple for generously hosting these workshops. Earlier drafts of the Introduction were presented at the 2015 Annual Convention of the International Studies Association, the 2015 General Conference of the European Consortium for Political Research, and the 2015 Annual Meeting of the American Political Science Association. We are grateful to Tana Johnson, Ronny Patz, and Carmela Lutmar for their remarks as discussants. Both the research and the workshops were supported in part by the Research Council of Norway through its Centres of Excellence Funding Scheme, project number 223274 – PluriCourts: The Legitimacy of the International Judiciary. We thank our colleagues at PluriCourts at the University of Oslo and participants at the 2015 PluriCourts Annual Conference for their comments. We are grateful for research assistance by Annette Hovdal, Claire Poppelwell-Scevak, and Eirik Torsvoll.

Introduction

1

A Framework for Evaluating the Performance of International Courts and Tribunals

THERESA SQUATRITO, ORAN R. YOUNG, ANDREAS FOLLESDAL, AND GEIR ULFSTEIN

Introduction

Many analysts have noted a trend toward the legalization of international affairs in recent decades (Goldstein et al. 2000). While the extent of this development is hard to measure, one significant feature of legalization is unmistakable. We have witnessed a proliferation of international courts and tribunals (ICs).[1] Such bodies now operate globally and in several regions of the world; they play significant roles in the application and interpretation of many elements of international law. ICs address issues of regional integration, trade, and economic relations. They have become important elements in human rights systems in Europe, the Americas, and Africa. ICs are integral to the development of international criminal law and help to determine territorial and maritime boundaries.

There is significant variation among ICs regarding not only their mandates, but also the practices they have adopted and the effects of their rulings. International courts vary greatly with regard to their level of activity. Some courts are extremely busy institutions. The European Court of Human Rights (ECtHR) and the Court of Justice of the European Union (CJEU)[2] both issue hundreds of decisions annually. The ECtHR issued 916 judgments responding to 3,659 applications in 2013, while the CJEU issued 1322 decisions by judgment or order in 2013.[3] On the other hand, there are courts

[1] We use the abbreviation ICs rather than ICTs to avoid confusion with international criminal tribunals.

[2] Formerly known as the European Court of Justice (ECJ).

[3] The figures for the CJEU include the decisions of the General Court and the Court of Justice. For statistics on the ECtHR's judicial activity, see www.echr.coe.int/Pages/home.aspx?p=reports&c= (accessed July 27, 2017). For statistics on the judicial activity of the CJEU, see http://curia.europa.eu/jcms/jcms/Jo2_7000/ (accessed July 27, 2017).

like the International Court of Justice (ICJ) that hear only a handful of cases in any given year. ICs differ also in their practices pertaining to access, transparency and confidentiality, fact-finding, standards of review, methods of interpretation, and more.

Some ICs have become "islands" of litigation, generally addressing a narrower set of legal questions than their mandates cover. Approximately 90 percent of the cases on the docket of the Andean Tribunal of Justice, for example, pertain to intellectual property law, though the mandate of the Court is much broader (Helfer et al. 2009). On the other hand, there are courts that have exercised authority across the entire scope of their mandate; some have even expanded their jurisdiction. Similarly, some ICs have demonstrated judicial activism, while others have shown judicial restraint.

Several international courts have encountered serious problems, facing backlogs in their caseloads, backlash on the part of member states, or failure to become operational. The ECtHR, for example, is saddled with an overwhelming backlog of cases; it had a backlog of 99,900 applications in 2013. The Southern African Development Community (SADC) Tribunal's operations were suspended as a result of backlash on the part of Zimbabwe. Twenty ICs have never become operational or became defunct after deciding only a few cases (Romano 2014).

ICs have made varying contributions to global governance. First, ICs often contribute to state compliance with international legal commitments, though at times they have sparked defiance, as in the case of the SADC Tribunal. Some ICs have been able to influence the behavior of states, encouraging them to adjust domestic laws to comply with international law. Others provide remedies by identifying appropriate compensatory measures for noncompliance. Second, some ICs have influenced the establishment and the work of other ICs, while others have not had such effects. The International Criminal Court (ICC), for instance, has been shaped by the International Criminal Tribunal for the former Yugoslavia (ICTY) and the International Criminal Tribunal for Rwanda (ICTR). Third, ICs have contributed to broader processes of global governance. The CJEU, for example, has been central to the institutionalization of regional integration in Europe (Burley and Mattli 1993; Mattli and Slaughter 1998; Stone Sweet 2004); the Dispute Settlement Mechanism (DSM) of the World Trade Organization (WTO) has facilitated trade relations globally (Rosendorff 2005; Goldstein et al. 2007; Davis 2012). Evidence has established a link between international criminal prosecutions and processes of democratization (Sikkink 2011). Some attribute the judicialization of international affairs and constitutionalization of international law to the experiences of the CJEU, ECtHR, the WTO DSM, and others.

As a matter of fact, then, there is a great deal of variation in the *performance* of international courts. This observation raises several critical questions. How should we think about performance in this context? How can we measure performance in specific cases? Why do some ICs perform better than others? What are the determinants of the performance of these courts? Are there ways to improve the performance of international courts? These are the concerns that motivate the contributions to this book.

The Study of Judicial Performance

While prior studies have tended to focus on specific questions relating either to the design or to the effects of international courts, we develop an integrated framework for the study of the performance of ICs. Using this framework, the contributors to this volume present empirical assessments of the performance of international courts that consider both the results that courts produce and the procedures guiding their operation. We explore factors that may explain the patterns of performance we observe.

This study of IC performance takes a broad comparative approach covering the full array of international courts and tribunals. We define the universe of cases to encompass international judicial bodies that: (1) decide the question(s) brought before them on the basis of international law; (2) follow pre-determined rules of procedure; (3) issue legally binding decisions or opinions; (4) are composed of independent members; and (5) require that at least one party to a dispute be a state or an international organization (Romano et al. 2014: 6). While some analysts may argue that international criminal tribunals do not fulfill the fifth criterion, the office of a prosecutor, an organ of an international organization, is one of the parties to disputes in international criminal tribunals (Romano et al. 2014: 7). While ICs can issue nonbinding opinions (i.e., advisory opinions) in addition to legally binding decisions, this definition excludes quasi-judicial bodies, such as the United Nations human rights treaty bodies, which issue only nonbinding recommendations. In addition to permanent bodies, we include ad hoc judicial bodies that meet these criteria, such as investor-state arbitration tribunals.[4] This allows us to assess the extent to which permanence contributes to performance. We include a range of ICs spanning several issue areas, including human rights, trade, investment, and criminal law.

We are interested both in the outcomes courts produce and the processes through which they arrive at judgments. Drawing on research dealing with the performance of international organizations (Gutner and Thompson 2010), we label these dimensions *outcome performance* and *process performance*. Outcome performance refers to the degree to which ICs attain substantive goals. Process performance, on the other hand, is a matter of the degree to which IC practices measure up to intended or aspired procedural standards.

There are several reasons to study the performance of international courts. For one thing, the performance of these courts affects their legitimacy. As Buchanan and Keohane argue, "If an institution exhibits a pattern of egregious disparity between its actual performance, on the one hand, and its self-proclaimed procedures or major goals, on the other, its legitimacy is seriously called into question" (2006: 422). A court's performance may also affect levels of popular support or the politicization of international legal processes (e.g., see Helfer and Alter 2013). Understanding the performance of ICs has implications as well for the design and reform of international courts. Knowing the determinants of good and bad performance can help in identifying what reform efforts are merited and how reform should proceed. Observers of the European Court of Human Rights, for example, have noted that reform efforts have been informed by policy-relevant assessments of the Court's performance. In addition, the performance of ICs can have implications for the effectiveness of international regimes or governance systems in which they are embedded. Thus, studying IC performance may advance our understanding of effectiveness of international regimes or governance systems.

The study of performance draws on existing research on the performance of international organizations (Gutner and Thompson 2010; Tallberg et al. 2016) and international environmental institutions (Mitchell 2008) as well as research on the effectiveness of international courts (Shany 2014) and international regimes or governance systems (Young 1999; Miles et al. 2002; Hovi et al. 2003; Breitmeier et al. 2006). The literature

[4] Permanence does not refer to whether the court or tribunal itself is permanent. Instead, it means that "they are made of a group of judges who are sitting permanently and are not selected ad hoc by the parties for any given case" (Romano 2011: 262).

on international regimes, governance systems, and social institutions more broadly has focused on the extent to which these arrangements contribute to solving problems (e.g., the depletion of stratospheric ozone, the occurrence of genocide) or steering systems toward socially desirable outcomes (e.g., increased trade, enhanced respect for human rights). The term effectiveness in this literature refers to a measure of the success of regimes and governance systems in solving problems or moving systems toward desired outcomes.

International courts, in our view, are tools or mechanisms that play a number of roles in regimes or governance systems. It is worth differentiating among several distinct roles in this regard. First, courts play roles within individual regimes or governance systems by providing authoritative interpretations of the meaning of a regime's rules, adapting rules to new circumstances, resolving disagreements among parties regarding the meaning of the rules, and helping to ensure compliance on the part of those subject to a regime's rules. Second, courts help to sort out tensions or conflicts between individual regimes or governance systems. This is typically a matter of determining the spheres of applicability of different rules or determining which rules take precedence over others in cases of conflict. Third, courts play a broader role in ensuring that the operations of international regimes or governance systems conform to overarching principles, norms, and values applicable above the level of individual regimes or governance systems. In many cases, this is a matter of ensuring that individual regimes or governance systems adhere to procedural norms like those associated with the idea of fairness.

To know whether regimes or governance systems are effective, then, we argue that it is imperative to ask whether international courts perform their roles well or poorly. The existence of courts that perform well can and often will contribute to the effectiveness of international regimes or governance systems, but there is nothing automatic about this relationship. It is possible to imagine regimes that are successful in solving various problems even in the absence of courts that perform well. Conversely, we can imagine regimes that fail to solve problems, despite the existence of courts that perform their roles well. The relationship between the effectiveness of international regimes or governance systems and the performance of international courts is a matter that merits careful analysis.

Assessing the performance of international courts, on this account, is a matter that extends beyond the intentions of those who create them. Creators may or may not articulate the roles they expect international courts to play. Moreover, creators may not agree on what roles courts are intended to have. Whether or not the creators are explicit about these matters, however, we can ask questions about the performance of a court in interpreting and adapting rules, sorting out tensions among different regimes, and encouraging adherence to broader principles and norms. As Mitchell observes in his general account of institutional performance, "performance analysis seeks to identify how much an institution contributed to whatever progress was made toward a specified goal" (2008: 79). But as he goes on to say, the relevant goals may be specified by "the creators of the institution, other interested parties, or the evaluator" rather than reflecting only the intentions of the creators (79). In this sense, our focus on performance is similar to Shany's analysis of the "effectiveness" of international courts comparing ". . . actual impacts with desired outcomes, or performance with expectations . . . in the eyes of multiple constituencies" (2014: 6). Unlike Shany, however, we employ the concept of performance to capture a broad set of goals identified by analysts as well as relevant constituencies.

There is an inescapable normative dimension to any study of the performance of international courts. A study of the performance of ICs that looks beyond the intentions of the creators is compatible with evidence suggesting that the effects of these courts go well beyond initial intentions. As Caron argues: "When assessing the value . . . of international courts and tribunals scholars should not only proceed in terms of how well a given institution serves its constituted ends, but also how well it serves the unstated purposes" (2006: 410). More generally, there are normatively grounded differences among observers regarding the proper interpretation of a regime's rules, the precedence granted to one regime vis-à-vis another, and the broader principles to be applied to the operations of regimes. Those who agree that a court performs well, therefore, may be more or less satisfied with the results in normative terms. But this should not detract from efforts to determine how well international courts play their roles and to identify factors that explain variance in performance.

Assessing Performance

Performance as an explanandum is a multifaceted concept. In everyday usage it has two distinct but related meanings. First, as a verb, to perform is simply to fulfill an obligation or complete a task. Second, as a noun, performance refers to the manner in which a task in completed. Thus to

> address the issue of performance, as applied to the social world, is to address both the outcomes produced and the process—the effort, efficiency and skill—by which goals are pursued by an individual or organization
>
> (Gutner and Thompson 2010: 231).

We build on this formulation, adopting Gutner and Thompson's distinction between outcomes and processes and adapting it for application to ICs. Thus, one dimension of performance is *outcome performance*, covering the full range of outcomes that result, either directly or indirectly, from the operation of a court.[5] The second dimension is *process performance* associated with the way in which international courts exercise their authority.

To assess both dimensions of performance, we need criteria against which outcomes and processes are compared. As Gutner and Thompson observe, "[e]stablishing a baseline is important because it is only against a particular set of objectives and in the context of a given timeframe that performance can be assessed" (2010: 240). But the selection of appropriate criteria against which performance is compared depends not only on the mandate of a court but also on the perspective of the researcher. Thus, Mitchell notes that while "[i]nstitutions can be evaluated against either the primary or the subsidiary goals for which they were designed . . . they can also be evaluated against the goals of actors outside an institution in question" (2008: 80).

It follows that the criteria of evaluation can vary considerably. Still, we endeavor to develop realistic criteria based on common understandings of international courts. We start by identifying the functions or roles that analysts typically ascribe to international courts. Some of these are clearly intended by creators of ICs, as reflected in their constitutive documents. Others are roles that ICs serve in practice, irrespective of creators' intentions. We then posit that these are plausible criteria against which the performance of courts can be evaluated. We do not claim that these criteria apply equally to all courts. Nor do we assume that they are exhaustive. Rather, our intention is to provide a common analytical starting point for comparison across ICs. We recognize that it is necessary to contextualize

[5] We use outcome here as a generic term to encompass a broad set of results. For these purposes, we do not distinguish outcomes from outputs and impacts, as is typical in comparative politics literature or in regime effectiveness literature. In other words, the outputs of an international court (or their judgments) are among the range of outcomes resulting from the IC's operation. The same applies to impacts.

criteria on a case-by-case basis, which all the contributions to this volume do. We also recognize that courts rarely bear sole responsibility for the production of specific outcomes. Our objective is to make judgments regarding the proportion of the variance in outcomes that we can attribute to the activities of specific courts.

The analysis of *outcome performance* is a matter of assessing the results of court activities. This means evaluating the extent to which the actions of courts contribute to the attainment of substantive goals. The relevant goals may be framed at the level of specific cases, the level of the governance system to which cases belong, or the level of the development of international society as a whole. Thus, the relevant criteria may range from a narrow conception of performance to much broader conceptions. Drawing on existing literature, however, we approach outcome performance in terms of the roles or functions of courts in various social settings. Specifically, we identify criteria dealing with dispute settlement, clarification of the law, and compliance.

The first criterion involves the function of settling disputes. To what extent are courts able to settle disputes? How effectively do they do so? Extensive research suggests that international courts and tribunals do contribute to the settlement of disputes (Alter 2013; Bogdandy and Venzke 2013; Alvarez 2014; Shany 2014). Traditional perspectives on the dispute settlement function of ICs focus on the settlement of disputes between states. More recently, several ICs have begun to address disputes between private parties as well as states. Human rights courts, for instance, often have jurisdiction over disputes between private actors and states. International organizations also may be involved in cases that come before ICs, as in cases where the UN General Assembly requests advisory opinions from the ICJ, or when the CJEU reviews disputes between the Commission of the European Union and a member state. While dispute settlement is generally recognized as an important role of ICs, it is not a criterion that applies to all courts. Many scholars conclude that international criminal courts or tribunals prosecute crimes rather than acting to settle disputes (Alter 2013; Bogdandy and Venzke 2013). Still, dispute settlement is an important focus in our examination of the performance of ICs. Are they good at settling disputes? What enables courts to settle disputes successfully?

A second criterion for assessing the outcome performance of international courts is clarification of the law. Most treaties establishing courts assign them the task of "interpreting" the law. Several scholars also emphasize the importance of clarifying the law (Alter and Helfer 2010;

Bogdandy and Venzke 2013; Alvarez 2014; Helfer 2014).[6] Law, including international law, comprises abstract or general rules. These rules cannot anticipate all possible circumstances to which they will apply. Also, states may disagree on the content of rules and thus intentionally adopt imprecise language in legal agreements. The result is that legal rules are often incomplete and ambiguous with regard to their application. ICs frequently are called upon to interpret the law and to clarify how general rules apply to specific circumstances.

Clarifying the law can take a number of forms. International courts may interpret the scope of legal rules. The ICJ and the ICTY, for example, have redefined the scope of laws of war to apply to internal conflicts (Haye 2008). Clarifying the law also may require ICs to order or prioritize different rules. A central question frequently brought before courts involves determining whether specific rules are superior or subordinate to one another. Similarly, ordering occurs when an international court determines whether a law is *jus cogens* or customary law. By determining that a law such as the prohibition of torture is *jus cogens*, the court is asserting that the prohibition of torture is a supreme law. In such cases, courts clarify the law by determining the hierarchy of rules. Beyond this, ICs may determine how rules balance against one another in order to reconcile conflicting rules. This may entail the balancing of rules within a single legal regime or the balancing of rules across legal regimes. An instance of the former involves the efforts of the ECtHR to clarify the law by determining how to balance the rights of one individual against those of another or against societal interests. The latter arises when courts help to adjudicate conflict between international trade law and international environmental law, as in the judgment of the WTO's Appellate Body (AB) in the *Shrimp-Turtle* case. The clarification of the law sometimes involves very limited adjustments to legal rules. At other times, clarification may lead to extensive revisions in the law, causing some observers to speak of the role of courts in developing the law, lawmaking, or even in constitutionalizing international law.

A third criterion for evaluating outcome performance centers on the expectation that ICs facilitate compliance with international law. Some scholars refer to international courts as having enforcement or compliance functions (Shelton 2009; Alter 2013) or even treat compliance as

[6] Not all scholars use the terminology of *clarification*. They may speak of lawmaking, gap-filling, developing the law, or other similar terms.

a measure of performance (Guzman 2008).[7] ICs can play this role either by providing incentives to comply with legal commitments or by providing remedies in response to noncompliance. Courts may encourage compliance through a process of social sanctioning, in effect delegitimizing actors or behaviors that do not comply with community norms or social expectations. Social sanctioning by ICs can enhance compliance through three distinct mechanisms. Such sanctions can damage an actor's reputation, causing a loss of status. Alternatively, the judgments of an IC may encourage more powerful actors, such as states or in some instances international organizations, to exercise their power to compel compliance. These more powerful actors may use the ruling of an international court to enhance the legitimacy of their exercise of power. Such exercises of power may range from the distribution of aid and trade benefits to benefits pertaining to membership and positions within international organizations and even to retaliatory measures and military actions. A third (and arguably most significant) mechanism comes into play when ICs' decisions strengthen domestic compliance constituencies, including domestic electorates and NGOs. Such constituencies may hold the executive to account for violations of international law by shifting political support to the opposition party or mobilizing social groups to demand domestic policy changes. Research suggests that all these mechanisms make a difference in specific cases (Dai 2005; Simmons 2009; Hafner-Burton 2013; Helfer and Voeten 2014).

In some cases, international courts may be able to influence compliance directly, through the imposition of penalties and other forms of punishment and through the monitoring of implementation. Some ICs have the authority to impose monetary penalties. The CJEU, for example, can impose penalties on states in response to noncompliance. ICs may also be able to require that compensation be paid to a wronged party. For example, the Inter-American Court of Human Rights (IACtHR) has authority to require monetary compensation be given to victims, which may incentivize states to adapt their behavior to comply with applicable laws. Monetary penalties can also include the authorization of retaliatory measures that have economic consequences. The WTO's Dispute Settlement Understanding, for instance, allows a state to use countermeasures against another state that fails to comply with the ruling of a panel or the Appellate Body. Alternatively, some ICs have the authority to impose sanctions in the form of physical punishment. International

7 For a discussion of the latter, see Shany (2014).

criminal courts can impose incarceration on guilty parties. Also, Article 94(2) of the UN Charter authorizes the Security Council to take measures (including the use of force) against states that fail to comply with ICJ decisions, thereby threatening peace and security (Bogdandy and Venzke 2013).[8]

Beyond this, an IC may enhance incentives to comply by initiating a process of monitoring the implementation of its decisions, often through an international body linked to the court. When the ECtHR finds that a law has been violated, for instance, the Committee of Ministers of the Council of Europe monitors the implementation of the Court's judgment. The WTO's Dispute Settlement Body plays a similar role in monitoring compliance with decisions of panels and the AB. In a more decentralized process, monitoring of implementation also may occur through actions of domestic entities. As in the case of social sanctioning, it is unclear exactly how effective these mechanisms are at influencing compliance. Further research regarding all these mechanisms should help to illuminate the performance of ICs.

Process performance, on the other hand, has to do with how courts go about performing their roles and whether their operations conform to various standards of proper judicial practice, fairness, and efficiency. To assess process performance is thus to look at judicial procedures. Relevant procedures include how courts receive claims and how they handle claims once received. They also include how courts process evidence, deliberate, arrive at decisions, and develop arguments as well as how they interact with disputing and other interested parties. Simply put, the analysis of process performance encompasses the evaluation of the full range of judicial procedures.[9] Our thinking about process performance draws on the work of Gutner and Thompson (2010), which differs from the approach of Shany (2014) who treats judicial procedures primarily as a determinant of goal attainment.

Criteria for evaluating process performance rest on normative preferences regarding judicial procedures. These preferences may or may not be specified by the framers of an IC. If we posit a preference for processes that are fair, for example, we can evaluate the extent to which an international court's procedures meet major standards of procedural

[8] In practice, the Council has not exercised this authority.

[9] We view judicial appointment processes as external to the judicial proceedings, and thus do not include it per se in process performance. Nevertheless, judicial appointment processes may be instrumental in shaping the performance of courts.

fairness. Broadly speaking, the standards we apply in assessing the process performance of ICs follow rule of law principles familiar from the study of domestic courts. Such principles accentuate matters of procedural fairness or procedural justice. Additional criteria relevant to the evaluation of process performance include matters of efficiency covering both the time it takes to render judgments on specific cases and the material costs of operating a judicial system. In cases where caseloads are heavy and resources are limited, the ability of a court to handle individual cases with minimal expenditure of time and resources becomes particularly important. Other criteria for process performance may include standards relating to methods and procedures of judicial decision-making (e.g., transparency, reasoning and interpretation, fact-finding).

Outcome performance and process performance are distinct. In principle, at least, a court may perform well in settling disputes or encouraging compliance, even when its performance with regard to process standards is relatively poor. Nevertheless, many analysts have taken an interest in the relationship between the two, exploring whether performing well in terms of process contributes to outcome performance. The issue here resembles the debate about the extent to which "good" governance contributes to effective governance. Process performance may be valued as an end in itself, but many value process performance on instrumental grounds on the assumption that performing well in process terms contributes positively to performing well in outcome terms. In our view, this is a matter worthy of systematic analysis among those interested in the performance of international courts.

Table 1.1 summarizes this discussion of criteria for assessing the performance of ICs and provides a template for the substantive chapters in this volume.

Table 1.1 *The performance of ICs*

	Performance Dimension	
	Process	Outcome
Performance Criteria	• Procedural fairness • Efficiency standards • Standards of legal reasoning and interpretation	• Dispute settlement • Clarification of law • Compliance

Levels of Analysis

Implicit in our discussion so far is a focus on the individual case or judicial action. Strictly speaking, what courts do is to accept or decline to intervene in the claims of those seeking judicial intervention and to render judgments on those cases that make it onto their dockets. But it is relevant to think about the consequences of the judgments of international courts at other levels as well. In this regard, we distinguish among the micro-, meso-, and macro-levels, corresponding roughly to the level of the individual case, the level of the issue areas or governance arrangements to which cases belong, and the level of the overarching system in which cases arise. In simple terms, the meso- and macro-levels concern how courts perform in relation to broader outcomes or processes, as opposed to outcomes or processes at the level of a specific dispute or legal case.

Like all other courts, ICs render judgments regarding specific cases arising within their sphere of jurisdiction. Individual cases may take the form of a dispute between two or more states, a dispute between one or more state and a nonstate actor, or an evaluation of allegations that an individual's behavior constitutes criminal actions. Performance at this level, which we call micro-level performance, constitutes the initial concern in any assessment of the performance of international courts. Though courts may seek to arrive at decisions on the narrowest possible grounds to minimize the consequences or impacts of their actions beyond the cases at hand, this is not the only level of analysis at which we can assess the performance of courts. In the course of handing down judgments, the actions of courts often produce effects extending well beyond the level of the individual cases. Thus, we can look to IC performance beyond specific cases to examine how ICs produce effects involving broader outcomes and processes.

When the judgments of ICs affect an issue area or governance system, we characterize the results as meso-level performance. Many regional integration regimes, for example, seek to promote economic and political integration among their members. In connection with these regimes, we can ask whether and how the judgments of a related international court have contributed to the pursuit of this goal. The CJEU provides a well-documented instance of an international court playing a vital role in advancing economic and political integration (Burley and Mattli 1993; Helfer and Slaughter 1997; Mattli and Slaughter 1998; Stone Sweet and Brunell 1998). Similarly, regional human rights regimes often seek to strengthen human rights law and policy. Some analyses of the performance of the ECtHR adopt this perspective, asking how the Court has contributed to the achievement of this goal (Helfer and Voeten 2014). Another way to think about performance at the meso-level is to ask whether the activities of a court have contributed to the prevention of disputes and behavioral change across the relevant governance system. International courts can contribute to dispute prevention by reducing uncertainty about the precise meaning of rules and encouraging parties to settle disputes before adjudication arises (e.g., Busch and Reinhardt 2006; Kim 2008; Gilligan et al. 2010). Similarly, parties may adjust their behavior ex ante to avoid incurring costs associated with judicial oversight. An IC thus may perform well if it reduces the number of cases brought before it in the long term. A central debate concerning the performance of international criminal courts and tribunals, for example, centers on the question of whether they play a role in deterring war crimes going forward (Wippman 1999; Akhavan 2001; Gilligan 2006; Rodman 2008; Kim and Sikkink 2010).

A third level of performance, which we call macro-level performance, directs attention to the impacts of an international court's activity on international society more generally. Of course, the higher the level of analysis, the more abstract the criteria for evaluating performance become and the longer the causal chains involved. Nevertheless, it is worth asking whether the activities of international courts (individually or collectively) make a difference in terms of the character or state of international society (Alter 2014). Thus, some observers have asked whether the activities of the WTO's dispute panels or AB have empowered developing nations. Similarly, the activities of courts in some settings have contributed to judicialization in other settings. There is evidence to suggest that the activities of ICTY and the ICTR influenced the international community's decision to establish the ICC. Similarly, the CJEU has served as a model for those seeking to create judicial mechanisms to handle disputes and other legal problems in a number of other regions (Alter 2012).

For the most part, the discussion of levels of performance addresses what we have called outcome performance. But it is worth asking whether there are similar distinctions with regard to process performance. Process performance at the micro-level centers on matters like procedural fairness and efficiency. These process considerations remain important at the meso-level, but we are also concerned with the development of a coherent or internally consistent body of law. At the macro-level, we can ask whether international courts are playing a role in spreading and strengthening the influence of the collection of practices generally described in terms of the rule of law. Although the primary reason to differentiate among levels involves outcome performance, then, there is a parallel set of distinctions relating to process performance that are of interest in the study of the performance of international courts.

Before taking the next step, we want to draw attention to the fact that there are challenges to explaining variations in performance across ICs or over time with regard to the same court. The central point is that links between outcomes of interest and the actions of courts are often difficult to establish precisely or conclusively. Sometimes the causal chain is short and the causal mechanisms are simple. If we ask questions about the decisions of courts regarding the acceptance of cases for consideration or about the contents of the judgment they render with regard to a specific case, there is no doubt about the causal connections. Courts are authors of their own decisions. But as soon as we proceed beyond these simple links, the causal connections become more complex. If the parties to a dispute choose to adjust their behavior to comply with the terms of a judicial judgment, for example, can we attribute their actions solely to the authority of the court? It does not take much analysis to realize that the decisions of parties regarding compliance are influenced by a range of factors that extend beyond the actions of the relevant courts. Establishing causal connections between the activities of courts and outcomes of interest becomes progressively more difficult as we move from the micro-level to the macro-level because causality becomes more complex and causal chains become longer. It is hard enough to establish causal connections at the micro-level. Proving that courts make a difference beyond the level of specific cases in issue domains like human rights or trade requires the use of clever methodological strategies. Demonstrating that the actions of courts influence the nature of international society as a whole is still more challenging. Despite these difficulties, it would be a mistake to conclude that courts are unimportant at the meso- and macro-levels. But it is important to exercise caution in arriving at judgments regarding the performance of courts at these levels. Still, we take the view that it is worthwhile to consider these higher levels of performance to gain a comprehensive understanding of the performance of ICs and to assess the significance of arguments regarding the legalization in international society.

Determinants of Performance

Obviously, tracking the performance of international courts is a demanding task. But assume for the moment that we have a clear understanding of the concept of performance and some ability empirically to measure or track patterns and variations in the performance of the ICs of interest to this project. The next challenge is to seek explanations for the variations and patterns in performance we are able to document. We want to know why some courts do better than others in terms of performance, whether there are significant variations in performance among courts operating in different issue areas or in different regions of the world, and why the performance of the same court may rise and fall over the course of time. This leads to a search for the determinants of performance. In more formal terms, if we think of performance as the dependent variable (or perhaps as a suite of dependent variables) in this context, we now want to direct attention to the search for independent variables that allow us to explain or account for variance in the dependent variable.

Several introductory comments are in order as we embark on this journey. To begin with, we want to evaluate performance in terms of two dimensions (process and outcome performance), three levels (micro-, meso-, and macro-level performance), and four issue areas (trade, investment, human rights, and criminal actions). There is no reason to assume a priori that the performance of courts will be uniform or formative across dimensions, levels, or issues. High performance with regard to the dimension of process may not translate into high performance with regard to outcomes. High performance at the micro-level need not lead to high performance at the meso-level, much less the macro-level. The fact that courts perform well in one issue area (e.g., investment) tells us little about how well they will perform in other issue areas. Our initial expectation is that we are likely to encounter a great deal of variance in examining the performance of international courts across the dimensions, levels, and issue areas.

In all cases, moreover, we must come to grips with issues of causal inference. It is helpful, as a point of departure, to identify associations or correlations between variations we are able to document regarding performance and factors that we hypothesize to be determinants of performance. But how can we be sure that the relationships we are examining are not spurious? If we observe that disputants accept the judgments of courts more readily in social settings in which power is highly concentrated, for instance, can we conclude that the concentration of power is the key determinant? Similarly, if courts have more success in clarifying the law in settings characterized by a high level of consensus regarding principles of judicial interpretation, are we justified in treating consensus as the essential determinant of success? Causal inference can also be complicated by complex causality. In some cases, the causal chain is short and comparatively simple. This is particularly true at the micro-level where we are concerned with the ability of courts to render judgments regarding the cases that come before them, the likelihood that the parties will accept or comply with the judgments that courts hand down, and the prospect that the handling of cases will make a difference regarding the treatment of the problems at hand. But even here it is important to be cautious in drawing causal inferences about factors that determine the performance of courts. Many factors may come into play in determining whether parties comply with the judgments of a court, for example. And when we turn to the influence of the actions of courts at the meso- and macro-levels, it is clear that we are operating in the realm of complex causality. There are no magic solutions to the problem of demonstrating causality in this realm; all the contributors to this volume wrestle with this challenge in arriving at conclusions pertaining to their individual topics.

This is not to diminish, much less dismiss, research that traces the role of courts in international society. But it does mean that we will typically find ourselves dealing with issues featuring complex causality in the sense that the actions of courts are significant as elements of what we can think of as causal clusters. In some instances, we will want to make an effort to devise means to tease out the contributions of ICs or, in more formal terms, to determine the proportion of the variance in outcomes of interest attributable to the activities of courts. In other cases, however, it may be sufficient to consider the influence of clusters of determinants, without making a sustained effort to separate out the influence of the activities of courts from a range of other factors. As we move toward the meso- and macro-levels, a focus on the character of such clusters seems likely to become increasingly important.

That said, we can identify some of the principal lines of argument that analysts bring to bear in efforts to explain the performance of courts. Our aim in this regard is not to spell out a set of precise hypotheses that we expect authors of substantive chapters to examine or "test" systematically in their contributions. Rather, we seek to identify and comment on the main types of explanations that those who think about such matters have articulated. Our expectation is that these observations will play a role in guiding the work of the substantive chapters in this volume, as well as future research, and that we can come back to in the conclusion to reflect on the relative importance of various factors in accounting for variations in the performance of international courts.

One way to think about determinants of the performance of courts is to turn to the main streams of analysis embedded in contemporary work on international relations more broadly: realism, liberalism, institutionalism, and constructivism. Realists focus on power and particularly on the configuration of power in specific settings in the search for explanations. Realists who study international law and courts place central importance on state interests and the distribution of power among states (Goldsmith and Posner 2005; Posner and Yoo 2005). This mode of analysis yields two main explanatory perspectives regarding the role of ICs. Is there a dominant state (i.e., what realists call a "hegemon") or a dominant coalition of states that provides backing for a court and supports its role in a given issue area? The idea here is that the performance of courts reflects in a general way the power structure prevailing in a given social setting. In this regard, we would expect the performance of courts to suffer in cases where the power structure is contested or in flux. Realists also look to matters of problem structure and ask whether the issues that give rise to cases that come before courts amount to coordination or collaboration problems (Goldsmith and Posner 2005). Similarly, realists expect better performance regarding issues involving low versus high politics (Zangl et al. 2012). While courts may do well on this account in handling coordination problems or low politics issues, their performance is expected to be poor if and when they tackle collaboration problems or issues of high politics.

Liberals and institutionalists, by contrast, think of the role of ICs as organizations that facilitate the operation of institutions in specific issue areas. This may be a matter of resolving ambiguities in the application of regulatory arrangements or resolving disagreements about the extent to which actors are complying with regulatory arrangements. In other cases, it will be a matter of sorting out situations in which there is disagreement regarding the requirements of regulatory measures associated with different regimes (e.g., trade regimes and environmental regimes). ICs on this account may be either general arrangements (e.g., the ICJ) whose jurisdiction allows them to address issues arising in many issue areas or more specialized arrangements (e.g., the ECtHR) whose jurisdiction extends to cases arising in a well-defined issue area. In the liberal view, domestic actors, and institutions influence the performance of international courts

(Helfer and Slaughter 1997; Mattli and Slaughter 1998; Alter 2001; Davis 2012). For example, performance may hinge on whether relevant state parties are democratic, the type of legal tradition, domestic courts, and domestic society. Institutionalism, on the other hand, views performance as a function of institutional design of ICs (Helfer and Slaughter 1997; Keohane et al. 2000; Helfer and Slaughter 2005; Zangl 2008; Zangl et al. 2012). Those who adopt this perspective deem access for private actors, independence, and enforcement capacity as well as the precision and obligation of international law to be instrumental to performance.

For their part, constructivists associate the role of ICs with systems of ideas embedded in society. A particularly powerful example is the idea of the rule of law with its presumption that disputants should resort to legal procedures to resolve their differences rather than falling back on the use of force and that legal proceedings constitute the appropriate means for determining whether or not parties are in compliance with prevailing rules in specific cases. A particularly important application of constructivism involves the growth of new rights and rules that may take precedence over the presumption of sovereign immunity. The creation and operation of international courts dealing with human rights, for example, is a function of the growth in recent decades of principles and rules relating to human rights that states are expected to adhere to regardless of the doctrine of sovereign immunity. The current effort to develop and make use of international laws dealing with criminal behavior is a particularly interesting example of the growth of a new international discourse governing the actions of states as well as individuals. The extent to which the International Criminal Court thrives in the coming years will be an important indicator of the growth of such a discourse on a global scale. In all cases, constructivists look to systems of ideas and the extent to which they are pervasive in international society for explanations of variance in the performance of ICs. For this reason, constructivists consider processes of socialization and norm internalization to be critical to understanding patterns of performance (Lutz and Sikkink 2001; Sikkink 2011; Goodman and Jinks 2013).

Another way to think about determinants of the performance of international courts is to compare and contrast the perspectives of political scientists and lawyers regarding factors that can account for variation in performance. Of course, such differences are not absolute. Political scientists often point to the importance of judicial politics as determinants of the performance of courts. The scope of this concern involves both intracourt dynamics and relations between courts and those who make the relevant rules and those who are responsible for implementing the judgments of courts in specific situations. Internal battles are common within courts, and it is reasonable to expect that the opinions of (near) unanimous courts will carry more weight when it comes to various measures of performance than those of deeply divided courts. Among other things, the opinions of deeply divided courts invite those on the losing side to try again with slightly different cases in the hope of getting a different outcome in new cases. Beyond this, courts may enjoy more or less comfortable relations with those responsible for making and implementing laws. Political scientists debate the extent to which performance hinges on how well aligned a court's decisions are with the preferences of states (Garrett et al. 1998; Cichowski 2007; Alter 2008; Carrubba et al. 2008; Stone Sweet and Brunell 2012; Stone Sweet and Brunell 2013). Embattled courts may suffer with regard to performance, even though they are highly visible players in addressing some social issues. On the other hand, courts that get along well with those who make and implement the rules may have little influence at the meso- and macro-levels. Another approach taken by some political scientists concerns the influence of various types of nonstate and substate actors. Strong performance of courts may or may not depend upon higher degrees of public support or perceived legitimacy (Gibson and Caldeira 1995; Gibson and Caldeira 1998). Similarly, performance may be associated with interactions with "compliance partners," such as national courts, domestic constituencies, and activists (Alter 2001; Dai 2005; Cichowski 2007; Simmons 2009; Alter 2014).

Lawyers, by contrast, often highlight the importance of factors such as jurisdiction, admissibility, and independence and impartiality (Helfer and Slaughter 1997; Shany 2014). Lawyers tend to pay greater attention to methods of judicial interpretation. They often differentiate between activist courts that endeavor to play an influential role regarding major social issues (e.g., the enlargement of civil and human rights) and more passive courts that seek to resolve the issues that come before them on narrow grounds. Similarly, there are differences between those who regard themselves as strict constructionists and seek to ground their opinions in the original meaning of prevailing rules and those who are willing to construe laws in such a way as to adapt them to changing circumstances or to advance social goals they espouse. The underlying idea in this connection is that matters pertaining to methods of interpretation may explain the performance of ICs in specific settings, though there is no reason to assume that one method or another will always strengthen the performance of courts.

Beyond this are a number of other perspectives on the determinants of performance that do not fit neatly into the categories outlined in the preceding paragraphs. While it is possible to devise arguments about the potential relevance of a wide range of factors, three additional perspectives have emerged in our preliminary discussions that deserve separate comment in connection with the thinking embedded in this project: (i) types of cases, (ii) the normative pull of judicial actions, and (iii) the role of leadership.

Traditional international law recognizes only states as subjects, an arrangement that limits litigation to cases involving two or more states willing to accept the jurisdiction of a court. But increasingly, states must accept the compulsory jurisdiction of a court if they want to become part of an international regime, and many international courts today consider a wider range of cases, including those in which private actors bring complaints against public authorities and those in which public authorities levy charges against individuals alleged to have engaged in criminal activities. This makes it possible to ask whether the performance of courts differs from one type of case to another. Cases in which both parties are states are notoriously difficult to deal with due to the barriers imposed by sovereignty and the ability of states to refuse to accept the jurisdiction of courts with regard to issues they do not intend to subject to the rule of law. It is interesting to ask, under the circumstances, whether we can expect international courts to perform better when they are dealing with cases involving nonstate actors.

Another line of thinking that is worthy of consideration centers on the issue of what some observers characterize as the "normative pull" of legal judgments. There is clearly a relationship between the normative principles embedded in the judgments of courts and the evolution of social discourses in any given societal setting. When courts get too far ahead of the state of the social discourse in an area like standards applicable to human rights, their decisions are apt to be ignored by most members of international society. Conversely, there are cases when social discourse evolves quickly, and the role of courts is to adapt legal standards to bring them into line with broader societal developments. In most cases, however, the decisions of courts are likely to be stimulants in the progressive development of international norms. The idea here is that the actions of courts exercise a normative pull that provides actors with an incentive to adapt existing norms or adopt new ones and adjust their behavior accordingly. We can ask, in this connection, whether there is an optimal balance between the prevailing practices and the normative content of court decisions as a determinant of the performance of international courts. Considerations of this sort are particularly relevant to efforts to assess the performance of ICs at what we have described as the meso-level.

Although leadership is discussed more often in the context of executive actions or legislative politics than in connection with the activities of courts, there is no doubt that judicial leadership can play a role as a determinant of the performance of international courts. Two distinct perspectives on leadership are notable in this context. One involves the ability of individual judges to forge consensus among the members of a court regarding both the content of judgments rendered in specific cases and the legal arguments crafted in support of these judgments. The other involves the ability of judges to articulate legal principles that gain credence at the societal level and emerge as influential determinants of legal and political practices beyond the confines of the case at hand. As those interested in the role of courts have observed regularly, the dicta articulated in legal opinions (even in cases where they are set forth in minority or dissenting opinions) can become influential going forward when they express normative principles in a concise and appealing manner or when they articulate sentiments that are nascent in the social discourses of a particular time and place. Here, again, it is interesting to think about the effects of the actions of courts at what we have characterized as the meso-level in contrast to the micro-level. A court does not have to compile a perfect record with regard to its performance at the micro-level in order to make a difference at the meso-level. A line of decisions that move the social discourse associated with a particular issue area in some well-defined direction can produce a significant effect at the meso-level that extends well beyond the disposition of individual cases.

As the observations in the preceding paragraphs suggest, there may be significant differences in the determinants of the performance of ICs across the levels of analysis we have identified. Of course, it is difficult to imagine that a court could make a real difference at the meso-level, much less the macro-level, if it performs poorly at the micro-level. But some courts might make a conscious effort to render decisions regarding specific cases on narrow grounds to minimize any impact their decisions have at the meso- and macro-levels. Conversely, the broader impacts of the actions of courts may survive setbacks with regard to the disposition of individual cases. What this suggests is that it is useful to draw clear distinctions among the three levels of analysis in examining the determinants of the performance of international courts. Causal chains become longer and more complex as we move from an assessment of the performance of courts at the micro-level to their performance at the meso- and especially the macro-levels. This means our judgments will become less robust as we move from one level to another, but this does not mean that ICs do not play influential roles with regard to the evolution of major issue areas or the character of international society as a whole. So long as we are careful to qualify our assessments appropriately, this seems to us to be a worthwhile line of analysis.

The Shape of Things to Come

The substantive chapters in this book comprise two major clusters of contributions followed by a conclusion that seeks to articulate preliminary responses to the questions we have formulated in this introductory chapter and to suggest fruitful avenues for further analysis.

Part I consists of a set of chapters providing broad assessments of the role of international courts in a number of distinct issue areas, including trade, investment, human rights, and international criminal law. Each of these chapters seeks to collect and synthesize existing research in the relevant issue area rather than to report the findings of new research. The authors of these chapters apply the performance criteria that we have identified in this chapter. But as we have argued, not all criteria equally apply to all ICs nor have we been exhaustive. We provide a general template that authors adapt to fit the issue area they discuss. Thus, the chapters in Part I apply the criteria that are most fitting for the issue they examine while also bearing in mind the state of existing research and debates of that issue area.

Part I begins with two chapters focused on adjudication of international economic law. In Chapter 2, Cosette Creamer and Anton Strezhnev assess the performance of ICs within the multilateral trade regime, focusing on interstate disputes and the WTO Dispute Settlement Mechanism. Drawing on existing literature and original data, Creamer and Strezhnev argue that the WTO DSM is most often able to facilitate the resolution of conflicts relating to market access. While there may be some question as to what "resolved" means, most WTO disputes are resolved in a manner acceptable to all parties and resulting in high levels of compliance. Less clear, however, is whether the WTO DSM encourages pre-litigation or post-litigation resolution. The authors argue that the dispute settlement mechanism has an informal role in clarifying international trade law, which states generally accept. Creamer and Strezhnev argue the WTO DSM process performance is weakened by its inability to ensure access to justice. Overrepresentation of the most powerful economies is problematic in the WTO DSM because disparities in legal capacity hinder equal access. The overrepresentation of powerful economies in the DSM also has implications for outcome performance, especially in terms of the development of law. Last, their chapter reviews other dispute settlement processes embedded within preferential trade agreements, such as the CJEU.

In Chapter 3, Daniel Behn evaluates the performance of international investment treaty arbitration. He argues that investment treaty arbitration has contributed to legal consistency emerging on legal rules in international investment law. Behn shows that the performance of international investment arbitration suffers from challenges of access as investment agreements do not offer universal coverage to investors and a disproportionate amount of litigation arises from only a portion of international investment agreements. In terms of outcomes, investors and respondent states tend to win at equal rates on the merits. But when considering jurisdictional decisions, discontinuances, and negotiated settlements, Behn shows that there is a prodeveloped state bias in investment arbitration. As for compliance, most arbitral judgments are enforced, even though there are notable instances of state defiance. The process performance of investment treaty arbitration is mixed. Behn argues that while there is increasing transparency in the regime, the regime's performance suffers from lengthy resolution of disputes and a lack of diversity among the arbitrators appointed to sit on tribunals.

Turning to the performance of regional human rights courts, Chapter 4 by Dinah Shelton evaluates the performance of the ECtHR, the IACtHR, and the African Court of Human and Peoples' Rights (AfCHPR). Shelton discusses how internal structural factors, such as tenure and appointment of judges, and external structural factors, like a lack of resources, affect the performance of regional human rights courts. She argues that the regional human rights courts perform better than member states expect but not as well as victims would hope. Their process performance suffers from limited access, lengthy proceedings, and the courts' inability to address widespread and serious violations. The outcome performance of the regional human rights courts is mixed due to variation in the degree of deference granted to states and the forms of redress provided to victims. Nevertheless, she argues all three courts generally perform well in terms of generating compliance with their decisions, even though compliance with the IACtHR is lower than its European counterpart. In addition, they have contributed to the development of normative principles relating to human rights.

Chapter 5 by Nobuo Hayashi examines the outcome performance of international criminal courts and tribunals (ICTs). Of interest here is one particularly controversial aspect of ICTs' outcome performance: whether they contribute to the development of international humanitarian law (IHL) and international criminal law (ICL). Non-retroactivity and strict interpretation, two cardinal principles of criminal justice, make reliance on custom as a source of punishable violations of IHL awkward. Yet, ICTs have engaged routinely in what some regard as interstitial lawmaking by their judges. This chapter argues that custom as a source of ICL will endure despite the Rome Statute's relatively high degree of codification, and that ICT judges will continue to claim to find customary rules even where the evidence for them is thin or nonexistent. It will therefore be crucial to see how states, the preeminent makers of today's customary international law, will respond to such claims. The chapter reveals that, while some forward-looking pronouncements find subsequent support amongst states and become codified, others elicit very different reactions. State involvement in ICT adjudication can sometimes make a difference, but not always. Hayashi concludes that overall the normative contribution of ICTs to IHL and ICL has been more mixed than is often claimed.

The chapters in Part II then turn to efforts to identify factors relevant to understanding the performance of courts. Rather than revisiting familiar themes, these chapters seek to illuminate important determinants of IC performance that have eluded rigorous assessment in prior work on ICs. The point is not to argue that familiar themes (e.g., the court's jurisdiction, judicial appointment procedures, legitimacy, etc.) are unimportant but rather to add to an understanding of factors that have not been highlighted in previous studies of the performance of ICs. These chapters feature original research that applies the concept of performance to concrete instances of IC performance. Each chapter contributes to our understanding of whether, how and why IOs perform as they do. The chapters in Part II are methodologically and empirically diverse. While some chapters dig into the performance of a single IC in a single case, others compare across several ICs. Some chapters examine process performance and others outcome performance. The chapters feature statistical data analysis as well as qualitative data analysis. The richness is the variation of these chapters illustrates how the concept of performance can be empirically applied across the dimensions, levels, and issues areas pertaining to international law and courts.

In Chapter 6, Hyeran Jo, Mitchell Radtke, and Beth Simmons analyze the ability of the ICC to deter. Focusing on outcome performance, they argue that the ICC's performance should be assessed in terms of its ability to deter crimes that are subject to its jurisdiction. The chapter presents two kinds of evidence to access the outcome performance of the ICC: first, whether it has had an imprint on domestic law, and second, whether there is evidence that the ICC or the domestic laws it has encouraged have had deterrent effects. The chapter relies on broad-based evidence to evaluate the ICC's deterrence effects, while also considering in depth the case of Uganda. Using a time-series intervention analysis, the authors provide robust evidence that violence against civilians by state agents and rebels dropped off significantly following the ICC's intervention in Uganda. While it is not conclusive, this finding constitutes significant evidence that the ICC has performed well against one exceedingly important criterion: deterring the killing of civilians in the context of civil wars.

Chapter 7 by Benjamin Faude explores the link between institutional fragmentation and IC performance. Faude considers how the proliferation of ICs challenges the commonly held assumption that ICs do not interact with one another. His central argument is that forum shopping may occur as a result of institutional fragmentation and that this can generate a return to politicized resolution of interstate conflicts. Divergent decisions from ICs with overlapping jurisdiction may compromise the performance of ICs and lead parties to solve their disputes outside of international judicial bodies. However, if ICs take each other's case law into account, they may be able to boost each other's performance, effectively foreclosing forum-shopping opportunities. Judicial dialogue and informal recognition of the judgments of other ICs as precedential may lead to the clear allocation of competencies among overlapping ICs or to the reconciliation of their jurisprudence. Faude looks at these dynamics in disputes involving softwood lumber brought before the DSMs of the North American Free Trade Agreement and the WTO.

Jeff Dunoff and Mark Pollack focus in Chapter 8 on process performance. The authors broaden the theoretical and methodological approaches used in evaluating court performance by introducing "practice theory" to evaluate judicial performance. They argue that to understand the performance of international courts it is necessary to assess the performances of judges. Judicial performances are based not only on court statutes and rules, but also are created by judges themselves in the practices they adopt. Dunoff and Pollack explain that judicial practices exist throughout a dispute's lifecycle and include multiple performances of judges, ranging from their private deliberations with colleagues to their off-the-bench activities such as delivering speeches. The chapter highlights the evidentiary and fact-finding practices of the International Court of Justice, offering contrasts to other ICs, and links these practices to the outcome performance of the Court.

In Chapter 9, Nicole De Silva explores how ICs try to influence their own performance by focusing on strategies of socialization. De Silva argues that ICs can formulate policies and practices aimed directly at socializing actors into the norms, rules, and procedures that underpin the performance of ICs. In these strategies, ICs move beyond adjudication and their mandated activities, developing policies and practices that feature diplomacy, training, and outreach, for socializing relevant actors in their legal regimes. The chapter presents a framework for conceptualizing ICs' socialization strategies and their influence on the actual and perceived performance of ICs. De Silva shows how ICs can formulate socialization strategies in response to challenges to their actual and perceived performance, thus highlighting a realm of IC decision-making and activity that has received little attention in existing scholarship. The chapter's analysis of ICs' reported policies and practices shows that these socialization strategies are an important means by which ICs aim to influence their performance and actors' perceptions of it.

Chapter 10 by Chiara Giorgetti concentrates on factors relating to compliance. Specifically, Giorgetti reviews the compliance mechanisms international courts use and discusses political, sociological, and other factors that affect compliance. She argues that compliance with court judgments is significant in determining whether a court is effective and performs as expected. She applies this line of analysis to four ICs: the ICJ, ECtHR, tribunals under the auspices of the International Convention for the Settlement of Investment Disputes, and the United Nations Claims Commission. The aim is to offer an appraisal of a variety of mechanisms that mirror the full panoply of existing compliance mechanisms as well as to evaluate their operability in "real life." Giorgetti argues that these formal mechanisms of compliance contribute to judgment compliance to varying degrees. Several legal factors affect compliance, including the types of remedies involved, the cost of compliance, the kind of case, and the composition of the court. Giorgetti also explains how external political pressure and features of the state, such as its domestic judicial system, contribute to compliance with IC judgments.

In Chapter 11, Steinar Andresen asks what the analysis of IC performance can learn from the literature on international regimes. Andresen argues that there is much to learn from this literature, especially for understanding the meso-level performance of ICs. This chapter discusses how regime effectiveness literature reveals particular methodological challenges in assessments of ICs' performance. Specifically, while we may be able to attribute causal significance to an IC, determining how much an IC matters is difficult. He encourages scholars to view ICs as intermediate variables, in the sense that they channel and guide human interaction in the issue areas in which they operate. Additionally, he argues that the regime literature suggests that it is pertinent to focus on problem structure, asking to what extent ICs are able to deal effectively with difficult or "malign" issues. He also points to other explanatory factors worth considering, especially the broader context, including adherence to "the rule of law" and the problem-solving capacity of ICs. Commenting on the impact of courts in the area of human rights, Andresen suggests the performance of regional human rights courts is linked to how long they have existed, their participatory scope, and the severity of the challenges facing them.

Part III summarizes key findings and discusses future directions for research on the performance of international courts. Chapter 12 by Theresa Squatrito focuses on methodological considerations for future research on IC performance. She discusses the operationalization and measurement of performance, reviewing existing and possible approaches to measurement and their advantages and disadvantages. In addition, she canvases some options for methods that researchers might use to evaluate and explain IC performance. In particular, she discusses five methods – experimental designs, meta-analysis, qualitative comparative analysis, counterfactual analysis, and multimethods research – and how they might be useful for future research on the performance of international courts.

Chapter 13 returns to our basic questions about the performance of ICs. How well have ICs performed, and does performance vary by issue area? What are the determinants of performance in this realm? What can we expect regarding trends in performance during the foreseeable future? We note that much of the work carried out in this field so far highlights what we have described as outcome performance at the micro-level. Even in this realm, our contributors are on more solid ground in describing performance than in explaining the patterns they identify. This is understandable given the challenges of arriving at convincing causal judgments regarding this category of performance, much less process performance in contrast to outcome performance and performance at other levels. This means that there is a broad range of issues relating to the performance of ICs that remain to be examined by analysts seeking to assess the judicialization of international affairs and more specifically the roles that ICs play in this development. While progress in addressing these issues will require a combination of ingenuity and hard work, it is hard to exaggerate the importance of deepening our understanding of this subject.

References

Akhavan, Payam. 2001. "Beyond Impunity: Can International Criminal Justice Prevent Future Atrocities?," *American Journal of International Law* 95(1): 7–31.

Alter, Karen J. 2001. *Establishing the Supremacy of European Law: The Making of an International Rule of Law in Europe*. Oxford: Oxford University Press.

2008. "Agents or Trustees? International Courts in Their Political Context," *European Journal of International Relations* 14(1): 33–63.

2012. "The Global Spread of European Style International Courts," *West European Politics* 35(1): 135–154.

2013. "The Multiple Roles of International Courts and Tribunals: Enforcement, Dispute Settlement, Constitutional and Administrative Review," in Dunoff, Jeffrey and Pollack, Mark (eds.), *Interdisciplinary Perspectives on International Law and International Relations*. Cambridge: Cambridge University Press, pp. 345–370.

2014. *The New Terrain of International Law: Courts, Politics, Rights*. Princeton: Princeton University Press.

Alter, Karen J. and Helfer, Laurence R. 2010. "Nature or Nurture? Judicial Lawmaking in the European Court of Justice and the Andean Tribunal of Justice," *International Organization* 64(4): 563–592.

Alvarez, José. 2014. "What Are International Judges For? The Main Functions of International Adjudication," in Romano, Cesare P. R., Alter, Karen J., and Shany, Yuval (eds.), *The Oxford Handbook of International Adjudication*. Oxford: Oxford University Press, pp. 159–178.

Bogdandy, Armin Von and Venzke, Ingo. 2013. "On the Functions of International Courts: An Appraisal in Light of Their Burgeoning Public Authority," *Leiden Journal of International Law* 26(1): 49–72.

Breitmeier, Helmut, Young, Oran R., and Zürn, Michael. 2006. *Analyzing International Environmental Regimes*. Cambridge, MA: MIT Press.

Buchanan, Allen and Keohane, Robert. 2006. "The Legitimacy of Global Governance Institutions," *Ethics and International Affairs* 20(4): 405–437.

Burley, Anne-Marie and Mattli, Walter. 1993. "Europe before the Court: A Political Theory of Legal Integration," *International Organization* 47(1): 41–76.

Busch, Marc L. and Reinhardt, Eric. 2006. "Three's a Crowd: Third Parties and WTO Dispute Settlement," *World Politics* 58(3): 446–477.

Caron, David C. 2006. "Towards a Political Theory of International Courts and Tribunals," *Berkeley Journal of International Law* 24(2): 401–422.

Carrubba, Clifford J., Gabel, Matthew, and Hankla, Charles. 2008. "Judicial Behavior under Political Constraints: Evidence from the European Court of Justice," *American Political Science Review* 102(4): 435–452.

Cichowski, Rachel A. 2007. *The European Court and Civil Society: Litigation, Mobilization and Governance*. Cambridge: Cambridge University Press.

Dai, Xinyuan. 2005. "Why Comply? The Domestic Constituency Mechanisms," *International Organization* 59(2): 363–398.

Davis, Christina. 2012. *Why Adjudicate?: Enforcing Trade Rules in the WTO*. Princeton: Princeton University Press.

Garrett, Geoffrey, Kelemen, R. Daniel, and Schulz, Heiner. 1998. "The European Court of Justice, National Governments, and Legal Integration in the European Union," *International Organization* 52(1): 149–176.

Gibson, James L. and Caldeira, Gregory A. 1995. "The Legitimacy of Transnational Legal Institutions: Compliance, Support, and the European Court of Justice," *American Journal of Political Science* 39(2): 459–489.

1998. "Changes in the Legitimacy of the European Court of Justice: A Post-Maastricht Analysis," *British Journal of Political Science* 28(1): 63–91.

Gilligan, Michael J. 2006. "Is Enforcement Necessary for Effectiveness? A Model of the International Criminal Regime," *International Organization* 60(4): 935–967.

Gilligan, Michael, Rosendorff, B. Peter, and Johns, Leslie. 2010. "Strengthening International Courts and the Early Settlement of Disputes," *Journal of Conflict Resolution* 54(1): 5–38.

Goldsmith, Jack and Posner, Eric A. 2005. *The Limits of International Law*. Oxford: Oxford University Press.

Goldstein, Judith, Kahler, Miles, Keohane, Robert O., and Slaughter, Anne-Marie. 2000. "Introduction: Legalization and World Politics," *International Organization* 54(3): 385–399.

Goldstein, Judith L., Rivers, Douglas, and Tomz, Michael. 2007. "Institutions in International Relations: Understanding the Effects of the GATT and the WTO on World Trade," *International Organization* 61(1): 37–67.

PART I

2

Court Performance within the Multilateral Trade Regime

COSETTE D. CREAMER AND ANTON STREZHNEV

Introduction

International and regional courts play a growing and critical role in facilitating world trade. Some adjudicate disputes between states parties to free trade agreements, others rule on cases brought by private actors against governments, and a few even hear challenges brought by the regime's surveillance authority. Nowhere is the extensive role played by trade courts more evident than within the regime created to liberalize international trade – and its institutional product, the World Trade Organization (WTO) – such that the vast majority of existing research on trade courts focuses on the WTO's Dispute Settlement Mechanism (DSM).

The WTO's dispute settlement system – created in 1995 – replaced the more diplomatic and power-oriented system operating under the General Agreement on Tariffs and Trade (GATT) with detailed procedures elaborated within the Dispute Settlement Understanding (DSU). Although many viewed the prior GATT system as largely successful in resolving disputes (Hudec 1999: 8), it was considerably less judicialized and characterized by blocked rulings, work delays, fragmentation, and inconsistent legal interpretations. The DSU sought to address many of these shortcomings and established a unified system that set strict timelines, guaranteed the right to a binding panel ruling, created an appeals body to ensure legal consistency, specified deadlines for compliance with adopted rulings, and if compliance did not occur, provided for the authorization of bilateral sanctions. In short, it is by any account far more legalized than the GATT system, a move that generated both hopeful enthusiasm and cautious concern (Goldstein and Martin 2000).

In the twenty-odd years since the DSM began operating, economists, trade lawyers, and interdisciplinary scholars have undertaken considerable empirical research on its operation. This intensive focus likely stems from the relative success of the system and the greater availability of high-quality dispute data compared to regional trade regimes or other issue areas. The vast majority of this work examines the determinants of resort to the WTO's Dispute Settlement System (DSS),[1] with most agreeing that system usage reflects countries' economic size and legal capacity (Horn and Mavroidis 2007). As this chapter will demonstrate, a growing number of studies have begun to focus on the DSM's *performance* as conceptualized within this volume, although there is still much work to be done (Squatrito et al. 2018).

Unlike a few regional economic courts, such as the Court of Justice for the European Union (CJEU) or the Andean Tribunal of Justice (ATJ), the WTO relies exclusively on member states to initiate dispute hearings and infringement proceedings. While we recognize that disputes initiated by private actors or a regime's surveillance authority may play an important role in some agreements, this chapter focuses primarily on interstate disputes and the extensive body of scholarship concerning the WTO DSM's performance in facilitating their resolution.

This chapter first reviews the subset of this literature that relates to the DSM's performance in promoting the goals of dispute settlement and compliance in the trade context. The first section notes that while dispute settlement has been studied extensively, the potential ways in which the DSM's decisions enable the resolution of trade disagreements remain underexamined. Moreover, the DSM's performance with respect to compliance with its recommendations, or WTO law more generally, remains an open question. There exists a substantial gap between whether a dispute is notified as settled or resolved and perfect government compliance with a ruling: the former rarely implies the latter. Determining compliance with rulings and presumably WTO law represents a challenging empirical task, particularly since full compliance is rare and evaluating the extent of partial compliance requires expert knowledge of domestic trade law.

The second section of the chapter then turns to review studies on outcome performance, in terms of law clarification. In addition to dispute settlement, the DSM serves to develop and interpret trade law. Despite the absence of any formal rule of precedent, recent research demonstrates that the WTO, through its rulings, has developed a *de*

[1] Following WTO conventions, this chapter uses DSS to refer to the entire legal, institutional, and organizational system established to facilitate the resolution of disputes between member governments. The DSM refers collectively to the WTO's adjudicative bodies – the dispute panels and Appellate Body.

facto system of precedent that supplements formal treaty lawmaking. This section suggests a number of promising avenues for future study of this phenomenon.

With respect to the process standard of fairness, the third section examines a burgeoning body of research on the extent to which the WTO structure facilitates or promotes fair and equal access to the DSM, for developing countries in particular. It also discusses the ways in which the WTO's judicial bodies have sought to reduce the salience of informal barriers – such as legal expertise – in generating inequality among states. The fourth section then briefly discusses existing studies of regional trade courts and the relationship of dispute settlement mechanisms contained within preferential trade agreements to that of the WTO. We finally conclude by identifying promising directions for future research into the role and performance of trade courts in the multilateral trade regime.

WTO Performance in Settling Disputes

Dispute Settlement, Ruling Implementation, and Compliance

The vast majority of empirical research on the WTO's DSS seeks to explain a country's decision to initiate and empanel a dispute, or its broader participation within the system. Studies on the determinants of dispute participation provide critical insight into the types of cases and parties heard by the DSM, but this section brackets these questions to focus on studies that evaluate the DSM's outcome performance in facilitating dispute settlement and enhancing compliance with WTO rules.[2]

Evaluations of the WTO system are generally positive about its ability to settle disputes, especially when compared to the GATT system or other state-to-state dispute settlement mechanisms (Ginsburg and McAdams 2004; Davey 2009). Descriptive statistics on performance in this sense abound, perhaps inspired by Robert Hudec's groundbreaking and comprehensive analysis of GATT dispute resolution which found successful resolution of around 90 percent of legally valid claims (Hudec 1993). A number of descriptive overviews have identified similarly high success rates for dispute settlement under the more legalized WTO (Busch and Reinhardt 2000; Iida 2004; Davey 2005; Wilson 2007; McRae 2008; Davey 2009; Lee 2011; Davey 2014).

[2] For a good overview of earlier studies on dispute initiation and participation within the WTO, see Horn and Mavroidis (2007).

For example, Davey (2005) pins the rate of full and partial implementation of DSM rulings during the WTO's first ten years at 83 percent. Bruce Wilson (2007), former Director of the WTO Secretariat's Legal Affairs Division, observed that in almost all cases a member found to be in breach would later comply with WTO law. Yet if one closely examines the details of how disputes are settled, the record becomes a bit murkier. As William J. Davey has persuasively argued, the "picture ... is not so rosy if one looks beyond general statistics and considers the quality and timeliness of compliance actions" (Davey 2009: 42), with considerable room for improvement. In more recent work, Davey (2014: 690) has suggested that implementation was not achieved in a "timely manner" in many instances, and that for some cases labeled as "resolved," it is "likely that the complainants have not pursued the matter – for cost or whatever reasons – even though they believe that full implementation has not occurred." In a similar vein, Horlick and Coleman (2007) calculated for the first decade of WTO dispute settlement a 6.1 percent rate of open noncompliance (a government publicly declares it does not intend to comply with a ruling), a relatively high figure given that this type of noncompliance is arguably the most detrimental to confidence in the system.

Rates of successful settlement or resolution across studies are rarely comparable, largely due to different conceptualizations of and measures for dispute outcomes. This is partly a function of the nature of the WTO system. The implementation and compliance phase of the WTO's dispute settlement process begins immediately following the circulation and adoption by the Dispute Settlement Body (DSB) of an Appellate Body or dispute panel report.[3] If the DSM finds a government's trade measure in breach of WTO rules, it recommends it be "brought into conformity" with WTO law and may even suggest ways in which this could be achieved.[4] Within the thirty days following report adoption by the DSB, the losing government must notify the DSB whether it intends to implement the ruling and the actions it has taken to comply. In many

[3] The DSB is the political body responsible for administering the WTO dispute settlement system. The DSB establishes panels, adopts panel and Appellate Body reports, monitors implementation of its recommendations, and authorizes compensation and the suspension of concessions. Understanding on the Rules and Procedures Governing the Settlement of Disputes, Marrakesh Agreement Establishing the World Trade Organization, Annex 2, 1869 UNTS 401, 33 ILM 1226 (1994) [hereinafter DSU], Arts. 2.1, 6, 16, 21, 22.

[4] See DSU, Article 19. It is within the dispute panel's discretion to include recommended methods of implementation, and it seems to be an exceptional occurrence.

instances, immediate compliance (within the thirty-day period) is impracticable, given that implementation may require extensive restructuring of a regulatory system or the passage of controversial legislation.[5] For this reason, a government often is afforded a reasonable period of time (RPT) to enact the necessary reforms (Zdouc 2005; Qian 2012).

A losing party is not considered in "breach" of its WTO obligations – and thus able to be subject to retaliation – until expiration of the RPT. If compliance is not achieved within this period, the defaulting member can voluntarily offer "compensation," which involves the lifting of other trade barriers by the losing party.[6] If no satisfactory compensation can be agreed upon, the winning party can request authorization from the DSB to take countermeasures or suspend concessions.[7] Countermeasures are bilateral and unlike compensation involve the *raising* of trade barriers by the winning party.

Notably, governments can claim they are in compliance with a ruling after making minimal – and perhaps insufficient – reforms to the challenged measure. The increasing tendency of governments to do so – either strategically or due to ambiguity concerning what implementation requires – has led to a rise in so-called "compliance proceedings." Complainant governments typically initiate DSU Article 21.5 compliance proceedings to challenge the respondent's notified implementation as falling short in some respect(s). These proceedings effectively delay the end of dispute resolution for several years, with some suggesting that respondent governments use deficient implementation to extend the time during which they can retain WTO-inconsistent measures without the added costs of authorized trade retaliation (Horlick and Coleman

[5] Governments have notified implementation immediately or within thirty days of report adoption in a mere fourteen disputes (11.2 percent) decided between 1996 and 2013. Descriptive data on WTO disputes within this chapter cover 141 total disputes decided between 1996 and 2013, with the unit of analysis at the dispute- and not report-level to avoid artificially inflating the data by counting all disputing dyads. Although disputes are initiated by different parties at different times, once it moves to the compliance stage, the timeline applies uniformly to all disputing parties. Data is taken from Creamer (2017).

[6] DSU, Article 22. Because the winning party has to agree to be compensated and to the specific amount offered, compensation is a rare event.

[7] DSU, Article 21. A request for authorization of retaliatory concessions has been made for 15.2 percent of disputes requiring implementation (17 percent of those that reach the "breach" stage), although complaining governments followed through and were granted authorization to retaliate in less than half of these initial requests.

2007; Brewster 2011).[8] Compliance proceedings have been initiated for nearly a quarter (23.2 percent) of disputes requiring implementation, a little over half of which were subsequently appealed. Not surprisingly then, disputes subject to compliance proceedings take on average twice as many days to reach resolution compared to those for which compliance panels are not requested.

The compliance phase of WTO dispute settlement thus may drag on for years. More critically, disputing parties can negotiate a settlement or achieve partial – but still acceptable – compliance, at any point during these proceedings. In other words, WTO disputes can and often are concluded in ways that do not always result in the offending measure being withdrawn. The winning party ultimately gets to decide if it is satisfied with the losing party's implementation of the recommendations or if it wishes to challenge the respondent's alleged compliance. Nothing stipulates that the type of implementation "agreed upon" by the disputing parties must follow the findings of the dispute report. For this reason, it may be misleading to suggest that the WTO's judicial bodies themselves decisively settle any given dispute.[9] In other words, identifying for any given dispute whether it was merely resolved satisfactorily between parties, resulted in implementation of the WTO ruling, or contributed to compliance with WTO rules more generally is not a straightforward endeavor.

These difficulties and complexities are likely compounded in relation to some of the WTO's newer members. Many of these countries have regulatory systems unfamiliar to other WTO members, and reforming laws on the books to implement rulings within some countries may "count" for less than for countries with robust legal institutions (Webster 2014: 572–574). The non-transparency of the compliance phase of WTO dispute settlement and the degree of privately held information complicate these measurement issues even further. For many disputes resolved through mutual agreement, only the parties know what deal has been negotiated. Moreover, the respondent government's incentive is often to behave opportunistically and not reveal the truth publicly (Mavroidis 2015: 23).

Many existing studies explicitly acknowledge the difficulties of tallying compliance records at both the second-order (implementation of ruling

[8] Though the timing of compliance proceedings – whether it should occur before or after the DSB's authorization to suspend concessions – was heavily disputed early on. See further (Valles and McGivern 2000; Zimmerman 2006).

[9] It may also be misleading to speak of compliance with a ruling, although for the sake of convenience this chapter uses dispute settlement, resolution, and compliance interchangeably.

recommendations) and first-order (compliance with WTO rules) levels, but still attempt to provide some overarching picture. As there exists no off-the-shelf, standardized measure of dispute implementation or compliance, comparisons across empirical studies are difficult. How, then, does the WTO DSM perform in terms of the very basic outcome performance goal of settling the underlying trade dispute? If we examine simply whether the dispute is considered "resolved" by the parties in terms of being removed from the DSB's agenda or whether it is considered "ongoing," nearly a quarter (twenty-nine disputes in total) of the 125 disputes requiring implementation remain ongoing or unresolved as of December 2014. In other words, over three quarters of disputes submitted to the WTO's judicial bodies have been resolved in a manner mutually satisfying to all parties. Notably, the proportion of disputes considered ongoing has not fluctuated considerably since 2001, despite the fact that the number of empaneled disputes has steadily increased over time (see Figure 2.1).

As noted previously, a number of distinct outcomes could qualify as the dispute being considered "resolved." We consider a dispute to result in "compliance" when a government notifies the WTO that it has fully implemented a ruling and this notification is not contested by the

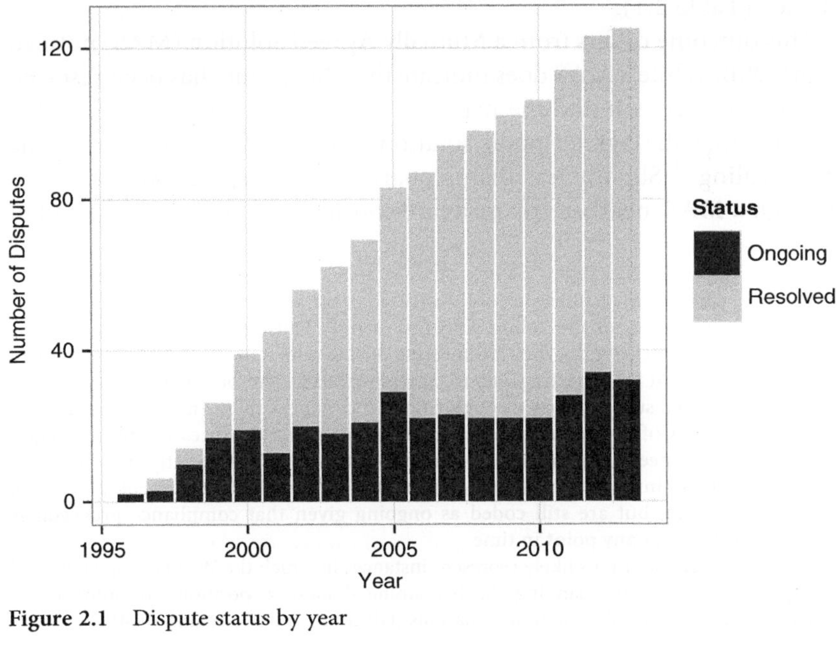

Figure 2.1 Dispute status by year

Table 2.1 *Status of WTO disputes, as of December 31, 2014*

Outcome Type	% In-Breach Disputes	Average Time In-Breach (days)
Compliance (implicit or explicit acceptance)	51.4%	145.1
Mutually Agreed Solution	21.6%	1,162.8
Ongoing	26.1%	1,988.2
New Dispute	0.9%	429

Figures calculated using only those disputes for which implementation was required and not resolved prior to expiration of the RPT (officially considered "in-breach"). N=111.

complaining party.[10] To be sure, public notification of implementation by the losing party – and implicit or even explicit acquiescence by the winning party – does not always capture perfect compliance with a judgment. Still, it does provide a close approximation, particularly given the winning party's incentives to achieve full compliance following a lengthy and costly litigation. A little more than half of the empaneled WTO disputes that ruled against the respondent between 1995 and 2014 have been resolved through notified and accepted compliance (Table 2.1).

This outcome differs from a Mutually Agreed Solution (MAS) notified to the DSB. While a MAS does indicate that the dispute has been resolved (in that all parties found the negotiated solution acceptable), it is often the case that the agreed-upon solution does not fully conform to the WTO ruling.[11] Slightly less than a quarter of all disputes were resolved through a MAS, nearly as many as are considered ongoing by the end of

[10] We code a dispute as resulting in compliance when the respondent government notifies full implementation of the ruling, and this is not challenged or questioned by the complaining state(s) within the DSB meeting during which implementation is notified or any subsequent DSB meetings (up to December 2014), and/or when implementation is not challenged subsequently through compliance proceedings. In a few cases following notification of implementation, the complaining party expressed dissatisfaction during a DSB meeting with the steps taken but did not subsequently insist on DSB surveillance or initiate compliance proceedings. These cases represent a form of accepted breach, but are still coded as ongoing given that compliance proceedings may be initiated at any point in time.

[11] Mutually agreed solutions likely represent instances in which the WTO ruling facilitated dispute settlement by changing the bargaining dynamics, positions, or information asymmetries within subsequent negotiations (Ginsburg and McAdams 2004).

2014 (Table 2.1). Finally, disputes considered ongoing may also fall into one of a number of categories: under surveillance within the DSB, in the compliance proceeding or retaliatory concessions phases, or the subject of continuing bilateral negotiations.

In addition to attempting to identify discrete dispute outcomes, a few studies focus on dispute duration. There is some evidence that the move from the GATT system to the more legalized WTO system has contributed to shortening the lifespan of trade disputes involving the US on average, though the size and strength of this finding is not large (Grinols and Perrelli 2002; Grinols and Perrelli 2006). That is, disputes are being resolved more quickly under the new as compared to the old regime, but this cannot be attributed entirely to the new system *per se*. The timeliness of dispute settlement and ruling implementation represents another aspect of the quality of compliance (Davey 2014: 692) and an important aspect of evaluating the WTO's outcome performance, but little existing research attempts to explain variation in how quickly trade disputes are settled following a WTO ruling (for notable exceptions see Spilker 2012; Brewster and Chilton 2014).

Compliance with adopted reports *could* indicate better outcome performance at both the micro- and meso-levels as conceptualized within this volume, as it provides a rough proxy for WTO rule conformity and dispute resolution (Epstein et al. 2009). That being said, we caution that focusing exclusively on dispute resolution or report implementation provides at best a simplified and limited understanding of outcome performance. First, report implementation does not help us understand the "shadow" effect that the DSM may have on future disputes, in the form of early settlement during pre-litigation negotiations or preemptive conformance (Busch and Reinhardt 2002; Vazquez and Jackson 2002; Busch and Reinhardt 2003). Second, compliance rates with issued rulings tell us nothing about the *erga omnes* effects of the rulings or the DSM more broadly. The direct correlation between report-compliance and WTO norm-compliance (even for the respondent government in that dispute and surely with respect to other trade relations) is questionable. Finally, report implementation does not capture the interaction between adjudication and negotiation in the post-ruling stage of the dispute, which represents a potential mechanism through which the DSM contributes to dispute resolution. The following section discusses this and other ways in which WTO adjudication may impact outcome performance goals at the micro-level, before turning to the meso- and macro-levels.

Determinants of WTO Outcome Performance: The Micro-level

Most existing studies on the performance of trade courts focus on whether the mere existence of a judicialized mechanism impacts settlement *prior* to litigation. For example, Busch and Reinhardt (2003) find a greater likelihood of pre-litigation settlement within the WTO compared to under the GATT system, save for developing country complainants or US-EU disputes. In a similar vein, Guzman and Simmons (2002) find that disputes involving non-continuous measures tend to pre-litigation settlement, although not for disputing democratic dyads. Fewer studies examine how trade courts impact post-adjudication behavior and their performance in this respect.

How might we expect a trade court's operations to facilitate dispute settlement and/or ruling implementation? Surprisingly, there has been little theorizing about the factors leading to different dispute outcomes and the theoretical models which have been developed (largely formal) are rarely evaluated through empirical testing. Existing scholarship anecdotally suggests that dispute resolution or implementation could occur for any number of reasons, including factors relating to domestic political economy, side payments, reputation costs, or the credibility of enforcement threats in the case of noncompliance. As discussed previously, WTO rulings could facilitate or incentivize dispute settlement even if the parties do not follow the DSB's recommendations to the letter, by revealing previously confidential information or a government's degree of commitment to a given policy position, as well as by clarifying the quality and strength of alternative legal interpretations. For example, Johns and Rosendorff (2009) argue that a key function of adjudication in the WTO is to provide information about the legal validity and anticipated consequences of a government trade policy. Such information in turn provides consumers and industry groups with the information necessary to lobby their government (Mansfield et al. 2002; Rosendorff 2005).

Existing literature also tends to emphasize various pressures on, or incentives for, breaching states to conform to international rules. Although the contribution of retaliatory concessions to direct enforcement of rulings is widely debated and its normative desirability questioned, there exists no systematic empirical analysis of whether and if so how retaliation (or the threat thereof) induces compliance. Similarly, there exists no research on whether monitoring by the DSB of report implementation has any discernible effect on settlement or compliance. This is a surprising oversight in need of further study, particularly given the amount of time trade lawyers spend engaging in debates over the WTO's system of remedies.

On adjudication's indirect enforcement role, Johns (2012) theorizes one way in which dispute rulings help coordinate enforcement by states not party to the dispute. The focal point of a court ruling facilitates the ability of third parties to impose costs on recalcitrant noncompliers, with states developing reputations for supplying "enforcement" in this respect. While the WTO system does not provide an institutionalized mechanism for third-party punishments, as it is predicated on bilateral suspensions of concessions, it is possible that third parties are able to impose such costs or pressures informally. Such costs could be material – such as the threat of future litigation if an offending measure is not repealed – or social – via shaming and public criticism within the DSB during discussion of monitoring implementation and surveillance reports. While we might be able to extend Johns' (2012) model to the WTO, to date the DSM's ability to facilitate such third-party indirect enforcement has not been examined empirically and represents a promising line of future research.

Few studies explicitly evaluate the relative influence of a court's informational and enforcement roles, similar to the institutionalist and neorealist perspectives described in this volume's introductory chapter. Sattler, Spilker, and Bernauer (2014) provide one of the few existing empirical studies to do so in the context of WTO disputes from 1995 to 2006. They find strong support for the conclusion that WTO dispute settlement primarily performs as an enforcement device, and much weaker support for the argument that it reduces complexity and clarifies trade law. Still, information provided by a trade court ruling could impact subsequent (or contemporaneous) negotiations, either between the disputing parties or with a third party. While some studies find that the most effective compliance bargaining takes place prior to the DSM's ruling (Busch and Reinhardt 2002), negotiations do continue during and after report adoption.[12]

Although the system emphasizes that prompt compliance with WTO rulings is central to its effectiveness, it also permits states to maintain

[12] Indeed, although the DSU attempts to "insulate the legal process from political dynamics, the dispute settlement system, at its core, remains focused on the resolution of bilateral disputes to the satisfaction of the contending states" (Tallberg and Smith 2014: 126). Regardless of whether there exists an international law obligation to comply with the letter of a dispute ruling (Schwartz and Sykes 2002; Jackson 2004), the DSS was designed to resolve trade conflicts through – first and foremost – private negotiations (Tallberg and Smith 2014: 120).

offending policies and simply accept retaliatory actions from injured states while negotiations continue (Schwartz and Sykes 2002; Brewster 2013). Rulings could thus encourage negotiated settlements in the shadow of concluded litigation. In theory, a ruling could reduce information asymmetries, alter the bargaining strength of the disputing parties, or shift the size of the overlapping win-set in ways that facilitate dispute resolution, even if the agreed settlement does not necessarily conform to the WTO-covered agreements or report findings. Much more work needs to be done on the extent to which WTO rulings impact subsequent bargaining dynamics and whether – and if so how – dispute reports facilitate settlement. Such research is particularly important as the systemic preference for mutually agreed solutions may lead to greater flexibility in outcomes (Tallberg and Smith 2014: 126) but could also "result in a deal . . . that disregards broader systemic interests of non-participant third parties" (Jackson 2006: 146). Future research in this vein should pay close attention to the broader effects of post-adjudication settlements.[13]

In terms of explaining variation in dispute duration, the same country-dyads that resolve some of their trade disputes quickly may fail to resolve others for decades. This suggests that the *timing* of resolution cannot be explained by state-level characteristics (such as a country's political system or economic power) alone. Some studies do look to factors that vary across disputes and tend to focus on the problem structure of the disputed issue-area or the domestic politics of compliance. With the notable exception of Rachel Brewster and Adam Chilton's (2014) study of US compliance, existing studies also tend to overlook how various domestic actors respond to WTO rulings.[14] As they aptly argue, this supply-side of compliance is equally important given that government institutions possess different policy preferences, face different demands, and encounter different obstacles when it comes to free trade and trade policy reform (Brewster and Chilton 2014: 217–218).

There may thus be strong reasons to expect that the government institution responsible for implementation of a WTO ruling will influence the type and speed of compliance achieved, and that trade courts'

13 Jackson (2012) provides one of the few case studies on post-adjudication compliance bargaining. Using an interview with a key advisor to Antigua and Barbuda during compliance bargaining with the US, she demonstrates how a small state can successfully attain bargaining leverage and prevail against a much more powerful country.

14 Though see Davis and Shirato (2007) for a focus on industry incentives to litigate within the WTO.

performance may be highly conditioned by the domestic politics of "losing" governments. Brewster and Chilton (2014) find that in the US, dispute duration was highly dependent on the involvement of Congress in implementing WTO recommendations. Hoffman and Kim (2009) similarly argue that implementation of WTO rulings depends on the relative domestic political weight of special interest groups benefiting from the *status quo*. Controlling for a range of other factors that likely influence the fact and timing of compliance, they find that continued noncompliance is greatest when it concerns trade measures benefiting influential economic sectors. Spilker (2012) also finds evidence to suggest that the domestic political economy of trade disputes matters, with compliance involving complex instruments for trade protection significantly more difficult to achieve in a timely manner. The suggestive findings of these few studies indicate that the political economy and domestic politics of WTO compliance represents an area ripe for further research.

WTO Outcome Performance: The Meso- and Macro-levels

There exists shockingly little research on meso-level performance of the WTO, in terms of the broader impact of DSM rulings on WTO rule compliance among states not directly party to the dispute. Systematic analysis of such *erga omnes* effects is made difficult by the fact that creating "a convincing data set on compliance with treaty law in this area would be a mind-boggling endeavor" particularly given the absence of an obvious unit of analysis (Simmons 2010: 284). Studies that attempt to identify such effects produce limited findings. For example, Busch, Raciborski, and Reinhardt (2008) find that the US is less likely to investigate and impose antidumping duties against countries that are members of the WTO. They argue this demonstrates that the WTO legal regime deters protectionist practices against fellow members, particularly those unable to credibly threaten retaliation, by clarifying policy standards and providing for enforcement through judicial review.

Evaluating the macro-level effects of WTO adjudication on broader economic trends, particularly trade flows between disputing parties, is a slightly more manageable task given the availability of a broad range of economic indicators. In one of the most sophisticated analyses to date, Bechtel and Sattler (2015) find that participation within a WTO dispute as a complainant increases its sectoral exports to the defendant by nearly eight million USD three years after a panel ruling. Even more striking, these positive economic benefits flow not only to the country carrying the costs of challenging a trade measure but to the "free riding" third-party participants as well. The authors suggest that evidence for such economic spillover from participating in disputes demonstrates the limited role power and legal capacity play in determining the WTO's broader redistributive effects (but see Bown and Reynolds 2014).

The WTO's Role in Trade Law Clarification

International courts not only resolve conflicts among parties. They also clarify states' legal obligations, a role consistent with "incomplete contracting" explanations for why states choose to delegate to third parties. Abbott and Snidal (2000) note that because states cannot write agreements that anticipate all possible future contingencies, judicial and quasi-judicial bodies frequently are tasked with interpreting the meaning and scope of treaty rights and obligations.

The WTO DSM is tasked with facilitating the resolution of specific disputes among parties. It is not mandated to issue general rulings regarding the interpretation of provisions of covered agreements. Whether the DSM is successful in "clarifying" international trade law thus depends on whether interpretations made in the context of one particular dispute are considered relevant to disputes between other members. Do DSM rulings form a coherent body of precedent for future disputes? Formally, there is no rule of *stare decisis* within the DSU. WTO rulings bind only the disputing parties and not the membership as a whole (Pauwelyn 2003: 46), a point confirmed by the Appellate Body within one of its first decisions, *Japan—Taxes on Alcoholic Beverages.*[15]

Nevertheless, the informal practices of the WTO are such that prior decisions of the DSM – and particularly the Appellate Body – play an important role in how subsequent panels interpret the law. Panelists frequently cite previously adopted panel and Appellate Body reports and the disputants themselves often appeal to precedent within their oral and written arguments. These citation practices have intensified over time (Pauwelyn 2016). Legal scholars have long noted the existence of a *de facto* form of legal precedent within the WTO (Bhala 1999a; Bhala 1999b; Blackmore 2003). It is not merely that panels find previous reports instructive. In some cases, they treat interpretations of law within adopted reports as binding on their own reasoning. Beyond simply citing

[15] Appellate Body Report, *Japan—Taxes on Alcoholic Beverages*, WT/DS8/AB/R, WT/DS10/AB/R, WT/DS11/AB/R (November 1, 1996).

past decisions, some Appellate Body reports have harshly criticized panels under review for failing to take into account prior jurisprudence. Roughly twelve years after it ruled in *Japan—Alcoholic Beverages II*, the Appellate Body noted in dicta that:

> ... the legal interpretation embodied in adopted panel and Appellate Body reports becomes part and parcel of the *acquis* of the WTO dispute settlement system. Ensuring "security and predictability" [...] implies that, absent cogent reasons, an adjudicatory body will resolve the same legal question in the same way in a subsequent case.[16]

Why would member states accept a *de facto* precedent system in the absence of any formal mandate? The Appellate Body often defends its adherence to precedent by noting that WTO members depend on the institution to provide predictability in dispute resolution; similar disputes should be settled in similar ways. This appeal to the will of the members as a whole in order to justify a rule of precedent illustrates an essential tension within the WTO system. The DSU envisions the DSS as a member-centric system. The core purpose of the DSS is to facilitate the resolution of disputes among states, with negotiation strongly favored over adjudication.[17] In this sense, the DSM plays an ostensibly passive role in international trade law – resolving conflicts between parties over existing agreements rather than actively imposing new legal obligations on its membership. However, the DSU also recognizes the need for a strong institutional underpinning in order to facilitate bargaining among the parties.[18] The DSM is meant to do more than simply serve as a mediator among members. It has an independent role in clarifying and interpreting the obligations of states under the multilateral trade regime.

The tension between being a member-centered organization and a source of legal clarification appears in the last sentence of DSU Article 3.2. Dispute settlement panels must clarify the obligations incumbent on members, but the act of clarification *must not* have the effect of adding to those obligations in unanticipated ways. This is something of a contradiction. Interpreting previously non-litigated provisions by definition changes *some* states' perceptions of their obligations in practice. If it didn't, there would be no need to litigate the provisions! The line between correctly interpreting an existing obligation and introducing a new one is very thin. The dispute settlement system

[16] Appellate Body Report, *United States—Final Anti-Dumping Measures on Stainless Steel from Mexico*, WT/DS344/AB/R (May 20, 2008).

[17] DSU, Article 3.7. [18] DSU, Article 3.2.

must therefore strike a difficult balance between clarifying unsettled elements of trade law while taking care not to appear to be "inventing" novel obligations for members. Classic models of international relations see states as loathe to sacrifice sovereignty over policymaking to international institutions, particularly when there is risk of adverse policy outcomes (Koremenos et al. 2001). Under principal-agent models of delegation, states (principals) would likely take efforts to restrain such adverse decisions by courts (agents) by retaining some form of ultimate control over the latter's decisions. Indeed, a core element of public international law is the principle that states cannot be bound by international obligations without their consent. Yet, as Alter (2008) argues, the relationship between international courts and their member states does not fit the typical assumptions of the principal-agent framework. States do not have expansive recontracting abilities with respect to courts – they are limited in their ability to explicitly sanction agents for outcomes they dislike since that would undermine the entire purpose of delegation. Courts are "trustees" called upon to exercise independent judgment for the benefit of beneficiary states. The mandate contained within DSU Article 3.2 suggests that some members do not want the DSS to serve *only* as a forum for bargaining; they demand that the DSM develop a body of jurisprudence that builds on the covered agreements.

There is, however, no consensus among members as to whether and how the WTO should choose to exercise its clarification role. While some states vehemently reject certain applications of precedent as imposing unforeseen obligations on states,[19] other states actively lobby for it. For example, the Appellate Body in *US—Stainless Steel* noted the European Communities' argument that:

> panels are not only *expected* to follow Appellate Body conclusions in earlier disputes, *especially where the issues are the same*, but are also *de jure* obliged to follow the findings of the Appellate Body where the Appellate Body has interpreted the same legal questions. This is consistent with the need to provide security and predictability to the multilateral trading system, as well as the need for prompt settlement of disputes.[20]

It is no wonder then that the Appellate Body, when justifying its citation of previous reports, emphasizes the importance that members themselves

[19] See, for example, the discussion in Alter (2008) of the US reaction to the Appellate Body's decision in *US – Lamb Meat.*

[20] Appellate Body Report, *United States—Final Anti-Dumping Measures on Stainless Steel from Mexico*, WT/DS344/AB/R (May 20, 2008), para. 51.

place on predictability and the role of precedent in facilitating dispute resolution.

Is this focus on members' interests enough to consider the WTO successful in clarifying international trade law? Given the absence of a formal mandate for precedent-setting, it may be that what passes for clarification is the maximum that the membership will tolerate. However, the importance of the DSM's clarification role has only grown in recent years, as multilateral negotiations on new treaties under the WTO's auspices have ground to a halt. In this context, concerns over member-state backlash may be constraining the WTO from serving a more expansive clarification purpose. The current round of WTO talks – the Doha round started in 2001 – has stalled and parties have largely been unable to reach agreement on further liberalization concessions (Gantz 2013: 1). While members were able to salvage an agreement at the 2013 Ministerial Conference in Bali on Trade Facilitation, the scope of concessions in this agreement is far smaller than the broad liberalization package envisioned at the outset of Doha (Wolfe 2015). Additionally, ratification and entry into force of the Trade Facilitation Agreement remains another obstacle that members must overcome. The WTO system remains, at the moment, in a kind of maintenance mode for global trade governance, with no additional multilateral accords joining the set of covered agreements and codifying new elements of trade law. Goldstein and Steinberg (2008) note that most of the multilateral liberalization gains in recent years have resulted from DSS litigation and law-making rather than negotiated concessions. The primary function of the WTO as a whole has thus been less to facilitate negotiations for further trade concessions among member states, and more to clarify and resolve disputes regarding the applicability of existing obligations.

Alternatives to informal precedent-setting for providing clarity in the law are limited by political factors, making panel and Appellate Body reports the primary way in which the WTO as a whole exercises its interpretive role. Article 9.2 of the WTO Agreement permits the Ministerial Conference and General Council to adopt authoritative interpretations of provisions within the covered agreements. These interpretations have been considered by the Appellate Body as binding on all WTO members.[21] However, as Creamer and Godzimirska (2016) note,

[21] For example, the AB in *US—Clove Cigarettes* described these interpretations as having "pervasive legal effect" and "binding on all Members." Appellate Body Report, *United States—Measures Affecting the Production and Sale of Clove Cigarettes*, WT/DS406/AB/R (April 24, 2012), para. 250.

the formal requirement of support from three-fourths of members (and in practice consensus) has resulted in nonuse of this mechanism. With respect to contested points of law, such consensus has been impossible to reach among members, and the WTO's political bodies are largely unable to exercise their clarification role in a formal manner.

What does research say about whether this rule of *de facto* precedent contributes to an effective, transparent, and predictable system of jurisprudence? This remains an open question. Part of the difficulty in developing a clear answer stems from the fact that the WTO is a member-driven organization. The DSM provides interpretations only when the members demand them, typically by filing a dispute. It is thus not possible to directly attribute a failure to clarify some elements of law to institutional inadequacy alone. An ideal study of this question would first need to establish some sort of underlying "demand" for clarification (on specific provisions or issue areas) to which the corresponding observed "supply" might be compared. Given evidence that access to the DSM is highly uneven across member states, it would be insufficient to simply look at the provisions litigated in disputes. Just as failure to clarify is not evidence of ineffectiveness, the existence of clarification is not evidence of effectiveness, particularly if clarifications systematically favor a subset of members.

The most straightforward benchmark for establishing whether the WTO has been successful in clarifying the law is simply whether states internalize panel and Appellate Body interpretations. That is, do member states consider the system of informal precedent to be legitimate, or at the very least an acceptable practice within the WTO? Understanding the extent to which members approve of a rule of *de facto* precedent would help to further determine whether the WTO has been successful in managing the balance between interpreting states' obligations under existing agreements while refraining from imposing new obligations.

Empirical evidence shows that states and private actors behave as though precedent matters in the WTO and that reports adopted by the DSB inform not only the dispute to which they apply but how states bargain over future disputes. In this sense, the WTO has been effective in its clarification role – the reasoning of panel and Appellate Body reports are accepted by members as meaningful guidance for resolving trade disputes *in general* rather than solely for the parties involved. However, studies also suggest that political pressures limit the provision of precedent. Only a fraction of WTO members actively litigates within the DSS and empirical analyses of when panels refrain from precedent-setting suggest that panels are responsive to the concerns of powerful members.

Very few studies look directly at whether governments explicitly care about precedent, but many describe downstream evidence of state behavior that suggests attentiveness to the implications of a decision beyond the immediate dispute. For example, research on forum shopping in international trade argues that governments selectively choose to litigate disputes within the WTO DSS in lieu of regional mechanisms when they value the global precedential impact of a particular dispute. In a case study of two disputes filed by the US and Mexico under the WTO and North American Free Trade Agreement (NAFTA) respectively, Busch (2007) suggests that each party's choice of forum that was driven by the desirability of setting a broader precedent with all trading partners. If WTO reports had no precedential value to governments, we would not likely observe patterns of regional vs. global institutional sorting in dispute resolution.

While the theoretical argument for forum shopping is relatively straightforward, systematic empirical evidence for forum selection in international trade remains scarce. This is partly because researchers rarely can observe the entire universe of *potential* disputes that could have been filed but were not and therefore have zero variation with which to determine whether precedent shapes the disputes states choose to litigate. Some progress on this question could be made by narrowing the focus to disputes filed by a single country, as Davis and Shirato (2007) and Davis (2012) do. However, both of these studies focus on determining the domestic political and economic factors motivating dispute choice, leaving open the question of whether institutional aspects of the WTO also play a role. It would be worth revisiting these analyses to consider the interaction between precedent and the issue areas being litigated, particularly as there is now greater longitudinal variation as more and more cases are litigated each year.

Another observable implication of responsiveness to precedent involves the behavior of third parties to disputes, who are permitted limited involvement in panel proceedings including the opportunity to submit official statements on the case. Busch and Reinhardt (2006) show that high levels of third-party involvement in a dispute reduces the probability that the disputants will come to a mutually agreeable settlement before a decision is issued. When many third parties become involved, they signal the desire of the membership for the DSM to take a formal stance on the points of law being contested by the complainant and respondent rather than accept a negotiated settlement where the legal question remains to be litigated. While this result provides some indirect evidence of attention to precedent, subsequent research should look towards finding evidence of explicit precedent-seeking by third parties. An extended analysis of third-party statements that builds on the coding rules used in Busch and Reinhardt (2006) to determine which issues are brought up by third parties might consider also coding the extent to which third parties demand that panels rule – or refrain from ruling – on particular questions.

Pelc (2014) is one of the few studies that addresses the question of members' interest in precedent directly and provides evidence that governments may file disputes *exclusively* for their precedential value. The evidence presented shows that governments engage in costly litigation over industries that are insignificant in terms of commercial benefit in order to obtain favorable precedent for future, more relevant disputes. Pelc finds that – all else equal – disputes that have less commercial value to their participants have greater "precedential value" as measured by the dispute's centrality in terms of subsequent citations to it (either direct or indirect) by the parties.

The citation network of the WTO is a very promising source of information about the WTO's law clarification role. However, analyzing the network is not an easy task and the correct approach to summarizing relevant network attributes is often unclear. In particular, subsequent empirical research on WTO citations should build on Pelc (2014) by more clearly defining how to measure "precedential value" specifically in the WTO context. Pelc (2014) relies primarily on network centrality measures developed in the social networks and computer science literatures, borrowing somewhat from an analogous study of the importance of precedent in the US Supreme Court (Fowler and Jeon 2008).[22] These centrality measures, while popular as summaries of what nodes should be considered "important," are often difficult to incorporate meaningfully into a subsequent statistical analysis. First, researchers rarely account for the fact that centrality is a noisy estimate. It is measured with *error*, and failure to account for this error correctly in the analysis may lead to incorrect inferences.

Second, because they are measures of some latent and unobserved concept, centrality scores by themselves do not have a meaningful scale. It is not clear exactly what a one-unit change in centrality means. This

[22] It is worth noting that the measures used by Pelc (2014) and Fowler and Jeon (2008) differ in how they are computed. Pelc (2014) focuses on inward-citations while Fowler and Jeon (2008) considers both outward and inward citations to be indicative of "precedential" authority. However, both measures are similar in type in that they use summaries of links among nodes (decisions) to develop node-level measures of importance.

creates problems for assessing the substantive significance of any observed effect. Finally, centrality measures may be measuring the wrong concept when it comes to precedential impact. What matters is not how generally cited a case is in subsequent disputes, but rather the effect of precedent's existence on a panel's legal reasoning (and subsequent behavior of the litigants). Panels cite cases for a variety of reasons and not all citations are necessarily positive or substantively engage the reasoning of the cited report, which is not necessarily reflected in aggregate measures like centrality. This is not to say that centrality measures do not provide valuable insights about how cases relate to one another, but rather that future research should consider alternative modelling strategies.[23]

Is the DSM effective at further clarifying the rules of the multilateral trade regime? The fact that both states and subsequent panels pay attention to the precedential value of reports demonstrates the existence of a serious *de facto* precedent system. Moreover, the DSM is not inventing this system out of thin air, but rather responding to members' demands for predictability and consistency within WTO jurisprudence. In this sense, the DSM is effective in its clarifying role because members respond to, rather than ignore, past panel and Appellate Body reports. However, effectiveness in outcome does not imply that the process behind it is particularly fair or representative of *all* members' interests.

Not all governments' demands for precedent are heard equally. Indeed, it appears to be the case that powerful countries are the ones shaping most of WTO jurisprudence. Among disputes brought before the Appellate Body, a majority have involved the United States, and the top three AB participants are the US, EU, and Canada (Pauwelyn 2016). The distribution of participation frequency is highly right-skewed, with only twenty-nine countries having ever appeared as a disputing party within AB proceedings. Pauwelyn (2016) further notes that only 72 out of 131 WTO members have been involved as third parties. While the distribution of main participants is to be expected given the distribution of disputes that are litigated – large economies are those most likely to have disputes brought against them – the fact that precedents tend to be set in disputes involving the most powerful actors suggests that panels' provision of "gap-filling" is not neutral. Creamer and Godzimirska (2016) further note that the most active members not only have more opportunities to present arguments for particular interpretations, but

[23] Latent space network models as developed by Hoff, Raftery, and Handcock (2002) provide one possible alternative.

also dominate statements made after reports are adopted. As political in addition to legal actors, WTO panels are responsive to the interests of active *members*.

If powerful members were invested in precedent-building for its own sake, then such overrepresentation would not implicate the overall effectiveness of the WTO's clarification role; panels would clarify what needed to be clarified. However, as the strategic account of precedent demand illustrates, states seek rulings because they are advantageous to them in constraining others' future behavior, not necessarily because they represent the mark of good jurisprudence.

One paradox noted by Pelc (2014) is that despite being positioned to set advantageous precedents, powerful states have often opposed a strong rule of precedent for panels, with the US being particularly recalcitrant. Even the European Union, often considered highly supportive of the trend towards greater WTO judicialization (Krüger 2013), has varied somewhat across disputes in how "binding" it believes precedent should be. On one hand, its third-party submission in *US—Stainless Steel (Mexico)* argued that Appellate Body rulings must be treated as authoritative, even though they do not formally bind nonparties to the dispute.[24] On the other, when its antidumping duties were challenged by India in *EC—Bed Linens*, in response to India's citation of the panel report in *Mexico—High Fructose Corn Syrup*, the EC highlighted its noninvolvement in the cited dispute as a reason to ignore the original panel's reasoning.[25]

Not only do governments vary in the scope of clarification that they demand, WTO panels also vary in how much "lawmaking" they choose to supply. Consistent with the underlying conflict between interpreting the law and avoiding the imposition of new trade obligations, Busch and Pelc (2010) show that political factors influence the extent to which the WTO dispute panels are willing to engage in such a clarifying role. Third-party involvement with respect to the scope of a ruling is particularly salient. Specifically, panels vary in the extent to which they invoke "judicial economy" – refusing to rule on a point brought by the litigants by deeming it unnecessary to the final outcome. Such exercises of economy are cases where panels explicitly *refuse* to contribute to the overall body of case law on a particular disputed provision. Panels that invoke

[24] Third Party Submission by the European Communities, *United States—Final Anti-Dumping Measures on Stainless Steel from Mexico*, WT/DS344/AB/R (May 20, 2008).

[25] Annex 2–3, Oral Statement of the European Communities, First Meeting of the Panel. Panel Report, *European Communities—Anti-Dumping Duties on Imports of Cotton-Type Bed Linen from India*, WT/DS141/R (October 30, 2000).

judicial economy explicitly state their intention to *not* set a precedent on a particular question as it is not relevant to the dispute at hand. Busch and Pelc (2010) show that panels are more likely to exercise judicial economy when more third parties make "mixed" submissions before the panel, that is, submissions not entirely in favor of either the complainant or respondent. These mixed submissions, Busch and Pelc (2010) argue, signal to panels that the membership at large is ambivalent about the consequences of a particular interpretation of law on future disputes concerning similar issues. This is consistent with panels' frequent insistence that the use of precedent is ultimately meant to be in the interests of member states. When the members are unsure of the value of such clarity, evidence suggests that the DSM responds by tempering its "gap-filling" mandate. However, empirical patterns in the use of judicial economy are not necessarily neutral. Brutger and Morse (2015) find that when the US or EU lose a dispute, the panel is more likely to exercise judicial economy, thus tailoring the precedential consequences of an adverse decision to the benefit of the strongest members. Future research on this question should elaborate on the distributional implications of judicial economy more generally. While initial evidence is suggestive, no comprehensive study currently exists on whether judicial economy tends to result in less precedent-setting for legal questions on which the major economies are particularly sensitive.

The evidence that more powerful countries are more capable of litigating *with the aim* of establishing favorable precedents tempers a generally optimistic assessment of the WTO's performance in clarifying the law. While the development of a robust *de facto* precedent rule has permitted the law to develop in the absence of consensus over interpretation, the way in which this system operates raises important questions about the *process* of accessing the WTO's dispute resolution proceedings. Clarification of law is as much a distributional question within the WTO as it is a purely legal one. Is the WTO clarifying law for the purpose of the membership as a whole, or for the benefit of its most powerful stakeholders? Answering this question requires examining an element of *process* performance – whether the DSM is successful in facilitating equal access for all members.

Process Performance and Access to the DSM

While most empirical work on the WTO has focused largely on outcome performance, one element of process performance has also attracted a significant amount of research: the extent to which certain countries are disadvantaged in their ability to access the DSS. It is clear that the most common users of the DSM are the wealthiest WTO members. This is in part because they are subject to the majority of complaints, given that the overall value of removing a particular trade barrier is greatest for the largest markets. However, developing countries are also underrepresented as claimants and third parties, which suggests that the WTO may be failing to live up to the procedural criterion of facilitating equal justice for members. Moreover, disparities in access have strong implications for outcome performance. Countries may fail to comply with treaty obligations and maintain measures that violate WTO-covered agreements because the affected parties cannot litigate. Why this participation divide exists remains only a partially answered question. In particular, future work should examine whether access gaps can be ameliorated by policy measures such as legal assistance or whether disparities in access are a result of more entrenched structural factors within the institution itself.

What accounts for the significant disparity between developing and developed economies in utilizing the DSM? Structural factors inherent to international trade are one explanation. Horn et al. (1999) find that states with highly diversified export sectors are more likely to file complaints since they are more likely to encounter disputes. However, subsequent research demonstrates that state capacity also plays an important role in predicting who files. Because litigation is costly, developing countries' lack of resources or legal capacity is commonly cited as an explanation for low levels of dispute participation. Bown (2005) find that even when accounting for the stakes of a dispute, a country's income level is positively associated with joining a dispute as complainant or third party. Guzman and Simmons (2005) also suggest that legal capacity matters for selection of respondents when developing countries *do* file. Countries with less human and legal capital tend to focus on the largest violators, given that litigation costs often outweigh the benefits gained from smaller cases. Data from surveys of WTO members by Busch, Reinhardt, and Shaffer (2009) further confirms the salience of legal capacity in deterring countries from filing disputes. Roughly two-thirds of delegations surveyed cited legal capacity issues (such as litigation costs) as reasons for not filing a complaint. Moreover, some 88 percent of members stated that the advantages of large economies stem from their legal expertise and experience with the WTO.

To what extent can this barrier to access be overcome? The empirical evidence appears to be mixed. On one hand, it may be possible for developing economies to "bootstrap" their way to expanded access.

Davis and Bermeo (2009) argue that legal capacity is largely a fixed cost for developing countries. Once countries get over the initial hurdle of litigating, they become much more active participants, which may explain the comparatively high rates of participation by some developing countries such as Brazil or the Philippines. They find that past experience as either claimant or respondent is strongly predictive of subsequent filings, suggesting that once countries overcome the initial start-up costs to litigation, capacity is endogenous to participation. Additionally, Davis and Bermeo (2009) find that assistance from the Advisory Centre on WTO Law (ACWL), which provides members with legal advice and training for WTO disputes, also correlates with higher dispute initiation, suggesting that interventions aimed at increasing capacity may help improve access for developing countries.

However, interview data from Busch, Reinhardt, and Shaffer (2009) suggests that access to legal aid may not entirely solve developing countries' capacity problems. As suggested by some delegations, a baseline level of capacity is necessary in order to incorporate assistance from the ACWL or private law firms. One major barrier cited was lack of institutional support from home governments and weak continuity in expertise among government officials. Institutional career paths mean that ministry officials that obtain experience working with the WTO are regularly replaced by new and inexperienced appointees, limiting the accumulation of institutional knowledge. Additionally, because legal assistance is not randomly assigned, observed correlations between assistance and filing may reflect differences in underlying capacity to *access* assistance in the first place.

Legal aid alone may not be able to replicate the strong "treatment" of dispute participation itself in enhancing developing country legal capacity. A valuable task for future research would be to identify the factors that drive countries to take that initial leap and file that first dispute. Beyond filing, another underexamined area concerning participation is what happens to developing countries *once they file*. Are states on equal footing throughout the course of the process, or does capacity also affect states' ability to win cases? One study on this question found that members with greater government efficiency and regulatory quality are more likely to obtain positive panel rulings while other measures of legal capacity (such as delegation size in Geneva) are uncorrelated with success (Zeng 2013). While promising, such observational studies of dispute outcomes are uniquely challenging from an empirical standpoint. Because some disputes result in a settlement rather than a final ruling from a panel, studies that look at outcomes such as whether states win or lose implicitly select for only those disputes that do not settle. This may result in a form of selection bias if the independent variable of interest also affects propensity for settlement. If countries with weaker legal capacity are more or less likely to reach a mutually agreeable settlement, then the types of disputes observed for countries with strong legal capacity might not be valid counterfactuals for the types of disputes observed for weaker capacity states. In general, researchers analyzing observational data on dispute outcomes should be aware of lurking variables that affect not only the independent variable of interest and the outcome, but also those that affect settlement and outcome.

Of all the areas of process performance, equal access appears to be the one where the DSM falls most short of its goals. Disparities in filing are pervasive and cannot be attributed to trade patterns alone. Wealthier countries are overrepresented in disputes due to higher legal capacity and propensity to file. The implications of this go beyond fairness and equity. Because DSM panels functionally make new trade law via a *de facto* system of precedent, the questions on which panels rule are disproportionately those that involve wealthier economies. Faced with seemingly insurmountable barriers to initiating trade disputes, developing countries get less of a say in the issues that get brought before the DSM. Determining the underlying causes of and identifying the most promising remedies for correcting these inequalities in access represent essential areas of investigation for scholars of the WTO and international trade law more broadly.

Regional Trade Courts

Preferential trade agreements (PTAs) have expanded exponentially over the past few decades. At the time of the WTO's establishment in 1995, only forty-three regional PTAs were in force (Chase et al. 2013: 13). By mid-2015, 264 physical PTAs were notified to the WTO[26] and even more were in force.[27] PTAs have also become quite expansive in coverage, moving from limited tariff reduction to issues such as standards harmonization, competition, and investment. Critically, they have

[26] See World Trade Organization, *Regional Trade Agreements Information System (RTA-IS)*, available at: http://rtais.wto.org/UI/publicsummarytable.aspx (accessed July 2017).

[27] A recent study collected and examined 589 PTAs concluded between 1947 and 2009 (Allee and Elsig 2015).

increasingly incorporated detailed and legalized forms of dispute settlement. Nearly all contain some procedure for resolving disputes, and most contemporary agreements provide for mandatory and binding dispute settlement (Donaldson and Lester 2009; Chase et al. 2013; Allee and Elsig 2015).[28]

Although the number of PTA Dispute Settlement Mechanisms (PTA-DSMs) have expanded in step with the number of PTAs, very few interstate disputes have been initiated thereunder and the vast majority of mechanisms have not been used at all.[29] While limited or nonuse cannot be taken as a direct indicator of performance, it does make assessment and comparative evaluation of trade court performance in the realm of inter-governmental disputes difficult. Some DSMs, such as those under NAFTA and the United States-Israel Free Trade Agreement, have seen a few government-to-government disputes (Donaldson and Lester 2009: 368), but overall only a few of the more judicialized systems have experienced a level of activity conducive to systematic empirical analysis. The reasons posited for this nonuse relative to the WTO system vary across courts and regions. For example, some African PTA tribunals struggle with lack of resources or infrastructure and thus have little or no reported activity (Porges 2011: 492).

Notably, two of the most active tribunals within regional integration communities – the Court of Justice for the European Union (CJEU) and the Andean Tribunal of Justice – are often viewed as largely successful in promoting greater economic integration within their respective regions (Weiler 1991; Alter 2001; Alter and Helfer 2010; Alter, Saldias, and Helfer 2012; Saldias 2014; Phelan 2015). Yet for the most part, each has relied heavily on a "preliminary reference" mechanism, which are case referrals from national courts that are not interstate disputes, to develop community law and ensure member state compliance.[30] The reliance on and

[28] Within Allee and Elsig (2015)'s sample of 589 PTAs, 83 percent contained a dispute settlement provision. Of these, 46 percent provided for arbitration by an ad hoc panel while only thirty-one PTAs creating standing dispute settlement bodies, many of which are situated within broader regional economic integration agreements (Allee and Elsig 2015: 327–328).

[29] The 2011 World Trade Report (WTO 2011: 130) found that "the vast majority of provisions in regional and bilateral trade agreements are never the subject of any dispute settlement proceedings, even where a right to invoke proceedings exists."

[30] The preliminary reference or ruling system consists of national courts requesting interpretations of regional law from the tribunal, and relies heavily on the strength of the doctrines of direct effect (requiring that regional obligations are enforced through national courts) and supremacy (requiring that in case of conflict, national courts must apply community rather than national law) (Weiler 1991; Alter and Helfer 2010).

success of this procedure in the EU was such that the enforcement by domestic courts of EU law "came to supplement and even overtake the use of the infringement procedure before the CJEU by the European Commission and the Member States" (Phelan 2015: 843). Although the European Commission continues to play an important role in monitoring compliance in the EU by launching infringement claims, similar to the role played by the Secretary-General within the Andean Community, infringement procedures initiated by member states are considerably less central than they are within the WTO.

Most existing scholarship on regional economic DSMs focuses on explaining variation in their design, specifically their degree of judicialization (Smith 2000; Jo and Namgung 2012; Allee and Elsig 2015) or specific enforcement and flexibility features (Phelan 2015). Dispute settlement mechanisms contained within regional agreements or PTAs can roughly be categorized into tribunal-based dispute settlement and panel-based (ad hoc) dispute settlement mechanisms (Porges 2011; Chase et al. 2013). Existing studies suggest that there is limited innovation in the design of PTA-DSMs, and that most which adopt a judicial or quasi-judicial mechanism are structured like the WTO dispute panel process. Only five PTA-DSMs include an appellate stage.[31] Regional economic or trade courts also vary in the extent to which they form part of a broader economic integration regime, and only a few constitute deeply integrating regional courts, such as the CJEU, the European Free Trade Area (EFTA) Court, the ATJ, Mercosur, and the Central American Common Market (CACM). In terms of explaining institutional design, Smith (2000) finds that states with relatively high economic power favor less legalized dispute settlement provisions within PTAs, which is why standing economic tribunals (such as the CJEU) tend to exist only within PTAs for which power asymmetry is low. In contrast, the EU Commission tends to prefer ad hoc or nonjudicialized arbitration procedures in its PTAs with non-EU countries (Garcia Bercero 2006), which some argue allows it to maintain economic advantages (Broude 2007). Arnold and Rittberger (2013) similarly find that the reforms of Mercosur's dispute settlement system in 2002 – reforms that significantly legalized the system – were strongly favored by Uruguay and Paraguay, and less so by the larger economies of Argentina and Brazil.

[31] Mercosur, ASEAN, CJEU, East African Court of Justice, and the South African Development Community (SADC) Tribunal (now disbanded).

As for panel-based dispute settlement, Porges (2011) records twenty-five known arbitral decisions in PTA formal proceedings (relating to sixteen separate disputes) by mid-2011, compared to the 136 panel reports issued between 1995 and 2011 within the WTO. She attributes this low level of PTA disputes to the fact that many of these agreements are new and implementation takes time, thus the probability of disputes arising over failure to implement remains low. She also suggests that PTA institutions and the repeated interactions involved help to reduce trade conflicts and that if conflicts do arise, the WTO is likely to be a more attractive forum. Like others, she suggests that factors contributing to this preference include: the "familiarity" and experience of WTO institutions, available recourse to retaliatory concessions, experienced and seemingly neutral dispute panelists, dispute settlement costs, higher reputational costs of noncompliance within the WTO, existing case law, appellate review, and the WTO secretariat staff (Davey 2006; Busch 2007; Porges 2011; Lewis and Van den Bossche 2013).

Because of this potential for jurisdictional overlap, a growing body of scholarship focuses on jurisdictional conflict, "fragmentation," or "forum shopping" between regional or PTA-based mechanisms and the WTO's DSM (Alter and Meunier 2006; Kwak and Marceau 2006; Busch 2007; Henckels 2008; Davis 2009; Hillman 2009; Marceau and Wyatt 2010; Yang 2012; Flett 2015). In fact, nearly half of existing PTAs that create an internal DSM also provide for an external option, typically through the WTO DSM, and most permit the complainant to choose the forum (Allee and Elsig 2015: 331). However, it appears that concerns about forum shopping or substitution effects may be slightly overstated (but see Faude 2018). For example, Mavroidis and Sapir (2015) recently concluded that the signature of a PTA with the EU or US leads to a decrease in WTO litigation between the parties, but not to the appearance of new disputes under the PTA.

Conclusion

As described by member governments and WTO officials, at its core the WTO is a "member-driven" organization. The dispute settlement mechanism is built around serving the interests of members with respect to facilitating the resolution of conflicts over market access. The WTO's ability to do so effectively depends on how it encourages members to reach mutually acceptable solutions and, when negotiations fail, how well it can compel members found in breach to conform their laws to WTO rules. This chapter first summarized existing research on the DSM's performance in contributing to these outcome goals, noting that operationalizing the concept of "compliance" remains a tricky empirical task. While open noncompliance with adopted decisions is relatively rare, both time-to-resolution and the degree of report implementation vary substantially across disputes. We note that post-litigation bargaining between the parties plays an important and understudied role in determining the extent to which losing parties implement the DSB's recommendations. Are WTO rulings effective at discouraging noncompliance because of the potential for punitive consequences via suspension of concessions or other more informal costs, or because they reduce information asymmetries and facilitate subsequent bargaining between the parties? This remains an open research question and has significant implications for understanding the connection between dispute outcomes and state behavior. In particular, it is not clear how important noncompliance costs are to ruling implementation and which actors (international or domestic) impose the most salient costs.

Beyond resolving disputes, the dispute settlement mechanism has also taken on an informal role as a source of clarification in international trade law. Panel and Appellate Body reports follow an ad hoc system of precedent under which interpretations of past reports should be adhered to absent cogent reasons to ignore. While the Appellate Body has taken care to emphasize that reports are only binding on the disputing parties, panelists, and indeed the Appellate Body, often argue that adherence to precedent is important for providing members with transparency in dispute resolution. In the absence of more member-driven sources of clarification via negotiated agreements or authoritative interpretations, much of the development of international trade law in the last decade has taken place through reports adopted by the DSB. One pressing and open research question relates to the extent to which this precedent-making system sufficiently represents the interests of *all* members as opposed to those of the most powerful economies. Some recent studies suggest that governments use precedent strategically in order to increase their chances of success in future disputes. If this is the case, then overrepresentation of the most influential countries may result in the adoption of interpretations that are largely in the interests of a small fraction of members. A promising line of future research could seek to connect WTO precedent setting to pretrial bargains among states. Does more clarity facilitate successful bargaining without the need to resort to trial, and in whose interest is precedent being set? Ultimately, understanding whether the WTO Dispute Settlement Mechanism is performing well requires an examination of the distributional consequences of WTO jurisprudence. The WTO may very well be member-driven, but much more research is needed to understand which members are driving the WTO and their intended destination.

References

Abbott, Kenneth W. and Snidal, Duncan. 2000. "Hard and Soft Law in International Governance," *International Organization* 54(3): 421–456.

Allee, Todd and Elsig, Manfred. 2015. "Dispute Settlement Provisions in PTAs: New Data and New Concepts," in Dür, Andreas and Elsig, Manfred (eds.), *Trade Cooperation: The Purpose, Design and Effects of Preferential Trade Agreements*. Cambridge: Cambridge University Press, pp. 319–350.

Alter, Karen J. 2008. "Agents or Trustees? International Courts in Their Political Context," *European Journal of International Relations* 14(1): 33–63.

2001. *Establishing the Supremacy of European Law: The Making of an International Rule of Law in Europe*. Oxford: Oxford University Press.

Alter, Karen J. and Helfer, Laurence R. 2010. "Nature or Nurture? Judicial Lawmaking in the European Court of Justice and the Andean Tribunal of Justice," *International Organization* 64(4): 563–592.

Alter, Karen J. and Meunier, Sophie, 2006. "Nested and Overlapping Regimes in the Transatlantic Banana Trade Dispute," *Journal of European Public Policy* 13(3): 362–382.

Alter, Karen J., Saldias, Osvaldo, and Helfer, Laurence R. 2012. "Transplanting the European Court of Justice: The Experience of the Andean Tribunal of Justice," *American Journal of Comparative Law* 60(3): 629–694.

Arnold, Christian and Rittberger, Berthold. 2013. "The Legalization of Dispute Resolution in Mercosur," *Journal of Politics in Latin America* 5(3): 97–132.

Bechtel, Michael M. and Sattler, Thomas. 2015. "What Is Litigation in the World Trade Organization Worth?," *International Organization* 69(2): 375–403.

Bhala, Raj. 1999a. "The Myth About Stare Decisis and International Trade Law: Part One of a Trilogy," *American University International Law Review* 14(4): 845–956.

1999b. "The Precedent Setters: De Facto Stare Decisis in WTO Adjudication: Part Two of a Trilogy," *Journal of Transnational Law and Policy* 9(1): 1–151.

Blackmore, Dana T. 2003. "Eradicating the Long-Standing Existence of a No-Precedent Rule in International Trade Law-Looking Toward Stare Decisis in WTO Dispute Settlement," *North Carolina Journal of International Law* 29(3): 487–519.

Bown, Chad P. 2005. "Participation in WTO Dispute Settlement: Complainants, Interested Parties, and Free Riders," *World Bank Economic Review* 19(2): 287–310.

Bown, Chad P. and Reynolds, Kara M. 2014. "Trade Flows and Trade Disputes," *Review of International Organizations* 10(2): 145–177.

Brewster, Rachel. 2011. "The Remedy Gap: Institutional Design, Retaliation, and Trade Law Enforcement," *George Washington Law Review* 80(1): 102–158.

2013. "Pricing Compliance: When Formal Remedies Displace Reputational Sanctions," *Harvard International Law Journal* 54(2): 259–314.

Brewster, Rachel and Chilton, Adam. 2014. "Supplying Compliance: Why and When the United States Complies with WTO Rulings," *Yale Journal of International Law* 39(2): 201–247.

Broude, Tomer. 2007. "From *Pax Mercatoria* to *Pax Europea*: How Trade Dispute Procedures Serve the EC's Regional Hegemony," in Stephan, Paul B. (ed.), *Economics of European Union Law*. Northampton, MA: Edward Elgar Publishing, pp. 319–334.

Brutger, Ryan and Morse, Julia C. 2015. "Balancing Law and Politics: Judicial Incentives in WTO Dispute Settlement," *Review of International Organizations* 10(2): 179–205.

Busch, Marc L. 2007. "Overlapping Institutions, Forum Shopping, and Dispute Settlement in International Trade," *International Organization* 61(04): 735–761.

Busch, Marc L. and Pelc, Krzysztof J. 2010. "The Politics of Judicial Economy at the World Trade Organization," *International Organization* 64(2): 257–279.

Busch, Marc L. and Reinhardt, Eric. 2000. "Bargaining in the Shadow of the Law: Early Settlement in GATT/WTO Disputes," *Fordham International Law Journal* 24(1): 158–172.

2002. "Testing International Trade Law: Empirical Studies of GATT/WTO Dispute Settlement," in Kennedy, Daniel L. M. and Southwick, James D. (eds.), *The Political Economy of International Trade Law: Essays in Honor of Robert Hudec*. Cambridge: Cambridge University Press, pp. 457–481.

2003. "Transatlantic Trade Conflicts and GATT/WTO Dispute Settlement," in Petersmann, Ernst-Ulrich and Pollack, Mark A. (eds.), *Transatlantic Economic Disputes: The EU, the US, and the WTO*. Oxford: Oxford University Press, pp. 465–486.

2006. "Three's a Crowd: Third Parties and WTO Dispute Settlement," *World Politics* 58(3): 446–77.

Busch, Marc L., Raciborski, Rafal, and Reinhardt, Eric. 2008. "Does the Rule of Law Matter? The WTO and US Antidumping Investigations," Working Paper, Georgetown University.

Busch, Marc L., Reinhardt, Eric, and Shaffer, Gregory. 2009. "Does Legal Capacity Matter? A Survey of WTO Members," *World Trade Review* 8(4): 559–77.

Chase, Claude, Yanovich, Alan, Crawford, Jo-Ann, and Ugaz, Pamela. 2013. "Mapping of Dispute Settlement Mechanisms in Regional Trade

3

Performance of Investment Treaty Arbitration

DANIEL BEHN

Introduction

The development of the modern investment treaty regime represents one of the most remarkable extensions of international law in the postwar period. Largely built on a network of over 3,000 bilateral investment treaties (BITs) and regional free trade agreements (FTAs), a handful of plurilateral investment treaties, as well as customary international law, foreign investors are granted beneficiary rights aimed at the protection of their investments.[1] While each international investment agreement (IIA) is a stand-alone agreement with considerable diversity, agreements typically include: prohibition against expropriation without adequate compensation, full protection and security, fair and equitable treatment, national treatment, most-favored nation treatment, free transfer of capital, and investor-state dispute settlement (ISDS) provisions. Combined, it has been claimed that "no other category of private individuals" is "given such expansive rights in international law as are private actors investing across borders."[2]

Primarily, however, the development of this regime is not exceptional solely for the expansiveness of the substantive rights granted to foreign investors under IIAs, but rather for the combination of such rights with the robustness of the ISDS mechanisms offered to foreign investors. Investment treaty arbitration (ITA), as permitted under the majority of IIAs in force, grants beneficiary rights to foreign investors for the initiation of arbitral claims against the state hosting their investments without

[1] Plurilateral treaties include, *inter alia*: the Energy Charter Treaty; the North American Free Trade Agreement; the Dominican Republic-Central American Free Trade Agreement; the Trans-Pacific Partnership; the Organization of the Islamic Conference Agreement for the Promotion, Protection, and Guarantee of Investments; and the Association of South-East Asian Nations Comprehensive Investment Agreement.

[2] B. Simmons, "Bargaining over BITs, Arbitrating Awards: The Regime for Protection and Promotion of International Investment," *World Politics*, 66, no. 1 (2014), 42.

the consent of their home state or the requirement (in almost all cases) to first exhaust domestic remedies.

ITA is thus distinct in relation to many of the other standing international courts presented in this volume; and because of this decentralized structure – combined with a striking number of disputes that have emerged prominently since 1990 – it is a system of adjudication that has garnered significant scholarly and critical attention. With close to 900 ITAs registered to date (through August 1, 2017), as well as an unknown number of instances in which the threat of treaty arbitration has been used as a bargaining tool, states hosting foreign investors increasingly find themselves having to defend their laws and policies before, and in, the shadow of investment treaty tribunals.

Many of these ITAs have resulted in sizable compensation awards for actions that states believe are both legitimate and within their exclusive purview as sovereigns;[3] and it is this increasing resort to ITA by aggrieved foreign investors that has led many (including some states) in recent years to reassess the utility of such a system of adjudication.[4] At the same time, ITA continues on a growth trajectory, and while mere use does not connote good performance, its practice to date indicates a successful form of dispute settlement by most measures. However, is it possible that ITA is performing too well?

As with any international legal order, the modern IIA regime might serve multiple purposes, but it appears that one purpose stands out as the primary driver for the development and maintenance of the regime as it is currently practiced: providing effective legal remedies to foreign investors in the event a dispute arises in the state hosting their investments (all other purposes are ancillary). From that perspective, ITA appears to be performing this function. This purpose (providing for investment treaty arbitration) is a response to a long-standing historical problem facing foreign investors investing abroad; and this form of adjudication – while arguably flawed – could be seen as providing an alternative, more effective, rule of law promoting, and peaceful form of dispute settlement when

[3] D. Behn, "Legitimacy, Evolution and Growth in Investment Treaty Arbitration: Empirically Evaluating the State-of-the-Art," *Georgetown Journal of International Law*, 46, no. 2 (2015), 363.

[4] M. Langford, D. Behn, and O. K. Fauchald, "Backlash and State Strategies in International Investment Law" in T. Gammeltoft-Hansen and T. Aalberts (eds.), *The Changing Practices of International Law: Sovereignty, Law and Politics in a Globalizing World* (Cambridge: Cambridge University Press, 2017).

compared to previous modes established to solve the problems relating to disputes that arise in the context of foreign investment.

Arguments in support of ITA hold that while this form of adjudication has issues worthy of reform,[5] efforts to dismantle the regime would only do away with treaty-based arbitration, not the underlying disputes (in fact, it might even increase the number of disputes). Therefore, the question is whether alternatives to ITA would not backtrack global governance in this area to a position prior to the advent of investment treaty arbitration: an era that was considered so problematic for foreign investment protection that ITA was developed as a response. However, given ITA's exclusive purpose, the strongest argument against its practice is whether it is needed at all anymore: i.e., was the development of this form of adjudication a response to a particular historical problem (inadequate local remedies in weak rule of law states) that is no longer present?

This contribution aims to evaluate the performance of this form of international adjudication in light of this singular purpose thesis. In doing so, this chapter will look at how ITA is performing in terms of its access, outcome, and process performance in individual cases and its performance in the aggregate as a (global) system of adjudication.

The Purpose of Investment Treaty Arbitration in Historical Context

Before attempting to evaluate the performance of ITA, it is important to assess how the international regime on foreign investment has developed across time, what goals it has tried to achieve and what types of problems it has sought (explicitly or implicitly) to overcome.

Investment treaty arbitration is a recent phenomenon. While the practice of ITA has emerged as a prominent form of international adjudication in the past twenty-five years, it is only in the past fifty years that ITA has even been possible. The first modern IIA was signed in 1959,[6] but the first

[5] One particularly strong reform measure currently being floated is for the establishment of an international investment court. The purpose of establishing such a court would be to alleviate concerns, not with the utility of having international dispute settlement for foreign investors, but with charges that the structure of arbitration is ill-suited for the resolution of these kinds of disputes. However, it is important to note that the current proposals for an international investment court do not propose a "court," but a more institutionalized form of arbitration that includes an appellate review mechanism.

[6] *Pakistan-Germany BIT* (1959).

IIA that included ISDS provisions was not signed until 1967.[7] Prior to this, there was no mechanism for ITA as it is currently practiced. While there have long been examples of dispute settlement provisions being embedded in various types of treaties signed by states, the specific type of adjudication permitted in modern IIAs is new.[8]

Most IIAs present a foreign investor with a standing offer to arbitrate a dispute directly with a state hosting their investment should a treaty breach occur, thus bypassing previous requirements of diplomatic espousal under international law. Further, these arbitrations will be composed on an ad hoc basis with relative autonomy from other disputes arising out of other IIAs. Combined, these structural characteristics of ITA make it a system of adjudication that is unfamiliar in the history of international law.

In the following subsections, the purpose of this system of adjudication will be examined as a means of putting its recent practice in historical context. While the overall practice of ITA is relatively new (from about 1990), the underlying issues concerning the treatment of foreign aliens in the international system are long-standing and can help in understanding why IIAs emerged in the post-Second World War period. The historical development of modern IIAs can be seen as a partial response to two sets of problems grouped broadly into the following categories: (1) providing alternatives to diplomatic espousal and "gunboat diplomacy"; and (2) providing solutions to problems arising out of commercial contracts with states.

Alternatives to Diplomatic Espousal

Historically speaking, the modern IIA regime grew out of the broader category of public international law relating to the treatment of foreign aliens. Typically, an alien residing in a foreign sovereign territory will be subject primarily to the laws and customs of the state in which she is residing. However, international legal rules developed so as to protect foreign aliens from domestic rules and procedures that fall below an international minimum standard of treatment.[9] The default rule is that

[7] *Chad-Italy BIT* (1967) (never entered into force). The first BIT with ISDS to enter into force was the *Netherlands-Indonesia BIT* (1969).

[8] J. Paulsson, "Arbitration without Privity," *ICSID Review*, 10, no. 2 (1995), 232.

[9] E. Root, "The Basis of Protection to Citizens Residing Abroad," *American Journal of International Law*, 4, no. 3, (1910), 517; E. Borchard, "The Minimum Standard of Treatment of Aliens," *Michigan Law Review*, 38, no. 4 (1940), 445.

the foreign alien is subject to the law of the state where she is residing unless the application of such laws fall below a minimum standard. However, even if the foreign alien has been treated in a manner below the minimum standard, how does she gain recourse to the law if individuals or companies are not directly subject to international law?

Until very recently, the customary international law on diplomatic protection has provided a good answer to this question. Diplomatic protection permits the home state of a foreign alien to espouse a claim against the state where the foreign alien was injured. In the past two hundred years, diplomatic protection claims have been espoused three ways: (1) directly between the governments of the home state of the foreign alien and the state where the injury occurred; (2) as legal proceedings before the International Court of Justice (ICJ);[10] or (3) through the establishment of international claims commissions.[11] However, in the post–Second World War period, the traditional use of diplomatic protection or espousal for remedying injuries to foreign aliens (particularly the narrower category of foreign investors) has largely been replaced by the ISDS provisions in IIAs. Since the first modern IIA was signed, there have only been three foreign investment-related cases involving diplomatic espousal brought before the ICJ.[12]

The ISDS provisions in IIAs represent a significant shift away from the traditional model of diplomatic espousal and can be seen as one of the underlying structural objectives or goals of IIAs: states choosing to allow direct rights of action to foreign investors for breaches to the underlying IIA. The exact reasons as to why states have chosen this option is not entirely clear historically, but is often attributed to the perceived benefits of "depoliticizing" international disputes and the political and economic efficiencies that can be gained when an international dispute involving a foreign alien can be directly resolved with the state where the injury occurred without directly involving the foreign alien's home state.

[10] Also including its predecessor, the Permanent Court of International Justice.

[11] "The Jay Treaty arbitrations marked the beginning of a long line of development, which reached its high noon around the year 1900 and continued until well after World War I. During this period, *ad hoc* interstate arbitration became the dominant method of resolving international claims. In a comprehensive survey, A. M. Sruyt has catalogued around 380 international arbitrations that were conducted during the period 1776–1925." V. Heiskanen, "Arbitrating Mass Investor Claims: Lessons of International Claims Commissions" in B. Macmahon (ed.), *Multiple Party Actions in International Arbitration* (Oxford: Oxford University Press, 2009), 299.

[12] These include: *Barcelona Traction* (*Belgium* v. *Spain*), 1970 ICJ Rep. 3; *ELSI* (*US* v. *Italy*) 1989 ICJ Rep. 15; and *Diallo* (*Guinea* v. *DRC*) 2012 ICJ Rep. 324.

In the past, disputes requiring diplomatic espousal of foreign alien claims have – at times – escalated into what has been called "gunboat diplomacy," whereby the home state of the foreign alien threatens or uses force against the state where the foreign alien was injured.[13] Many of these examples of gunboat diplomacy occurred in states that had already declared independence in the nineteenth century (i.e., Latin American states); and without sufficient international legal remedies (none had been sufficiently developed prior to the First World War), imperial powers frequently used their military prowess to intimidate or pressure certain states into providing remedies for injured foreign aliens. The post–Second World War international legal development that provides an alternative to gunboat diplomacy (i.e., ITA) has been seen by some states as a beneficial alternative.

In historical terms then, one of the performance criteria that could be used to evaluate ITA is whether the move away from diplomatic espousal for these types of international disputes has actually improved relations between states and the extent to which the robustness of legal dispute resolution for conflicts between foreigners and the states in which they invest has reduced the real or potential risk of gunboat diplomacy.

Alternatives to Commercial Arbitration with States

One additional goal of the modern IIA regime can be identified by looking at the history of colonialism and the contractual arrangements between foreign investors and states that emerged in the period before and after decolonization. There is an argument that the emergence of IIAs can be largely attributed to the geopolitics associated with the process of decolonization and the perceived lack of legal protections for foreign investors in newly independent states.[14] During the colonial era, imperial states were able to protect the investments of their citizens by

13 Great Britain intervened militarily in Latin American states on at least forty occasions between 1820 and 1914.

14 However, considering that most early BITs did not include ISDS provisions, it is more likely that early IIA practice was little more than a signaling of friendly relations between developing and developed economies, with little expectation from developing states that they would become subject to investment treaty disputes. There is a good argument that some of these early IIAs were intended to develop relationships between former colonial powers and potential markets that had been closed to them previously (i.e., the colonies of other colonial powers). Of the 403 IIAs signed before 1990, over half (207) were signed between a colonial power and a former colony. However, only sixteen IIAs were signed by a colonial power and *their* former colony.

extending their sovereign control over colonial territories. Foreign investment in the colonies was not really foreign at all (at least not foreign capital initiating in the imperial state of that colony). There was little need for international legal protections that were distinct from the legal protections already available to foreign aliens (i.e., citizens of the imperial state) operating within the territory of the colony.

However, as states began to decolonize in the post–Second World War period, some foreign investors were placed in a vulnerable position: Many newly independent states sought to denounce historical oppression from the colonial powers by declaring that foreigners residing or investing within the sovereign territory of these newly formed states would not be afforded any special rights independent of the rights granted to nationals.

At the international level, this policy was initially pursued at the United Nations (UN) through declarations on permanent sovereignty over natural resources (PSNR)[15] in what later came to be described as the new international economic order (NIEO).[16] These declarations asserted, inter alia, that sovereign states had the autonomy to shape their own policies on how foreign investors would be treated within their territory. Many of the former colonies were (are) rich in resources, and they believed that – as newly independent states – those resources were exclusively theirs to exploit and the nationalization of natural resource operations was legal and did not require compensation commensurate with the customary international law standard.

During this period, many newly independent states pursued nationalization policies (especially in the extractive industries). The practice of nationalization signaled two problems for foreign investment protection. The first problem was that some foreign investors found that the nationalization of their assets might not be compensated at the level required by customary international law. The second problem was that even if their contracts or concessions with states included strong dispute settlement mechanisms calling for international arbitration, enforcing a favorable award against a state was not always a straightforward process. Many arbitrations that did result from nationalizations in the 1950s

[15] UN, General Assembly Resolution, *Right to Exploit Freely Natural Wealth and Resources*, 626 (December 21, 1952); UN, General Assembly Resolution, *Permanent Sovereignty Over Natural Resources*, 1803 (XVII) (December 14, 1962); UN, General Assembly Resolution, *Permanent Sovereignty Over Natural Resources*, 3171 (XXVIII) (December 17, 1973).

[16] UN, General Assembly Resolution, *Declaration on the Establishment of a New International Economic Order*, A/RES/S-6/3201 (May 1, 1974).

through the 1970s demonstrated that there would be considerable difficulty at the enforcement stage of the proceedings.

So, while some newly independent states made broad declarations on the international stage through the PSNR and NIEO declarations, nationalized their natural resource operations, and signaled that contract-based arbitration might not be a viable means to protect foreign investments, many of these same states also knew that they would not be able to develop their economies without foreign capital and expertise. The main question to arise in this context was how these states could convince foreign investors that their investments would be adequately protected. For some investors and states, the continued practice of signing contracts and concessions with arbitration clauses would be sufficient. However, for others, more robust solutions would have to develop; and two did: (1) the signing of the International Centre for Settlement of Investment Disputes (ICSID) Convention; and (2) the signing of BITs between capital-exporting and capital-importing states.

As to the first solution, the ICSID Convention was ratified in 1965. The ICSID Convention does two things of critical significance: (1) it allows for contracts to be "internationalized," thus overcoming the perceived problem during the NIEO that contracts would be subject to national expropriation laws (and their significantly lower rates of compensation); and (2) it requires that final arbitral awards be directly enforceable against states without the requirement of further enforcement procedures in domestic courts. It was thought that the inclusion of an ICSID arbitration clause in a contract with a state could remedy both of these issues.

The second solution was for some capital-exporting states to sign BITs with capital-importing states. While it remains unclear whether these early BITs were only pursued as a response to the problems of foreign asset protection that emerged after decolonization, some have argued that these agreements emerged as a means of defecting from the broader policy objectives pursued at the international level through the PSNR and NIEO declarations.[17] Regardless of exact reasons, IIAs became increasingly popular between the 1960s and the 1980s and would explode in the 1990s following the collapse of the Soviet Union and the rise of the so-called "Washington consensus." By the end of the first decade of the twenty-first century, over 3,000 of these agreements had been signed (see Figure 3.1).

[17] A. Guzman, "Why LDCs Sign Treaties that Hurt Them: Explaining the Popularity of Bilateral Investment Treaties," *Virginia Journal of International Law*, 38 (1997), 639.

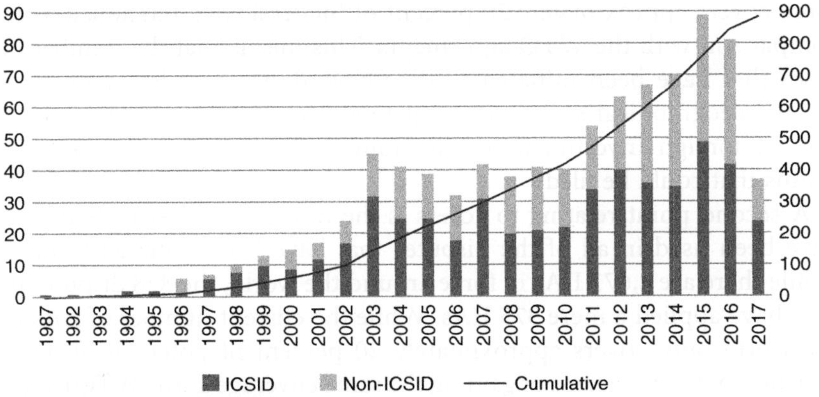

Figure 3.2 ITAs initiated by year (1987–2017)
Source: Data compiled by author from PITAD through August 1, 2017. Data on file with author

of the biggest issues in regard to performance at the individual case level relates to *access* to ITA rather than its processes or outcomes. As a largely bilateral treaty regime, the coverage of treaties allowing for ITA is limited to those states that have agreed to such bilateral relationships. If an assessment of the performance of ITA refers to the number of cases that have arisen to date, an equally relevant assessment is the number of cases that have not arisen because of issues relating to access to this form of adjudication. Two points on this issue of access are illustrative.

First, one must put the number of IIAs into perspective. While 3,327 IIAs have been signed (through August 1, 2017), 3,171 of which are current,[25] significantly fewer agreements have been ratified and are in force: a total of 2,673.[26] Furthermore, if one were to take the number of bilateral relationships represented by the WTO agreements with its current membership of 162 states, there would have to be 13,041[27] BITs to reach the same amount of coverage. Without taking into consideration the vast differences between foreign investment flows between states and the fact that some plurilateral investment agreements provide much more coverage than a single BIT,[28] the number of IIAs currently in

[25] 156 of signed IIAs have been terminated.

[26] 654 IIAs that have been signed but are not force. [27] (162*161)/2

[28] For example, the recently signed – but not yet ratified (and may never be ratified following the US withdrawal in January 2017) – Trans-Pacific Partnership covers twelve states which alone would count as the equivalent of sixty-six bilateral agreements.

force covers approximately 20 percent of bilateral state relationships in comparison with the WTO agreements. This means that the number of cases that have been initiated to date have done so as based on very limited geographical scope. A multilateral arrangement for the protection of foreign investment would dramatically increase the potential claims that could be filed.

A second point relating to access is the modest number of IIAs that have been used in all of the disputes that have been initiated to date. While there are 2,673 IIAs in force around the world, the 878 disputes to date have applied a mere 375 IIAs. While the current number of IIAs in the world only covers approximately 20 percent of potential bilateral pairings (at least in terms of gaining the same coverage as the WTO), only 14 percent of IIAs in force have been used in actual ITA cases. For critics of the use of ITA, this type of limited access may be a positive restriction. But if one is to assess this in terms of performance, one could easily argue that the current structure of investment treaty arbitration is so restrictive and selective that it leaves vast swaths of foreign investors without treaty protections and also disproportionately targets specific states that have been repeat respondent states in investment treaty arbitrations under the same treaty. For example, Map 3.1 shows the most frequently invoked treaties in ITA.[29] Remarkably, just six IIAs have been used in 25 percent (219 cases) of all ITAs registered to date.

The limited number of IIAs that have been used in ITA – and the high instances of a small number of treaties being invoked multiple times – demonstrates the uneven coverage and the uneven use of these agreements. In addition to issue of access, the pattern of use also raises a number of performance-related questions. Are certain respondent states being targeted? Are IIAs used reciprocally? And if not, what types of states are frequently sued in investment treaty arbitration?

On the issue of targeting, one can deduce from the data that the use of ITA tends to cluster around a small number of states. While there have been 111 different states as respondents in ITA cases, only thirty of those states have been sued once. The remaining eighty-one states have all received more than one claim. Fifteen states have between five and nine claims against them and twenty-three states have ten or more.

As Map 3.2 demonstrates, the top six respondent states in ITA constitute 26 percent of all claims initiated to date (225 cases). While some of the clustering of states can be explained by particular events (Argentina) or

[29] Ibid.

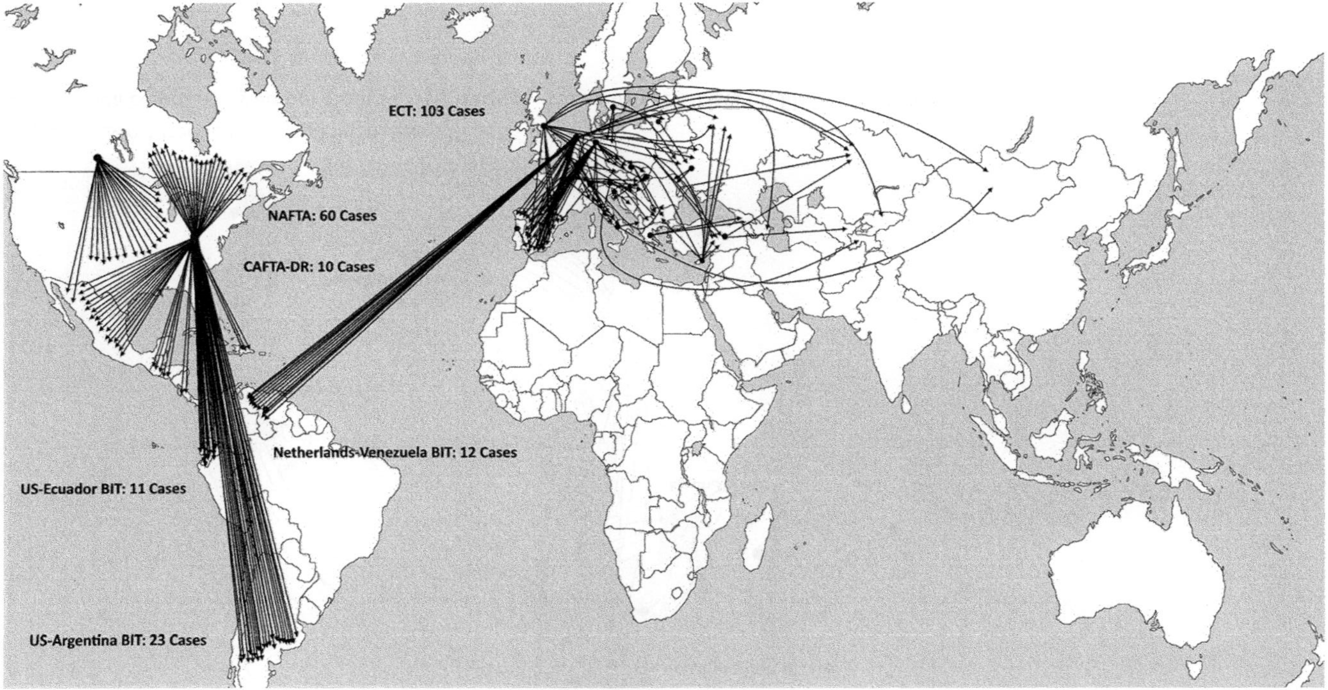

Map 3.1 Most frequently invoked IIAs in ITA

Source: Data compiled by author from PITAD through August 1, 2017. Data on file with author

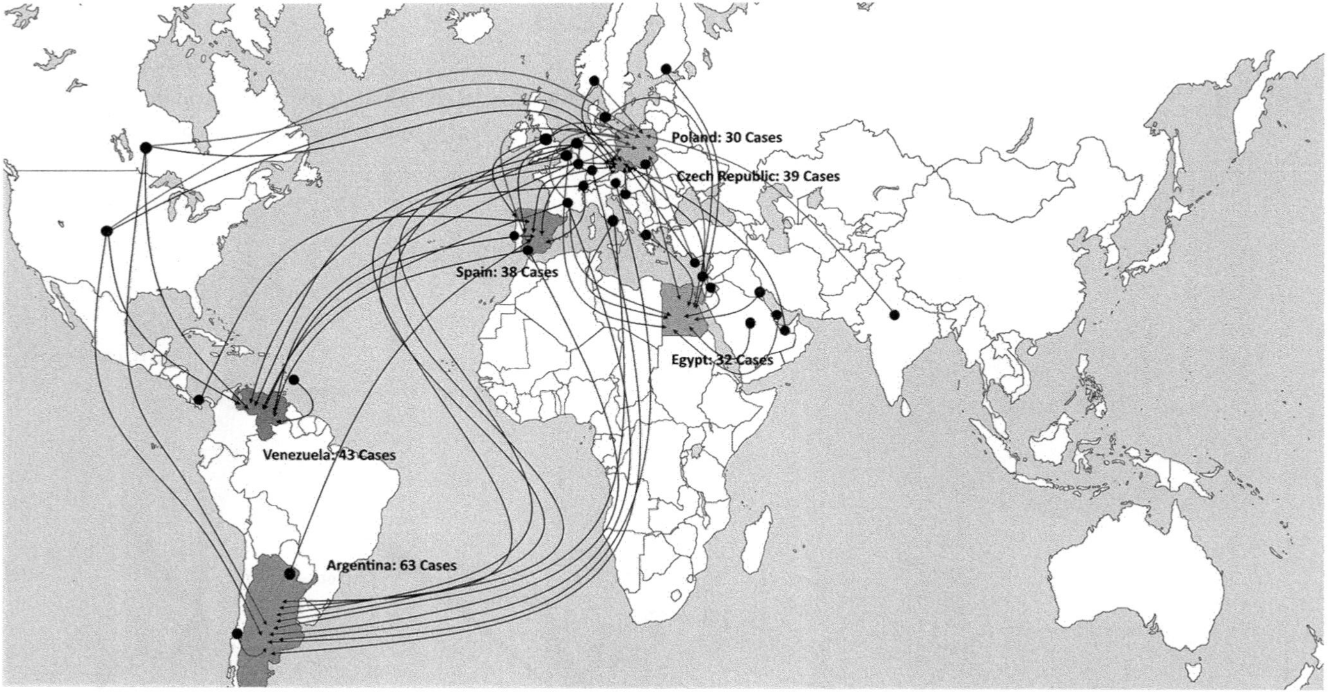

Map 3.2 Most frequent respondent states in ITA
Source: Data compiled by author from PITAD through August 1, 2017. Data on file with author

policy choices (Venezuela, Ecuador, and Spain), others are less obvious as to why they have attracted so many claims (Egypt, Czech Republic, and Poland).

While it is possible that the fact that Egypt, Czech Republic, and Poland have attracted a high number of ITA claims is explained by significant number of IIAs that these states have ratified, there are a number of other states with high numbers of IIAs that have received relatively few (or no) disputes (e.g., Turkey, China, Belarus, Iran, Malaysia, and Vietnam). Looking at those states that have been sued most frequently, there is one final consideration: particular treaties or types of treaties. Cases arising under the North American Free Trade Agreement (NAFTA) explain nearly all of the cases against Canada (twenty-five out of twenty-six cases), the US (eighteen out of eighteen cases), and Mexico (nineteen out of twenty-six cases). Further, in the case of Poland, Spain, and the Czech Republic, 87 out of 107 of the cases that have been filed against these states arise under the Energy Charter Treaty (ECT) or an intra-European Union (EU) BIT.

While all IIAs, especially BITs, are designed to be reciprocal, in operation they are used primarily unidirectionally. For example, of the 878 registered cases, there is only one treaty that has been invoked reciprocally.[30] Further, ITA disputes tend to be brought by investors from a capital-exporting state against a capital-importing state; this pattern correlates with the development status of states. In other words, the vast majority of ITAs brought to date have been initiated by claimant-investors from states with a higher development status than the respondent state. For example, Table 3.1 below shows that 87 percent of the 878 cases initiated have been brought by claimant-investors from a high-income state (as measured by the World Bank income categories). Further, there are only twenty-six cases where the development status of the home state of the claimant-investor is lower than the development status of the respondent host state.

On the respondent side of the dispute, the development status of states is distributed more evenly, with the highest percentage of respondent states falling in the upper middle-income group. Interestingly, there are very few cases brought against low-income states. While this challenges many perceptions that ITA is used by powerful economic actors from the developed world against poorer developing states, the reality is more nuanced. Very poor states tend to be excluded from many forms of

[30] *Spain-Argentina BIT* (1992).

Table 3.1 *Registered ITA cases by host and home state World Bank income groups*

		Claimant-investor home state				
		High income	Upper middle income	Lower middle income	Low income	Sum (878 cases)
Respondent state	High income	229 *25.9%*	21 *2.4%*	5 *1.0%*	0 *0.0%*	255 *28.9%*
	Upper middle income	336 *38.3%*	43 *4.9%*	0 *0.0%*	0 *0.0%*	385 *43.8%*
	Lower middle income	174 19.8%	40 4.5%	2 0.1%	0 0.0%	216 24.7%
	Low income	21 *2.4%*	2 *0.1%*	0 *0.0%*	0 *0.0%*	23 *2.7%*
	Sum (878 cases)	760 *86.5%*	106 *12.1%*	12 *1.4%*	0 *0.0%*	878 *100.0%*

Source: Data compiled by author from PITAD through August 1, 2017. Data on file with author

international economic governance and investment treaty arbitration is no exception. There is no evidence of targeting against low-income states, primarily because foreign investment flowing into these states is very low in the first place. However, there is an issue of targeting in ITA, but to date the targeting has been against more developed states (see Map 3.2). The exceptions in this regard are Egypt and Ecuador.

Overall, one can say that ITA has been used by claimant-investors in well-developed economies against respondents from slightly less-developed – but not low-income – states. In many ways, this makes sense. The signing of IIAs over the past sixty years reflects this pattern. If the purpose of IIAs was to provide legal protections for foreign investors in capital-exporting states who are investing in capital-importing states, the performance of ITA to date supports this pattern. It is an entirely different question, however, as to whether this *should* be the way that ITA is performing.

Even when claimant-investors have access to ITA they tend to use it sparingly; and the majority of cases that have been brought to date appear to be claims of last resort. For example, the global number of registered multinationals and their subsidiaries in 2007 was at least 858,000.[31] This means that the 878 cases to date may be a mere fraction of potential claims. This fact may foster additional instability for the regime as ITA becomes more popular and well known as a means for adjudicating international disputes. There is a potential for thousands of cases entering the pipeline in the coming decades. Take a further example on the limited number of cases filed to date: there are currently thirty-eight investment treaty arbitrations (all based on the ECT) that have been filed against Spain (three have been concluded) in relation to the incentivization of renewable energy. However, one source claims that there have been over 650,000 domestic court cases that have been filed in relation to the same issues being litigated in the treaty-based arbitrations.[32]

Further, while there are a number of home states of claimant-investors that use ITA frequently (see Map 3.3), there are very few examples of repeat claimant-investors. The top six home states of claimant-investors accounts for 54 percent of all cases initiated to date (468 cases). On the issue of repeat claimant-investors, 771 cases (out of 878) were brought by a foreign investor that had never brought an ITA case before. Of the remaining 107 cases, there are a number of examples of entities using ITA more than once; and a few examples of entities using ITA repeatedly against the same state (e.g., Yukos shareholders – Russia, Uzan family claims – Turkey, and Bogdanov family claims – Moldova) and against multiple states (e.g., SGS, Impregilo, Phillip Morris, ExxonMobil, ConocoPhillips, EDF, Vivendi, France Telecom, AES, and RSM).

The conclusion that these illustrations capture is that ITA as it is currently practiced represents a small fraction of potential cases and the limitations in treaty coverage have resulted in a small number of states having to respond to a disproportionately high number of cases (and repeatedly in many instances). In terms of performance deficits, the clearest issue for ITA relates to the fact that many foreign investors do not have access to ITA and those that do have access appear to bring suits disproportionately against a small number of targeted states.

[31] UNCTAD, *World Investment Report* (2007).

[32] D. Behn and O. K. Fauchald, "Governments under Cross-Fire: Renewable Energy and International Economic Tribunals," *Manchester Journal of International Economic Law*, 12, no. 2 (2015), 117.

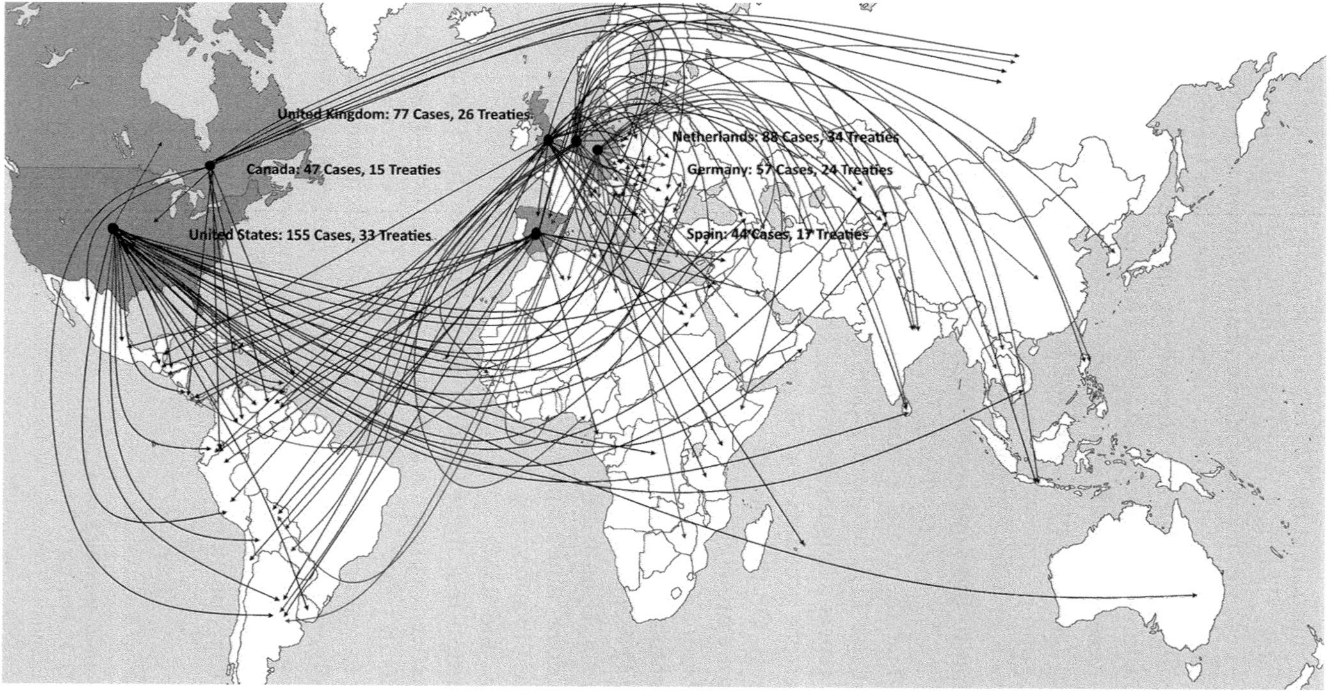

Map 3.3 Most frequent investor home states in ITA

Source: Data compiled by author from PITAD through August 1, 2017. Data on file with author

Outcome Performance

Moving from patterns of use to patterns of outcomes, this section will assess the performance of ITA in relation to outcomes in specific cases. Given the number of cases that have been filed to date, how has ITA performed in terms of its ability to resolve particular disputes? Further, what performance deficits can be identified, and are they able to be improved?

While ITA has been on a growth trajectory, the early days of ITA were fairly modest. There was a thirty-year gap between the signing of the first BIT and the first treaty-based arbitration. The first treaty-based investment dispute was initiated in the late-1980s and rendered an award in 1990.[33] Before this date, there were a number of ICSID arbitrations but they were all based on ICSID arbitration clauses in investment contracts with states or in a host state's foreign investment law that included recourse to ICSID arbitration in the event of a dispute. While there continues to be some practice of foreign investment law-based or contract-based ICISD arbitrations, they are now in the distinct minority when compared to treaty-based arbitrations.

Through the 1990s, there were only a handful of ITA cases that were initiated and an even smaller number that reached final awards. Almost all of these cases were arbitrations administered according to the ICSID Convention. However, there were a few ad hoc tribunals established under the UNCITRAL arbitration rules during this decade as well. The first known UNCITRAL treaty-based arbitration issued an award in 1995.[34] Towards the end of the 1990s, a number of cases based on NAFTA were also initiated. Most of these early cases were brought by US investors against Mexico, but there were also a few important cases brought by Canadian investors against the US, and by US investors against Canada.

By the turn of the twenty-first century, there were approximately forty-three ITA cases that had been initiated, and after 2000 the annual number of initiated claims starts to increase substantially. The 2000s saw an additional 334 cases registered; and the period of 2010 through the present added 501. Overall, of the 878 registered ITA cases, 388 cases have reached final awards, 124 cases have settled, 67 cases were discontinued, and 299 cases remain pending. From this dataset, we see that the cases resolved through final decisions in the first instance

[33] *Asian Agricultural Products Limited (AAPL)* v. *Sri Lanka* (ICSID Case No. ARB/87/3).
[34] *Saar Papier* v. *Poland* (UNCITRAL) 1994.

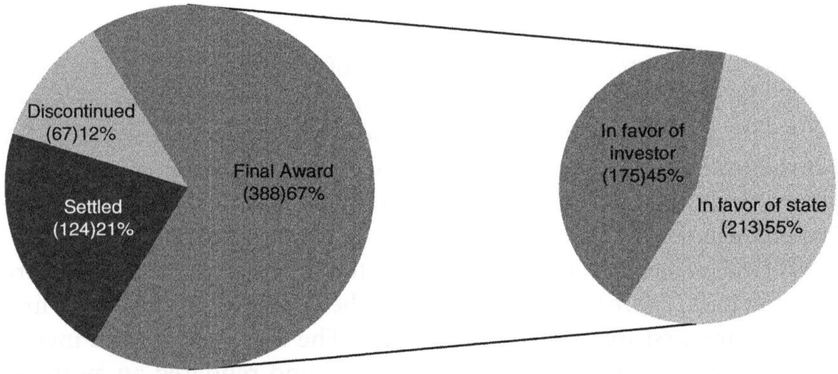

Figure 3.3 Finally resolved ITA cases (1990–2017)
Source: PITAD through August 1, 2017

(i.e., not including annulments at ICSID or set-aside proceedings in domestic courts) found in favor of the claimant-investor in 175 instances and found in favor of the respondent state in 213 instances (see Figure 3.3).

Including just these cases that were resolved in the form of final awards in the first instance, the win-loss rate does not appear problematic on its face. Claimant-investors win 45 percent of the time. However, we can assume a significant number of settled were resolved in favor of the claimant-investor, even if the investor did not secure its preferred or ideal remedy in these cases. Taking the settled cases as representing (at least partial) win for the claimant-investor, the win rates rise from 45 percent to approximately 67 percent.

Before briefly turning to some of the critiques relating to outcomes and structural bias in the ITA regime, it is interesting to divide up the cases between jurisdictional decisions and merits decisions. In doing so, we see that tribunals in an ITA case accept jurisdiction in 72 percent of disputes (278 out of 388 cases ending in a final award).

There are a number of reasons why tribunals accept jurisdiction in the vast number of claims brought before them: some are probably completely benign, others may be less so. In many ways, the nature of investment treaty arbitration means that cases of this type are often brought as a last resort, and given the seriousness of a private entity bringing suit against a foreign state (the "seriousness" thesis), a high number of cases of questionable jurisdiction are not entering into the system in the first place. However, an alternative argument – of the less benign type – is that

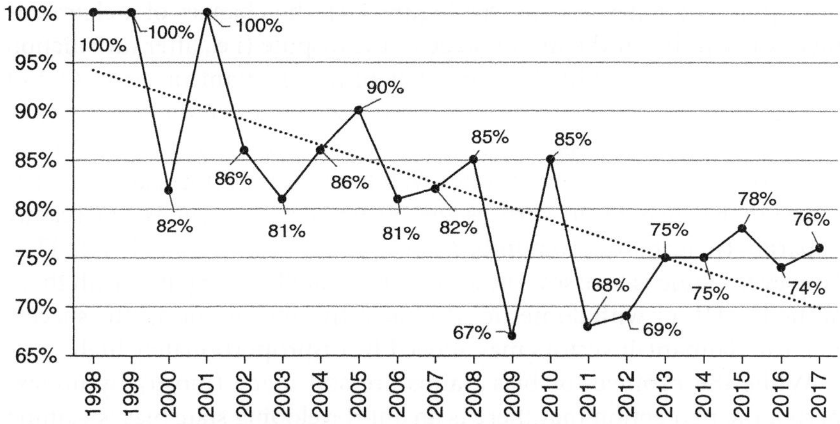

Figure 3.4 Jurisdictional decisions in finally resolved cases (across time)
Source: Data compiled by author from PITAD through August 1, 2017. Data on file with author

tribunals have been systematically expanding their jurisdiction in ITAs across time (in order to benefit from more cases and more arbitral appointments) by defining key terms such as what constitutes an eligible "foreign investor" and "foreign investment" in a liberal manner (the "expansiveness" thesis).

A study, using content analysis to assess the jurisdictional aspects of early ITAs, supports the expansiveness thesis.[35] However, Figure 3.4 shows that the expansiveness thesis does not hold across time. Tribunals before 2005 accepted jurisdiction on average in about 85 percent of the cases, while cases brought in the last ten years drop to about 70 percent. The conclusions that can be drawn from these numbers is that there may have been some early expansiveness in interpretations on jurisdictional issues, but that the more recent trend is that tribunals may either be restricting their jurisdictional interpretations (the opposite of the "expansiveness" thesis) or that there are more dubious cases entering the system (the opposite of the "seriousness" thesis).

In addition to the issues of jurisdiction, one of the fundamental critiques against ITA outcomes is that there is a proinvestor bias, reflected in claimant-investors winning a high percentage of claims. While there appears to be a near 45 percent to 55 percent split in favor

[35] G. Van Harten, "Arbitrator Behavior in Asymmetrical Adjudication: An Empirical Study of Investment Treaty Arbitration," *Osgoode Hall Law Journal*, 50, no. 1 (2012), 211.

of respondent states overall (see Figure 3.3), the chances of a claimant-investor winning at the merits stage of the dispute (i.e., after jurisdiction has been accepted) shifts back in favor of the claimant-investor. Out of 288 cases where an ITA tribunal accepts jurisdiction and decides on the merits of the dispute, claimant-investors have succeeded in 161 out of 288 cases (55 percent success rate). While the success rates at the merits stage of the dispute do surpass the 50 percent mark, it is not readily apparent (in terms of raw numbers) of a systemic proinvestor bias in ITA. However, if one is to assess the success rates in ITA compared with those at the ECtHR or with domestic administrative review courts, the success rate for claimant-investors may indeed be disproportionately high.

While the proinvestor bias claims are still made (mostly by nonexperts), the perception that there is an antideveloping state bias is gaining more traction in scholarly literature of late. Prior to the mid-2000s, there were not a sufficient number of ITAs to warrant systematic empirical analysis of the types of states being sued, the type of claimants bringing suit, and the outcomes of these cases. However, from the mid-2000s onwards, a number of critiques emerged in the context of investment treaty disputes. In response, earlier studies indicated that there was not a statistically significant relationship between outcomes and the development status of the respondent state.[36] One of the key caveats with these studies is that there were not many cases against developed states in the early jurisprudence.

More recent studies bring some of these early results into question.[37] As more cases enter the system and as more developed (and emerging economy) states are sued, the universe of ITAs that have reached a final award (388) has significantly expanded. This is a large increase over the approximately 140 cases included in earlier studies. Using a dataset of all cases reaching a final award in the first instance, a recent study shows that there is a statistically significant relationship between the gross domestic product (GDP) per capita of the state being sued and its likelihood to lose a case.[38] This correlation indicates that the poorer the state is the more likely it is to lose an ITA. This is troubling in regard to issues relating to the legitimacy of ITA but also raise questions about its performance.

[36] S. Franck, "Conflating Politics and Development: Examining Investment Treaty Outcomes," *Virginia Journal of International Law*, 55 (2014), 55.

[37] D. Behn, T. Berge, and M. Langford, "Poor States or Poor Governance: Explaining Outcomes in Investment Treaty Arbitration," *Northwestern Journal of International Law and Business*, forthcoming (2018).

[38] Ibid.

If a system of adjudication produces a systemic bias against respondent states on the basis of their relative wealth, we should certainly be concerned. Anecdotally, it is interesting to note that the US (a high-income state) has famously never lost an ITA case, while Zimbabwe and Burundi (low-income states) have never defeated an investor claim.[39]

Before turning to issues of process performance, there are a few additional issues relating to outcome performance that are worthy of mention. These include issues of a lack of diversity in the subject-matter of cases, the exorbitant size of compensation awards, and the losing state's lack of compliance with monetary awards. To test these claims and to assess them in regard to outcome performance, we look to see if there are any aggregate patterns in outcomes across these selective issues areas.

The subject-matter of ITAs brought before 2000 were largely related (but certainly not exclusively) to projects in the extractive industries. However, in more recent years there has been a significant diversification of the types of cases.[40] This can be viewed as a positive or negative development depending on one's perspective. It is positive in the sense that, as a general system of adjudication, ITA looks less and less like a system that is tailor-made for the energy and extractive industries. It might be viewed as a negative development, however, as more and more cases arise out of foreign investments that were not originally envisioned as the types of investments that should be eligible for protections under IIAs. For example, there is a trend towards disputes involving the financial services sector and other service industries.

Looking at all ITA cases registered to date (878), we see a considerable diversity of the types of cases that have been resolved. Figure 3.5 shows the distribution and subject-matter diversity for all registered. Despite this diversification, the extractive industry and energy sector disputes are still the two most represented economic sectors using ITA (17 percent for the extractive industries and 19 percent for the electricity/energy generation sectors). And there is still the perception that claimant-investors tend to do disproportionately well in these types of cases in terms of win percentages and the monetary compensation awarded. However, it is important to note, that the manufacturing, construction and finance sectors now each constitute a double-digit percentage of the caseload, which is a dramatic shift if compared with the early ITA caseload where the percentages for these sectors were either negligible or in the low single digits.

[39] PITAD. [40] Behn, "Legitimacy, Evolution and Growth in ITA."

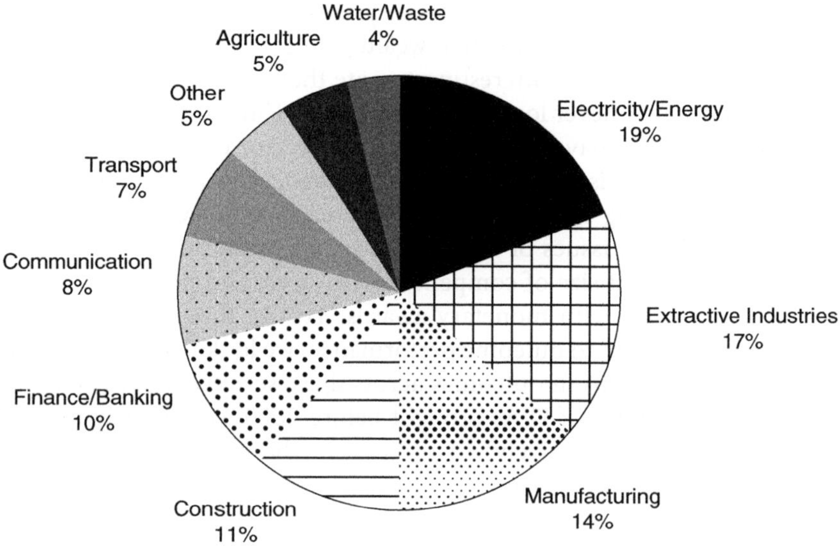

Figure 3.5 Economic sector distribution for all registered ITA cases (1990–2017)
Source: Data compiled by author from PITAD through August 1, 2017. Data on file with author

In terms of outcomes, there are a few interesting patterns worth noting that largely confirm the aforementioned perceptions. If we look at the win-loss ratios for all finally resolved ITA cases in the extractive industry and electricity/energy generation sectors versus cases involving all other economic sectors, there are two striking differences in the outcomes. First, ITAs involving the extractive industries or energy sectors are much more likely to settle; and second, in these cases, the respondent state has a much lower chance of successfully defending itself against a claim (in comparison to outcomes in the other economic sectors). For extractive industry and electricity/energy generation cases that have been fully resolved (182 cases), claimant-investors win 35 percent of the time, lose 31 percent, settle 25 percent, and discontinue 9 percent. For all other economic sectors (397 cases), claimant-investors win 28 percent of the time, lose 39 percent, settle 20 percent, and discontinue 13 percent.

However, it is not very surprising that cases in these two sectors are more likely to settle and that the state is less likely to succeed in defending itself against such claims. This is because many of these cases concern very large projects (with massive sunk costs) that become subject to various types of nationalizations/expropriations where the issue in dispute is more in relation to the level of compensation than to whether the state is liable. In regard to performance, the difference in outcome patterns between these two sectors and all other economic sectors is not very problematic; however, ITA cases in the extractive industry and electricity/energy generation sectors do tend to be more visible and high profile than others, and as such, these cases (where states lose or settle much more often than they win) might contribute to creating perceptions that the ITA system is unbalanced in favor of claimant-investors.

Turning to the amounts of compensation awarded to successful claimant-investors in ITAs, there are a number of patterns worth noting. The issue of compensation levels has been one of the more controversial areas in ITA. With a number of high-profile cases awarding claimant-investors in excess of one billion US dollars (USD),[41] questions about the fairness and reasonableness of such compensation has continually entered the discourse. However, looking at the awards to date with the highest dollar amounts attached to them, they all relate to expropriations in the extractive industries. These cases, with the exception of the three Yukos awards (which were found to be indirect expropriations by Russia), were all *direct* expropriations where the respondent states (Ecuador and Venezuela, respectively) likely knew that they would be found liable for breaches to the relevant IIA because they had not offered adequate compensation for the direct expropriations according to the standards of international law.

While the massive monetary awards are the ones that have grabbed the headlines, the overall levels of compensation awarded to winning claimant-investors are considerably more modest in the aggregate. This does not discount the fact that some cases have awarded compensation awards to winning cases where the USD amount of the award is significant in terms of the annual GDP of a particular state (e.g., a 935 million USD award against Libya or a 266 million USD award against Lebanon), these

[41] There are six cases where the claimant-investor was awarded in excess of one billion USD: *Hulley Enterprises* v. *Russia* (PCA UNCITRAL) (40 billion USD); *Veteran Petroleum* v. *Russia* (PCA UNCITRAL) 2014 (8.2 billion USD); *Yukos Universal* v. *Russia* (PCA UNCITRAL) 2014 (1.8 billion USD); *Occidental* v. *Ecuador* (ICSID Case No. ARB/06/11) (1.8 billion USD) 2014; *Venezuela Holdings* v. *Venezuela* (ICSID Case No. ARB/07/27) 2015 (1.6 billion USD); *Crystallex* v. *Venezuela* (ICSID Case No. ARB(AF)/11/2) 2016 (1.4 billion USD). However, it is equally important to note that annulment committees have significantly reduced the amount of compensation awarded in *Occidental* and *Venezuela Holdings*, and the three *Yukos* awards have been set-aside in the courts of the Netherlands (pending high court review).

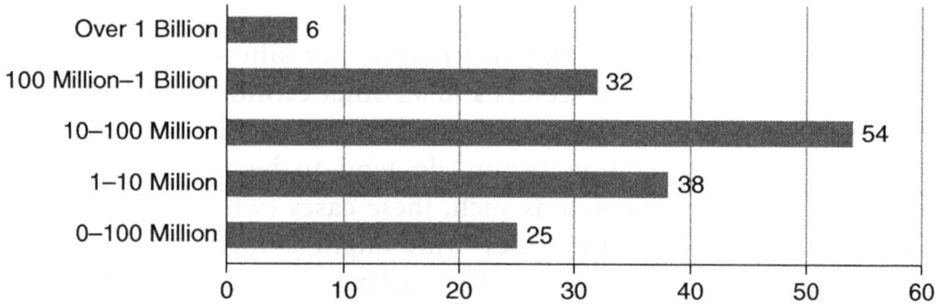

Figure 3.6 ITA compensation ranges in USD (155 cases)
Source: Data compiled by author from PITAD through August 1, 2017. Data on file with author

awards remain the distinct minority in ITA. Of the 175 cases to date where the claimant-investor has won at the liability/merits stage of the proceedings, there are ten cases where the amount of damages awarded remains pending (only a liability award has been rendered to date) and ten cases where the amount awarded is unknown. Thus, of the 155 cases where a claimant-investor has won on the merits and the amount of compensation awarded is known (see Figure 3.6), the distribution is highest in the 10 to 100 million USD range with fifty-four awards fitting into that category. However, there are also sixty-three awards totaling less than 10 million.

Interestingly, of the twenty-five awards where the claimant-investor is awarded less than one million USD, there are five cases where the tribunal found a breach of the IIA but awarded no compensation to the claimant-investor. Taking out the six awards where over one billion USD was awarded and the five awards where no compensation was awarded, the average compensation (149 awards) amounts to approximately 72.8 million USD and the grand total awarded equals approximately 10.2 billion USD in total across the entire universe of ITAs. While this number sounds substantial for sure, it may appear slightly more modest if reflecting the trillions and trillions of foreign direct investment (FDI) flows that have occurred global since the first ITA award was rendered in 1990. In other words, the amount of compensation awarded to claimant-investors might be found to be egregious in particular cases, but in the aggregate the amounts awarded to date do not appear to be particularly troubling.

The final issue to be discussed in terms of outcome performance is that of compliance with awards rendered against respondent states in ITA.

As discussed in the first section of this chapter, the difficulty in compelling a state to satisfy an international arbitral award against it is a long-standing problem. While the New York Convention has been in place for over sixty years and has been very effective in enforcing and recognizing international commercial arbitration awards, its effectiveness in enforcing treaty-based arbitration awards has been a bit more mixed due to the complexities associated with issues of sovereignty when the award is being enforced against a state. The ICSID Convention sought to overcome the problems associated with enforcing an award against a state: Article 53 of the ICSID Convention bypasses the need for national court recognition under the New York Convention. For the early ICSID cases, this innovation seemed to be working as many early awards were paid without significant challenge. The direct enforceability of awards under the ICSID Convention was systemically challenged for the first time following Argentina's financial collapse in 2001.

Argentina has been steadfast in refusing to enforce ICSID awards, arguing that despite reference to the direct enforceability of awards in the ICSID Convention, the Argentinian constitution requires all payments out of the state treasury to be first authorized through a court judgment. Given the high number of ICSID awards against Argentina in the past ten years, this noncompliance has put considerable strain on the regime overall. While Argentina has recently satisfied many of its outstanding awards through negotiated settlements, some final awards remain unsatisfied.

In addition to the Argentinian cases, Zimbabwe, Russia, Kyrgyzstan, and Thailand have all refused to comply with any awards rendered against them.[42] In addition, a number of respondent states delayed or refused enforcement in individual cases: Guatemala, Kazakhstan, Mexico, and Venezuela.[43] These states have a record of complying with some awards and rigorously fighting enforcement in others.

Interestingly, in the Russian case, many of the awards rendered against the state have been fought in domestic courts through set-aside proceedings, and with substantial success to date. So far, all of the awards

[42] The cases listed in this section only include treaty-based awards (and may not be exhaustive). In addition to the states listed, there are a few states that have not complied with contract-based ICSID awards or settlement agreements. Primarily, these include: Lao PDR, Dominican Republic, Democratic Republic of Congo, Ukraine, and Turkmenistan. See Langford, Behn, and Fauchald, "Backlash and State Strategies in International Investment Law."

[43] Ibid.

rendered against Russia in the Yukos saga have been set-aside in the domestic courts of Sweden and the Netherlands (the seats of these arbitrations). This appears to be an increasingly popular strategy by losing respondent states in ITA: challenge any award rendered against it in the domestic courts at the enforcement state of the proceedings. As the legitimacy of ITA continues to be questioned, domestic courts are playing an increasing role in policing the enforceability of ITA awards that many respondent states believe they should not be obligated to pay. As more and more awards enter the pipeline, one could predict that the challenge to awards in domestic courts at the enforcement stage of the proceedings will continue to increase.

Process Performance

The process of ITA has been the subject of intense debate. Many critics are concerned that arbitration is not the appropriate model of adjudication for the type of public law disputes arbitrators in ITA are asked to resolve. The argument against arbitration claims that courts with tenured judges provide more institutional safeguards than do ad hoc arbitrators;[44] and that these safeguards help ensure that international legal disputes of this type are not as susceptible to particular forms of bias or other structural incentives that might favor private investors over measures taken by the state in the public interest.

One of the proposed solutions to this critique would be to establish an international investment court that would have many design features of the dispute settlement understanding (DSU) of the WTO. In September 2015, the European Commission proposed such a solution as a substitute to ISDS provisions in future IIAs it signs with third states.[45] Such a court-style mechanism has now made its way into the *EU-Vietnam FTA*, the *EU-Canada FTA* (CETA), and has been proposed as part of the ongoing negotiations over the *Trans-Atlantic Trade and Investment Partnership* (TTIP) between the EU and the US. What this investment court system (ICS) seeks to accomplish is to do away with the system of party-appointed arbitrators (a process that critics claim results in a proinvestor bias due to the perverse incentives that such

[44] See e.g., G. Van Harten, *Investment Treaty Arbitration and Public Law* (Oxford: Oxford University Press, 2007).

[45] European Commission, "Commission Draft Text TTIP – Investment" September 16, 2015. Available at: http://trade.ec. europa.eu/doclib/html/153807.htm (accessed August 1, 2017).

a system creates) and to add an appellate review system that will help reduce the perceived inconsistency of investment treaty outcomes. While such a court-type system could possible replace ITA in the long run, there are a number of institutional difficulties that will prevent a quick transition to such a system from taking place.[46]

While the proposal for an ICS is garnering significant attention of late, more pragmatic considerations in the immediate future might be to reform particular aspects of the processes associated with ITA. To assess what these reforms might be, and how they might assist in increasing the performance of ITA, this section will look at a few features of treaty-based arbitration that have been variously viewed as problematic: (1) issues relating to transparency; (2) issues relating to the length of proceedings; and (3) issues relating to a system that favors repeat arbitrators.

Looking first at issues of transparency, there is a significant perception that ITA is a secretive process that is conducted behind closed doors with low levels of transparency. This critique of the process of ITA has been around for a long time and is premised on the fact that many of the institutional design features of investment treaty arbitration are borrowed from international commercial arbitration where the default rule is one of confidentiality. Transparency in ITA can be divided into two major categories: (1) transparency in the proceedings (i.e., open hearings); and (2) transparency in the existence of a dispute and in the awards rendered. While there are some examples of tribunals opening up their hearings to the public (mostly in the context of NAFTA and CAFTA-DR cases), it remains a fairly rare occurrence. On the other hand, transparency through publicly available awards is something that has been changing rapidly in ITA in recent years.[47] The default assumption of confidentiality and secrecy is no longer accurate.

[46] Primarily, there are significant costs that will be imposed on states in establishing a standing court for each agreement (mostly bilateral) that a state signs. One of the benefits of investment treaty arbitration is that the costs for individual cases can be high, but they are significantly less so than the establishment of a permanent court system that might not have many disputes brought before. For example, it may make sense to establish a permanent court for the TTIP, but less so under a Norway-Mozambique BIT. A long-term alternative to bilateral court system would be to establish a multilateral framework that would cover all existing IIAs.

[47] As of April 2014, the *UNCITRAL Rules on Transparency in Treaty-based Investor-State Arbitration* came into effect (but will only cover arbitrations based on IIAs signed after April 1, 2014). See UNCITRAL *Rules on Transparency* 2014. Available at: www.uncitral.org/uncitral/uncitral_texts/arbitration/2014Transparency.html (accessed

In regard to the transparency of ITA, it turns out that the likelihood that parties will seek to keep proceedings and awards secret is a product of the institutional setting of the arbitration. Looking specifically at the institutional distribution of cases, one can see that the majority of ITAs registered to date (878 cases) have been administered by ICSID (59 percent). However, non-ICSID cases are encroaching on ICSID's market dominance. It is now that 41 percent of all ITA cases have either been administered with no institutional backing (181 ad hoc UNCITRAL tribunals) or they have been administered by either the PCA (ninety-four cases) or a regional international commercial arbitration center (seventy-six cases).[48]

If an ITA case is administered by ICSID, there is a presumption of transparency and in fact there are only about 9 percent of all ICSID cases that have been resolved to date where the final award remains confidential. Furthermore, ICSID also provides a publicly available registry that logs all of the cases that have been initiated and resolved. This means for ICSID cases, there is public knowledge of the existence of a dispute and the awards in almost all cases are also publicly available. The picture of transparency in non-ICSID cases is certainly opaquer and without any legal requirement that even the occurrence of a dispute be known to the public, there is a much higher likelihood in non-ICSID cases that some disputes will not even be known, let alone that an award will be made publicly available. While the number of confidential ICSID awards currently hovers around 10 percent, approximately one-third of all non-ICSID cases are not publicly available.

Overall, out of the 388 ITA cases that have reached a final award, 76 percent (or 294 awards) are publicly available. However, this is only the number for known cases. In other words, there may be a number of non-ICSID cases that are not even known (because there is no formal registry for these cases). The chances of this being a large number is fairly low though; knowledge about most cases (and who won the case), even if

August 1, 2017). Further, in March 2015, the *Mauritius Convention on Transparency* opened for signatures. As of August 1, 2017, eighteen states have signed the Convention (with only one ratification). See *Mauritius Convention on Transparency*. Available at: www.uncitral.org/uncitral/en/uncitral_texts/arbitration/2014Transparency_Convention.html (accessed August 1, 2017).

48 The SCC is the most frequently used international commercial arbitration center (forty-one fully resolved disputes), followed by the International Chamber of Commerce (four fully resolved disputes), the LCIA (four fully resolved disputes), the Moscow Chamber of Commerce and Industry (three fully resolved disputes), and the Cairo Regional Centre for International Commercial Arbitration (two fully resolved disputes).

the awards are not made public, increasingly get leaked into the public domain at some point.

One issue in relation to transparency that is interesting to look at is which parties might be seeking to keep awards in particular cases confidential. Of the 24 percent of cases whose awards remain confidential (ninety-four cases), the claimant-investors won sixty-two of these cases (66 percent) and lost in thirty-two cases. Of the 76 percent of cases that are publicly available, the claimant-investor won 137 of these cases (46 percent) and lost in 157 cases. These descriptive statistics suggest that cases where the claimant-investor wins are, on average, more likely to be kept confidential. Without investigating the circumstances of these cases more closely, one could speculate that confidentiality in ITA may not be driven by claimant-investors but by respondent states seeking to keep awards in losing cases confidential.[49] Respondent states may want to minimize the fallout that could come from the details of a loss becoming public knowledge.

The next procedural performance issue to discuss is the length of proceedings in ITA. Examining Figure 3.7, it becomes readily apparent that these disputes take a long time to resolve. On average, ITAs take over three and a half years to resolve in the first instance. This does not include the amount of time that is often spent at the enforcement stage of the proceedings in domestic courts (which can take upwards of five years depending on the number of appellate review stages that are possible in a particular domestic system) or through the annulment process in ICSID cases (average of about two years). Further, if an ICSID case is annulled by an ad hoc annulment committee, it is possible for the case to be resubmitted again as a first instance tribunal. There are a number of examples of ITAs of this type taking in excess of ten years to become finally resolved. It is unknown whether an ICS as proposed by the European Commission would reduce the length of proceedings in investment treaty cases because the current ITA system does not have a formal appellate review process. Adding such a process through a court system would theoretically add significant time to any dispute.

Further, those who believe that ITA should be a faster alternative to using domestic courts charge that the amount of time taken to resolve

[49] The assumption here is that a winning claimant-investor has a lower incentive to keep a case confidential and that given the overall win rate for claimant-investors in cases where awards remain confidential is significantly higher (66 percent) than the overall win rate for claimant-investors (45 percent) in all cases, it may be that respondent states do not want to make these awards publicly available.

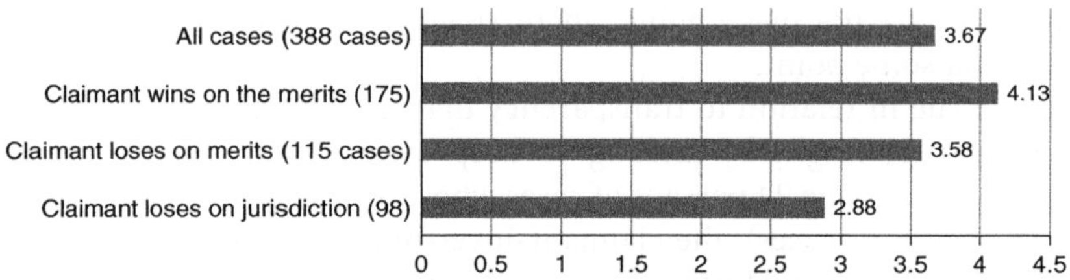

Figure 3.7 Average length of ITA proceedings (in years)
Source: Data compiled by author from PITAD through August 1, 2017. Data on file with author

a dispute is problematic. Certainly, it is difficult to argue that ITA is faster than many domestic courts. However, making such analogies is a possible misnomer because ITA has very little in common with the types of arbitration that tend to be more efficient and faster than domestic courts (i.e., employment arbitration or consumer contract arbitration). In fact, ITA cases can often be more complex and time intensive than the vast majority of domestic court litigation. Many ITAs produce thousands of pages of factual evidence and awards can easily run into the hundreds of pages. It is therefore unsurprising that typically ITA cases take a long time to resolve. However, the type of disputes that ITA appears to favor (large, complex litigation) undermines the possibility for any type of small claims mechanism to develop. In terms of performance and legitimacy, ITA would benefit from a process that would allow relatively small investments and investors to use the system. Currently, ITA – for reasons of both time and expense – is *de facto* foreclosed to foreign investors with claims smaller than about 10 million USD.

The final issue relating to the process performance of ITA is to empirically assess the system of party-appointments and the repeat appointment of a small cadre of arbitrators. ITA is built, procedurally, on the system developed in the context of international commercial arbitration. The default rule is that each party to the dispute appoints an arbitrator and the president of the tribunal is then appointed by agreement of either the two coarbitrators or the parties. For most cases, this default rule works well. However, such a process is often charged as being incapable of impartiality because the very nature of an appointment-based system is to appoint an arbitrator that the party believes is most likely to support her version of the case. But what most critics fail to realize is that one party to the dispute is not picking all three arbitrators on a tribunal; rather they only get to pick one. This means that actually there is very little possibility for one of the party-appointed arbitrators on a tribunal to excessively influence the outcome. Further, and in practice, it is the president of the tribunal that is tasked with making the ultimate decision in a particular dispute.

As such, the party-appointed arbitrators may play less of a role in the final outcome than is often assumed. Nonetheless, one of the biggest complaints about ITA is its system of party-appointed arbitrators. The alternative to such a system is to either convert to a court-style system with permanent tenured judges resolving disputes or for a system of institutional appointments.

In addition to problems with the system of party-appointed arbitrators is the system of repeat appointments. ITA is increasingly dominated by a small group of elite arbitrators that are repeatedly selected by parties in the vast majority of disputes. To date, in the 878 cases that have been registered, there have been 652 different arbitrators that have accepted appointments in these cases (this does not include the 152 pending cases where no arbitrators have been selected yet). Of these 652 different arbitrators, over half (350) of them have sat in only one case. However, while these one-time arbitrators are in the clear majority, it is the numbers of repeat-appointed arbitrators that is interesting. There is a large percentage of arbitrators (32 percent), constituting 208 individuals, who have been appointed between two and nine times in ITA cases; and there are sixty-three arbitrators that have ten or more appointments. The most fantastic statistic in this regard is that these sixty-three arbitrators have taken 58 percent of all possible appointments in fully constituted ITA cases to date (722 cases). It is clear that there is a core group of arbitrators that dominate in investment treaty arbitration.[50]

One of the main issues with the high clustering of repeat arbitrators in ITAs is that charge that there is a dearth of diversity among those gaining repeat appointments. Of the 652 arbitrators appointed to date, 68 percent of them have nationalities from states in either North America or Western Europe. Further, only 4 percent of all arbitrators are women.[51] Considering that the majority of ITA cases are against states in the developing world, the fact that so many arbitrators are from the global

[50] The two most often appointed ITA arbitrators are Gabrielle Kaufmann-Kohler (forty-eight) and Brigitte Stern (eighty-seven).

[51] The irony here is that only thirty-eight women have been appointed as arbitrators in ITA cases but the two most often appointed arbitrators (accounting for 135 appointments combined) are women.

North and so few are women is problematic. Overall, it appears that ITA does in fact have a diversity problem, but it is unclear how a structural shift to a court system or a system of institutional appointments would improve the diversity of the system. In fact, it may even exasperate the problem by drastically reducing the number of individuals eligible to sit on investment treaty tribunals (i.e., the ICS proposal calls for fifteen individuals to accept permanent appointments).

Conclusions

Assessing the overall performance of an entire system of adjudication within the confines of a short book chapter is no easy task. What this contribution has sought to provide is an overview of the entire system of ITA as it has been practiced to date. The effect of such an exercise was to highlight some of the performance deficits that have occurred in its practice and to objectively assess (with empirical evidence) the overall performance of ITA in terms of its historical purpose.

One of the problems with objectively assessing the performance of ITA is that it is a system of adjudication with a high degree of normative polarization whereby most issues are evaluated through a normative lens. For many, ITA has been in a legitimacy crisis for the past decade and debates about the use and legitimacy (and performance) of ITA often turn into heated exchanges about issues of unfairness and unjustness in global economic governance more generally. For critics of the regime, no performance benchmarks are worthy: The system is rotten and should be dismantled. For those with more moderate views, ITA does in fact seem to be performing its functions fairly well, especially when viewed in terms of historical purpose.

In fact, this contribution highlights that one area where ITA could improve its performance is through increased access. One of the main deficits identified is that there are too few foreign investors with access to legal protections that can be enforced through binding arbitration. Such a finding would actually call for an expansion of ITA, not its constriction. In terms of the process of ITA, this chapter identified that while becoming increasingly transparent, disputes take a long time to resolve and that there appears to be a severe lack of diversity among the arbitrators appointed to sit on tribunals. In terms of outcomes, the most problematic issue in regard to its performance is that, while the win-loss ratios overall appear fairly balanced, there seems to be a bias against developing states that is unlikely to be justifiable.

Overall, assessing ITA in terms of its performance has provided a neutral framework for evaluating a system of adjudication on objective, empirically based terms. Such an approach is valuable in identifying where ITA can be improved. While arguably flawed in certain respects, investment treaty arbitration does seem to be serving a valuable function and should be worthy of reform. Such reforms might eventually lead to a system of adjudication that takes the form of a standing international court or one that is based on a multilateral treaty where issues of access and balance between states and investors can be fine-tuned and improved. However, given the problems that ITA has sought to address in the aggregate (i.e., the historical problem of enforcing rights for foreign aliens investing abroad), ITA does appear to be performing commensurate with its historic purpose.

4

Performance of Regional Human Rights Courts

DINAH SHELTON

Regional human rights courts exist in Europe, the Americas, and Africa; in 2014 the League of Arab States approved the creation of a further regional court, but it is not functioning as of the beginning of 2016 (International Commission of Jurists 2015). A growing number of subregional courts also hear human rights cases, but their jurisdiction extends to other matters as well and they are not included among the human rights courts discussed herein.

Assessing the performance of the three regional courts involves what the courts do and how they do it, examining who decides, how decisions are reached, what is decided, and whether litigants comply with judgments. The contribution of the regional courts to the global human rights project can also be evaluated. The perspectives of litigants and lawyers who use the court, the broader membership of states in the regional organization, the public, and the international community as a whole may differ on each of these issues based on their particular interests and what they perceive as the primary function of the regional court.

In general, it can be said that the regional courts probably perform better than the member states intended, but not as well as victims of violations hope or expect. "Better" in evaluating a regional judicial body means providing accessible and fair proceedings in which judges apply the law in a consistent, independent, and unbiased manner to credible findings of fact, granting remedies consistent with international norms and the purpose of the litigation, and contributing to the improvement of human rights in the states in the region.

Any court's performance is inextricably interwoven with legitimacy; performance can enhance or undermine legitimacy but, equally, legitimacy can positively or negatively influence performance. Courts perceived as legitimate are more likely to receive better funding, more staff, and a higher quality of judges than courts viewed less favorably. External events in a region, including civil wars, military coups, or a strengthening

Governments nominate the judges in all three systems; in the Inter-American and African systems the state parties also elect them, providing a considerable degree of control over the composition of the courts. The European system differs in having government nominations, followed by the Parliamentary Assembly composed of legislators from member states vetting and electing the judges, a process that lessens governmental control, but one that nonetheless is not free of problems (Limbach 2003: 18; Engel 2012; Dzehtsiarou and Coffey 2014: 288). The Parliamentary Assembly itself has been highly critical of the nomination process in some countries, especially on the issues of independence, transparency, and gender balance (Drzemczewski 2015). Independent candidates are not always nominated nor is independence honored once judges are elected. They have been personally criticized for their decisions (Voeten 2008: 419–422) and one was allegedly physically attacked in Russia (Dzehtsiarou and Coffey 2014: 284–285, n. 45). In one instance a former judge of the European Court successfully challenged his own country for actions taken against him after he returned to his State.[3]

European and American judges frequently come from universities or government service. The African Court is unique in thus far electing a majority of judges with prior domestic judicial experience, a factor that could affect both the process and the outcome of cases, as well as compliance over time. Judges with judicial experience may be better equipped to decide issues of evidence, procedure, and case management. In addition, if domestic courts are held in high regard this could enhance the reputation of the regional court. The prior judicial experience of African judges could also facilitate their relations with other judges in the national systems and encourage incorporation and application of the regional norms and court decisions. It is difficult to evaluate the impact at present, however, given the relatively short period in which the African Court has been operating. Experience from the other systems suggests that the absence of judicial experience among regional court judges can negatively affect relations with national judiciaries.

The Inter-American Court has less diversity than the other courts, despite the clear cultural, linguistic, and legal divide in the OAS between the English-speaking, common law Northern states, and Latin American states with their civil law and predominantly Hispanic, Catholic traditions. For most of its existence, the Court has been comprised of Latin American men, due to the failure of the English-speaking North to ratify

[3] *Baka* v. *Hungary* [2016] ECtHR App. No. 20261/12.

the Convention and the failure of all states parties to nominate women to the Court. This relative homogeneity has played out in the performance of the Court, especially in its frequent application of concepts like *jura novit curia* (Shelton 2013) and *jus cogens* and its use of civil law methods of weighing evidence (Alvaro 2012). The parties to the African Court opted for greater diversity and have elected the eleven members based on equitable representation of gender, the five major African regions, and the major legal systems.

All of the courts allow separate and dissenting opinions, which often reflect linguistic differences and the various legal traditions from which the judges emerge. Dissenting opinions can be positive for the reputation of the court, indicating that it gave full consideration to the different arguments and interests at stake. The practice can also enhance the perception of independent judges and transparency, and can stimulate further evaluation of the legal analysis in a case. Nonetheless, a prevalence of such opinions may reinforce linguistic and cultural differences.

The size of the courts affects the perception and the reality of their judicial role; the judges on the smaller courts are perceived to represent the region as a whole rather than having a representational role to play in regard to their own state. In Europe the national judge sits on cases coming from his or her country, something not permitted in the other two courts. The European system is defended on the ground of diversity: a case may be filed in any national language of the forty-seven member states and often the national judge is the only member of the panel capable of reading the file and informing other judges about the cultural, legal, and societal interests at stake (given the Court's caseload it is unclear that judges actually have or take the time to read the files).

National representation can give the member states and the public as a whole the impression that judges should act to represent the interests of their own country (Dzehtsiarou and Coffey 2014: 274). It may influence the outcome of a proceeding, especially when the panel is divided, as well as compliance. If the national judge joins a judgment against the country, the judgment may be seen as more credible and legitimate. However, to the extent a national judge consistently or frequently dissents, it may undermine willingness to comply by suggesting that the Court is biased or lacks full understanding of the context of the case (Cali 2010). National representation also creates a procedural anomaly because the national judge sits not only in the Chamber, but also in the Grand Chamber to review of his or her own Chamber decision, contrary to the principle *nemo judex in causa sua*.

Problems resulting from including the national judge on cases are exacerbated when the elected judge is not available or cannot sit in a particular case, requiring an ad hoc judge. As a result of concern about state manipulation of ad hoc judges, the contracting parties no longer can directly appoint them, but criticism continues (Parliamentary Assembly 2011: para. 14). Concerns about the independence of national judges led the Inter-American Court in 2009 to issue an advisory opinion ending the practice of ad hoc judges except in interstate cases.[4] The Court subsequently revised its rules of procedure to prohibit any judge from sitting on a case brought by alleged human rights victims against his or her own state.

External Structural Factors

All regional courts are established within the framework of a larger political body which retains control over the nomination and election of judges, budget and staffing, and the normative framework. All of the courts complain about a lack of resources, with the Inter-American Court referred to as "the poorest international court in the world" in the size of its budget (Garcia-Sayan 2012: 105). The African Court began operating with no registry, offices, equipment, resources, budget or rules of Court. By 2014, the operational budget from member states was US$6,607,632 with an additional US$2,362,315 for programs coming from external sources, including the European Union. The Court noted, however, that many staff members and judges continue to lack basic furniture and working equipment, necessitating a manual case management system (AfCHPR 2013).

Restricting financial support for the courts is one way political bodies can reduce the performance of the courts, limiting their ability to meet, travel to promote the court or gather evidence, also forcing them to engage in outside fund-raising. To maintain their effectiveness, the regional courts do engage in outside fund-raising. Some states have complained that outside donors can influence the processing or outcome of cases, while civil society organizations instead see the ability to obtain external resources as increasing the independence of the courts. Without

[4] *Article 55 American Convention on Human Rights* (2009) IACtHR Advisory Opinion OC-20/09.

these external resources, the courts would be hampered in developing electronic resources important to communicating with litigants, developing a database of jurisprudence and complaints, and disseminating information to the public.

Lack of resources has an impact on performance because of the need to translate judgments into the various languages of the Court or region as a whole; the practice of the Inter-American and African Courts is generally to draft the original judgment in the primary language of the applicant and respondent state, later translating into the other languages. The European Court's working languages are French and English; in recent years it has sought and obtained funding to translate and post versions of its judgments in the national languages of some of the member states. The quality of translations varies widely and texts can have substantial errors or inconsistencies from one version to another. A comparison of two judgments of the African Court, one drafted in English, one in French, show inconsistencies perhaps due to translation errors, but also possibly due to differences between civil law and common law concepts and approaches to reparations.[5]

The courts are also dependent on political bodies for enforcement action in the event of noncompliance with judgments. This requires the courts to retain state support. In turn the political bodies must be informed of the performance and concerns of the courts. The African Court has complained to the African Union's Council about its decision in 2012 limiting the number and timing of the Court's reports to once a year (AfCHPR 2013). There was no response and the Court has not published a report since 2013, limiting access to information about its activities.

The Committee of Ministers (CoM), a political body composed of the foreign affairs ministers of all the member states or their permanent diplomatic representatives, oversees compliance with the European Court's judgments. In theory this structure gives the European system the most robust follow-up procedure. In practice, it has affected outcomes because the European Court has effectively delegated some of its judicial functions to the Committee of Ministers as part of its "enforcement" role. Unlike the Inter-American Court, the European Court has generally refrained from indicating the kind of measures that national authorities must undertake to remedy a violation and prevent its

[5] *Mtikila* v. *Tanzania* [2014] AfCHPR App. No. 011/2011, para 27; *Zongo et al.* v. *Burkina Faso* [2015] AfCHPR App. No. 013/2011, para 20.

recurrence. The CoM confirmed in a recent report that "as regards the nature and scope of other execution measures, whether individual or general, the judgments are generally silent" (CoM 2013: 24).

In the Inter-American and African systems, relations with the human rights commissions are also an important structural factor affecting the performance of the courts, as was the situation earlier in Europe (Frowein 2015: 2). The IACHR acts as a filter: Cases cannot come directly to the Inter-American Court and the IACHR has discretion to send a case forward or not. After criticism of its early reluctance to send matters to the Court, the Commission changed its rules and now presumptively transmits all cases in which it has found a violation and the state has failed to comply with its recommendations. In the African system, the Commission also acts in part as a filter in deciding whether or not to submit cases; direct access to the Court is available but only against the eight states that have filed a declaration accepting this procedure.

Relations between the regional commissions and the courts sometimes can be competitive, as each seeks to maximize its resources from the budget of the parent organization and its reputation among the member states and public. This has led to periods of tension, especially when a court has been critical of the performance of its commission, e.g., when the Inter-American Court rejected the IACHR's interpretation of its own powers[6] or disagreed with it on matters of fact or substantive law.[7] By contrast, the African Court generally cites decisions of the African Commission favorably and as persuasive authority, invoking them before referring to judgments of other regional courts or to UN practice.[8] The African Court's unique practice in this respect serves to enhance the legitimacy and credibility of the African Commission, an important element in the regional system, given the paucity of states that have accepted the Court's optional jurisdiction to receive individual communications; for individuals and groups from most states in the region, the African Commission is the only regional venue available. The Court's support for the Commission may also reflect a desire to enhance its reputation and avoid the diversion of cases to subregional tribunals like ECOWAS and SADC.

[6] *X* v. *Y* (*Las Palmeras Case*) (2001) IACtHR (ser. C) No. 196, para 34; *X* v. *Y* (*Genie Lacayo Case*) (1997) IACtHR (ser. C) No. 30, para 93.

[7] *Case of the Five Pensioners* v. *Peru* (2003) IACtHR (ser. C) No. 98, paras. 146–148; *Castillo Petruzzi* v. *X* (1999) IACtHR (ser. C) No. 52, paras. 102–103; *Las Palmeras*, para. 47.

[8] *In the Matter of Alex Thomas* v. *United Republic of Tanzania* [2015] AfCHPR App. No. 005/2013.

Another important external constituency is the public. Regional courts need the support and visibility that can be created through engaging public opinion, including NGOs, victims of human rights abuses, and international jurists. These actors must perceive that a court is operating in a judicial way: giving cogent public reasons for its decisions, acting impartially, and affording due process. James Cavallaro and Stephanie Erin Brewer have highlighted the need for lawyers representing applicants to coordinate litigation with "social movements ... and others carrying on long-term advocacy campaigns or pushing for better policies" (2008: 770). They see this as related to performance in large part because international tribunals are most likely to be effective when their procedures and jurisprudence are relevant to such actors' long-term efforts to advance human rights.

Positive public attention is critical to the long-term success of regional courts and they ignore this constituency at their peril (Helfer & Slaughter 1997: 312). Indeed, it is reported that in the United Kingdom, where debates about the European Court regularly feature on the front pages of newspapers following high-profile judgments against the state, public support for the European Court had decreased from 71 percent approval in June of 1996 to 19 percent by February of 2011 (Voeten 2013: 418). Lack of public support may encourage noncompliance with specific judgments and may lend support to government efforts to curtail the Court.

The courts understand the need for outreach to the public. Judges on the African Court have complained about the overall lack of awareness about the existence of the Court throughout Africa, as well as a dearth of knowledge about who can apply to it and how they may do so (Akuffo 2012: para. 20; AfCHPR 2013). In response, the Court has undertaken an increasing number of activities to enhance public awareness, holding colloquia, seminars, and conferences throughout the region, to which it attributes the increase in applications since 2011. The Inter-American Court has also made efforts to disseminate information about its work. It publishes an Annual Report containing summaries of proceedings and the full text of its judgments. All records related to the Court's cases, including parties' briefs, evidentiary documents, and transcripts of public hearings, are also available through the Court's library in Costa Rica in their original languages.

Process Performance

This section evaluates the process performance of the regional human rights courts in terms of two criteria. First, it evaluates performance in terms of access to justice. Second, it evaluates process performance concerning the processing and hearing of cases.

Access to Justice

None of the regional courts is able to open the courthouse door widely. Jurisdictional and admissibility requirements set forth in the treaties limit the cases that can be considered. The European Court dismisses the overwhelming percentage of all applications and in recent years has been increasingly restricting individual access to the Court in response to a growing backlog. Protocol No. 14, which entered into force June 1, 2010, added a new admissibility criterion requiring the Court to declare inadmissible any individual application where "the applicant has not suffered a significant disadvantage, unless respect for human rights as defined in the Convention and the Protocols thereto requires an examination of the application on the merits and provided that no case may be rejected on this ground which has not been duly considered by a domestic tribunal" (ECHR, Art. 35(3)(b)). Protocol No. 15 will further restrict access, after all forty-seven Contracting Parties ratify it, by removing the concluding safeguard about domestic remedies and shortening the period of time to apply to the Court from six months to four months.

The Court itself has introduced stricter formal requirements for submitting an application and has established a policy of ranking cases in seven categories, giving priority consideration to the first three categories (ECtHR 2009b). According to the Court, the old chronological approach meant that certain very serious allegations of human rights violations were taking too long to be examined, especially applications coming from countries with the highest volume of complaints (ECtHR 2015). As of December 31, 2014, there were 7,386 applications in the priority group, likely precluding for the foreseeable future any consideration of cases in the remaining categories despite their merits.

The European Court's Registry plays a central role in case processing. It undertakes an initial evaluation of applications and a nonjudicial rapporteur from the Registry decides whether the application should be assigned to a single judge, a Committee or a Chamber. The Registry assists the single judges, transmitting the lists of cases deemed inadmissible to them for approval (ECtHR 2016: Rule 18A). As Iain Cameron has noted and judges on the Court have confirmed, the lists transmitted electronically to the single judges contain only one or two sentence summaries of each matter recommended for dismissal; the judges do not see the applications (2013: 25, 31) and a few judges have complained of feeling that they are expected to "rubber-stamp" the decisions of the Registry. Once the application is rejected, the author of it is sent a form letter so indicating, without explanation or reasoned decision, simply stating that "taking account of all the elements in its possession, and to the extent that it is able to evaluate the allegations formulated," the Court sees no reason to proceed.[9]

It is not surprising that governments would seek to limit admissibility: between 1959 and 2011, 93 percent of all judgments on the merits resulted in the finding of at least one violation (ECtHR 2011); for 2014, the rate of violations found was 85 percent (ECtHR 2015). Limiting admissibility means limiting condemnation, a result most likely in repetitive cases that come to the Court due to noncompliance by the state with prior judgments. The problem is arguably not one exclusively for the Court: Member states as well as the Court have failed to insist on compliance with prior judgments on the part of the four states that account for approximately 60 percent of the Court's caseload. As a result, the system risks losing support among the public by placing the onus on it instead of the noncomplying governments. This problem is exacerbated by a change in the subject matter of cases: In 2014, although a quarter of the cases continued to concern the right to a fair trial, which has historically accounted for the most applications, another quarter of the judgments found violations of the right to life or the prohibition of torture. The system will lose its credibility if violations of this type are not halted and redressed.

The Inter-American and African systems are also receiving more cases, but the numbers are small compared to the European system. The lack of direct access by victims partly explains the situation. The African Court has facilitated filing by having no filing fee and allowing applications to be submitted by post, fax, email, or in person, with one original filed in any African Union language. The Court assumes the cost of making copies and translations and has instituted a program of legal aid.

Processing and Hearing the Cases

The regional courts face a number of problems related to time. First, the time it takes to get a case to courts has an impact on the ability to make

[9] *Gagliano Giorgi* v. *Italy* [2012] ECtHR App. No. 23563/07, para 40.

credible determinations of contested facts. After the applicant has spent seven to ten years exhausting local remedies (and procedures before regional commissions), forensic evidence and witnesses are often missing; memories have faded; and documents have disappeared. Decisions often have to be made almost exclusively on the basis of the credibility of the applicant and the government. This is a particular problem for applicants in the European Court which has established "proof beyond a reasonable doubt" as its standard for finding a violation. The part-time nature of the Inter-American and African Courts adds to the timeliness problem: hearings are not always granted and usually truncate the time for argument and presentation of the case. Prerequisite Commission proceedings mean cases take longer to get before the courts and to judgment. Even in the European Court, the case load means the time for each case is strictly limited and many cases will not be heard at all within a reasonable period of time. The ability of litigants to proceed directly to the African Court, together with its small caseload, has allowed for quicker well-reasoned decisions despite it being a part-time court with a small registry.

For cases that are heard, the regional tribunals have implied various judicial powers in order to ensure the fairness of their proceedings and preserve the object of complaints procedures. The courts make use of precautionary or interim measures, although they are expressly authorized only for the Inter-American and the African courts. The adoption of such measures has given rise to controversy and negative reaction on the part of some states, partly because of the type of measures issued, and partly because the regional tribunals have concluded that such measures are legally binding (Pasqualucci 2005: 13–14). The latter is particularly debated in the European system, where interim measures lack a textual basis in the Convention and the European Court reversed earlier judgments denying the binding nature of such measures.[10]

The regional courts face particular problems in dealing with cases alleging widespread and serious violations, including summary executions, disappearances, torture, and prolonged arbitrary detention. These cases usually require the court to engage in extensive fact-finding to determine state responsibility, but the ability of regional courts to engage in fact-finding is limited by resources, time, and expertise. They may have to rely on circumstantial evidence, presumptions and inferences, leading

[10] *Mamatkulov and Askarov* v. *Turkey* [2005] ECtHR App. Nos. 46827/99 and 46951/99, paras. 123–29.

defendant governments to question the credibility of their findings attributing responsibility.[11] As a result, there is a risk that those governments engaged in the most egregious violations will be unwilling or unable to halt and remedy the violations being committed.

Ultimately, the commitment to human rights of the member states is determinative. If the level of respect for human rights norms on the domestic level is low, and domestic institutions are not effective, judgments are not implemented and the workload of human rights bodies becomes unmanageable. In this regard, scholars argue that on the whole the African human rights system remains inadequately equipped in norms and procedures to effectively protect human rights and Africa needs to develop its commitment to respect for human rights (Matua 1999; Isanga 2013).

Regional court procedures and case management are influenced by judicial recognition of the disparity of power between the applicants and the respondent governments. First, the three courts have adopted default judgment procedures to presume the merits of applications if the government refuses to answer; this has served to encourage responses from governments. Such participation enhances the credibility of judgments ultimately reached because the issues are then fully litigated. Second, courts will presume true any noncontested facts; in some instances governments, particularly in the Inter-American system, have conceded the merits of a complaint in an effort to avoid having the facts set forth in the judgment, but the Court has insisted on the right to know the truth as a form of justice for the victims and society as a whole. Third, the courts have insisted that governments must come forward with evidence that they control and which cannot otherwise be obtained by litigants or the Court.[12] Presumptions and inferences may also be used, as when an applicant has been in state custody and appears with injuries; the burden is placed on the government to provide convincing evidence of how those injuries occurred.[13]

In terms of participation, procedural reforms in 2009 have significantly altered the role of the Inter-American Commission in Court proceedings. Formerly, the Commission functioned as the party opposing the state and bore primary responsibility for prosecuting the case.

[11] *Kurt* v. *Turkey* [1998] ECtHR App. No. 24276/94.

[12] *Velasquez Rodriguez* v. *Honduras* (1988) IACtHR (ser. C) No. 4; *Cyprus* v. *Turkey* (Reparations) [2001] ECtHR App. No. 25781/94.

[13] *Selmouni* v. *France* [1999] ECtHR App. No. 25803/94; *Miguel Castro Castro Prison v. Peru* (2006) IACtHR (ser. C) No. 16.

The alleged victims were permitted to intervene throughout the proceedings by submitting briefs, evidence, and motions through their counsel. This model was more similar to a criminal proceeding prosecuted by a district attorney, as opposed to a civil proceeding where the victim brings claims through private counsel. The 2009 reforms gave the alleged victims greater control of the legal proceedings, while relegating the Commission to a supporting role particularly in proposing measures of nonrepetition. Nonetheless, some governments have expressed the view that allowing two accusatory parties unfairly tilts the procedure against them.

Finally, the role of third parties, such as *amici curiae* and intervening states, is an important part of the process that can affect the outcome. Each court has allowed and some have encouraged the participation of *amici*. State interventions in cases before the European Court have undoubtedly helped the Court to determine whether or not a European consensus exists on human rights issues presented to it, helping thereby to build support for its judgments not only in the particular state accused of a violation, but in other states in the region, preventing future violations. In the African Court, several states and the African Commission have submitted observations on requests for advisory opinions and the Court has cited their views in reaching its decisions.

Outcome Performance

All courts are expected to decide cases in accordance with the law, developing and consistently applying basic principles and methodologies. For international tribunals these principles and methodologies should conform to general international law, to avoid contributing to concerns about the "fragmentation" of international law (ILC 2005; Sicilianos 2012). The European and the Inter-American courts have large bodies of case law that can be evaluated in this regard. The African Court decided its first matters only in 2011 and issued its first judgments on merits and reparations in 2013, allowing only tentative comments on its methodology.

Regional context influences the methodology and the outcome of cases, in part due to the judges' general understanding of their region's commitment to human rights and in part resulting from the type of cases brought. Judgments pronounced in cases where the facts are in dispute or the matter involves sensitive issues of national security, political questions, moral values, and long-standing traditions can articulate specific doctrines that are later, often inappropriately, applied more generally. The European *Lawless* case, for example, led to the original formulation of the European margin of appreciation doctrine to deal with a national security matter;[14] the doctrine has subsequently been applied to all manner of cases, although it has evolved to include a range of "broad" and "narrow" margins. Similarly, the European Court announced its requirement of "proof beyond a reasonable doubt" in a case in which the respondent government was accused of a systematic practice of torture, allegations that constituted criminal conduct; the Court may have deemed it appropriate under the circumstances to require this high standard of proof. Once the standard was announced, however, the Court began to apply it consistently, irrespective of the subject matter of the dispute, until widespread opposition led the Court to proclaim that it means something different (and undefined) in human rights cases than it means in criminal cases.[15]

The American and African regional contexts differ from the European in ways that influence the contents of judgments. From the beginning the newer courts have faced more systematic violations of nonderogable rights by repressive regimes, internal armed conflicts, and weaker domestic institutions than the European Court encountered, at least before the admission of new members following the end of the Cold War; in fact, the Inter-American Court did not have a living applicant until the case of *Loayza Tamayo* in 1997.[16] The types of violations and lack of domestic commitment to human rights have led to stronger and more detailed reparations orders by the Inter-American Court, which has made expansive use of its remedial powers.

For its part, the African Court's first merits decisions have involved sensitive regional matters in a region where states are still heavily committed to the doctrine of nonintervention in domestic matters. The *Mtikila* case asked the African Court to examine the state's organization of elections and political rights, matters which the government argued should be considered political questions outside the Court's competence. The Court disagreed and gave little deference to Tanzania's arguments about the need to afford it broad discretion in organizing its political system, given its history and social values. The Court's ability and willingness to engage in this scrutiny may have been strengthened by the African Union's recent

[14] *Lawless* v. *Ireland (No. 3)* [1961] ECtHR App. No. 332/57.
[15] *Mathew* v. *Netherlands* [2005] ECtHR App. No. 24919/03.
[16] *Loayza Tamayo* v. *Peru* (1997) IACtHR (ser. C) No. 33.

It may also be thought that the more states influence ICT proceedings by litigating, making representations with ICTs, or reacting publicly to their rulings, the likelier it is that they embrace IHL and ICL developed through international crimes trials. This chapter shows grounds to be somewhat skeptical. Whereas involvement in ICT judicial lawmaking has generated outcomes acceptable to states in some cases, this has not occurred in others. The situation becomes even more varied where states are not involved.

State of ICTs

Since Nuremberg and Tokyo, the world has had five ICTs. The International Criminal Tribunal for the Former Yugoslavia (ICTY) has indicated 161 individuals and completed proceedings with regard to 154 of them. Of those, eighty-three have been sentenced and nineteen acquitted; thirteen have had their cases transferred to national courts. Thirty-seven cases were terminated due to the withdrawal of indictments or the death of the accused. Proceedings are ongoing for seven accused.

By the time it completed its mandate in December 2015, the International Criminal Tribunal for Rwanda (ICTR) had concluded proceedings for eighty-five accused persons, resulting in sixty-one convictions and fourteen acquittals. Two indictments had been withdrawn and two accused had died before judgment. The ICTR transferred five proceedings to national courts and five fugitives to Rwanda.

Meanwhile, a UN Mechanism for International Criminal Tribunals (MICT) was set up in 2010. The mechanism has inherited three ICTR fugitives and two ICTY accused for retrial. The MICT is also responsible for all ICTR appellate proceedings for which notice was filed on or after July 1, 2012, and all ICTY appellate proceedings for which notice was filed on or after July 1, 2013.

The Special Court for Sierra Leone (SCSL) indicted thirteen individuals, ten of whom were brought to trial (two had died and one is still at large). Trial proceedings against one accused were terminated following his death. The SCSL completed its mandate in December 2013. A Residual SCSL retains jurisdiction over the sole remaining accused.

The Special Tribunal for Lebanon (STL) has so far indicted five accused in connection with the assassination of a former Lebanese prime minister. In January 2014, four of them had their case proceed to trial in absentia. The case concerning the fifth accused was joined shortly thereafter.

The Rome Statute of the International Criminal Court (ICC) came into force on July 1, 2002. Since then, twenty-three cases have been brought before the Court. The ICC has entered nine convictions, acquitted one accused, terminated proceedings against two individuals before reaching judgment, declined to confirm charges against four persons, and declared one case inadmissible. The ICC Prosecutor is now investigating ten situations and monitoring another ten.

ICT Judges as "Supplanters" of State Prerogatives in IHL and ICL Development

The ICTY's 1995 *Tadić Jurisdiction Decision* observes that international law's "[s]tate-sovereignty-oriented approach has been gradually supplanted by a human-being-oriented approach."[1] Much has since been written about ICTs' contribution to the "humanization" of IHL and the substantive development of ICL (Meron 1998a; Danner 2006; Schabas 2011; Kolb 2013). For critics, judges effectively rewrite these laws to the detriment of legitimate military considerations (Reeves and Thurnher 2013). Hayashi (2017) has considered this alleged bias and not found evidence to support it, at least for the ICTY.

Michael N. Schmitt (2010: 822) asserts that ICTs "supplant states in their role as the arbiter of the balance" between military necessity and humanity. In other words, ICTs develop IHL and ICL without state involvement (Murphy 2000).

International courts and other nonstate actors play an increasingly active role in contemporary international lawmaking (Boyle and Chinkin 2006; Hakimi 2016; Wouters and Hamid 2016). Nevertheless, the idea that only states enact international law by concluding treaties and forming custom remains our mainstream understanding (Mettraux 2005; Ochoa 2007; Kolb 2013). Finding that ICT judges create binding rules for states would undercut this idea.

Also, proceedings before other international courts and tribunals involve at least one state as a litigant. States provide input by arguing about applicable law. ICTs are different. Although states do appear before ICTs regarding certain issues, they do so infrequently. Consequently, ICT judges often identify and articulate relevant international law

[1] *Prosecutor* v. *Duško Tadić a/k/a "Dule,"* Case No. IT-94-1-AR72, Decision on the Defence Motion for Interlocutory Appeal on Jurisdiction, October 2, 1995, para. 97.

without state input (Van den Herik 2016). When this occurs, it is important to see if and how states respond.

Further, states' reactions matter when ICT rulings purport to modify their rights and obligations. ICL does not deal directly with the rights and obligations of states (Cançado Trindade 2010; Van den Herik 2016). Occasionally, however, the latter become the subject of judicial pronouncement by ICTs. How such pronouncements are grounded and how states regard them are matters of real concern.

Who Creates IHL and ICL?

Do ICTs accept indicia other than state practice and *opinio juris* as capable of creating custom? Do they give themselves the power to determine what rules of international law bind states, even where supporting authorities are scarce or absent? Is custom as a source of law diminishing in contemporary IHL and ICL and, with it, the role of ICTs in their normative development?

Redefining Custom

Customary law is supposed to be based on evidence of state practice and *opino juris*, yet whether ICTs have adequately relied upon such evidence when discovering custom has been the subject of critique. Several examples highlight how ICTs rulings on customary law can be controversial.

The *Tadić* Appeals Chamber concluded that, by 1991, customary law had ascribed individual criminal responsibility to serious violations of Article 3 common to the four 1949 Geneva Conventions, as well as breaches of "certain fundamental principles and rules regarding means and methods of combat" committed in non-international armed conflicts.[2] Commentators generally agree that this finding was at best progressive (Shahabuddeen 2004; Schabas 2007), and at worst premature (La Haye 2008).

The *Martić Rule 61* Chamber concluded that customary IHL prohibits belligerent reprisals directed against civilians during hostilities.[3] When reaffirming the technique's customary prohibition,[4] the *Kupreškić* Trial Chamber relied, *inter alia*, on the Martens Clause. In the chamber's view,

[2] *Tadić* Jurisdiction Decision, paras. 131–134.

[3] *Prosecutor* v. *Milan Martić*, Case No. IT-95-11-R61, Decision, March 8, 1996, paras. 15–17.

[4] *Prosecutor* v. *Zoran Kupreškić et al.*, Case No. IT-95-16-T, Judgment, January 14, 2000, paras. 527–534.

the clause effectively reverses the long-held presumption of freedom of action under international law – i.e., from being permitted unless specifically prohibited to being prohibited unless specifically permitted.

With few exceptions (Orakhelashvili 2008; Quéguiner 2008; Lepard 2016), reactions to the *Martić* Rue 61 Decision and the *Kupreškić* Trial Judgment have been largely cautious (Henckaerts and Doswald-Beck 2005) or disapproving (Kalshoven 2003; UK Ministry of Defence 2004; Greenwood 2006; Newton 2010). In particular, *Kupreškić*'s suggestion that inconsistent state practice may be disregarded in favor of humanitarian principles and public conscience when ascertaining customary rules has been heavily criticized (Darcy 2003; Skordas 2003; Cryer et al. 2010; Schlütter 2010; Günther 2011). In 2007, eleven years after its Rule 61 Decision, the *Martić* Trial Chamber implicitly conceded that belligerent reprisals against civilians in hostilities may be lawful.[5]

The *Kunarac* Appeals Chamber held that "there was nothing in . . . customary international law at the time of the alleged acts [in 1992–1993] which required proof of the existence of a plan or policy to commit these crimes" as a contextual element of crimes against humanity.[6] Commentators found the authorities offered selective and of questionable value (Schabas 2008; Van den Herik 2010; Van den Herik 2016). Similarly, the *Galić* Appeal Judgment's majority finding that, by 1992–1993, customary ICL had criminalized "acts and threats of violence the primary purpose of which is to spread terror among the civilian population"[7] attracted criticisms[8] (Cryer 2005–2006; Schlütter 2010; Bartels 2017).

The *Hadžihasanović* Trial and Appeals Chambers rejected the defense's argument that command responsibility as a customary mode of liability did not apply to non-international armed conflicts in 1991. Rather than finding affirmative pre-1991 state practice and *opinio juris*, the Trial Chamber held that nowhere in the material available had command responsibility's applicability in non-international armed

[5] *Prosecutor* v. *Milan Martić*, Case No. IT-95–11-T, Judgment, June 12, 2007, paras. 465–468. See also *Prosecutor* v. *Milan Martić*, Case No. IT-95–11-A, Judgment, October 8, 2008, paras. 263–267.

[6] *Prosecutor* v. *Dragoljub Kunarac et al.*, Case No. IT-96–23&IT-96–23/1-A, Judgment, June 12, 2002, para. 98.

[7] *Prosecutor* v. *Stanislav Galić*, Case No. IT-98–29-A, Judgment, November 30, 2006, paras. 86–98.

[8] Ibid., Separate and Partially Dissenting Opinion of Judge Schomburg.

conflict been explicitly denied.[9] The Appeals Chamber agreed,[10] adding that the criminal responsibility of a commander is what logically results where IHL embraces the notions of individual criminal responsibility and of organized military forces operating under responsible command.[11] This reasoning has been criticized as rather broadly deductive (Cryer 2010). Meanwhile, that Chamber's majority ruled that this mode of liability does not customarily cover those who assume command authority only after the crimes have been committed. The majority not only relied on a limited number of authorities[12] but also, curiously, derided the dissenting judges for engaging in *a contrario* reasoning themselves.[13] Subsequent ICTY[14] and ICTR[15] rulings, as well as scholarly commentary (Orie 2012), have since generated considerable uncertainty over the veracity of the *Hadžihasanović* Appeals Chamber's majority ruling.

The ICTY's *Naletilić and Martinović* Trial Chamber that forced labor in breach of Geneva Conventions III and IV constitutes a customary war crime. It did not cite any authority whatsoever.[16]

At the SCSL, the *Norman* Appeal Chamber's majority ruled that it had become a customary war crime by 1996 to recruit or enlist children or to use them to participate actively in hostilities.[17] Although *Norman* has received some support[18] (Smith 2004; Meron 2014), critics found it unpersuasive in view of the paucity of relevant authorities cited[19] (Van Schaak 2008; Cryer 2012; Kirakosyan 2012; Vasiliev 2016).

[9] *Prosecutor* v. *Enver Hadžihasanović, Mehmed Alagić and Amir Kubura*, Case No. IT-01-47-PT, Decision on Joint Challenge to Jurisdiction, November 12, 2002, paras. 68–93, 150–167.

[10] *Prosecutor* v. *Enver Hadžihasanović, Mehmed Alagić and Amir Kubura*, Case No. IT-01-47-AR72, Decision on Interlocutory Appeal Challenging Jurisdiction in Relation to Command Responsibility, July 16, 2003, paras. 27, 31.

[11] Ibid., paras. 13–23. [12] Ibid., para. 53. [13] Ibid., para. 54.

[14] *Prosecutor* v. *Naser Orić*, Case No. IT-03-68-T, Judgment, June 30, 2006, para. 335; *Prosecutor* v. *Naser Orić*, Case No. IT-03-68-A, Judgment, July 3, 2008, paras. 161–168; Declaration of Judge Shahabuddeen; Partially Dissenting Opinion and Declaration of Judge Liu; Separate and Partially Dissenting Opinion of Judge Schomburg.

[15] *Prosecutor* v. *Augustin Ndindiliyimana et al.*, Case No. ICTR-00-56-T, Judgment and Sentence, May 17, 2011, paras. 1960–1961; *Augustin Bizimungu* v. *Prosecutor*, Case No. ICTR-00-56B-A, June 30, 2014, paras. 369–370; Separate Declaration of Judge Liu.

[16] *Prosecutor* v. *Mladen Naletilić aka "Tuta" and Vinko Martinović aka "Štela,"* Case No. IT-98-34-T, Judgment, March 31, 2003, para. 250.

[17] *Prosecutor* v. *Sam Hinga Norman*, Case No. SCSL-2004-14-AR72(E), Decision on Preliminary Motion Based on Lack of Jurisdiction (Child Recruitment), May 31, 2004.

[18] *Prosecutor* v. *Thomas Lubanga Dyilo*, Case No. ICC-01/04-01/06, Decision on the Confirmation of Charges, January 29, 2007, paras. 299, 311.

[19] *Norman* Child Recruitment Decision, Dissenting Opinion of Justice Robertson.

Whether customary international law defines and criminalizes terrorism has long been debated (Duffy 2015). In 2011, the STL's Appeals Chamber concluded that it did.[20] According to the Chamber, the oft-cited controversies surrounding the notion's motive requirement were "covered by the *Nicaragua* principle,"[21] in effect a degree of leeway recognized by the International Court of Justice (ICJ) in its 1986 *Nicaragua Judgment* that tolerates certain discrepancies amongst the behavior of some states when determining the existence of a customary rule.[22] The methodology used and the conclusion reached have found support (Scharf 2011; Ventura 2011) as well as criticism (Gillett and Schuster 2011; Saul 2012; Jurdi 2014).

Several explanations have been offered for the generally "thin" evidence of state practice examined by ICTs. First, ICTs simply *assume* that states recognize weighty humanitarian principles deserving of recognition as such (Kirgis 1987; Meron 1991). Second, ICTs in the early days of their work have found it inevitable to *postulate* the customary rule they needed (Kolb 2013). Third, in some situations, the silence or inaction of a state in response to a potentially custom-generating event may constitute passive conduct (Villiger 1985; Ryngaert 2015).

ICTs as Law-Givers

Despite our standard position that states create customary international law, in some respects it may resemble more closely the creation of judge-made rules in the English common law (Schabas 2009; Bradley 2016). Indeed, one may challenge the very assumption that "finding [custom] is an objective exercise that stands apart from the messy process for making [it]" (Hakimi 2016: 170). Some ICT rulings arguably compound this methodological ambiguity, exacerbating the suspicion that ICT judges create new law where preexisting rules do not suit their purposes and that they impermissibly apply it retroactively or by analogy.

In 1997, for example, the ICTY *Erdemović* Appeals Chamber's majority rejected duress as a complete defense to the taking of innocent lives.[23]

[20] Case No. STL-11–01/1, Interlocutory Decision on the Applicable Law: Terrorism, Conspiracy, Homicide, Perpetration, Cumulative Charging, February 16, 2011, paras. 83–110.

[21] Ibid., para. 100.

[22] *Military and Paramilitary Activities in and against Nicaragua (Nicaragua* v. *United States of America)*, Merits Judgment, 1986 ICJ Rep. 14, para. 186.

[23] *Prosecutor* v. *Dražen Erdemović*, Case No. IT-96–22-A, *Judgment*, October 7, 1997, para. 19, disposition.

No relevant customary rule or general principle of law was found.[24] The majority nevertheless noted: "It would be naive to believe that international law operates and develops wholly divorced from considerations of social and economic policy . . . At the municipal level, criminal law and criminal policy are closely intertwined. There is no reason why this should be any different in international criminal law."[25]

Judge McDonald, one of the two judges forming the majority, defended the role of ICT judges in international public policymaking when she observed:

> [A]n international tribunal has an obligation to recognize the highest standards of international humanitarian law and develop a normative framework that reflects the purposes of Geneva law and incorporates the moral essence of a humane and just society . . . As war itself has changed, the laws of war should follow. Yet, because the international community has clung passionately, politically, to the immovable rock of State sovereignty that keeps alive and keeps dominant archaic perceptions of warfare, the pace of the law has been far slower than the pace of the war (McDonald 1998, 50–51).

Several commentators criticized the use of policy considerations by the *Erdemović* Appeals Chamber's majority (Turns 1998; Newman 2000; Fichtelberg 2008).

The *Tadić* Appeal Judgment finds that Article 4 of Geneva Convention IV protects Bosnian Muslim victims against actions of Bosnian Serbs, despite the fact that the article only protects those "in the hands of a Party to the conflict or Occupying Power of which they are not nationals." In this judgment's view, "nationality" is understood on ethnic allegiance. The judgment cites: (a) the absence of diplomatic protection as an eligibility requirement for neutral and cobelligerent nationals under Article 4; (b) the article's preparatory works suggesting the protection of refugees who had fled to territory now under occupation by their state of nationality; and (c) today's prevalence of interethnic conflicts.[26] Subsequent ICTY rulings supporting this construal refer, without much elaboration, to the object and purpose test and preparatory works.[27]

24 Ibid., Joint Separate Opinion of Judge McDonald and Judge Vohrah, paras. 55, 67, and 72.

25 Ibid., para. 78.

26 *Prosecutor* v. *Duško Tadić*, Case No. IT-94-1-A, Judgment, July 15, 1999, paras. 164–166.

27 *Prosecutor* v. *Zlatko Aleksovski*, Case No. IT-95-14/1-A, Judgment, March 24, 2000, paras. 151–152; *Prosecutor* v. *Zejnil Delalić et al. ("Čelebići Case")*, Case No. IT-96-21-A, Judgment, February 20, 2001, paras. 64–73.

According to the *Galić* Trial Chamber's majority, Additional Protocol I (API) *qua* treaty law, together with a special agreement concluded amongst the warring parties in Bosnia and Herzegovina (BiH), indicated that certain Article 51(2) violations had become subject to criminal sanctions by 1992.[28] Commentators have complained that the majority had departed from the ICTY's established law requiring a finding of customary criminalization[29] (Mettraux 2005) and that, in so doing, the majority had acted *ultra vires* (Swart 2010).

The SCSL's *AFRC* Trial Chamber interpreted "using children under the age of 15 years to participate actively in hostilities" to encompass putting their lives directly at risk in combat, such as the provision of logistical support to maintain military operations.[30] The *Taylor* Trial Chamber was more cautious, adding that the said risk "may" also include combat-related support activities and that the question will be assessed on a case-by-case basis.[31] *Taylor* arguably keeps active participation closer in substance to direct participation, an IHL notion commonly deemed synonymous with active participation that requires a specific threshold of harm and a causal link between the activities and the operation (Melzer 2009; Nicholson 2017). The ICC's *Lubanga* Trial Chamber chose to interpret "active participation" to include both "direct" and "indirect" participation,[32] although its majority refused to consider whether sexual violence against children amounted to their "use."[33] These rulings have divided commentators between those who fear that children would enjoy less IHL protection as a result (Guibert and Blumenstock 2007; Vité 2012; Wagner 2013; McBride 2014) and those unconvinced by such concerns (Smith 2004; Graf 2012; Nicholson 2017).

The notion that judges are interstitial lawmakers (Shapiro 1981; Shahabuddeen 1996) is not without controversy. For our purposes, this idea also involves the possibility that it leads judges to breach the prohibition against applying criminal provisions retroactively. Hayashi (2009) has suggested a slightly different line of reasoning. According to

28 *Prosecutor* v. *Stanislav Galić*, Case No. IT-98-29-T, Judgment, December 5, 2003, paras. 127–128.

29 Ibid., Separate and Partially Dissenting Opinion of Judge Nieto-Navia, paras. 112–113.

30 *Prosecutor* v. *Alex Tamba Brima et al.*, Case No. SCSL-2004-16-T, June 20, 2007, paras. 736–737.

31 *Prosecutor* v. *Charles Ghankay Taylor*, Case No. SCSL-03-01-T, Judgment, May 18, 2012, para. 444.

32 *Prosecutor* v. *Thomas Lubanga Dyilo*, Case No. ICC-01/04-01/06, Judgment pursuant to Article 74 of the Statute, March 14, 2012, paras. 624–628.

33 Ibid., paras. 629–630. But see Separate and Dissenting Opinion of Judge Odio Benito, paras. 2–21.

one school of modern legal positivism, what validates law is the combination of two kinds of rules. On the one hand are "primary rules of obligation" (Hart 1994: 94) that establish substantive standards of behavior (e.g., do not kill prisoners of war) addressed to actual duty-bearers. On the other are "secondary rules," including those called "rules of adjudication" (Hart 1994: 97) (e.g., those who kill prisoners of war shall be punished as war criminals) that delineate the powers and functions of law-applying officials. It follows that the principle of non-retroactivity would be satisfied if:

(i) The substantive prohibition bound the duty-bearer when he or she committed its breach; and
(ii) The penal provision empowered the law-applying official to determine and punish that breach when he or she was seized of the case.

In most instances of alleged lawmaking by ICT judges, at least the primary rules of obligation did exist when it was breached. What remains to be established is whether, when suspects were brought to trial, relevant law properly authorized the judge to impose penal sanctions for these breaches. This may be a somewhat less onerous enquiry.

Others argue that the prohibition against retroactive criminalization is less stringent in ICL than in domestic criminal law (Werle and Jessberger 2014). Deliberate wrongdoers should not be permitted to take advantage of the law's formal limitations (Meron 1995). Nonretroactivity is a necessary safeguard against arbitrary exercise of state power. Since ICTs are not instruments of such power, they are less constrained by it (Cassese and Gaeta 2013).

Some distinguish existing penal rules being foreseeably adapted through interpretive techniques to new situations, from new offences being created[34] (Cassese and Gaeta 2013). How far such adaptations can go without infringing another criminal law principle, that is, that criminal provisions may not be applied by analogy, is unclear (Akande 2009a; Schlütter 2010).

Custom and ICTs as Finders-Creators of IHL and ICL in Decline?

Regardless, suspicions that ICTs have created new law, and that they applied it retroactively, analogously, or as a matter of public policy, linger

[34] *Prosecutor* v. *Zlatko Aleksovski*, Case No. IT-95-14/1-A, Judgment, March 24, 2000, paras. 126–127.

(Van Schaack 2008). Due process safeguards require that fair advance notice of penal sanctions be available to potential defendants[35] (Fletcher and Ohlin 2005).

It is therefore tempting to think that the danger of judicial lawmaking is subsiding. Commentators suggest that custom is declining in today's ICL. The jurisprudence of the two ad hoc tribunals, veritable drivers of ICL's era of judicial lawmaking, has become more settled (Kolb 2014). The field has gradually shifted to an era of codified rules characterized by the ICC's Rome Statute (Van den Herik 2016).

The ICTY and ICTR must ground their "power to convict an accused of any crime listed in the Statute[s] on its existence qua custom at the time this crime was alleged committed."[36] In his report to the Security Council, the UN Secretary-General famously observed that the ICTY should apply rules that are "beyond any doubt part of customary law" (UN Secretary-General 1993: 9). The nebulousness surrounding the Tribunals' applicable rules and their lawmaking role (Grover 2010) arguably prompted those negotiating the Rome Statute to avoid reference to custom (DeGuzman 2008), thereby betraying their distrust of ICC judges (Cassese 1999; Hunt 2004).

Neither custom nor ICTs' role as its finders-creators is likely to diminish, however (Arajärvi 2014; Meron 2014; Guzman and Hsiang 2016). First, even with the narrowing lacunae left amongst its detailed provisions, interpreting the Rome Statute will continue to involve custom (Bufalini 2015). Article 31(3) empowers the ICC to consider grounds for excluding criminal responsibility other than those enumerated in Article 31(1). Other examples include open-ended provisions, for example, Article 7(1)(k) designating "other inhumane acts" as a crime against humanity[37] (Heinsch 2010; Ambos 2014).

35 *Prosecutor* v. *Enver Hadžihasanović, Mehmed Alagić and Amir Kubura*, Case No. IT-01–47-PT, Decision on Joint Challenge to Jurisdiction, November 12, 2002, para. 62.

36 *Prosecutor* v. *Milan Milutinović, Nikola Šainović and Dragoljub Ojdanić*, Case No. IT-99–37-AR72, Decision on Dragoljub Ojdanić's Motion Challenging Jurisdiction – Joint Criminal Enterprise, May 21, 2003, para. 9. See also *Celebic* Appeal Judgment, para. 178; *Prosecutor* v. *Enver Hadžihasanović, Mehmed Alagić and Amir Kubura*, Case No. IT-01–47-AR72, Decision on Interlocutory Appeal Challenging Jurisdiction in Relation to Command Responsibility, July 16, 2003, para. 44.

37 *Prosecutor* v. *Germain Katanga and Mathieu Ngudjolo Chui*, Case No. ICC-01/04–01/07, Decision on the Confirmation of Charges, September 30, 2008, para. 448; *Prosecutor* v. *Jean-Pierre Bemba Gombo*, Case No. ICC-01/05–01/08, Judgment Pursuant to Article 74 of the Statute, March 21, 2016, para. 85.

The same can be said of the destruction of property and deportation or forcible transfer, crimes that require the absence of military necessity as one of their elements. The ICC's case law on them has so far remained limited and superficial. Given the growing number of pending charges built around these offences, however, the Court is likely to assess military necessity as a negative element under customary ICL (Hayashi 2017b).

Second, custom may become contentious when adjudicating acts committed on the territory of a nonparty state and by a nonparty national (Milanovic 2011; Bartels 2017). The ICC, though permanent, effectively functions as an ad hoc jurisdiction when the UN Security Council refers situations encompassing such cases. The ICC should then satisfy itself that the criminal provisions it is to apply have passed into custom by the relevant time.

Despite suggestions to the contrary (Kirsch 2006; Cryer 2015), the customary status of some Rome Statute crimes is doubtful (Gaeta 1999; von Hebel and Robinson 1999; McCormack and Robertson 1999; Sadat 2000; Robinson 2001; Bennouna 2002; Dörmann 2003; Cryer 2009; Kreß 2009).[38] The ICC's *Banda* case is interesting in this regard (Bartels 2017). Banda, a Sudanese national, is charged with the war crime of intentionally directing attacks against personnel, installations, materials, units, and vehicles involved in a peacekeeping mission for events that took place in Darfur, Sudan in 2007.[39] Sudan is party neither to the Rome Statute nor to the 1994 Convention on the Safety of United Nations and Associated Personnel. Arguably, the customary status of the offence stipulated under Article 8(2)(e)(iii) is in issue for *Banda*.

Third, even with the development of its case law, the ICC will need to examine subsequent custom. The ICC is unlikely to deal with numerous cases with broadly similar sets of facts, ranges of criminal acts, theories of liability, or circumstances surrounding accused persons. Rather, most cases will raise novel legal issues and concern situations that are more or less unique to each of them.

Fourth, despite the ICC's fifteen-year presence, new ad hoc ICTs continue to be created. They will face situations where the customary status of an offence needs to be determined. This prospect should not be underestimated, because these ICTs' creation will be not only ad hoc but

[38] *Prosecutor* v. *Radislav Krstić*, Case No. IT-98-33-A, Judgment, April 19, 2004, para. 224.

[39] *Prosecutor* v. *Abdallah Banda Abakaer Nourain and Saleh Mohammed Jerbo Jamus*, Case No. ICC-02/05-03/09, Corrigendum of the "Decision on the Confirmation of Charges," March 7, 2011, para. 163.

also post hoc, and any post hoc ICT must satisfy itself that the law it applies is not retroactive (Akande 2009a).

States as Interested Third Parties

As seen above, ICTs have occasionally taken it upon themselves to find or develop customary IHL and ICL. Let us now consider where states – whose practice and *opinio juris* according to standard thought are what creates custom – come in.

In some scenarios, states formally participate in the formation and application of certain rules by ICTs. In these instances, the question is whether such engagements influence the outcome. In other scenarios, states neither litigate nor make official representations on the matter. Not having "participated" in the deliberative process, would states accept their rights and obligations as described by ICTs?

Where States Participate

The ICTY's permanent judges adopt and amend its Rules of Procedure and Evidence (RPEs). These rules are judge-made law *par excellence* (Swart 2002; Sluiter 2010). Rule 54 stipulates that, "[a]t the request of either party or *proprio motu*, a Judge or a Trial Chamber may issue such orders, summonses, subpoenas, warrants and transfer orders as may be necessary for the purposes of an investigation or for the preparation or conduct of the trial." This provision, read in conjunction with Article 29 of the ICTY Statute, obligates states to cooperate with the Tribunal, including the production of evidence and servicing of documents.

In 1997, Croatia challenged an ICTY subpoena in connection with the *Blaškić* case. Croatia, as well as BiH and other *amici*, submitted written and oral submissions before the Trial Chamber that eventually upheld the subpoena. Croatia appealed. Canada, China, the Netherlands, New Zealand, and Norway, in addition to several groups and individuals, filed *amici* briefs. The Appeals Chamber held that Article 29 empowers the ICTY to issue orders binding on states (but not subpoenas, insofar as they are understood as injunctions accompanied by threat of penalty);[40] that state officials acting in their official capacity are susceptible neither to

[40] *Prosecutor* v. *Tihomir Blaškić*, Case No. IT-95-14-AR108bis, Judgment on the Request of the Republic of Croatia for Review of the Decision of Trial Chamber II of July 18, 1997, October 29, 1997, paras. 25–31.

namely: (a) that any person, regardless of his or her official capacity, is capable of assuming individual criminal responsibility for crimes punishable under international law (an ICL principle); (b) that head of state immunity claims are unopposable vis-à-vis ICTs (a court's personal scope of jurisdiction); and (c) that an ICT arrest warrant obligates a state to act inconsistently with its immunity-related obligations owed towards third states (a modification to existing interstate obligations).

Only the first proposition is uncontroversial. Regarding the second proposition, it has been suggested that customary international law contains an exception whereby head of state immunity does not apply to an ICT[85] (Gaeta 2009). Another view holds that Security Council referrals effectively override any such immunity[86] (Akande 2009b). Both arguments have been contested, however[87] (Kiyani 2013). Whether the third proposition is true may depend on the mode of an ICT's creation and the scope of its binding authority. The proposition at issue directly contradicts Article 98(1) of the Rome Statute:

> The [ICC] may not proceed with a request for surrender or assistance which would require the requested State to act inconsistently with its obligations under international law with respect to the State or diplomatic immunity of a person or property of a third State, unless the Court can first obtain the cooperation of that third State for the waiver of the immunity.

In *Arrest Warrant*, the ICJ ruled that head of state immunity was customarily opposable vis-à-vis national jurisdictions even for charges of war crimes and crimes against humanity[88] and that, by issuing an arrest warrant against the then serving Congolese foreign minister for such crimes, Belgium violated its obligation towards the Democratic Republic of the Congo.[89] In view of this, and absent Sudan's waiver with respect to Al Bashir, Article 98(1) of the Rome Statute would bar the ICC from requesting states parties to arrest and surrender him. It follows that ICC requests for Al Bashir's arrest and surrender are arguably *ultra vires*[90]

[85] *Arrest Warrant of 11 April 2000 (Democratic Republic of the Congo* v. *Belgium)*, Judgment, 2002 ICJ Rep. 3, para. 61; *Prosecutor* v. *Charles Ghankay Taylor*, Case No. SCSL-2003-01-I, Decision on Immunity from Jurisdiction, May 31, 2004, paras. 49–51.

[86] *Prosecutor* v. *Omar Hassan Ahmad Al Bashir*, Case No. ICC-02/05-01/09, Decision under Article 87(7) of the Rome Statute on the Non-Compliance by South Africa with Request by the Court for the Arrest and Surrender of Omar Al Bashir, July 6, 2017, paras. 84–97.

[87] Ibid., Minority Opinion of Judge Marc Perrin de Brichambaut, paras. 64–83, 92–96.

[88] *Arrest Warrant*, paras. 51, 53–55, 58–59.

[89] Ibid., para. 78(2).

[90] See also *Al Bashir* South Africa Non-Compliance Decision Minority Opinion of Judge Marc Perrin de Brichambaut, paras. 50–51, 54–58. But see South Africa Non-Compliance Decision, paras. 96–106.

(Gaeta 2009). Whether armed with sound legal arguments or not, increasingly bold defiance amongst some states parties vis-à-vis Al Bashir's arrest warrants is likely to continue.

Conclusion

ICTs' claims that a given rule is part of extant IHL or ICL would be unproblematic if the positions had already been widely accepted, or if they were the result of a thorough and careful analysis of state practice and *opinio juris*. ICTs would be treading well within the traditional, state-driven realm of customary international law. Nevertheless, ICTs sometimes find custom based on evidence that is limited in quality and quantity. Occasionally, they even act as if they are not just finders but also creators of rules. Such behavior is not easily reconcilable with the criminal law principle of nonretroactivity. Despite such concerns and custom's predicted decline, ICTs are likely to engage in judicial lawmaking for the foreseeable future.

Whether states accept ICT-made law is a separate question. With or without state involvement in the deliberative process, the record so far appears to be uneven. While litigation and representation by states have brought about accommodations in some cases, success has not been replicated in others. Outcomes are even less consistent where states are not formally involved. They codified some novel ICT findings. Other rulings failed to garner state support, lost coherence amid discord amongst judges and alleged informal pressure, or met with vocal opposition from interested states.

ICTs' contribution to the development of IHL and ICL is difficult to gauge. Forward-looking legal pronouncements are not enough. Given varied state reactions, ICTs' outcome performance in this department appears mixed. Try as they may, perhaps ICTs have not yet "supplanted" states in their role as IHL and ICL developers.

References

Akande, Dapo. 2004. "International Law Immunities and the International Criminal Court," *American Journal of International Law* 98(3): 407–433.

2009a. "Sources of International Criminal Law," in Cassese, Antonio, Acquaviva, Guido, and Akande, Dapo et al. (eds.), *The Oxford Companion to International Criminal Justice*. Oxford: Oxford University Press, pp. 41–53.

2009b. "The Legal Nature of Security Council Referrals to the ICC and Its Impact on Al Bashir's Immunities," *Journal of International Criminal Justice* 7(2): 333–352.

Aksenova, Marina. 2015. "The Specific Direction Requirement for Aiding and Abetting: A Call for Revisiting Comparative Criminal Law," *Cambridge Journal of International and Comparative Law* 4(1): 88–107.

Alamuddin, Amal and Webb, Philippa. 2010. "Expanding Jurisdiction over War Crimes under Article 8 of the ICC Statute," *Journal of International Criminal Justice* 8(5): 1219–1243.

Ambos, Kai. 2014. *Treatise on International Criminal Law*. Vol. 2. Oxford: Oxford University Press.

Appel, Benjamin J. 2016. "In the Shadow of the International Criminal Court: Does the ICC Deter Human Rights Violations?," *Journal of Conflict Resolution* 60: 1–26.

Arajärvi, Noora. 2014. *The Changing Nature of Customary International Law: Methods of Interpreting the Concept of Custom in International Criminal Tribunals*. Abingdon: Routledge.

Bachmann, Klaus and Fatić, Aleksandar. 2015. *The UN International Criminal Tribunals: Transition without Justice?* Abingdon: Routledge.

Bartels, Rogier. 2017. "Legitimacy and ICC Jurisdiction Following Security Council Referrals: Conduct on the Territory of Non-Party States and the Legality Principle," in Hayashi, Nobuo, Bailliet, Cecilia. M., and Nicholson, Joanna (eds.), *The Legitimacy of International Criminal Tribunals*. Cambridge: Cambridge University Press.

Bennouna, Mohamed. 2002. "The Statute's Rules on Crimes and Existing or Developing International Law," in Cassese, Antonio, Gaeta, Paola, and Jones, John R. W. D. (eds.), *The Rome Statute of the International Criminal Court*. Oxford: Oxford University Press, pp. 1101–1107.

Blank, Laurie R. 2012. "Operational Law Experts Roundtable on the *Gotovina* Judgment: Military Operations, Battlefield Reality and the Judgment's Impact on Effective Implementation and Enforcement of International Humanitarian Law," *Public Law & Legal Theory Research Paper Series Research Paper No. 12–186*. Atlanta: Emory University School of Law.

Boelaert-Suominen, Sonja. 2000. "Commentary: The Yugoslavia Tribunal and the Common Core of Humanitarian Law Applicable to All Armed Conflicts," *Leiden Journal of International Law* 13(3): 619–653.

Bogoeva, Julija. 2016. "International Judges and Government Interests: The Case of President Meron," *FICHL Policy Brief Series No. 48 (2016)*.

Bohlander, Michael (ed.), 2007. *International Criminal Justice: A Critical Analysis of Institutions and Procedures*. London: Cameron May.

Boyle, Alan and Chinkin, Christine. 2006. *The Making of International Law*. Oxford: Oxford University Press.

Bradley, Curtis A. 2016. "Customary International Law Adjudication as Common Law Adjudication," in Bradley, Curtis A. (ed.), *Custom's Future International Law in a Changing World.* Cambridge: Cambridge University Press, pp. 34–61.

Bufalini, Alessandro. 2015. "The Principle of Legality and the Role of Customary International Law in the Interpretation of the ICC Statute," *Law and Practice of International Courts and Tribunals* 14(2): 233–254.

Cançado Trindade, Augusto Antônio. 2010. *International Law for Humankind: Towards a New Jus Gentium.* Leiden: Martinus Nijhoff Publishers.

Cassese, Antonio 1999. "The Statute of the International Criminal Court: Some Preliminary Reflections," *European Journal of International Law* 10(1): 144–171.

Cassese, Antonio and Gaeta, P. 2013. *Cassese's International Criminal Law.* 3rd edn. Oxford: Oxford University Press.

Choi, Jonathan H. 2014. "Early Release in International Criminal Law," *Yale Law Journal* 123(6): 1784–1828.

Clark, Janine Natalya. 2013. "Courting Controversy: The ICTY's Acquittal of Croatian Generals Gotovina and Markač," *Journal of International Criminal Justice* 11(2): 399–423.

2014. *International Trials and Reconciliation: Assessing the Impact of the International Criminal Tribunal for the Former Yugoslavia.* Abingdon: Routledge.

2015. "'Specific Direction' and the Fragmentation of International Jurisprudence on Aiding and Abetting: Perišić and Beyond," *International Criminal Law Review* 15(3): 411–451.

Corn, Geoffrey S. and Corn, Gary P. 2012. "The Law of Operational Targeting: Viewing the LOAC Through an Operational Lens," *Texas International Law Journal* 47(2): 337–380.

Cryer, Robert. 2005–2006. "*Prosecutor v. Galić* and the War Crime of Terror Bombing," *Israel Defense Forces Law Review* 2: 75–101.

2009. "Royalism and the King: Article 21 of the Rome Statute and the Politics of Sources," *New Criminal Law Review* 12(3): 390–405.

2010. "The *Ad Hoc* Tribunals and the Law of Command Responsibility: A Quiet Earthquake," in Darcy, Shane and Powderly, Joseph (eds.), *Judicial Creativity at the International Criminal Tribunals.* Oxford: Oxford University Press, pp. 159–183.

2012. "International Criminal Justice in Historical Context: The Post-Second World War Trials and Modern International Criminal Justice," in Boas, Gideon, Schabas, William A., and Scharf, Michael P. (eds.), *International Criminal Justice: Legitimacy and Coherence.* Cheltenham: Edward Elgar, pp. 145–189.

2015. "The ICC and Its Relationship to Non-States Parties," in Stahn, Carsten (ed.), *The Law and Practice of the International Criminal Court*. Oxford: Oxford University Press, pp. 260–280.

Cryer, Robert, Friman, Hakan, Robinson, Darryl, and Wilmshurst, Elizabeth (eds.). 2010. *An Introduction to International Criminal Law and Procedure*. 2nd edn. Cambridge: Cambridge University Press.

Damaska, Mirjan R. 2008. "What Is the Point of International Criminal Justice?," *Chicago-Kent Law Review* 83(1): 329–365.

Danner, Allison Marston. 2006. "When Courts Make Law: How the International Criminal Tribunals Recast the Laws of War," *Vanderbilt Law Review* 59(1): 1–65.

Darcy, Shane. 2003. "The Evolution of the Law of Belligerent Reprisals," *Military Law Review* 175: 184–251.

2010. "Bridging the Gaps in the Law of Armed Conflict? International Criminal Tribunals and the Development of Humanitarian Law," in Quénivet, Noëlle and Shah-Davis, Shilan (eds.), *International Law and Armed Conflict: Challenges in the 21st Century*. The Hague: T. M. C. Asser Press, pp. 319–337.

2014. "Assistance, Direction and Control: Untangling International Judicial Opinion on Individual and State Responsibility for War Crimes by Non-State Actors," *International Review of the Red Cross* 96(893): 243–273.

DeGuzman, Margaret McAuliffe. 2008. "Applicable Law: Article 21," in Triffterer, Otto (ed.), *Commentary on the Rome Statute of the International Criminal Court: Observers' Notes, Article by Article*. 2nd edn. Baden-Baden: C. H. Beck Hart Nomos, pp. 435–446.

Dietrich, John. 2014. "The Limited Prospects of Deterrence by the International Criminal Court: Lessons from Domestic Experience," *International Social Science Review* 88(3): 1–26.

Dörmann, Knut. 2003. "War Crimes under the Rome Statute of the International Criminal Court, with a Special Focus on the Negotiations on the Elements of Crimes," *Max Planck Yearbook of United Nations Law* 7: 341–407.

Drumbl, Mark A. 2007. *Atrocity, Punishment and International Law*. Cambridge: Cambridge University Press.

Duffy, Helen. 2015. *The "War on Terror" and the Framework of International Law*. 2nd edn. Cambridge: Cambridge University Press.

Fichtelverg, Aaron. 2008. "Liberal Values in International Criminal Law: A Critique of *Erdemovic*," *Journal of International Criminal Justice* 6(1): 3–19.

Fischer, Martina and Simić, Olivera (eds.), 2016. *Transitional Justice and Reconciliation: Lessons from the Balkans*. Abington: Routledge.

Fletcher, George P. and Ohlin, Jens David. 2005. "Reclaiming Fundamental Principles of Criminal Law in the Darfur Case," *Journal of International Criminal Justice* 3(3): 539–561.

Gaeta, Paola. 1999. "The Defence of Superior Orders: The Statute of the International Criminal Court versus Customary International Law," *European Journal of International Law* 10(1): 172–191.

2009. "Does President Al Bashir Enjoy Immunity from Arrest?," *Journal of International Criminal Justice* 7(2): 315–332.

Gillett, Matthew and Schuster, Matthias. 2011. "Fast-Track Justice: The Special Tribunal for Lebanon Defines Terrorism," *Journal of International Criminal Justice* 9(5): 989–1020.

Graf, Roman. 2012. "The International Criminal Court and Child Soldiers: An Appraisal of the *Lubanga* Judgment," *Journal of International Criminal Justice* 10(4): 945–969.

Greenawalt, Alexander K. A. 2014. "International Criminal Law for Retributivists," *University of Pennsylvania Journal of International Law* 35(4): 969–1044.

Greenwood, Christopher. 1989. "The Twilight of the Law of Belligerent Reprisals," *Netherlands Yearbook of International Law* 20: 35–69.

2006. "Belligerent Reprisals in the Jurisprudence of the International Criminal Tribunal for the former Yugoslavia," in Greenwood, Christopher (ed.), *Essays on War in International Law*. London: Cameron May, pp. 331–351.

Grover, Leena. 2010. "A Call to Arms: Fundamental Dilemmas Confronting the Interpretation of Crimes in the Rome Statute of the International Criminal Court," *European Journal of International Law* 21(3): 543–583.

Guibert, Nulwenn and Blumenstock, Tilman. 2007. "The First Judgment of the Special Court for Sierra Leone: A Missed Opportunity?," *The Law and Practice of International Courts and Tribunals* 6(3): 367–391.

Günther, Klaus. 2011. "Beyond Dispute: International Judicial Institutions as Lawmakers: Judicial Lawmaking, Discourse Theory, and the ICTY on Belligerent Reprisals," *German Law Journal* 12(5): 1261–1278.

Guzman, Andrew T. and Hsiang, Jerome. 2016. "Reinvigorating Customary International Law," in Bradley, Curtis A. (ed.), *Custom's Future: International Law in a Changing World*. Cambridge: Cambridge University Press, pp. 275–304.

Hakimi, Monica. 2016. "Custom's Method and Process: Lessons from Humanitarian Law," in Bradley, Curtis A. (ed.), *Custom's Future: International Law in a Changing World*. Cambridge: Cambridge University Press, pp. 148–171.

Haque, Adil Ahmad. 2005. "Group Violence and Group Vengeance: Toward a Retributivist Theory of International Criminal Law," *Buffalo Criminal Law Review* 9(1): 272–328.

Harhoff, Frederik. 2016. "Mystery Lane: A Note on Independence and Impartiality in International Criminal Trials," *FICHL Policy Brief Series* No. 47 *(2016)*.

Hart, H. L. A. 1994. *The Concept of Law*. 2nd edn. Oxford: Oxford University Press.

Hayashi, Nobuo. 2009. "Critical Essays: Eve La Haye on *War Crimes in Internal Armed Conflicts*," *Nordic Journal of Human Rights* 27(3): 357–365.

2017a. "Is the Yugoslav Tribunal Guilty of Hyper-Humanising International Humanitarian Law?," in Hayashi, Nobuo, Bailliet, Cecilia M., and Nicholson, Joanna (eds.), *The Legitimacy of International Criminal Tribunals*. Cambridge: Cambridge University Press.

2017b. *Military Necessity*. Leiden: Leiden University Repository.

Heinsch, Robert. 2010. "The Crime of Aggression After Kampala: Success or Burden for the Future?," *Goettingen Journal of International Law* 2(2): 713–743.

Henckaerts, Jean-Marie and Doswald-Beck, Louise. 2005. *Customary International Humanitarian Law: Volume I: Rules*. Cambridge: Cambridge University Press.

Higgins, Rosalyn. 1998. "The International Court of Justice and Human Rights," in Wellens, Karel (ed.), *International Law: Theory and Practice: Essays in Honour of Eric Suy*. The Hague: Martinus Nijhoff Publishers, pp. 691–706.

Huffman, Walter B. 2012. "Margin of Error: Potential Pitfalls of the Rulings in *The Prosecutor v. Ante Gotovina*," *Military Law Review* 211: 1–56.

Hunt, David. 2004. "The International Criminal Court: High Hopes, 'Creative Ambiguity' and an Unfortunate Mistrust in International Judges," *Journal of International Criminal Justice* 2(1): 56–70.

International Law Commission. 2002. *Rapport final sur la succession en matière de traités*.

Jo, Hyeran, Radtke, Mitchell, and Simmons, Beth A. 2018. "*Assessing the International Criminal Court*," Chapter 6 in this volume.

Jurdi, Nidal Nabil. 2014. "The Crime of Terrorism in Lebanese and International Law," in Alamuddin, Amal, Jurdi, Nidal Nabil, and Tolbert, David (eds.), *The Special Tribunal for Lebanon: Law and Practice*. Oxford: Oxford University Press, pp. 73–87.

Kalshoven, Frits. 1990. "Belligerent Reprisals Revisited," *Netherlands Yearbook of International Law* 21: 43–80.

2003. "Reprisals and the Protection of Civilians: Two Recent Decision of the Yugoslav Tribunal," in Vohrah, Lal Chand, Pocar, Fausto, Featherstone, Yvonne, Fourmy, Olivier, Graham, Christine, and Hocking, John et al. (eds.), *Man's Inhumanity to Man: Essays on International Law in Honour of Antonio Cassese*. The Hague: Kluwer Law International, pp. 481–510.

Kamminga, Menno T. 1996. "State Succession in Respect of Human Rights Treaties," *European Journal of International Law* 7(4): 469–484.

2005. *Preliminary Report "Human Rights Treaties and State Succession"*. Strasbourg: European Commission for Democracy Through Law.

Kelder, Jessica M., Holá, Barbora, and van Wijk, Joris. 2014. "Rehabilitation and Early Release of Perpetrators of International Crimes: A Case Study of the ICTY and ICTR," *International Criminal Law Review* 14(6): 1177–1203.

Kirakosyan, Yeghishe. 2012. "Finding Custom: The ICJ and the International Criminal Courts and Tribunals Compared," in Van den Herik, Larissa and Stahn, Carsten (eds.), *The Diversification and Fragmentation of International Criminal Law*. Leiden: Martinus Nijhoff Publishers, pp. 149–162.

Kirgis, Frederic L. 1987. "Custom on a Sliding Scale," *American Journal of International Law* 81(1): 146–151.

Kirsch, Philippe. 2006. "Customary International Humanitarian Law, Its Enforcement, and the Role of the International Criminal Court," in Maybee, Larry and Chakka, Benarji (eds.), *Custom as a Source of International Humanitarian Law: Proceedings of the Conference to Mark the Publication of the ICRC Study "Customary International Humanitarian Law."* New Delhi: International Committee of the Red Cross, pp. 79–85.

Kiyani, Asad G. 2013. "Al-Bashir & the ICC: The Problem of Head of State Immunity," *Chinese Yearbook of International Law* 12(3): 467–508.

Kolb, Robert. 2013. "The Main Epochs of Modern International Humanitarian Law Since 1864 and Their Related Dominant Legal Constructions," in Larsen, Kjetil Mujezinovic, Cooper, Camilla Guldahl, and Nystuen, Gro (eds.), *Searching for a "Principle of Humanity" in International Humanitarian Law*. Cambridge: Cambridge University Press, pp. 23–71.

2014. "The Jurisprudence of the Yugoslav and Rwandan Criminal Tribunals on Their Jurisdiction and on International Crimes (2004–2014)," *British Yearbook of International Law* 84(1): 131–186.

Krieger, Heike. 2012. "Cases of State Succession, State Responsibility and Outbreak of Hostilities," in Dörr, Oliver and Schmalenbach, Kirsten (eds.), *Vienna Convention on the Law of Treaties: A Commentary*. Berlin: Springer, pp. 1239–1266.

Kreß, Claus. 2009. "The Crime of Genocide and Contextual Elements: A Comment on the ICC Pre-Trial Chamber's Decision in the *Al-Bashir* Case," *Journal of International Criminal Justice* 7(2): 297–306.

Ku, Julian and Nzelibe, Jide. 2006. "Do International Criminal Tribunals Deter or Exacerbate Humanitarian Atrocities?," *Washington University Law Review* 84(4): 777–833.

La Haye, Eve. 2008. *War Crimes in Internal Armed Conflicts*. Cambridge: Cambridge University Press.

Lepard, Brian D. 2016. "Customary International Law as a Dynamic Process," in Bradley, Curtis A. (ed.), *Custom's Future: International Law in a Changing World*. Cambridge: Cambridge University Press, pp. 62–94.

Matheson, Michael J. 1987. "Session One: The United States Position on the Relation of Customary International Law to the 1977 Protocols Additional to the 1949 Geneva Conventions: Remarks of Michael J. Matheson," *American University Journal of International Law and Policy* 2(2): 419–431.

McCormack, Tim L. H. and Robertson, Susan. 1999. "Jurisdictional Aspects of the Rome Statute for the New International Criminal Court," *Melbourne University Law Review* 23(3): 635–667.

McDermott, Yvonne. 2016. *Fairness in International Criminal Trials.* Oxford: Oxford University Press.

McDonald, Gabrielle Kirk. 1998. "The Eleventh Annual Waldemar A. Solf Lecture: The Changing Nature of the Laws of War," *Military Law Review* 156: 30–51.

McBride, Julie. 2014. *The War Crime of Child Soldiers Recruitment.* The Hague: Asser Press.

Melzer, Nils. 2009. *Interpretive Guidance on the Notion of Direct Participation in Hostilities under International Humanitarian Law.* Geneva: International Committee of the Red Cross.

Meron, Theodor. 1991. *Human Rights and Humanitarian Norms as Customary Law.* Oxford: Clarendon Press.

1995. "International Criminalization of Internal Atrocities," *American Journal of International Law* 89(3): 554–577.

1998a. "The Hague Tribunal: Working to Clarify International Humanitarian Law," *American University International Law Review* 13(6): 1511–1518.

1998b. "War Crimes Law Comes of Age," *American Journal of International Law* 92(3): 462–468.

2014. "Customary Humanitarian Law Today: From the Academy to the Courtroom," in Clapham, Andrew and Gaeta, Paola (eds.), *The Oxford Handbook of International Law in Armed Conflict.* Oxford: Oxford University Press, pp. 37–49.

Mettraux, Gunénaël. 2005. *International Crimes and the Ad Hoc Tribunals.* Oxford: Oxford University Press.

Milanovic, Marko. 2011. "Is the Rome Statute Binding on Individuals? (And Why We Should Care)," *Journal of International Criminal Justice* 9(1): 25–52.

Ministère de la défense de la République français. 2012. *Manuel de droit des conflits armés.* Paris: Ministère de la defense.

Moir, Lindsay. 2005. "Towards the Unification of International Humanitarian Law?," in Burchill, Richard, White, Nigel D., and Morris, Justin (eds.), *International Conflict and Security Law: Essays in Memory of Hilaire McCoubrey.* Cambridge: Cambridge University Press, pp. 108–128.

Murphy, Peter W. 2000. "Judging War Criminals (book review)," *Texas International Law Journal* 35(2): 325–333.

Neuner, Matthias. 2002. "The Power of International Criminal Tribunals to Produce Evidence," in Roggemann, Herwig and Šarčević, Petar (eds.), *National Security and International Criminal Justice.* The Hague: Kluwer Law International, pp. 163–191.

Newman, Stephen C. 2000. "Duress as a Defense to War Crimes and Crimes Against Humanity – *Prosecutor v. Drazen Erdemovic*," *Military Law Review* 166: 158–171.

Newton, Michael A. 2010. "Reconsidering Reprisals," *Duke Journal of Comparative & International Law* 20(3): 361–388.

Nicholson, Joanna. 2017. *Fighting and Victimhood in International Criminal Law*. Leiden: Brill.

Office of General Counsel. 2015. *Department of Defense Law of War Manual*. Washington, D.C.: Department of Defense.

Ochoa, Christiana. 2007. "The Individual and Customary International Law Formation," *Virginia Journal of International Law* 48(1): 119–186.

O'Donohue, Jonathan. 2015. "The ICC and the ASP," in Stahn, Carsten (ed.), *The Law and Practice of the International Criminal Court*. Oxford: Oxford University Press, pp. 105–138.

Orakhelashvili, Alexander. 2008. "Review of Books: Perspectives on the ICRC Study on Customary International Humanitarian Law and The Handbook of International Humanitarian Law," *British Yearbook of International law* 79(1): 371–378.

Orentlicher, Diane F. 2008. *Shrinking the Space for Denial: The Impact of the ICTY in Serbia*. New York: Open Society institute.

Orie, Alphons M. M. 2012. "*Stare Decisis* in the ICTY Appeal System? Successor Responsibility in the *Hadžihasanović* Case," *Journal of International Criminal Justice* 10(3): 635–644.

Quéquiner, Jean-François. 2008. "The Principle of Distinction: Beyond an Obligation of Customary International Humanitarian Law," in Hensel, Howard M. (ed.), *The Legitimate Use of Military Force: The Just War Tradition and the Customary Law of Armed Conflict*. Hampshire, Burlington: Ashgate, pp. 161–187.

Rasulov, Akbar. 2003. "Revisiting State Succession to Humanitarian Treaties: Is There a Case for Automaticity?," *European Journal of International Law* 14(1): 141–170.

Reeves, Shane R. and Thurnher, Jeffrey S. 2013. "Are We Reaching a Tipping Point? How Contemporary Challenges Are Affecting the Military Necessity-Humanity Balance," *Harvard National Security Journal Features*: 1–12.

Robinson, Darryl. 2001. "The Elements for Crimes Against Humanity: Introduction," in Lee, Roy S. and Friman, Hakan (eds.), *The International Criminal Court: Elements of Crimes and Rules of Procedure and Evidence*. Ardsley, NY: Transnational Publishers, pp. 57–61.

Ryngaert, Cedric. 2015. *Jurisdiction in International Law*. 2nd edn. Oxford: Oxford University Press.

Sadat, Leila. 2000. "Custom, Codification and Some Thoughts about the Relationship between the Two: Article 10 of the ICC Statute," *De Paul Law Review* 49(4): 909–923.

Saul, Ben. 2012. "Civilizing the Exception: Universally Defining Terrorism," in Masferrer, Aniceto (ed.), *Post 9/11 and the State of Permanent Emergency: Security and Human Rights in Countering Terrorism*. Dordrecht: Springer, pp. 79–100.

Schabas, William A. 2007. *The UN International Criminal Tribunals*. Cambridge: Cambridge University Press.

2008. "State Policy as an Element of International Crimes," *Journal of Criminal Law and Criminology* 98(3): 953–982.

2009. "Customary Law or 'Judge-Made' Law: Judicial Creativity at the UN Criminal Tribunals," in Doria, José, Gasser, Hans-Peter, and Bassiouni, M. Cherif (eds.), *The Legal Regime of the International Criminal Court: Essays in Honour of Professor Igor Blishchenko*. Leiden: Martinus Nijhoff Publishers, pp. 77–101.

2011. *An Introduction to the International Criminal Court*. 4th edn. Cambridge: Cambridge University Press.

Scharf, Michael P. 2011. "Special Tribunal for Lebanon Issues Landmark Ruling on Definition of Terrorism and Modes of Participation," *ASIL Insights* 15(6).

Schlütter, Birgit. 2010. *Developments in Customary International Law: Theory and the Practice of the International Court of Justice and the International ad hoc Criminal Tribunals for Rwanda and Yugoslavia*. Leiden: Martinus Nijhoff Publishers.

Schmitt, Michael N. 2010. "Military Necessity and Humanity in International Humanitarian Law: Preserving the Delicate Balance," *Virginia Journal of International Law* 50(4): 795–839.

Schomburg, Wolfgang. 2009. "The Role of International Criminal Tribunals in Promoting Respect for Fair Trial Rights," *Northwestern Journal of International Human Rights* 8(1): 1–29.

Secretary-General of the United Nations. 1993. *Report of the Secretary-General pursuant to paragraph 2 of Security Council Resolution 808 (1993)*. S/25704, May 3, 1993.

Shahabuddeen, Mohamed. 1996. *Precedent in the World Court*. Cambridge: Cambridge University Press.

2004. "Does the Principle of Legality Stand in the Way of Progressive Development of Law?," *Journal of International Criminal Justice* 2(4): 1007–1017.

Shapiro, Martin. 1981. *Courts: A Comparative and Political Analysis*. Chicago: University of Chicago Press.

Skordas, Achilles. 2003. "Hegemonic Custom?," in Byers, Michael and Nolte, Georg (eds.). *United States Hegemony and the Foundation of International Law*. Cambridge: Cambridge University Press, pp. 317–347.

Sluiter, Göran. 2004. "Judicial Assistance," in Klip, André and Sluiter, Göran (eds.), *Annotated Leading Cases of International Criminal Tribunals: The*

International Criminal Tribunal for the Former Yugoslavia 2001, Vol. 7. Antwerp: Intersentia, pp. 243–247.

2010. "Procedural Lawmaking at the International Criminal Tribunals," in Darcy, Shane and Powderly, Joseph (eds.), *Judicial Creativity at the International Criminal Tribunals*. Oxford: Oxford University Press, pp. 315–331.

Smith, Alison. 2004. "Child Recruitment and the Special Court for Sierra Leone," *Journal of International Criminal Justice* 2(4): 1141–1153.

Sofaer, Abraham D. 1987. "The Position of the United States on Current Law of War Agreements: Remarks of Judge Abraham D. Sofaer, Legal Adviser, United States Department of State, January 22, 1987," *American University Journal of International Law and Policy* 2(2): 460–471.

Solis, Gary D. 2013. "The *Gotovina* Acquittal: A Sound Appellate Course Correction," *Military Law Review* 215: 78–107.

Stato Maggiore della Difesa. 1991. *Manuale di diritto umanitario*. SMD-G-014. Rome: Stato Maggiore della Difesa.

Stewart, James. 2003. "Towards a Single Definition of Armed Conflict in International Humanitarian Law: A Critique of International Armed Conflict," *International Review of the Red Cross* 850: 313–350.

Swart, Mia. 2002. "Ad Hoc Rules for Ad Hoc Tribunals? The Rule-Making Power of the Judges of the ICTY and ICTR," *South African Journal on Human Rights* 18(4): 570–589.

2010. "Judicial Lawmaking at the *ad hoc* Tribunals: The Creative Use of the Sources of International Law and 'Adventurous Interpretation'," *Heidelberg Journal of International Law* 70: 459–486.

Turns, David. 1998. "The International Criminal Tribunal for the Former Yugoslavia: The *Erdemovic* Case," *International and Comparative Law Quarterly* 47(2): 461–474.

UK Ministry of Defence. 2004. *The Manual of the Law of Armed Conflict*. Oxford: Oxford University Press.

Vallentgoed, Darren. 2013. "The Last Round? A Post-Gotovina Reassessment of the Legality of Using Artillery Against Built-Up Areas," *Journal of Conflict & Security Law* 18(1): 25–57.

Van den Herik, Larissa. 2010. "Using Custom to Reconceptualize Crimes Crimes Against Humanity," in Darcy, Shane and Powderly, Joseph (eds.), *Judicial Creativity at the International Criminal Tribunals*. Cambridge: Cambridge University Press, pp. 80–105.

2016. "The Decline of Customary International Law as a Source of International Criminal Law," in Bradley, Curtis A. (ed.), *Custom's Future: International Law in a Changing World*. Cambridge: Cambridge University Press, pp. 230–252.

Van Schaack, Beth. 2008. "*Crimen Sene Lege*: Judicial Lawmaking at the Intersection of Law and Morals," *The Georgetown Law Journal* 97(1): 119–192.

Vasiliev, Sergey. 2016. "The Making of International Criminal Law," in Brölmann, Catherine and Radi, Yannick (eds.), *Research Handbook on the Theory and Practice of International Lawmaking*. Glos: Edward Elgar, pp. 354–394.

Ventura, Manuel J. 2011. "Terrorism According to the STL's Interlocutory Decision on the Applicable Law: A Defining Moment or a Moment of Defining?," *Journal of International Criminal Justice* 9(5): 1021–1042.

2014. "Farewell 'Specific Direction': Aiding and Abetting War Crimes and Crimes Against Humanity in Perišić, Tayor, Šainović et al., and US Alien Tort Statute Jurisprudence," in Casey-Maslen, Stuart (ed.), *The War Report: Armed Conflict in 2013*. Oxford: Oxford University Press, pp. 511–553.

Villiger, Mark E. 1985. *Customary International Law and Treaties: A Study of Their Interaction and Interrelations with Special Consideration of the 1969 Vienna Convention on the Law of Treaties*. Dordrecht: Martinus Nijhoff Publishers.

Vité, Sylvain. 2012. "Between Consolidation and Innovation: The International Criminal Court's Trial Chamber Judgment in the *Lubanga* Case," *Yearbook of International Humanitarian Law* 15: 61–85.

Von Hebel, Herman and Robinson, Darryl. 1999. "Crimes within the Jurisdiction of the Court," in Lee, Roy S. (ed.), *The International Criminal Court: The Making of the Rome Statute: Issues, Negotiations, Results*. The Hague: Kluwer Law International, pp. 79–126.

Wagner, Natalie. 2013. "A Critical Assessment of Using Children to Participate Actively in Hostilities in Lubanga," *Criminal Law Forum* 24(2): 145–203.

Wedgwood, Ruth. 1998. "Case Analysis: International Criminal Tribunals and State Sources of Proof: The Case of Tihomir Blaškić," *Leiden Journal of International Law* 11(3): 635–654.

Werle, Gerhard and Jessberger, Florian. 2014. *Principles of International Criminal Law*. 3rd edn. Oxford: Oxford University Press.

Wierda, Marieke and Triolo, Anthony. 2012. "Resources," in Reydams, Luc, Wouters, Jan, and Ryngaert, Cedric (eds.), *International Prosecutors*. Oxford: Oxford University Press, pp. 113–170.

Wippman, David. 2006. "The Costs of International Justice," *American Journal of International Law* 100(4): 861–881.

Wilson, Richard Ashby. 2005. "Writing History: The Historical Record of the International Criminal Tribunal for the Former Yugoslavia," *Human Rights Quarterly* 27(3): 908–942.

2011. *Writing History in International Criminal Tribunals*. Cambridge: Cambridge University Press.

Wouters, Jan and Hamid, Linda. 2016. "Custom and Informal International Lawmaking," in Bradley, Curtis A. (ed.), *Custom's Future: International*

Law in a Changing World. Cambridge: Cambridge University Press, pp. 332–359.

Zacklin, Ralph. 2004. "The Failings of Ad Hoc International Criminal Tribunals," *Journal of International Criminal Justice* 2(2): 541–545.

Zimmermann, Andreas. 2006. "State Succession in Treaties," *Max Planck Encyclopedia of Public International Law*. Oxford: Oxford University Press.

PART II

6

Assessing the International Criminal Court

HYERAN JO, MITCHELL RADTKE, AND BETH A. SIMMONS

> Recognizing that such grave crimes threaten the peace, security and well-being of the world ... Determined to put an end to impunity for the perpetrators of these crimes and thus to contribute to the prevention of such crimes ...
>
> *Preamble, Rome Statute of the International Criminal Court*

One of the most important issues surrounding international courts is whether they can further the dual causes of peace and justice.[1] None has been more ambitious in this regard than the International Criminal Court (ICC). And yet the ICC has been the object of a good deal of criticism. Some people claim it has been an expensive use of resources that might have been directed to other purposes. Others claim that its accomplishments are meager because it has managed to try and convict so few people. And many commentators and researchers claim that the Court faces an inherent tension between the dual objectives of securing the peace and ending impunity for perpetrators of some of the most egregious crimes, including genocide, crimes against humanity, war crimes, and crimes of aggression.[2]

This chapter assesses the ability of the ICC to deter. In so doing, we follow the lead of the framing chapter and think not only about the Court's performance in the narrow sense (e.g., how many people have been tried?) but rather think about the ways in which the ICC has contributed to a broader culture that refuses to tolerate impunity for violations of international criminal law. Because we must limit our topic to manageable proportions (and because we are social scientists and not lawyers) our focus is primarily on *outcome performance* rather than process performance.[3] We focus on two outcomes alluded to in the

[1] The authors thank Terry Chapman, Sarah Nouwen, Jon Pevehouse, William Burke-White and the Editors for comments, and Kate Bryant and Dennis Ologho for research assistance.

[2] Rome Statute, Article 5(1)a-d.

[3] See Hayashi (2018) for a legal analysis of the performance of international criminal courts and tribunals.

introductory chapter: 1) reaching desired goals and 2) deterring atrocities against civilians.

As a criminal court, the ICC is much different than courts that settle disputes between states or disputes between private parties (e.g., investors) and states. The ICC fits four out of five of the criteria set out in the introduction. It decides issues of guilt or innocence on the basis of international law (greatly influenced in this case by domestic criminal procedures); it follows predetermined rules of procedure, detailed in the Rome Statute, its founding document; the Court issues legally binding decisions and is composed of independent judges. States are parties to the Rome Statute, but only individuals are on trial in the criminal cases that come before the Court.[4] The Office of the Prosecutor (OTP) has been empowered by the States Parties to bring criminal charges against individuals accused of violations of international criminal law.

There are many ways one could judge the ICC's performance. It might be evaluated based on its contribution to justice (Goodman and Jinks 2003), on its normative value (Bass 2003), on its capacity to offer societal "atonement" (Bikundo 2012), and/or on its legitimacy in the eyes of local victims (Clark 2013). We will concentrate on examining the extent to which the ICC succeeds in achieving its desired outcomes (Introduction). From the preamble quoted above, it is fairly clear that for most states this means moving the international criminal law system towards a relatively consistent and coherent set of rules and institutions – at the international, regional, and national level – that improve the possibility of deterring the most egregious human rights violations and war crimes. The Court understands its own mission as being "to help end impunity for the perpetrators of the most serious crimes of concern to the international community."[5] Indeed, in its referral to the ICC, Uganda (the first state to refer a case to the Court) appealed for "the suppression of the most serious crimes of concern to the international community as a whole," although it is widely recognized in this case that the intent was to wield a legal threat against rebels alone.[6] At the same time, the

4 States Parties may have an active role in admissibility proceedings. See for example Rome Statute, Articles 17–19.

5 ICC, Available at: www.icc-cpi.int/en_menus/icc/about%20the%20court/Pages/about%20the%20court.aspx (accessed July 6, 2017).

6 "Referral of the situation concerning the Lord's Resistance Army," submitted by The Republic of Uganda, December 16, 2003. PDF on file with authors. Note the (intentional?) error in the government's submission; the Court has since corrected reference to

purposes of the ICC were to be achieved while protecting state sovereignty to prosecute crimes committed in their jurisdictions, through complementarity.[7]

How should we then assess the performance of the Court? We present evidence of two kinds: First, we look for the imprint of the ICC on domestic law. In the case of the ICC, States Parties have strong incentives to reconcile domestic criminal statutes with international criminal law, since to do so allows them to take jurisdiction should they want to do so.[8] One of the major performance outcomes of the ICC is therefore the extent to which it has encouraged legal change within the domestic crime statutes of members. Second, we look for actual evidence that the ICC or the domestic laws it has encouraged have contributed to crime deterrence. Does the extension of the ICC jurisdiction through ratification actually deter the crimes it was designed to punish? Do changes in crime statutes that the ICC has stimulated done so?

Evidence exists that the ICC has performed well in this regard (Jo and Simmons 2016). We discuss broad-based evidence of its deterrence effects, but we also focus in on a specific and very violent case: that of Uganda. We believe there is some evidence that the ICC has deterred some heinous crimes even in this difficult case. We discuss the evidence that the ICC's jurisdiction and action have deterred both state agents and rebel groups from committing atrocities against civilians in this case. In so doing, we recognize that this may not be what the government of Uganda originally intended when they ratified the ICC. Nonetheless, as the introduction entreats us, we should look for evidence of court performance in individual cases as well as more

this referral as relating to the Situation in *Uganda* not the LRA, since referrals cannot specify individuals or specific groups to be investigated. The original referral reflects the government of Uganda's hope that the Court could be used to prosecute rebels alone. While this was in fact the decision of the OTP in this case, referrals inherently allow for investigation and indictments of any individuals. See the discussion in Nouwen (2013: 114–115).

[7] Concerns about preserving state sovereign via carefully worded complementary jurisdiction was a strong emphasis of many states during negotiation of the ICC statute. See paragraphs 91–93 and 100 of the United Nations Report of the Ad Hoc Committee on the Establishment of an International Criminal Court General Assembly Official Records, Fiftieth Session Supplement No. 22 (A/50/22). Available at: www.legal-tools.org/uploads/tx_ltpdb/doc21168.pdf (accessed July 6, 2017).

[8] A case is inadmissible when "The case is being investigated or prosecuted by a State which has jurisdiction over it" (Rome Statute, Article 17(1)(a)). If a state wants to have a credible objection to admissibility, then, there are clear incentives to define the crimes listed in Article 5(1)a-d in domestic criminal statutes.

broadly. The case of Uganda helps us to understand, in greater detail, just how international justice institutions, such as the ICC, become relevant on the ground.

Background on the ICC

The First Global Criminal Tribunal

The twentieth century has been a remarkable period of international judicialization.[9] International courts and court-like institutions have sprouted in surprising numbers to deal with specific functional problems, like conflict over trade agreements or disagreements over the application of the Law of the Sea, and regional concerns such as individual human rights. The ICC is different from nearly all of these institutions. Post-Cold War *internal* conflicts caused nongovernmental human rights, humanitarian organizations, and some states[10] to call for an end to impunity for crimes against humanity and genocide (Lee 1999, Pace and Schense 2002, Glasius 2006). International Criminal Tribunals for the former Yugoslavia and then Rwanda primed the international community to think about the creation of the International Criminal Court (Tochilovsky 2003, Danner 2006). After several years of negotiation, a standing court was established with the ability to prosecute high officials – even national leaders. Today, the ICC is the only international court devoted to the enforcement of international *criminal law*, holding *individuals* accountable for violations with the potential to imprison for life persons convicted of such crimes, operating potentially on a global scale.

The Court has jurisdiction over all potential cases of genocide, crimes against humanity, and war crimes that occur after July 1, 2002 in the territory of a state that has ratified the treaty or that are committed by a national of such a state.[11] Unlike the traditional model exemplified by the International Court of Justice (ICJ), the treaty creating the ICC does not allow States Parties to decide whether or

[9] On the development of international law and judicial institutions over the past few decades see (Abbott 2000; Keohane et al. 2000). On the development of "new style" ICs that give individuals a right to launch cases (in criminal cases, a prosecutor) see Alter (2011).

[10] See for example the Statement of Norway, November 12, 2001, available at www.iccnow.org/documents/Norway6thComm12Nov01.pdf (accessed July 6, 2017).

[11] Rome Statute, Art. 12(2). In addition, the Court has jurisdiction over any case referred to it by the United Nations Security Council under its Chapter VII authority, whether or not the state where the alleged crimes occurred has ratified the treaty.

not to accept the Court's jurisdiction on a case-by-case basis.[12] Furthermore, unlike the original draft treaty for the Court,[13] the Rome Statute invests a prosecutor with the ability to commence cases on her or his own initiative without relying solely on the referrals of states (Danner 2003: 513–15).[14] The Rome Statute does not allow States Parties to make reservations to its provisions.[15] Adherence is an all-or-nothing choice.[16] In addition, the ICC does not recognize any of the immunities traditionally accorded to heads of state and other senior officials under international law. In fact the treaty *overrides* any immunities that states may grant to presidential, parliamentary, or legislative officials in their domestic systems.[17] The result is a court much more independent of state control in the initiation of cases and far less protective of state sovereignty than was originally contemplated or has ever existed in modern history.

Enthusiasts of the ICC point out that its membership is very widespread. As of 2015, 123 states had ratified the Rome Statutes (Figure 6.1), thus becoming parties to the agreement and placing their nationals under the Court's (complimentary) jurisdiction. Detractors, however, see the glass as much more than half empty, with some of the most powerful and populous states in the world – including the United States, India, China, and Indonesia – as non–members. Some argue the Court has been overwhelmed, while others argue it has not done much. On this point, we simply let the facts speak for themselves: the ICC has issued twenty-nine arrest warrants (additionally, three wanted persons have died; thirteen individuals remain fugitives), heard twenty-three

[12] A nonparty state may also accept the jurisdiction of the Court on an ad hoc basis with regard to that particular situation. Rome Statute, Art. 12(3).

[13] "Draft Statute for the International Criminal Court," in *Report of the International Law Commission on the Work of its Forty-Sixth Session*, UN GAOR, 49th Sess., Supp. No. 10, at 43–45 (Art. 23 & Art. 25), UN Doc. A/49/10 (1994), *reprinted in* [1994] 2 *Yearbook of the International Law Commission* 46, UN Doc. A/CN.4/Ser.A/1994/Add.1 (Part 2).

[14] While frivolous or politically motivated prosecutions are a possibility (and one that has particularly concerned the United States), the Rome Statute has checks built into it to discourage a prosecutor from acting irresponsibly. These are described further in (Danner 2003).

[15] Rome Statute, Art. 120.

[16] The treaty does officially allow countries to decline to recognize the Court's jurisdiction for seven years after the state becomes a party to the treaty. Rome Statute, Art. 124. Furthermore, the Court does not have jurisdiction over crimes of aggression until 2017. See RC Resolution 6 "The Crime of Aggression" (Kampala Amendment, 2010). Available at: https://web.archive.org/web/20110616100534/http://www.icc-cpi.int/iccdocs/asp_docs/Resolutions/RC-Res.6-ENG.pdf (accessed July 6, 2017).

[17] Rome Statute, Art. 27.

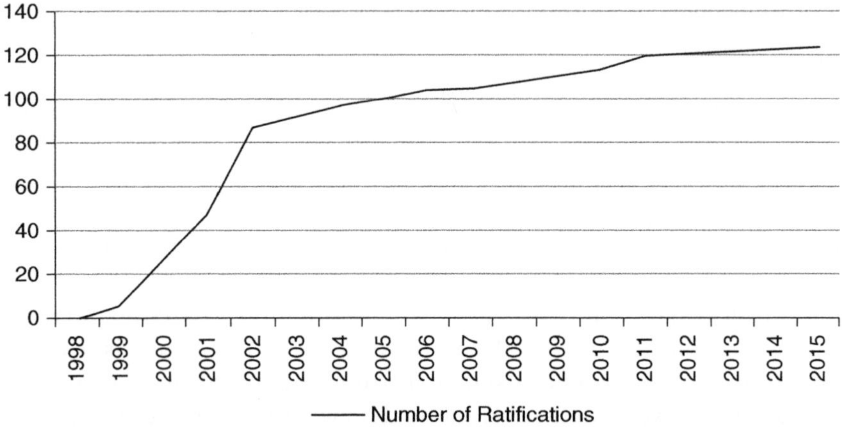

Figure 6.1 States parties to the ICC statutes

cases, and convicted nine individuals.[18] The Court is now examining crimes against humanity in Uganda, the Central African Republic, the DRC, Côte d'Ivoire, Sudan, Kenya, Libya, Georgia, and Mali, and has begun preliminary investigations to decide whether or not to proceed with indictments[19] in Afghanistan, Burundi, Colombia, Gabon, Guinea, Iraq/UK, Nigeria, Palestine, and Ukraine.

Prelude to Assessing Performance: How Salient is the ICC?

Much has been alleged – both positive and negative – about the consequences of establishing the Court. But one fact seems to have emerged: the ICC has received a notable amount of attention and likely has stimulated attention to international criminal law in general. In the English-speaking world anyway, bibliographic evidence shows that the ICC has now surpassed more traditional state-to-state dispute settlement bodies such as the ICJ in frequency in written discourse. A scan of billions of books (unfortunately, limited to English) shows references as a percentage of written words to the ICC exploded in the late 1990s and now surpasses written discussion of the much longer lived ICJ

[18] For a list of convicted individuals as of July 6, 2017, see https://www.icc-cpi.int/pages/defendants.aspx (accessed July 6, 2017).

[19] We use the words "indict," "indictment," and "indictee" to refer to persons for whom the ICC has served warrants and related processes. The word "indict" does not appear in the Rome Statute.

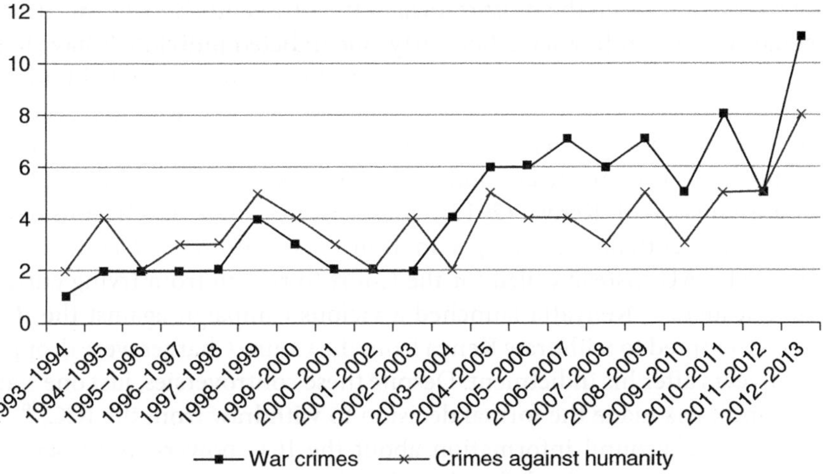

Figure 6.3 UN attention to ICC crimes: Number of United Nations General Assembly resolutions mentioning ICC crimes (1993–2013)
Source: Authors' database; based on resolutions at www.un.org/depts/dhl/resguide/gares_en.shtml

As the ICC has become more assertive and taken on a large number of cases, the international community has focused more and more attention on international crimes. Indeed, concern about crimes against humanity, war crimes, and related atrocities have spilled beyond the Prosecutor's office and have appeared more frequently in General Assembly resolutions since the ICC entered into force in 2002 (Figure 6.3). While we are not claiming the ICC per se has caused this thickening rhetoric, the international community, it seems, is paying much more attention to international crimes than it has done in the past.

Nonetheless, the ICC itself has become quite controversial, recently even among its States Parties. The European Union has been the Court's staunchest ally, pouring significant financial and political resources into its operation.[24] The United States has shifted from belligerently anti-ICC during the George W. Bush administration to intermittently helpful under the Obama administration. Many African states have taken the opposite tack. Despite the fact that many African states were among the first to "tie their hands" (Simmons and Danner 2010) by joining the ICC,

[24] Coalition for the International Criminal Court, "EU a Key Player in the ICC System," www.coalitionfortheicc.org/news/20150203/eu-key-player-icc-system (accessed July 12, 2017).

they have also been the most critical of the Prosecutor's focus on African situations and indictments (all thirty-one indicted individuals have been from Africa; about half are government officials and half rebel leaders). Many government officials initially thought the ICC would be useful in trying and punishing rebel opponents. But when the OTP decided to use its power to investigate and indict sitting leaders Bashir of Sudan (2009) and Kenyatta of Kenya (2013), the African Union (AU) considered (though eventually rejected) a motion to withdraw *en bloc* from the ICC. The AU instead called for the Court to refrain from trying current state leaders.[25] Kenyatta launched a vicious campaign against the ICC, and attempted to withdraw Kenya from the Court. Charges were dropped four years after his indictment. Despite these controversies, just one state, Burundi, has made the formal decision to withdraw from the ICC.[26]

This background information about the ICC powers, purposes and (un)popularity are food for thought. But its performance should be assessed systematically, and we suggest the best outcome performance measure is the extent to which the ICC has helped to deter the crimes within its jurisdiction. This can be done *indirectly* (through the development and encouragement of national capacities) and *directly*, by sending strong signals that impunity is a waning option.

The ICC and Deterrence: Theory and Mechanisms

In this section, we justify our focus on the capacity of the ICC to deter crimes within its jurisdiction as one of the most important aspects of its performance, of which there are potentially many. We cannot possibly address all aspects of institutional performance in a single paper. Nor is our expertise in process performance. We therefore concentrate on *outcome performance*. Second, we refrain from attempting to read the minds of the creators of the ICC by devising creative interpretations of the Court's purposes. Instead, we take seriously the plain meaning of the words of the preamble quoted above: *the ICC was meant, at least indirectly by addressing impunity, to contribute to the prevention of international crimes*. For us, this means the ICC was designed to deter the kinds

[25] "African Union says ICC Should Not Prosecute Sitting Leaders." The Guardian, October 12, 2013. www.theguardian.com/world/2013/oct/12/african-union-icc-kenyan-president (accessed July 12, 2017).

[26] Press Release, October 18, 2016, "Statement of the President of the Assembly of States Parties on the Process of withdrawal from the Rome Statute by Burundi." www.icc-cpi.int //Pages/item.aspx?name=pr1244 (accessed July 12, 2017).

of atrocities that are within its jurisdiction. Note this does not mean the ICC was created to put an end to war, although the preamble clearly expresses the idea that such crimes do "threaten the peace, security and well-being of the world ..." Nor should the ICC be judged by the (inevitable) fact that some perpetrators may not actually face trials. The preamble is clear that the purpose of the ICC is to "put an end to impunity," which means that there should no longer be *presumed exemption from punishment* or freedom from the injurious consequences of an action. The extension of jurisdiction via ratification ends *impunity* understood as exemption. *No one is exempt* from consequences flowing from the *obligation* to refrain from committing crimes under the ICC's jurisdiction. International criminal law applies to all, whether or not a specific individual actually faces trial. The number of trials held is, for our purposes, only relevant insofar as it undermines the ability of the ICC to contribute to the prevention of international crimes. The key performance indicator therefore should be: has the ICC contributed to *crime deterrence?*

We argue that it has. Prosecutorial deterrence refers to the omission of a criminal act out of fear of sanctions resulting from legal prosecution. People are increasingly likely to be deterred from violating the law when the chances and severity of a legal sanction, such as a fine, incarceration or capital punishment, increases. As such, law violation is a function of prosecution and sentencing. As the risk of more severe penalties is perceived to increase, the likelihood that an individual will commit a crime is reduced and the crime rate falls (holding any "utility" resulting from the violation constant).

For decades, the criminal deterrence literature has debated the question of exactly which elements of this rationalist model account for the deterrence of criminal behavior. The idea that severity of punishment largely drives deterrence (Grasmick and Bryjak 1980) fueled the move toward harsher sentencing in the United States in the 1980s. However, a growing consensus in the deterrence literature suggests that the swiftness and especially the *likelihood* of punishment may more effectively deter crime than severity of punishment (Kleiman 2009; Wright 2010). Empirical researchers employing surveys, experiments, and scenarios also conclude that the likelihood of punishment is key for deterring crimes ranging from tax evasion to theft to sexual assault (Nagin and Paternoster 1993; Nagin 1998).

Raising the risk of punishment where the rule of law is otherwise weak is precisely the *formal* role envisioned for the ICC. The Court was designed to do this in two ways. The first is through its own authority to prosecute. The Court's jurisdiction applies to cases of genocide, crimes against humanity, and war crimes[27] that occurred after July 1, 2002 in the territory of a state that has ratified the treaty or that is committed by a national of such a state or in cases referred to it by the UN Security Council (UNSC).[28] The Office of the Prosecutor ultimately decides which situations to pursue, but cases may be referred by member states (e.g., Uganda, the DRC, the Central African Republic, and Mali), the Security Council (Sudan and Libya), or initiated by the Prosecutor herself (Kenya and Côte d'Ivoire).

General deterrence is only possible if the Court's existence and actions raise the perceived likelihood that an individual will be tried and punished. Above we discussed the growing salience of international criminal law by various measures. As of 2017, the ICC prosecutor has indicted some forty persons, and a further ten situations are under preliminary examination for jurisdiction and admissibility. Prosecutorial deterrence theory implies that investigations, indictments and especially successful prosecutions should trigger a reassessment of the likelihood of punishment and a boost to general deterrence (Geerken and Gove 1975) – a result consistent with Kim and Sikkink's (2010) study of national human rights trials in transition countries.

The most common rejoinder of ICC skeptics is that nine investigations and thirty-five indictments is not much, and not enough to affect the behavior of governments and rebels locked in violent conflict with each other with civilians as pawns often in between. Our first response is that forty indictments is considerable, *compared to impunity*. But moreover, there is no reason we should suppose governments and rebels sift through evidence in a completely objective way. These actors are as susceptible as any other with a human brain in their heads to biases produced by availability heuristics. Availability heuristics, for example, make it far more likely that people will remember ICC investigations and warrants rather than their lack, as well as convictions rather than acquittals. The former are salient while the latter often go unnoticed. Just as an example, a look at google trends for 2012 shows a significant search trend for Thomas Lubanga Dyilo (who was convicted for war crimes in March 2012) yet nothing but a flat line for Mathieu Ngudjolo Chui

[27] See Rome Statute, Article 5. We refer to these below as "ICC crimes" or "international crimes."

[28] Rome Statute, Art. 12(2); Chapter VIII covers UNSC authority to refer.

(who was acquitted for similar crimes in December that same year). The name of the convicted man also has about 30 percent more google hits, and 230 percent more press coverage, as measured by articles in the Lexis-Nexis database, than the name of the acquitted man. Conviction is news; acquittal, not so much.[29] Note we are not claiming that rebels and government officials do these searches; we are simply demonstrating that small numbers of convictions do not undercut our deterrence argument for well-known psychological reasons. Arguably, the ICC is an institution that is likely to make the risk of punishment both salient and vivid.

The common rejoinder also neglects a crucial indirect deterrence mechanism. The Rome Statute's "complementarity regime" creates a channel for the ICC to support prosecutorial deterrence at the *national* level as well. The ICC is designed to complement, and not to preempt or substitute for national prosecution.[30] National courts have the option of investigating a case domestically before the ICC can adjudicate it.[31] As the Court's first prosecutor stated, "intervention by the ICC must be exceptional – it will only step in when states fail to genuinely act."[32] The ICC may nonetheless find a case admissible despite domestic action if the Court determines that "the state is unwilling or unable genuinely to carry out the investigation or prosecution."[33] Sudan's desultory investigations and prosecutions of crimes committed in Darfur provide an example of the kind of behavior the admissibility provisions were designed to override (ICC 2006).

This complementarity principle bolsters the ICC's prosecutorial deterrence to the extent that it creates incentives for states to strengthen their own legal capacities to try and convict individuals of international crimes (Dunoff and Trachtman 1999; Burke-White 2008). A recent ICC report to the United Nations notes several national legal reforms implemented after the launch of preliminary examinations, including reforms in Guinea, Colombia, and Georgia (ICC 2011). Sarah Nouwen (2013)

[29] The trial of Slobodan Milosevic provided an exceptionally poignant image of a national leader subjected to the humiliation of an international trial.

[30] See Rome Statute, Preamble (emphasizing that the ICC "shall be complementary to national criminal jurisdictions").

[31] See Rome Statute, Preamble and Art.1. For a discussion of the conditions under which domestic courts are likely to enforce international human rights law, see Lupu (2013).

[32] Moreno-Ocampo, Luis 2006. "A Global Web of Justice is up and Running," *International Herald Tribune*, June 12. Available at www.spiegel.de/international/the-international-criminal-court-a-global-web-of-justice-is-up-and-running-a-421098.html (accessed July 13, 2017).

[33] Rome Statute, Art. 17(1)(a).

documents how ICC investigations catalyzed legal reforms in Uganda and Sudan. Uganda's ICC implementing legislation was passed only recently, in 2010, but it facilitates prosecution of international crimes in the Ugandan High Court (Nouwen and Werner 2011).

The evidence that the Rome Statute has contributed to strengthening of the laws and institutions to deter international crimes is strong and systematic. A careful look at the dates of ratification and of domestic criminal law reform indicates that ICC ratification *precedes* most of these crime statute reforms, indicating that the reform cases are, in fact, plausibly connected with the ICC regime.[34] Among the forty-four ratifying countries, ten countries did not reform their crime statutes at all, twenty-eight countries implemented some reform, and six underwent substantial reform. Among nonratifying states, only two countries reformed their crime statutes to conform with ICC law. Note also that the list of crime statute reformers includes unlikely candidates in the absence of an ICC obligation: Uganda, Kenya, Niger, Cambodia, Georgia, Mali, Senegal, Burkina Faso, Central African Republic, Peru, Chile, Argentina, and Uruguay (Table 6.1). In a sample of over 100 states with a post-World War history of domestic civil war violence, Jo and Simmons (2016) report a strong statistical correlation between ICC ratification and changes in domestic crime statutes that strengthen the ability to prosecute international crimes. Thus, an *indirect* channel through which the ICC may exert prosecutorial deterrence is through stimulating domestic laws and structures that overtime enhance the ability of national courts to act (Stahn and El Zeidy 2011), theoretically bolstering prosecutorial deterrence. We consider this to be an indirect *multiplier* effect of the ICC itself. One might expect a certain asymmetry in the use of domestic law, since governments are likely to have much more influence over the domestic legal machinery than do their opponents, but as we show below in Uganda, government allies – local defense units, for example – have been prosecuted at least in some instances. Arguably, national courts have contributed to a broader system-wide expectation that impunity is no longer quietly tolerated (Sikkink 2011).[35]

[34] ICC Legal Tools, www.legal-tools.org/ (accessed July 13, 2017). The information from previous National Implementing Legislation Database (NILD) is now under "National Jurisdictions."

[35] Many legal experts consider the development of such national capacities to be the most important legacy of the ICC. See Slaughter and Burke-White (2006: 339–341) and Burke-White (2008).

Table 6.1 *ICC ratification and change in domestic crime statutes that reflect incorporation of ICC-consistent international criminal law*

	Domestic Crime Statute	No Domestic Crime Statute
ICC Ratification	Ratification → Domestic Crime Statute (23) Trinidad and Tobago, Costa Rica, Panama, Uganda, Kenya, Niger, Romania, UK, France, Cambodia, Georgia, Mali, Senegal, Burkina Faso, Central African Republic, South Africa, Bosnia & Herzegovina, Croatia, Peru, Chile, Argentina, Uruguay, Spain Domestic Crime Statute → ICC Ratification (6) Colombia Venezuela Macedonia Burundi Congo, Brazzaville Bangladesh	(24) Madagascar, Nigeria, Ghana, Sierra Leone, Liberia, Guinea, Lesotho, Mauritania, Surinam, Tajikistan, Djibouti, Afghanistan, Bolivia, Paraguay, Comoros, Gabon, DRC, Greece, Gambia, Chad, Mexico, Guatemala, Dominican Republic, Philippines
No ICC Ratification	(8) El Salvador, Nicaragua, Moldova, Azerbaijan, Rwanda, Ethiopia, Turkey, Indonesia	(35) Papua New Guinea, US, Cuba, Uzbekistan, China, India, Pakistan, Haiti, Russia, Guinea-Bissau, Togo, Cameroon, Myanmar, Sri Lanka, Nepal, Thailand, Cote d'Ivoire, Somalia, Eritrea, Angola, Mozambique, Zimbabwe, Morocco, Algeria, Tunisia, Libya, Sudan, Iran, Iraq, Egypt, Syria, Lebanon, Israel, Saudi Arabia, Yemen, Oman

Source: ICC legal tools main website: www.legal-tools.org/. Information is from previous National Implementing Legislation Database (NILD), which is now under "National Jurisdictions" (accessed July 13, 2017).

But do perpetrators and potential perpetrators take note? Qualitative research reveals such changes become part of leaders' updated calculations. For example, the former Colombian President Pastrana expressed concerns that he might get prosecuted by the ICC, and the paramilitary leader, Vincente Castano of the Autodefensas Unidas de Colombia, was "sharply aware and fearful of the possibility of ICC prosecution, a fear that reportedly directly contributed to his demobilization" (Grono and Wheeler 2015: 1233). Even some rebel groups have begun to assess risks in the ICC's shadow. For example, the two main rebel groups in Colombia – the Fuerzas Armadas Revolucionarias de Colombia and the Unión Camilista – Ejército de Liberación Nacional – have published internal documents assessing the likelihood of prosecution by the ICC or domestic courts (Cantor and Engstrom 2011). ICC investigations, indictments, and convictions or those triggered by complementarity are likely to encourage actual or potential perpetrators to reassess the risks of punishment – *relative to the status quo, which is often impunity* – and to moderate their behavior.

Moreover, there may be good reasons to think that changing domestic statutes matters. For one thing, it may increase the domestic capacity to prosecute egregious human rights violations domestically. The correlation coefficient between crime statute reform and domestic human rights trials in the next year is strong and positive,[36] which implies a clear positive relationship between enhanced crime statutes and trials. In other words, ratification of ICC statutes is associated with a chain of consequences: Ratification creates incentives to change domestic laws, which in turn are associated with prosecutions.[37] Recent research suggests this account is quite plausible. For example, Dancy and Montal (2017) find an increase in African countries' human rights related domestic trials of state agents, specifically after the ratification of Rome Statute. The authors note a significant increase in the number of human rights prosecutions and guilty verdicts following ICC

36 The trials variable is from Kim and Sikkink (2011). The correlation coefficient between reform and human rights trials is .176 (p-value: 0.000). Spearman correlation test for ordered variables returns a similar result. Spearman's rho is 0.166 with p-value of 0.000.

37 Dancy and Sikkink (2011–2012) also find quantitative as well as qualitative evidence that "countries that ratify treaties protecting core rights with individual accountability provisions are more likely to use human rights prosecutions than countries that have not ratified these treaties" (751).

investigation in Uganda[38] and DRC,[39] a moderate increase in the Central African Republic and Sudan, and no notable trends in the case of Cote d'Ivoire and Kenya (which are too recent to assess). We are not naïve enough to believe any of these cases represent international standards of justice, nor do they overturn the prevalent culture of impunity in these and similar cases, but they do suggest that some institutional change has occurred in some of the worst cases in which the ICC has had an influence.

In sum, we argue that ICC performance should be assessed in terms of its ability to deter the kinds of crimes under its jurisdiction. The ICC and the norms it embodies are highly salient institutions that have caught the attention of would-be perpetrators, and influence them to reassess their prospects for apprehension and punishment. Prosecutorial deterrence is therefore enhanced by conditions that make prosecution more likely in a given jurisdiction, such as ratification of the Rome Statute, passage of ICC implementing legislation, national trials or court reforms that make trials more probable and credible.[40] In the next section, we discuss the evidence for these propositions in one of the most violent cases: that of Uganda.

ICC's Deterrence Potential in Uganda

Uganda is one among eight situations currently on the ICC docket. Uganda was the very first situation the Court took up in July 2004, which gives us greater temporal coverage than is possible with other cases. The Ugandan government signed the Rome Statute in March 1999, ratified the Statute in June 2002, and self-referred its case to the Court

[38] Opinions vary as to whether the trial was impartial, credible, and fair Nouwen (2012a) notes that "The prosecution of Kwoyelo was prompted by opportunism rather than law or policy. Kwoyelo is considered of little use by the ruling party. Rather, Kwoyelo, as a Ugandan 'Tadic', could satisfy the ICD's institutional craving for a first case, and during the ICC Review Conference in Kampala the preparations for his case served to demonstrate the host country's commitment to international justice at home" (pp. 221–222). See also Nouwen 2012b: "Critics charge that Kwoyelo was politically convenient; his submission for amnesty was ignored; it was a political show before the Ugandan government hosted the ICC Review Conference in 2010; and that it was the only trial thus far taken up by the ICD."

[39] See also the Transitional Justice Research Collaborative, events history data on human rights trials https://transitionaljusticedata.com/.

[40] On the phenomenon of "enforcement spillovers" by which monitoring and enforcement increases compliance even in areas without monitoring or enforcement see Rincke and Traxler (2010).

in December 2003. The Ugandan military has fought the Lord's Resistance Army (LRA) for over two decades, and civilian abuse and brutality are well-documented on both sides (Schomerus 2007). Many observers think that the ICC failed in Uganda (Branch 2011) and are cynical about the Ugandan government's self-referral to the Court, suspecting the Court's bias (Clark 2011). Against this backdrop, we evaluate the effects of Court's actions in Uganda. Is there any evidence that the jurisdiction and actions of the Court have deterred ICC crimes? We focus specifically on violent attacks against civilians – one of several international crimes under the Court's jurisdiction. We argue that there is plausible evidence of a deterrent effect of the ICC, even in this case, one of the most violent situations in which the Court has been involved.

Background

When Ugandan strongman Idi Amin was overthrown in 1979, succession became a battle between two military factions: the Uganda National Liberation Army (UNLA) which was led by Milton Obote and the National Resistance Army (NRA) led by Yoweni Museveni. The UNLA was comprised of Northerners that mostly belonged to the Acholi people while the NRA was comprised of Southern and Western ethnic groups. These ethnic differences would vie for power for the next seven years.

In 1986, Museveni and his supporters secured governmental control when they overthrew the Uganda leader Tito Okello, a general from northern Uganda. After Museveni ascended to power, Acholi resistance groups were formed, the most prominent of which was the Holy Spirit Movement led by Alice Auma. Joseph Kony joined this group and established his own followers. When the Holy Spirit Movement was summarily defeated in November 1987 by Museveni's forces, Kony created the Lord's Resistance Army out of its remnants. Over the next twelve years, the LRA became Museveni's strongest opponent, establishing bases in Northern Uganda and Southern Sudan. It grew in size and power through an alliance with the Sudanese government, which saw them as a means to balance the power of Sudan People's Liberation Movement/Army (SPLM/A) in Southern Sudan as well as retribution for the Uganda government's support of the SPLM/A.

In December 1999, Uganda and Sudan agreed in Nairobi that they would no longer support rebel groups in each other's countries. When the Sudanese government agreed to let Ugandan military forces cross the border to pursue the LRA in 2002, Museveni launched a major military offensive, Operation Iron Fist, in March of that year, to root the LRA out of its bases. The next four years saw intense fighting between the LRA and Ugandan government forces with neither side gaining an upper hand. However, in January 2005, the government of Sudan and the SPLM/A negotiated the Comprehensive Peace Agreement. The agreement threatened the LRA's ability to keep bases in the region, and (likely in combination with pressure from the ICC, discussed below) encouraged Kony to make overtures for peace. The two sides held peace talks in the southern Sudan city of Juba in July 2006. The negotiations produced the Final Peace Agreement between the Government of Uganda and the LRA; however, Kony refused to sign the agreement in 2008. Meanwhile, the LRA began to shift their bases from Southern Sudan and Northern Uganda to northeast portions of the Democratic Republic of Congo (DRC) and Central African Republic (CAR). In response to provocative attacks, the DRC government launched Operation Rudia I in September 2008 and a second phase in May 2009 in order to push the LRA outside of its borders, basically ending the Juba peace process. When negotiations officially failed in November 2009, Museveni, with support from the DRC and South Sudan, launched a military offensive, Operation Lightning Thunder, in order to capture Kony.

The LRA suffered major defections in 2004 and 2008 (Wegner 2015) but the group continued to draw the outrage of the global community by perpetrating large-scale massacres on unarmed civilians during the Christmas seasons of 2008 and 2009. Facing public and NGO pressure, the United States passed the LRA Disarmament and Northern Uganda Recovery Act into law in May 2010, thus committing the US to provide military support in order to destroy the LRA and capture or kill its leadership. In support of that mission, President Barack Obama authorized the deployment of 100 military advisors in October 2011. However, the LRA has continued to survive to this day by hiding out in peripheral regions of the Democratic Republic of Congo and the Central African Republic.

ICC and Ugandan Military Attacks

Table 6.2 summarizes the key events described above, including not only military and political developments that might impact the LRA's behavior toward civilians, but also ICC interventions relevant to the situation, starting from 1997.

Table 6.2 *Major events for Lord's Resistance Army (1997–2014)*

Events	Dates
Uganda signs Rome Statute	**03/17/1999**
Nairobi Agreement	12/08/1999
Amnesty Act	01/21/2000
Operation Iron Fist	03/08/2002
Uganda ratifies Rome Statute	**06/14/2002**
ICC investigation into LRA	**07/28/2004**
Sudan's Comprehensive Peace Agreement	01/09/2005
ICC warrants for LRA	**10/13/2005**
Juba Peace Talks start	07/14/2006
Operation Rudia I (DRC)	09/2008
Juba Peace Talks fail	11/30/2008
Operation Lightning Thunder	12/2008–03/2009
Operation Rudia II (DRC)	05/2009
LRA Disarmament Act	05/24/2010
US deploys military advisors	10/14/2011
Four-nation AU force deployed	03/23/2012

Note: ICC events in bold

Examining data from the Armed Conflict and Location Event Data (ACLED v.2) from January 1, 1997 to March 28, 2010, reveals two general patterns.[41] First, government attacks on civilians decreased in magnitude during this time, and those that do occur are harder to attribute with certainty to the government. The number of "accused" (i.e., unsubstantiated) attacks increases as a share of total violations. Second, there is a reduction in coordinated actions by government forces, such as aerial bombardments, which suggests that the Ugandan chain of command may have refrained from coordinating military attacks against civilians, at least at the highest levels. Much of this change can be attributed to the diminished presence of LRA forces in northern Uganda and a decrease in the number of battles. But it is notable that the change in the government's military tactics coincides with ICC involvement as well.

[41] The data include government violence against civilians within and outside of Uganda, although the majority of violent instances occurred primarily within Uganda.

The demonstrated willingness of the ICC to prosecute may also have encouraged some changes in domestic law, institutions, and practice. After ICC ratification, Uganda began to reform its own capacity to detect and deter war crimes (Witte 2011). As noted in polls discussed above, in the mid-2000s, Ugandans had much more confidence in the ICC than in their own legal system. But since its encounter with the ICC, the state has invested in its domestic court system's capacity to try war crimes and crimes against humanity (Nouwen 2012). The ICC Bill (drafted in 2006, passed in 2010) is an example of the domestic legal changes the ICC stimulates and civil society increasingly demands.[42] The Uganda People's Defense Force's (UPDF) reduced violence toward civilians may be a result of both external monitoring by the international community (Allen and Vlassenroot 2010) and internal monitoring within the UPDF itself.

Moves to prosecute war crimes domestically are also evident. A remark by Uganda's President Museveni in 2004 reveals something of the shadow cast by the ICC on the domestic legal regime in Uganda: "I am ready to be investigated for war crimes ... and if any of our people were involved in any crimes, we will give him up to be tried by the ICC .... And in any case, if such cases are brought to our attention, we will try them ourselves."[43] We do not think that Museveni's political motivations are benign – many targets for such trials were largely "convenient" from the government's perspective – but they are associated with some change in Uganda's actual military behavior. For example, the government utilized military tribunals[44] to try its own soldiers. Local defense units, in particular, have in fact been charged with committing violence against civilians.[45] No one thinks the Museveni government is now free of human rights violations. But would the government of Uganda have

[42] For the discussion of civil society in Uganda, see Oola (2010). For example, the Uganda Victims Fund pressured government to consider victim's participation and reparations in the 2010 ICC Bill that set out the domestic judicial reform.

[43] Remarks by Luis Moreno, Ocampo, Committee of Legal Advisers on Public International Law, (CAHDI), 27th meeting, Strasbourg, March 18–19, 2004, p. 37. https://rm.coe.int/168004b99d (accessed July 13, 2017).

[44] Such a move has been criticized, however, because military tribunals lack transparency compared to civilian courts (Witte 2011).

[45] "Consideration of Reports Submitted by State Parties under Article 8, Paragraph 1, of the Optional Protocol to the Convention of the Rights of the Child on the Involvement of Children in Armed Conflict: Uganda" United Nations Committee on the Rights of the Child. CRC/C/OPAC/UGA/1, July 17, 2008. p. 32. http://tbinternet.ohchr.org/_layouts/treatybodyexternal/Download.aspx?symbolno=CRC%2FC%2FOPAC%2FUGA%2F1&Lang=en (accessed July 13, 2017).

adopted this series of measures – ranging from legal reform to military sanctioning – if it were not for ICC intervention? Our answer is probably not; it is rather unlikely that such measures would have been taken if the ICC regime was not in place and the OTP had not launched an investigation.

In short, the Court made it clear in 2004 that it was determined to prosecute. The Prosecutor's office opened an investigation in July 2004 and issued warrants in 2005, supported by international efforts to pressure Sudan to cut aid to the LRA (International Crisis Group 2004). The ICC's display of prosecutorial determination and the added threat of material pressure by the European Union and the United States may well have contributed to a perception on the part of the Ugandan government that the costs of law violation were likely to escalate.

ICC and the Lord's Resistance Army

The ICC may also have had some effect on rebel behavior in Uganda. The qualitative evidence suggests that ICC actions – in particular investigations – indirectly contributed to internal defections. True, the first wave of rebel defection came before the ICC entered into force: after the 2000 Amnesty Law.[46] By mid-2004, more than 5000 members surrendered and applied for amnesty. But even more defections came around the time of the announcement of the ICC's investigations in July 2004, the most prominent of which was the LRA's chief negotiator Sam Kolo in February of 2005 (Akhavan 2005). It is plausible to suppose that the defections were related purely to the success of Operation Iron Fist that started in March 2002, at which point LRA soldiers may have calculated the rebellion was in serious decline. But the fact that defections occurred in 2004 suggests the additional influence of ICC investigations.

Far from undermining the domestic amnesty process, ICC investigation of the situation in Uganda appears to have contributed to fissures within the rebel leadership (at least some of whom were prompted to jump ship) and to have encouraged defection of rank-and-file soldiers. The fact that Kony placed withdrawal of the ICC arrest warrants at the top of his negotiating agenda suggests that he and other LRA leaders were concerned about ICC indictments. (Despite these demands, Joseph Kony

[46] Note that the Government of Uganda adopted the Amnesty Act in 2000, after signing into the Rome Statute in 1999. As we argued elsewhere (Jo and Simmons 2016), signature is a weaker form of commitment than ratification. Therefore, we do not expect much deterrent effect upon signature alone.

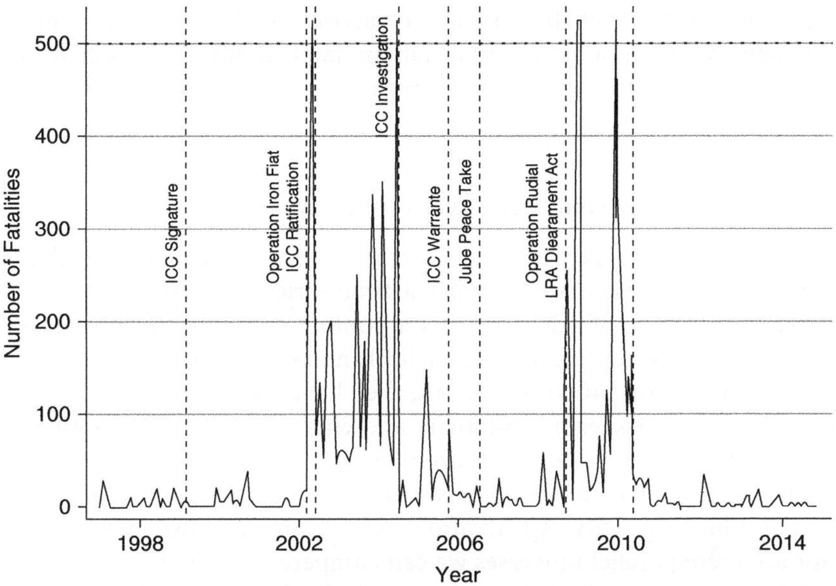

Figure 6.4 Monthly count of civilian fatalities from LRA attacks (1997–2014)
Note: Horizontal dotted line indicates scale break at 500 civilian fatalities.

was indicted on July 8, 2005 on twelve counts of crimes against humanity and twenty-one counts of war crimes.) Even if the weakening rebel position could be attributed in good part to Sudan's agreement to stop supporting the LRA, the increasing likelihood of prosecution by the ICC likely entered the rebel calculation.

Figure 6.4 graphs the monthly count of civilian fatalities associated with LRA attacks, as well as vertical markers indicating where the major military and diplomatic events and ICC actions, over time. We use monthly data of violence against civilians by the LRA from the Armed Conflict Location and Event Dataset (ACLED v.5). The data include rebel violence within and outside of Uganda, including Sudan, Central African Republic, and the Democratic Republic of Congo. As indicated by Table 6.2, there were four major ICC actions related to the prosecution of the LRA: Uganda's *ICC Signature,* Uganda's *ICC Ratification,* the ICC's *Investigation* and the ICC's issuance of *Arrest Warrants.* The figure shows that Uganda's signature on the Rome Statute and issue of arrest warrants for rebel leaders did little to perturb the series. In fact, there is a considerable spike in rebel attacks on civilians associated with ratification, though this is likely attributable to the launch of

Operation Iron Fist than with any action by the ICC. But more crucially, there is a precipitous fall in fatal attacks on civilians by rebels occurring just after the ICC began investigation of the situation in Uganda.

Time Series Intervention Analysis

Is the ICC in some way responsible for this welcome decline? In order to answer this question, we conduct a time-series intervention analysis. Previous analyses of ICC's effect on conflict behavior have relied on case studies and cross-national statistical analysis. Although these studies have made important contributions, they have shortcomings. Case studies alone raise issues of objectivity and cherry-picking information to support a particular interpretation of events.[47] Cross-national statistical studies often suffer from problems such as endogeneity, selection effects, and unit heterogeneity. ICC treatment effects are obviously not random; nor are there parallel universes we can compare.

We use a time-series intervention analysis of one critically important case to determine whether there is a statistically significant difference in the level of a group's violence before and after an ICC intervention, while accounting for alternative explanations as well as the series' random component. If we observe no difference, then we have no reason to believe that the ICC affected the outcome. But if we observe a difference within a case over time, we will have some evidence that the ICC affected the pattern of violence. Although we cannot necessarily generalize the ICC's effects outside of the specific case,[48] we can better isolate ICC intervention from other factors, while comparing LRA violence before and after the intervention.

The dependent variable in our intervention analysis of Uganda is graphed in Figure 6.4. The data reflect the count of civilian fatalities from LRA attacks per month,[49] both within Uganda and in neighboring

[47] Case studies of the ICC's performance should still be employed as they are invaluable in their ability to trace the process for how ICC interventions have their effect.

[48] For cross-national analyses on ICC crime deterrence, see Jo and Simmons (2016).

[49] The variable is observed daily in the ACLED dataset, but we aggregated to a monthly measure. We chose to aggregate because intervention analysis looks for changes in the mean of the series from immediately before the event to immediately after. It is very unlikely that these events would cause changes in LRA behavior just days after their occurrence. News travels slowly in these areas and major strategic decisions are usually not made hastily. Also, the aggregation allows for better noise component identification, since at a daily sampling interval, most observations are zero.

regions of the Democratic Republic of Congo, the Central African Republic, and Sudan. The data contain several outliers.[50] In particular, there are two extreme outliers for December 2008 and December 2009, which are nearly three and four times larger than the next highest data point, respectively. These outliers correspond to the Christmas and Makombo Massacres in northeast DRC. Since such outliers can cause our analysis to falsely present mean shifts that are not there, we logged the fatalities measure in our analysis.[51]

Intervention analysis involves two modeling decisions: whether the effects are permanent (mean-shifting) or temporary (non-mean-shifting) and whether the effects are abrupt or gradual (i.e., the rate at which the effects appear and subside). The effects reported in these models are assumed to permanently and abruptly shift the mean. Key events associated with the ICC constitute a "change of state" within Uganda and we expect them to have a permanent impact on the behavior of LRA. Moreover, we expect any change to be rather abrupt because these ICC events are expected to have a major impact on the lives of key leaders in the LRA, who have strong incentives to keep themselves informed and to change their behavior almost immediately.[52] In order to model the effects of events as permanent and abrupt shifts, each independent variable (binary indicators for *Signature, Ratification, Investigation*, and *Warrants*) is coded as zero for every month before the event and as one for every month after the event.[53] These interventions signal increased ICC authority and/or willingness to prosecute war crimes violations.

Since interventional analysis can lead to spurious results when key events of interest are correlated with other factors and events, we use two strategies to ensure that our results are robust: controlling for rival events and employing Bai-Perron breakpoint tests. For rival events, we include events other than ICC actions that likely caused the level of fighting to escalate or diminish. We control for two military operations: one by the Ugandan government (*Operation Iron Fist)* and one by the government

[50] The skewness statistic is 7.81 and the standard deviation of the series is nearly 218.

[51] Logging the measure also helps with concerns that the series does not have variance stationarity.

[52] We also checked the results with different combinations of modeling assumptions: (permanent, gradual), (temporary, abrupt), and (temporary, gradual). Permanent and abrupt models provide the best fit.

[53] In the time-series analysis of multiple interventions, the influence of each intervention only holds until the next event (see Montgomery et al. 2015: 471).

of the DRC (*Operations Rudia* I).[54] Moreover, we include a variable for the effect of the *Juba Peace Talks* and the introduction of the United States as a conflict actor with the passage of the *LRA Disarmament Act.* We also use a more general variable, *Battles*, which is the monthly count of battles between the LRA and governmental or international forces. The LRA's propensity to exhibit violence towards civilians might also have been the result of their wartime fortunes. Defeats might have left the group more desperate for civilian support and supplies causing them to use violence and coercion as a means to secure these necessities. We use a variable to account for this military balance (*Government Territory Gain*), which are monthly counts of battles in which the rebels or government claimed territory from the other side as indicated by ACLED. The purpose of these controls is to minimize the possibility that we are misattributing a reduction in violence toward civilians to the ICC rather than to other conditions.

Table 6.3 presents the results of intervention analysis of LRA violence. Model 1 estimates the effects of four ICC interventions: *Signature, Ratification, Investigation*, and *Warrants*. Of these, only two ICC interventions have a significant effect on the fatality series: ratification and investigation. Since the dependent variable is logged, the coefficients indicate a proportional change in the mean. Model 1 indicates that approximately three civilian casualties occurred each month from LRA attacks before Uganda ratified the Rome Statute, and after that event, the mean increased by more than thirty times to about 104 casualties per month. However, when the ICC demonstrated its determination actually to investigate crimes, this casualty rate plummeted by nearly 94 percent to a new mean of about 6.5 casualties per month.

The full model with rival events is displayed in Model 2. The results are revealing. It appears that ICC ratification effects are largely attributable to the start of *Operation Iron Fist.* Three other non-ICC events appear to have an effect on the series as well. The *Juba Peace Process* depressed the casualty rate while the collapse of this peace process, and the subsequent launching of *Operation Rudia I* increased the LRA violence towards civilians. This new, increased level of violence would persist until US involvement into the conflict (*LRA Disarmament Act*), when the number of casualties dropped to a rate lower than pre-*Rudia* levels.

[54] As a robustness check, we ran models with the two additional military offensives found in Table 2: *Operation Lightning Thunder* and *Operation Rudia II.* These operations appear to have no significant effect on either the attack or fatality series. We drop them from our main results to improve efficiency.

Table 6.3 *Intervention analysis on monthly count of logged civilian fatalities and LRA attacks (1997–2014)*

	ICC Events	Rival Events	**Battlefield Conditions**	Attacks as DV
Operation Iron Fist		4.35**	3.32**	11.97**
		(0.80)	(0.43)	(2.96)
ICC Ratification	2.79**	−0.52		
	(0.72)	(0.81)		
ICC Investigation	−2.80**	−2.40**	−2.04**	−12.52**
	(0.85)	(0.50)	(0.43)	(3.15)
ICC Signature	0.58	−0.08		
	(0.73)	(0.41)		
ICC Warrants	0.25	0.22		
	(0.74)	(0.63)		
Juba Peace Talks		−1.26*	−0.86	1.01
		(0.58)	(0.44)	(3.22)
Operation Rudia I		3.31**	3.12**	19.03**
		(0.46)	(0.45)	(3.33)
LRA Disarmament Act		−3.54**	−3.31**	−15.97**
		(0.41)	(0.41)	(2.98)
Battles			0.03*	0.33**
			(0.01)	(0.07)
Govt. Gains (-1)			0.06	1.33*
			(0.11)	(0.57)
AR(1)	0.46**	0.14*	0.18*	0.43**
	(0.06)	(0.07)	(0.07)	(0.06)
Constant	1.03	0.96**	0.76**	1.58
	(0.60)	(0.32)	(0.19)	(1.54)
Observations	215	215	214	214
Adjusted R-Squared	0.481	0.610	0.622	0.663
Bayesian Information Criterion	1333.58	1289.66	1267.81	2001.39
Durbin-Watson	2.13	1.97	2.03	2.04
Q Statistic P-value (Lags 1–36)	0.11	0.40	0.13	0.25

*p<0.05, ** p<0.01, two-tailed test
Mean of Logged Fatalities: 1.99
Mean of Attacks: 8.38
Moving average terms are included, but not shown

Even when we drop the events that were insignificant from Model 3, our five significant events remain: *Operation Iron Fist, ICC Investigation*, the *Juba Peace Process, Operation Rudia I*, and the *LRA Disarmament Act*.

In order to generate substantive results, we track the mean level of monthly casualties through time by rerunning Model 3 with just the significant events. The model estimates that the initial monthly civilian casualty rate from LRA attacks was about 2.5 deaths, which increased by 115.5 deaths to a new mean of about 118 monthly deaths after Operation Iron Fist. The ICC investigation was able to substantially decrease this loss of innocent life to about eleven deaths per month, meaning that 107 fewer people lost their lives each month, *even as the fighting raged on*. The end of open hostilities, that is the Juba Peace Process, decreased this rate further to about 3.5 deaths per month. However, when peace negotiations failed in late 2008 (near the period of Operation Rudia I), LRA-related civilian deaths spiked again to about 100 deaths per month until US assistance (*LRA Disarmament Act*) decreased this rate to about 2.8 deaths per month.

The final model in Table 6.3 (Model 4) switches our dependent variable from a logged measure of civilian casualties to the monthly number of LRA attacks on civilians. All events, with the exception of the Juba Peace Process, are still significant. Since the dependent variable is no longer logged, interpretation is straightforward.

Operation Iron Fist increased the mean level by twelve attacks, but this effect was essentially erased by the ICC investigation as the mean returns back to slightly below its initial level. The number of attacks greatly increased again with Operation Rudia I (by nineteen attacks per month), only falling with the passage of the LRA Disarmament Act.

Model 4 also shows a rather strong relationship between the intensity of fighting and the level of LRA violence towards civilians. Each additional battle increases the attack rate on civilians by 0.3. However, further examination of these two series reveals a remarkable pattern. Figure 6.5 shows the battles and attacks series together. Before the ICC investigation, the two series track each other rather closely; the two series are highly correlated (Pearson's r=0.74). But during the two-year period between the start of the ICC investigation and the Juba Peace Process (when fighting essentially fell to zero), correlation between the two series weakens substantially to 0.22.[55] This is at least suggestive evidence that

[55] There is a similar pattern between logged fatalities and battles. The correlation between the series is 0.68 before the investigation and falls to 0.28 after.

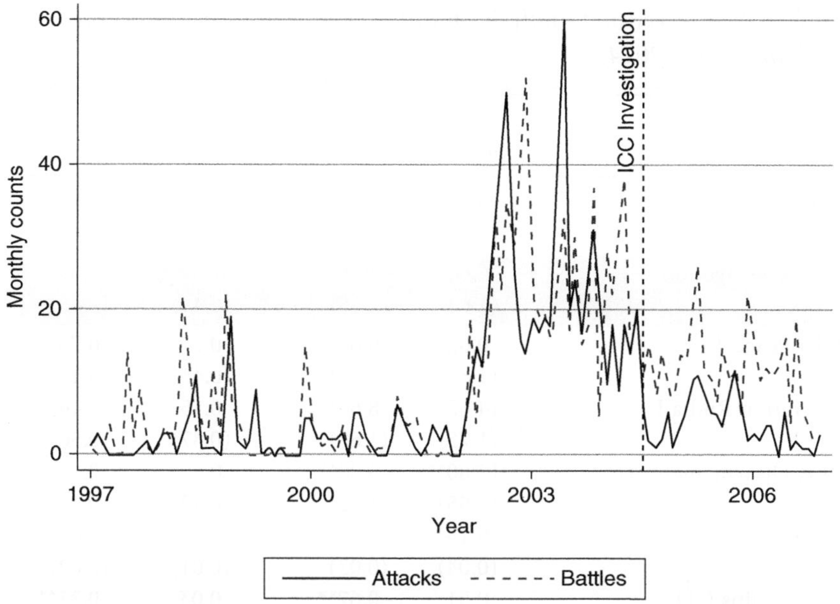

Figure 6.5 Monthly count of LRA attacks compared with number of battles (1997–2014)

the drop in civilian violence was the result of a conscious and concerted effort by Joseph Kony and LRA leadership to decrease violence against civilians during the investigation and not merely a consequence of battlefield dynamics.

We recognize several concerns and alternative explanations in establishing plausible causation between the ICC actions and violence patterns. First, substitution of violence might occur. Even though civilian fatalities are down after ICC investigations, what about other forms of violence (e.g., torture, rape, pillaging, etc.)? We investigated the violence substitution possibility by using the ACLED event descriptions to disaggregate LRA attacks into four different types: *Killings, Kidnappings, Pillaging,* and *Scorched Earth Tactics.*[56] Table 6.4 shows the results of intervention analysis with these four different series.[57] The key takeaway

[56] The authors used the "Notes" sections within ACLED's country-level datasets to ascertain these descriptions. Keywords for killings were killed, death and fatalities. For kidnappings, it was kidnapped and abducted. For pillaging, it was looted, raided, pillaged, robbed, or stole. For scorched earth, it was burned or torched.

[57] It was the authors' intention to test the effect of the ICC's efforts on the occurrence of rape. Unfortunately, this was not feasible due to the low event count in the ACLED data.

Table 6.4 *Intervention analysis on different type of LRA attacks on civilians (1997–2014)*

	Killings	Kidnappings	Pillaging	Scorched Earth
Operation Iron Fist	3.62*	2.48	1.23**	1.98**
	(1.49)	(1.47)	(0.42)	(0.48)
ICC Investigation	−4.64**	−3.26*	−1.87**	−2.59**
	(1.63)	(1.58)	(0.44)	(0.48)
Juba Peace Talks	0.62	0.66	0.77	0.76
	(1.63)	(1.63)	(0.45)	(0.48)
Operation Rudia I	14.60**	8.60**	0.15	−0.44
	(1.75)	(1.68)	(0.47)	(0.50)
LRA Disarmament Act	−12.80**	−5.90**	0.40	0.50
	(1.55)	(1.52)	(0.42)	(0.45)
Battles	0.15**	0.13**	0.06**	0.05**
	(0.04)	(0.03)	(0.01)	(0.02)
Govt. Gains (-1)	0.51	−0.67**	0.03	0.37**
	(0.31)	(0.25)	(0.09)	(0.12)
AR(1)	0.30**	0.43**	0.27**	0.15*
	(0.07)	(0.07)	(0.07)	(0.07)
Constant	0.42	0.41	0.06	−0.04
	(0.73)	(0.80)	(0.20)	(0.22)
Observations	214	214	214	214
Adjusted R-Squared	0.646	0.576	0.424	0.393
Bayesian Information	1773.95	1666.41	1237.14	1325.13
Durbin-Watson	2.08	1.97	2.01	2.00
Q Statistic P-value (Lags 1–36)	0.43	0.99	0.11	0.67

*p<0.05, ** p<0.01, two-tailed test
Mean of Killings: 3.52
Mean of Kidnappings: 2.91
Mean of Pillaging: 0.76
Mean of Scorched Earth: 0.59
Moving average terms are included, but not shown

Schomerus, Mareike. 2007. "The Lord's Resistance Army in Sudan: A History and Overview." Geneva: Small Arms Survey, Graduate Institute of International Studies. Available at www.smallarmssurveysudan.org/fileadmin/docs/working-papers/HSBA-WP-08-LRA.pdf (accessed July 16, 2017).

Sikkink, Kathryn. 2011. *The Justice Cascade: How Human Rights Prosecutions Are Changing World Politics*. New York: W. W. Norton & Company.

Simmons, Beth A. and Danner, Allison Marston. 2010. "Credible Commitments and the International Criminal Court," *International Organization* 64(2): 225–256.

Slaughter, Anne-Marie and Burke-White, William. 2006. "The Future of International Law Is Domestic (or, the European Way of Law)," *Harvard International Law Journal* 47(2): 327–352.

Stahn, Carsten and El Zeidy, Mohamed. 2011. *The International Criminal Court and Complementarity: From Theory to Practice (Volume I and II)*. Cambridge: Cambridge University Press.

Tochilovsky, Vladimir. 2003. "Globalizing Criminal Justice: Challenges for the International Criminal Court." *Global Governance* 9(3): 291–299.

UN System Standing Committee on Nutrition. 2004. "Nutrition in Crisis Situations." Report No. 2 – Summary. Geneva. Available at http://apps.who.int/disasters/repo/13489.pdf (accessed July 16, 2017).

Voeten, Erik. 2013. "Public Opinion and the Legitimacy of International Courts," *Theoretical Inquiries in Law* 14(2): 411–436.

Wegner, Patrick S. 2015. *The International Criminal Court in Ongoing Intrastate Conflicts: Navigating the Peace-Justice Divide*. Cambridge: Cambridge University Press.

Witte, Eric. 2011. "Putting Complementarity into Practice: Domestic Justice for International Crimes in DRC, Uganda, and Kenya," New York: *Open Society Foundations*. Available at www.opensocietyfoundations.org/sites/default/files/putting-complementarity-into-practice-20110120.pdf (accessed July 16, 2017).

Wright, Valerie. 2010. "Deterrence in Criminal Justice: Evaluating Certainty Vs. Severity of Punishment," Washington, DC: The Sentencing Project. Available at www.sentencingproject.org/wp-content/uploads/2016/01/Deterrence-in-Criminal-Justice.pdf (accessed July 16, 2017).

7

How the Fragmentation of the International Judiciary Affects the Performance of International Judicial Bodies

BENJAMIN FAUDE

Introduction[1]

Global governance is currently affected by two related developments: First, a proliferation of international institutions which results in an increased institutional density at the international level (Raustiala 2013).[2] Research on "institutional choice" (Jupille et al. 2013), "forum shopping" (Busch 2007), and "regime-shifting" (Helfer 2009) demonstrates that the central implication of institutional proliferation for state actors is that they gain the possibility to choose among different, potentially overlapping institutions to pursue their interests. Thus, contemporary world politics takes place not only *within* but also *across* international institutions (Morse and Keohane 2014). Second, international cooperation is becoming increasingly legalized (Abbott et al. 2000); that is, international rules are becoming more obligatory and precise. Furthermore, they are to a greater extent enforced by more or less independent judicial bodies (Abbott and Snidal 2000; Goldstein et al. 2000; Keohane et al. 2000). Thus, an integral part of legalization consists in the judicialization of international dispute settlement (Keohane et al. 2000; Zangl 2008; Rittberger et al. 2012; Zangl et al. 2012; Tallberg and McCall Smith 2014). The international judicial system comprises twenty-six permanent international courts and more than 100 court-like judicial bodies (Romano 2011; Alter 2014). As a cumulative result of these two developments, states can oftentimes select between overlapping international courts and tribunals (ICs) when they intend to file a complaint

[1] I thank Jeffrey Dunoff, Theresa Squatrito, and Oran Young for very helpful comments.

[2] This trend can be concluded from the fact that the number of international agreements has risen from 1634 in 1998 to 2403 in 2012 (Yearbook of International Organizations 2013).

(Busch 2007). In the absence of coordination among ICs with overlapping jurisdictions, this includes the possibility of submitting the same legal question either simultaneously or sequentially to multiple ICs. Thus, while legalization is deemed necessary to *prevent* opportunistic state behavior (Goldstein and Martin 2000), its institution-specific nature may also *change* the opportunistic behavior of states. They may use ICs in a strategic way against each other.

As a result, both the *process performance* and the *outcome performance* of ICs are influenced by interinstitutional effects (see Gutner and Thompson 2010; Squatrito et al., Chapter 1). A full-fledged analysis of the performance of ICs needs to take these effects into account. However, International Relations (IR) scholars conceptualize judicialization as taking place within clearly separable international institutions and assume ICs operate in isolation from each other (Abbott et al. 2000; Keohane et al. 2000; Alter 2008). Thus, they cannot grasp how the performance of ICs is affected by the fragmentation of the international judiciary (but see Voeten 2010; Axelrod 2014).[3] I submit that, given their proliferation (Shany 2003), the assumption of clearly separable ICs working in isolation from each other has become problematic (see Alter 2014).

Overcoming the institution-specific analysis of judicialization processes is therefore the purpose of this chapter. Its central argument is that the growing (but institution-specific) judicialization of international dispute settlement does not necessarily create a judicialized resolution of conflicts, as the literature on judicialization leads us to expect (Abbott et al. 2000: 409–410, 418–419; Keohane et al. 2000: 457; Alter 2008: 34; Zangl 2008). To the extent that multiple ICs hand down divergent judgments, the proliferation of ICs generates a return to a politicized resolution of interstate conflicts (Axelrod 2014). Because divergent judgments do not resolve interstate disputes, they compromise the perfomance of ICs. More precisely, ICs issuing divergent judgments neither increase legal certainty (see Goldstein et al. 2000: 398), nor boost

[3] The fragmentation of the international judiciary describes its overall structure, which consists of a multitude of international judicial bodies, but lacks a hierarchy of courts and other ways of formal coordination among them. Thus, neither is there a hierarchical order between ICs nor does a central coordinating instance regulate their relationships (Trachtman 2014: Chapters 10 and 11). Admittedly, the Vienna Convention on the Law of the Treaties (VCLT), particularly its Article 30, tries to regulate collisions in areas of overlapping jurisdictions. However, its rules are too vague to be effective and lack enforcement power (Safrin 2002: 624; Axelrod 2014). In sum, this structure enables the particular type of forum shopping that this chapter addresses.

compliance with international obligations (see Stone Sweet 1997; Goldstein et al. 2000: 397–398; Zangl 2008). In other words, divergent opinions compromise the ability of ICs to clarify the law by providing authoritative interpretations of their underlying treaties. Thus, the parties will often need to solve their dispute outside either international judicial body. I hypothesize that they will do so by way of bargaining, and that doing so will yield a different resolution of the dispute compared to that of an international judicial body. Thus, all in all, I develop a theoretical account for how forum shopping among overlapping ICs leads to a relapse from judicialized to politicized dispute resolution (see also Axelrod 2014).[4]

On a more general level, this chapter suggests that the way(s) in which ICs deal with influence emanating from judicial competitors constitutes an additional factor that shapes their performance. The ways in which international judicial bodies respond to "forum shopping" and, if necessary, to the judgments of competing ICs, influences their proximate performance concerning particular disputes as well as more far-reaching aspects of their performance (see Squatrito et al., Chapter 1). If competing international judicial bodies do not take each other's decisions into account, they mutually undermine each other's performance. If ICs, however, take each other's case law into account or even develop a persistent collision rule, they mutually support each other's performance. Consequently, they can effectively foreclose forum shopping opportunities by determining the applicability of overlapping rules. Thus, a judicial dialogue or an informal recognition of the judgments of other ICs as precedential may lead either to the clear allocation of competencies among overlapping ICs or to the reconciliation of their jurisprudence (see Voeten 2010; Pelc 2014; Squatrito et al. 2018). All in all, ICs can enhance, as well as reduce, tensions between overlapping international institutions. Thus, this chapter speaks directly to the performance criteria of (judicialized) dispute settlement and interinstitutional legal compatibility. With regard to the level of analysis, its theoretical reasoning as well as its empirical illustration is located at the microlevel of individual cases. However, I carve out the implications for the mesolevel of issue-areas (see Squatrito et al., Chapter 1).

[4] I thereby follow the notion of a social mechanism as a pathway or process by which an effect is produced (see Mayntz 2004; Gerring 2008).

The chapter is structured as follows. The first section starts by illustrating the significance of the phenomenon that an interstate dispute is handled by at least two overlapping ICs. It then develops the analytical framework in three steps. First, I elaborate on the conditions under which we can expect forum shopping among overlapping ICs and on the determinants of states' forum shopping behavior. Second, I draw one central consequence of forum shopping among overlapping ICs for the judicialization of international dispute settlement – the possibility of divergent decisions which leave the interstate dispute unresolved. Third, I theorize how divergent decisions of overlapping ICs cause the relapse from the judicialized mode of dispute settlement within ICs into the politicized mode of dispute settlement outside of them. In the second section, the chapter turns to the overlapping ICs in international trade governance. Here, I clarify the legal backdrop against which state actors, as well as economic ICs, are operating and show that, in the softwood lumber dispute between the US and Canada, forum shopping among the dispute settlement mechanisms (DSMs) of the North American Free Trade Agreement (NAFTA) and the World Trade Organization (WTO) has led to divergent decisions. As a consequence, the dispute backslid into politicized resolution via interstate bargaining. Thus, I demonstrate empirically how the DSMs of NAFTA and the WTO have mutually undermined each other's performance.

The Dynamics of Dispute Settlement by International Courts and Tribunals with Overlapping Jurisdictions

The purpose of this section is to develop a framework for analyzing how interinstitutional effects impact the *outcome performance* of ICs (see Squatrito et al., Chapter 1). My analytical framework focuses exclusively on state-to-state dispute settlement provisions and grasps all those interstate disputes that were examined by two or more international judicial bodies with overlapping jurisdictions. This does not necessarily imply that those international judicial bodies need to adopt a ruling on the case at hand. It is sufficient that they were engaged with the case. Before developing the analytical framework, I demonstrate how often this has been the case in international trade governance.

The Significance of the Problem

The more fragmented the international judiciary, the greater the interinstitutional challenge for the performance of ICs.[5] In other words, the more formally uncoordinated ICs there are in a particular issue-area of international governance, the higher the propensity of forum shopping and, consequently, of divergent judgments. Thus, the degree to which the international judiciary is fragmented, as well as the significance of forum shopping, varies by issue area. The international trade judiciary, for example, is highly fragmented. Between 1948 and 1994, 124 regional trade agreements (RTAs) were notified with the WTO. Since the creation of the WTO in 1995, an additional 535 agreements have been notified. Thus, the current total is 659 RTAs.[6] Most of these RTAs regulate the same issues as the WTO, such as trade in goods and services, intellectual property, sanitary and phytosanitary provisions, and technical barriers to trade (Hillman 2009: 195). According to the WTO (2013: 6), "[t]ogether with the proliferation of RTAs, there has been a proliferation of RTA-DSMs." By the end of 2012, 226 DSMs of RTAs were notified to the WTO (2013: 6); 147 of which use a "quasi-judicial model" of dispute settlement (i.e., an ad hoc adjudicatory body), 10 use a "judicial" model (i.e., a permanent adjudicatory body), and only 69 a "political" model based on interstate bargaining (WTO 2013: 13). Thus, all in all, as Caroline Henckels (2008: 574) puts it, "[g]iven the proliferation of FTAs in recent years and their substantive overlap with WTO law, forum selection has become an important part of international trade policy."

Against this backdrop, it comes as no surprise that interstate trade disputes are not exclusively handled by one IC, but occasionally also by two or more overlapping judicial bodies. Table 7.1 summarizes those interstate disputes that were addressed either simultaneously or sequentially by overlapping ICs, and involve at least one trade court (i.e., either the WTO Dispute Settlement Body [DSB] or a regional trade court). Those cases involve purely trade-related cases revolving around import restrictions and antidumping measures (the *Poultry* dispute, the *Sugar* dispute, and the *Softwood Lumber* dispute), as well as cases that require

[5] Please note that the fragmentation of the international judiciary is different from the fragmentation of international law (e.g., Fischer-Lescano and Teubner 2004; Benvenisti and Downs 2007). While the former denotes the structure of the international judicial bodies, the latter captures the structure of the legal rules that these bodies are supposed to interpret and apply.

[6] See Regional Trade Agreements: Facts and Figures. Available at: www.wto.org/english/tratop_e/region_e/regfac_e.htm (accessed on July 3, 2017).

Table 7.1 *Interstate disputes handled by overlapping International Courts and Tribunals*

Case	Opposing Parties	Involved DSMs	Content	Outcome
Swordfish	European Community Chile	WTO DSM ITLOS	Chile's prohibition of unloading and transit of highly migratory swordfish for foreigners	Negotiated out-of-court settlement (no decision of either court)
Softwood Lumber	Canada US	WTO DSM NAFTA DSM	US import restrictions on Canadian lumber	Negotiated out-of-court settlement: Softwood Lumber Agreement 2006
Sugar	US Mexico	WTO DSM NAFTA DSM	US quotas on Mexican cane sugar Mexican tariffs on US-imports of High Fructose Corn Syrup	Negotiated out-of-court settlement: Sugar Agreement 2006
Brazilian Tires	Brazil Uruguay EC	WTO DSM Mercosur DSM	Brazil's ban on the importation of retreaded (and used) tires	Divergent decisions of WTO AB and Mercosur DSM
Poultry	Brazil Argentina	WTO DSM Mercosur DSM	Argentina's antidumping measures on the import of Brazilian poultry	Divergent decisions of WTO panel and Mercosur DSM
MOX Plant	Ireland UK	OSPAR ITLOS ECJ	UK responsible for operating MOX nuclear plant Ireland fear release of nuclear substances into the Irish sea	*OSPAR*: Dismissal *ECJ*: Ireland breached EC processual obligations *UNCLOS Arbitral Tribunal*: Termination of suspended proceedings with parties' consent

balancing trade against nontrade interests, such as the protection of the environment and of public health (the *Swordfish* dispute, the *Brazilian tyres* dispute, and the *Mox Plant* dispute).

In the *Swordfish* dispute, Chile tried to protect swordfish by banning their import as well as their trans-shipment through Chilean ports. This measure caused the European Community (EC) to file a complaint with the WTO DSM.[7] In response, Chile filed a complaint with the International Tribunal for the Law of the Sea (ITLOS).[8] However, neither IC handed down a decision. The dispute was resolved in out-of-court negotiations (Axelrod 2014). The *Softwood Lumber* dispute between the US and Canada revolved around whether Canada subsidized its lumber industry in an unfair manner and whether the US, therefore, has the right to restrict imports of Canadian lumber (discussed in detail below).[9] In the *Sugar* dispute, Mexico initiated the dispute settlement procedure of NAFTA as a response to restrictions on the import of Mexican sugar by the US, which however blocked the establishment of a panel.[10] As a result, Mexico introduced an import tax on soft drinks sweetened with noncane sugar. This was clearly targeted at the US, which in turn complained with the WTO DSM that Mexico had violated its WTO national treatment obligation.[11] A discussion arose on whether the WTO DSM should exercise its jurisdiction and what legal norms it is entitled to interpret and apply – only those of the WTO or also those of NAFTA? In the end, a WTO panel as well as the

[7] See WTO DSB, *Chile – Measures Affecting the Transit and Importation of Swordfish*, WT/DS193/2, Request for Establishment of a Panel by the European Communities (November 7, 2000).

[8] See ITLOS Case Concerning the Conservation and Sustainable Exploitation of Swordfish Stocks in the South-Eastern Pacific Ocean, Order 2000/3 (December 20, 2000).

[9] See WTO Panel Report, *United States – Investigation of the International Trade Commission in Softwood Lumber from Canada*, Recourse to Article 21.5 of the DSU by Canada, WT/DS277/RW (November 15, 2005); Decision of the NAFTA Panel, *In the Matter of Certain Softwood Lumber Products from Canada: Final Affirmative Threat of Injury Determination*, Sec. File No. USA-CDA-2002–1904-7 (August 31, 2004); Decision of the NAFTA Extraordinary Challenge Committee, *In the Matter of Certain Softwood Lumber Products from Canada: Opinion and Order of the Extraordinary Challenge Committee*, Sec. File No. ECC-2004–1904-01USA (August 10, 2005).

[10] Decision of the NAFTA Panel, *Review of the Final Determination of the Antidumping Investigation on Imports of High Fructose Corn Syrup, originating from the United States of America. Final Decision*, Sec. File No. MEX-USA-98–1904-01 (August 3, 2001).

[11] See WTO Panel Report, *Anti-Dumping Investigations of High Fructose Corn Syrup (HFCS) from the United States*, WT/DS132/R: Mexico (January 28, 2000).

WTO Appellate Body exercised jurisdiction solely based upon WTO law. Both organs found Mexico's behavior to be inconsistent with certain regulations of the General Agreement on Tariffs and Trade (GATT).[12] However, the dispute was finally resolved by an out-of-court negotiated settlement – the sugar agreement (Henckels 2008: 576–579). The *Brazilian tyres* dispute concerning the restriction of the import of used tires for environmental and public health reasons by Brazil was arbitrated by an ad hoc Arbitral Tribunal of the Common Market of the South (Mercosur) and by a WTO panel, as well as the WTO Appellate Body. At the request of Uruguay, a Mercosur ad hoc Arbitral Tribunal found Brazil's behavior to be incompatible with Mercosur regulations, and it exempted the member states of Mercosur from the restrictions.[13] This prompted a second lawsuit with the WTO DSM, initiated by the EC, against the so-called "Mercosur-exemption."[14] The WTO panel found other measures by Brazil, but not the "Mercosur-exemption," to be inconsistent with WTO law. Subsequently, the WTO Appellate Body overruled the panel by deciding that the "Mercosur-exemption" constituted "arbitrary and unjustifiable discrimination," which is inconsistent with WTO law (Lavranos and Vielliard 2008). In the *Poultry* dispute, Brazil submitted legal questions on certain Argentinian antidumping measures on the import of poultry from Brazil to the Mercosur ad hoc Arbitral Tribunal[15] and, subsequent to an unfavorable decision of the former, to the WTO DSM. The WTO panel found that these Argentinian measures were partly inconsistent with the WTO Anti-Dumping Agreement.[16] Also in this case, it was discussed whether the WTO DSM should exercise its jurisdiction at all, but it insisted on doing so (Henckels 2008: 579). The *Mox Plant* dispute concerning the discharge of radioactive waste into the Irish Sea by

[12] See WTO Panel Report, *Mexico – Tax Measures on Soft Drinks and Other Beverages*, WT/DS308/R (October 7, 2005); WTO Appellate Body Report, *Mexico – Tax Measures on Soft Drinks and Other Beverages*, WT/DS308/AB/ R (March 6, 2006).

[13] See Mercosur ad hoc Arbitral Tribunal, *Uruguay v Brazil-Import prohibition of remoulded tyres from Uruguay* (January 9, 2002).

[14] See WTO Panel Report, *Brazil-Measures Affecting Imports of Retreated Tyres*, WT/DS332/R (June 12, 2007); Appellate Body Report, WT/DS332/AB/R (December 3, 2007).

[15] See Aplicación de Medidas Antidumping Contra la Exportación de Pollos Enteros, Provenientes de Brasil (Tribunal Ad Hoc del Mercosur 2001).

[16] See WTO Panel Report, *Argentina – Definitive Anti-Dumping Duties on Poultry from Brazil*, WT/DS241/R (April 22, 2003).

a British processing plant touched upon the United Nations Convention on the Law of the Sea (UNCLOS),[17] the Convention for the Protection of the Marine Environment of the North-East Atlantic (OSPAR Convention), and the Treaty Establishing the European Community (TEC).[18] Thus, the European Court of Justice (ECJ) ruled that Ireland's decision to submit this legal question to other tribunals was in breach of EC law. Remarkably, the UNCLOS arbitral tribunal suspended the proceedings, because it was of the opinion that the dispute would partly fall within the exclusive jurisdiction of the ECJ. In the end, Ireland withdrew the legal case against the UK (Henckels 2008: 587–588).

Despite the fact that trade-related ICs with high levels of judicialization (the WTO DSM, the ECJ, the NAFTA DSM, and the Mercosur DSM) were involved in these cases, the engagement of overlapping ICs has led to outcomes that diverge from the expectation of the legalization literature that judicialized dispute settlement procedures lead to judicialized dispute resolution (see Zangl 2008). In some cases, the disputing parties negotiated an out-of-court settlement; in others, divergent decisions made it more difficult to solve the dispute. In the *MOX Plant* dispute, however, overlapping jurisdictions led to interjudicial coordination.

All in all, compared to the magnitude of the fragmentation of the international judiciary, the sheer number of cases handled by more than one IC is comparatively low. What is more, the comparatively high degree of fragmentation of the international trade judiciary leads us to expect that forum shopping and divergent judicial decisions are more significant here than in other issue areas. Aware of these qualifications, I nevertheless hold that the qualitative effects these cases produce provide a justification for paying analytical attention to the distinctive dynamics of dispute settlement through overlapping ICs.

Forum Shopping under Conditions of "Jurisdictional Ambiguity"

The proliferation of ICs offers states a new opportunity to pursue their interests in interstate disputes: They can select between different ICs when they intend to file a complaint (Busch 2007). That is, when two

[17] See ITLOS, The MOX Plant Case (*Ireland* v. *United Kingdom*), Provisional Measures (www.itlos.org/cases/list-of-cases/case-no-10/, accessed July 3, 2017).

[18] Under the TEC member states agree not to submit a dispute concerning the interpretation or application of Community law to any court or tribunal other than the ECJ.

or more overlapping international institutions offer judicialized dispute settlement procedures, the overlapping members have the opportunity to select the most suitable IC (see Bièvre et al. 2014). In the absence of coordination among ICs with overlapping jurisdictions, this includes the possibility of submitting the same legal question, or particular aspects of the same legal question, either simultaneously or sequentially to multiple ICs that overlap in their jurisdictions (see Kwak and Marceau 2006: 467). In international trade governance, those states that are members of the WTO, and of at least one regional institution that accommodates an IC, have the opportunity to file a suit with their regional institution *and/or* with the global WTO DSM.

The possibility of forum shopping in the international judiciary raises three interconnected analytical questions: First, and most basically, why can we expect forum shopping among ICs to occur? Second, under which conditions can we expect it? Third, what determines forum shopping behavior among ICs?

First, we may expect the overlapping members to select among different ICs because they offer different incentive structures (Bièvre et al. 2014).[19] This is so for two reasons. On the one hand, they may apply different substantive rules. On the other hand, their respective procedures may give the complainant different leverage over the outcome, enable different levels of enforcement, and provide different sanctioning mechanisms. Thus, the overlapping members act on the assumption that it makes a difference whether they submit a legal question to one IC or the other.

Second, we can expect forum shopping among ICs in areas of "functional overlap" among international institutions that offer judicialized dispute settlement procedures to their members (Raustiala and Victor 2004).[20] Such areas are characterized by "judicial ambiguity" (Jupille 2004). Thus, all ICs have jurisdiction, defined as "the power to hear and determine a case" (King 1997: 6). If certain state behaviour refers to the rules of both or all institutions at the same time, a complainant has the opportunity to file a lawsuit with either of the available ICs. This is possible as long as – formal or informal – secondary rules do not clearly

[19] Overlapping members are those states that are subject to the jurisdictions of both overlapping international judicial bodies.

[20] Since this chapter focuses exclusively on state-to-state dispute settlement, the question of "access" is restricted to the question which states have "access" to more than one international DSM.

separate the jurisdictions of the overlapping judicial bodies from each other.

Third, the complainants can be expected to submit the legal question to the IC which they perceive to be most conducive to their interest in winning the case and which does not threaten to harm them in the future by setting an undesirable precedent (Busch 2007). Thus, state actors select the IC that promises the "greatest expected utility" (Bièvre et al. 2014). This implies that complainants select the judicial body based on differences in the applicable law (Which substantive rule is the defendant perceived to have violated most clearly? Are there any exemptions from general rules that allow for the behavior in question?), the ability to influence the judicial procedure (Does the respondent have the opportunity to block the establishment of a panel? Is there the possibility to appeal a decision? Are other members allowed to participate as third parties?), the intrusiveness of sanctioning mechanisms, and the enforceability of judicial decisions (compare Henckels 2008: 574).

One type of forum shopping is at the heart of this chapter:[21] the appeal to an IC regarding a legal question that was previously addressed by an overlapping IC, or is at least intrinsically related to the judgment of an overlapping judicial body (see Marceau and Wyatt 2010).[22] This specific type of forum shopping captures the following constellations: the decision of one IC leads respondents to either adapt their behavior in accordance with the legal decision or to maintain their current behavior. Either reaction may cause another lawsuit with the IC of an overlapping institution. Either the initial complainant to the dispute, or another complainant who is not satisfied with the behavioral adaptations of the respondent, has the opportunity to file a suit with the IC of an overlapping institution.

[21] Admittedly, focusing only on one this type of forum shopping restricts the generalizability of my theoretical argument. However, I deliberately focus on this type of forum shopping because it is most consequential for the performance of ICs.

[22] The *Brazilian Tyres* dispute and the *Sugar* dispute (see above) exemplify what is meant by closely related cases: In the *Brazilian Tyres* dispute, a Mercosur ruling triggered a new, but related legal case, initiated by the EC at the WTO DSM. In the *Sugar* dispute, the US blocked the establishment of a NAFTA panel, which, in the end, led to a dispute with the WTO DSM, initiated by the US, based on certain Mexican actions in response to the blockade of the NAFTA procedure by the US.

The Impact of Forum Shopping on the Performance of International Courts and Tribunals

When responding to the forum shopping of overlapping members, ICs with overlapping jurisdictions can mutually influence each other's performance. If they take each other's decisions into account when handing down decisions, or even develop a collision rule through case law, they mutually support each other's performance. In doing so, ICs may indeed sort out tensions between different regimes (see Squatrito et al., Chapter 1). However, this chapter focuses on the second possibility that overlapping ICs do not take each other's decisions into account and even decide the same legal question differently. If two decisions contradict or are at odds with each other, two ICs mutually undermine each other's performance.[23] In such cases, the interstate dispute cannot be resolved through judicialized dispute settlement. This is detrimental to the performance of ICs because inherent in a failure to settle disputes is a qualification of ICs' ability to provide authoritative interpretations of the meaning of legal rules and to ensure compliance with international rules (see Squatrito et al. 2018).

How do states react to divergent judgments? As long as no further judicial venue is available, they turn to politicized dispute settlement, because they are forced to solve their dispute by way of out-of-court negotiations (Axelrod 2014). These allow actors to draw directly on their exogenous power resources in order to reach favorable dispute resolution (see Elster 1989). The bargaining solution may therefore be expected to reflect the power disparities between the negotiators (see Alter 2008: 34). In international trade negotiations, a country's relative market size is the central determinant of its bargaining power (Steinberg 2002: 347–348; Drezner 2007). Large economies tend to be less dependent on trade and, therefore, have a greater retaliatory leverage than smaller economies (Arnold and Rittberger 2013; Tallberg and McCall Smith 2014).

Politicized dispute settlement outside of ICs contrasts with judicialized dispute settlement within ICs. In order to solve an interstate dispute, international judicial bodies interpret and apply legal rules according to established legal principles (Abbott and Snidal 2013). This includes a (quasi-)judicial process of *arguing* among the disputing parties and the judicial actor based upon the legal rules of the institution (Keohane et al. 2000: 457). In this process, the disputing parties can use their

[23] The probability that overlapping ICs adopt divergent decisions is highest if they interpret and apply divergent substantive norms, for example those of the WTO and the UNCLOS.

exogenous power resources and pursue their interests only insofar as they are able to connect them to valid institutional norms (Abbott et al. 2000: 409; Deitelhoff 2009: 35). The process of (quasi-) judicial arguing does not exclude judicial actors from pursuing strategic interests, such as adopting decisions that are complied with by major actors (Alter 2014: 32–67; Brutger and Morse 2015). To be sure, ICs face political constraints (Ginsburg 2014). However, arbitrators or judges address an interstate dispute according to a predefined procedure and apply valid institutional norms (Abbott and Snidal 2000: 430–431). Thus, the judicialization of dispute settlement procedures entails distinctive politics, which makes a politicized dispute resolution based on pure power-based bargaining impossible (Alter 2008: 47–48; Abbott and Snidal 2013). Divergent judicial opinions, however, repulse states from judicialized dispute settlement within ICs into politicized dispute settlement outside of them.

I expect the solution to an interstate dispute that is reached by politicized dispute settlement outside of ICs to differ from the solution that was reached by judicialized dispute settlement inside of them. In particular, I expect the solutions of interstate disputes that are reached via interstate bargaining to correspond more closely to the distribution of power between the opponents than the dispute resolutions reached via judicialized dispute settlement. At the same time, however, I assume that the rules of the overlapping institutions constrain politicized dispute settlement (Axelrod 2014). Adopting an out-of-court agreement which violates the legal rules of one of the institutions involved would create the danger of new litigation with its IC. In that sense, the overlapping legal rules constrain the bargaining space (Charney 1999; Axelrod 2014). Thus, politicized dispute settlement outside of ICs does not imply bargaining in an anarchical world in which legal constraints are completely absent. Even politicized dispute settlement takes place in the shadow of international law.

It is essential to distinguish this type of politicized dispute settlement from politicized dispute settlement taking place within international judicial bodies prior to the (quasi-)judicial arguing (see Koremenos and Betz 2013; Tallberg and McCall Smith 2014). Many ICs encourage states to solve their disputes by finding a mutually agreeable solution before the judicial procedure starts (Johns 2012). In this vein, politicized dispute settlement is the first step of judicialized dispute settlement. However, prior to litigation, the use of exogenous power resources by states is restricted, because it is always an option to switch into (quasi-) judicial arguing. Thus, politicized dispute resolution takes place in the

Furthermore, my analysis is limited to one specific matter of the overall dispute – whether Canadian imports of softwood lumber pose a threat of material injury to the US market.

The "methods of forest ownership and management" (Dunoff 2007: 3) differ between the US and Canada. In the US, almost all lumber is "produced from timber harvested on privately owned lands" (Dunoff 2007: 3). The price firms pay to harvest timber is determined by a competitive auction. In Canada, on the other hand, "94 percent of forests are owned by either federal or provincial governments" (Dunoff 2007: 3). Thus, the price to harvest the timber, known as the stumpage fee, is set administratively and in consideration of nonmarket based criteria, such as the revenue goals of Canadian provinces and the jobs created by harvesting operations (Dunoff 2007: 3). This stumpage fee is at the center of the *Softwood Lumber* dispute. The central claim of the US is that the stumpage fee is set below market levels by Canadian officials and that this results in an unfair subsidization of Canadian softwood lumber and in the dumping of Canadian softwood lumber onto the US market (Dunoff 2007). Based on that claim, the US repeatedly imposed AD and CVD on Canadian softwood lumber. Canada repeatedly called into question whether these actions correspond to international law and to US domestic law. In sum, the diverging "approaches in the economic and political governance of the softwood lumber industry" are at the core of this dispute (Guglya 2011: 176).

On April 1, 2001, the first SLA between the US and Canada expired. The SLA had introduced a system of Canadian voluntary export restraints (VER) on softwood lumber to the US (Williams 2010: 19). It provided that "14.7 billion board feet of Canadian lumber could enter the US market per year without a tax; thereafter an export tax would be imposed on a sliding scale" (Dunoff 2007: 5; Williams 2010: 22). On April 2, 2001, the US lumber industry requested the US Department of Commerce to charge AD and CVD against Canada. It was determined that "Canadian stumpage policies constituted countervailing subsidies," that "Canadian softwood lumber firms were dumping their products in the US market," and that "imported Canadian softwood lumber threatened the US industry with material injury" (Dunoff 2007: 5).[26] Consequently, in May 2002, the

[26] "Both NAFTA and the WTO Agreement require US domestic agencies to make three determinations prior to the levying of antidumping or countervailing duties in response. These are findings of dumping, subsidization, or the threat of either; material injury to

US Department of Commerce determined a combined AD/CVD rate of 27.22 percent.

With regard to the question whether Canadian imports of softwood lumber pose a threat of material injury to the US market, the DSMs of NAFTA's chapter 19, which applies US domestic law, and of the WTO, which applies WTO law, adopted divergent decisions. A NAFTA panel decided that Canadian imports of softwood lumber do not threaten to cause material injury to the US market.[27] It therefore "ordered the ITC [International Trade Commission] to issue a negative threat of injury determination" (Dunoff 2007: 12). Thus, "the NAFTA litigation resulted in a conclusive determination that Canadian softwood lumber imports neither caused nor threatened to cause material injury to US industry. As a matter of US law, absent injury, there is no basis for the imposition of antidumping and countervailing duties" (Dunoff 2007: 12). In reaction to that decision, the US engaged in forum shopping and filed another suit against Canada with the WTO DSM. Thus, "the ITC's injury determinations were also subject to a separate WTO proceeding" (Dunoff 2007: 13). The US again claimed that Canadian imports of softwood lumber threaten to cause material injury on the US market. Thus, the US submitted to the WTO DSM the same legal question that it had previously submitted to the NAFTA DSM. A WTO panel decided that such a threat was indeed given.[28] In doing so, the WTO panel diverged from the former decision of the NAFTA DSM that had been confirmed by the NAFTA Extraordinary Challenge Committee in the meantime.[29]

As a result, the forum shopping of the US led to divergent decisions by the two overlapping judicial bodies on the question whether Canadian subsidies threaten to injure the US market: NAFTA's ruling in favor of Canada implies that there is no threat of material injury to US firms, and hence, no right for the US to impose AD/CVD according to US domestic law. The decision of the WTO DSB to accept the claim that Canadian

a domestic industry or the threat thereof; a causal link between the activity and the injury" (Carmody 2006: 665).

27 Decision of the NAFTA Panel, In the Matter of Certain Softwood Lumber Products from Canada: Final Affirmative Threat of Injury Determination, Sec. File No. USA-CDA-2002–1904-7 (August 31, 2004).

28 WTO Panel Report, *United States – Investigation of the International Trade Commission in Softwood Lumber from Canada*, Recourse to Article 21.5 of the DSU by Canada, WT/DS277/RW (November 15, 2015).

29 Decision of the NAFTA Extraordinary Challenge Committee, In the Matter of Certain Softwood Lumber Products from Canada: Opinion and Order of the Extraordinary Challenge Committee, Sec. File No. ECC-2004–1904-01USA (August 10, 2005).

imports of softwood lumber threaten to cause material injury on the US market, on the other hand, allows the US to impose AD/CVDs on Canada (Pauwelyn 2006: 197). As a result, both judicial bodies did not resolve the dispute. Instead they added to legal uncertainty.

The divergent judgments of the overlapping judicial bodies of NAFTA and the WTO forced Canada and the US to solve their dispute via out-of-court negotiations. Thus, divergent decisions pushed states back from judicialized dispute settlement into politicized dispute settlement. As a result, they negotiated the SLA 2006. It entered into force on October 12, 2006 for a duration of seven years and a possible renewal of two years. The agreement stipulates the "revocation of countervailing and antidumping duties against Canadian Softwood Lumber" and "the return of over $4.4 billion in duties collected by the US since 2002" (Dunoff 2007: 12). Canada, on the other hand, committed itself to maintaining conditional restrictions on its softwood lumber exports to the US. Should prices fall under a specified price, Canadian regions have to impose an export tax or a quota (Dunoff 2007: 12). All in all, the SLA aims at limiting Canadian exports of softwood lumber to the US. However, the effective tariff rate of the agreement was lower than the existing tariffs and Canadian exports grew (Williams 2010: 28).

Conclusion

Interinstitutional dynamics have so far been neglected by IR scholarship on the judicialization of international dispute settlement (but see Voeten 2010; Axelrod 2014), which holds that the institution-specific judicialization of dispute settlement leads to increased legal certainty (see Goldstein et al. 2000: 398), boosts states' compliance with international obligations (Zangl 2008), and therefore raises the performance of international institutions. The implicit assumption behind these propositions is that ICs operate in isolation from each other. That is, the judicialization of international dispute settlement was conceptualized as taking place within clearly separable international institutions (Stone Sweet 1997; Abbott et al. 2000). This chapter demonstrates that this assumption is not accurate in areas of overlap among separately established international institutions that offer judicialized dispute settlement procedures to their members. In such areas, inter-institutional effects affect the performance of ICs. When handing down divergent judgments, those judicial bodies may mutually undermine compliance with their judgments and therefore each other's performance.

Thus, in the end, in areas of jurisdictional overlap, judicialized dispute settlement does not necessarily establish legal certainty, but may induce a relapse into politicized dispute settlement. Thus, forum shopping and the lack of coordination among overlapping ICs change dispute settlement in world politics. As soon as the jurisdictions of separately established ICs overlap, states may succeed in thwarting judicialized dispute settlement by submitting the same legal question to more than one international judicial body. As a result, overlapping judicial bodies may adopt different conclusions, which force the opponent parties to settle their dispute outside any international judicial body.

Since it features a high density of judicialized dispute settlement, international trade governance provides a laboratory for the study of interstate dispute resolution in areas of institutional overlap. There are simply more ICs in this issue area than in other issue areas. Thus, collisions between dispute settlement bodies are most likely to pop up in international trade governance. We should therefore be aware that I have applied my theoretical argument to a "most likely case".

How can the problem of divergent decisions be countered? The challenge is to develop "secondary rules" which disentangle the overlapping jurisdictions by clearly allocating competencies. Such a meta-coordination would dissolve the area of overlap and, therefore, foreclose forum shopping opportunities. Empirically, the development of a "secondary rule" can be observed, for example, in the relationship between the ECJ and the European Court of Human Rights (ECtHR), where the Solange principle was introduced to disentangle the overlapping jurisdictions (Lavranos 2008: 603–605). Developing a "secondary rule" between overlapping international judicial bodies is possible, but not unproblematic, because it involves a distributional conflict. The overlapping ICs may be assumed to be in a situation which resembles the "Battle of the Sexes" (Snidal 1985: 931–936). In order to secure their own turf, all courts have an interest in developing "secondary rules." However, the preferred solutions differ because each court has a natural incentive to struggle for dominance. Nevertheless, the relapse from judicialized dispute settlement into politicized dispute settlement is not inevitable. When ICs develop appropriate practices, they can counter the problems caused by the fragmentation of the international judiciary.

All in all, the performance of ICs with overlapping jurisdictions may be enhanced as well as reduced through interinstitutional influence. It therefore seems a promising avenue for further research to study on a comparative basis and over time how ICs position themselves against their competitors in the fragmented international judiciary. In other words, "positioning against competitors" may be seen as an additional factor which shapes the performance of ICs. This positioning may range from an "inward-looking perspective," which means that an IC interprets its treaty "in clinical isolation" from other treaties, to an "outward-looking perspective," which implies that it interprets the treaty by taking relevant other treaties into account ("systemic interpretation").

References

Abbott, Frederick M. 2000. "NAFTA and the Legalization of World Politics: A Case Study," *International Organization* 54(3): 519–547.

Abbott, Kenneth W., Keohane, Robert O., Moravcsik, Andrew, Slaughter, Anne-Marie, and Snidal, Duncan. 2000. "The Concept of Legalization," *International Organization* 54(3): 401–419.

Abbott, Kenneth W. and Snidal, Duncan. 2000. "Hard and Soft Law in International Governance," *International Organization* 54(3): 421–456.

2013. "Law, Legalization and Politics: An Agenda for the Next Generation of IL/IR Scholars," in Dunoff, Jeffrey L. and Pollack, Mark A. (eds.), *Interdisciplinary Perspectives on International Law and International Relations*. Cambridge: Cambridge University Press, pp. 33–56.

Alter, Karen J. 2000. "The European Union's Legal System and Domestic Policy: Spillover or Backlash," *International Organization* 54(3): 489–518.

2008. "Agents or Trustees? International Courts in their Political Context," *European Journal of International Relations* 14(1): 33–63.

2013. "The Multiple Roles of International Courts and Tribunals: Enforcement, Dispute Settlement, Constitutional and Administrative Review," in Dunoff, Jeffrey L. and Pollack, Mark A. (eds.), *Interdisciplinary Perspectives on International Law and International Relations*. Cambridge: Cambridge University Press, pp. 345–370.

2014. *The New Terrain of International Law: Courts, Politics, Rights*. Princeton, NJ: Princeton University Press.

Arnold, Christian and Rittberger, Berthold. 2013. "The Legalization of Dispute Resolution in Mercosur," *Journal of Politics in Latin America* 5(3): 97–132.

Axelrod, Mark. 2014. "Clash of the Treaties: Responding to Institutional Interplay in European Community-Chile Swordfish Negotiations," *European Journal of International Relations* 20(4): 987–1013.

Benvenisti, Eyal and Downs, George W. 2007. "The Empire's New Clothes: Political Economy and the Fragmentation of International Law," *Stanford Law Review* 60(2): 595–632.

Bezuijen, Jeanine. 2015. "Exploring the Causes for Change in Regional Third Party Dispute Settlement," *World Trade Review* 14(1): 59–81.

Bièvre, Dirk de, Poletti, Arlo, and Thomann, Lars. 2014. "To Enforce or Not to Enforce? Judicialization, Venue Shopping, and Global Regulatory Harmonization," *Regulation & Governance* 8(3): 269–286.

Brutger, Ryan and Morse, Julia C. 2015. "Balancing Law and Politics: Judicial Incentives in WTO Dispute Settlement," *The Review of International Organizations* 10(2): 179–205.

Burley, Anne-Marie and Mattli, Walter. 1993. "Europe before the Court: A Political Theory of Legal Integration," *International Organization* 47(1): 41–76.

Busch, Marc L. 2007. "Overlapping Institutions, Forum Shopping, and Dispute Settlement in International Trade," *International Organization* 61(4): 735–761.

Busch, Marc L. and Reinhardt, Eric. 2000. "Bargaining in the Shadow of the Law: Early Settlement in GATT/WTO Disputes," *Fordham International Law Journal* 24(1): 158–172.

Carmody, Chi. 2006. "Softwood Lumber Dispute (2001–2006)," *The American Journal of International Law* 100(3): 664–674.

Charney, Jonathan I. 1999. "The Proliferation of Courts and Tribunals: Piecing Together the Puzzle," *New York University Journal of International Law* 31: 697–708.

Davis, Christina L. 2009. "Overlapping Institutions in Trade Policy," *Perspectives on Politics* 7(1): 25–31.

Deitelhoff, Nicole. 2009. "The Discursive Process of Legalization: Charting Islands of Persuasion in the ICC Case," *International Organization* 63(1): 33–65.

Drezner, Daniel W. 2007. *All Politics is Global. Explaining International Regulatory Regimes.* Princeton, NJ: Princeton University Press.

Dunoff, Jeffrey L. 2007. *The Many Dimensions of Softwood Lumber.* Legal Studies Research Paper Series. Research Paper No. 2007–24. Temple University. Beasley School of Law.

Elster, Jon. 1989. *The Cement of Society: A Study of Social Order Studies in Rationality and Social Change.* Cambridge: Cambridge University Press.

Fischer-Lescano, Andreas and Teubner, Gunther. 2004. "Regime-Collisions: The Vain Search for Legal Unity in the Fragmentation of Global Law," *Michigan Journal of International Law* 25: 999–1046.

Gerring, John. 2008. "Review Article: The Mechanismic Worldview: Thinking Inside the Box," *British Journal of Political Science* 38(1): 161–179.

Gilligan, Michael, Johns, Leslie, and Rosendorff, B. Peter. 2010. "Strengthening International Courts and the Early Settlement of Disputes," *Journal of Conflict Resolution* 54(1): 5–38.

Ginsburg, Tom. 2014. "Political Constraints on International Courts," in Romano, Cesare, Alter, Karen J., and Shany, Yuval (eds.), *The Oxford Handbook on International Adjudication*. Oxford: Oxford University Press, pp. 483–502.

Goldstein, Judith, Kahler, Miles, Keohane, Robert O., and Slaughter, Anne-Marie. 2000. "Introduction: Legalization and World Politics," *International Organization* 54(3): 385–399.

Goldstein, Judith and Martin, Lisa L. 2000. "Legalization, Trade Liberalization, and Domestic Politics: A Cautionary Note," *International Organization* 54(3): 603–632.

Gomez-Mera, Laura and Molinari, Andrea. 2014. "Overlapping Institutions, Learning, and Dispute Initiation in Regional Trade Agreements: Evidence from South America," *International Studies Quarterly* 58(2): 269–281.

Guglya, L. 2011. "The Interplay of International Dispute Resolution Mechanisms: The Softwood Lumber Controversy," *Journal of International Dispute Settlement* 2(1): 175–207.

Gutner, Tamar and Thompson, Alexander. 2010. "The Politics of IO performance: A Framework," *The Review of International Organizations* 5(3): 227–248.

Helfer, Laurence R. 2009. "Regime Shifting in the International Intellectual Property System," *Perspectives on Politics* 7(1): 39–44.

Helfer, Laurence R. and Slaughter, Anne-Marie. 2005. "Why States Create International Tribunals: A Response to Professors Posner and Yoo," *California Law Review* 93: 899–956.

Henckels, C. 2008. "Overcoming Jurisdictional Isolationism at the WTO-FTA Nexus. A Potential Approach for the WTO," *European Journal of International Law* 19(3): 571–599.

Hillman, Jennifer. 2009. "Conflicts between Dispute Settlement Mechanisms in Regional Trade Agreements and the WTO – What Should WTO Do," *Cornell International Law Journal* 42(2): 193–208.

Johns, Leslie. 2012. "Courts as Coordinators. Endogenous Enforcement and Jurisdiction in International Adjudication," *Journal of Conflict Resolution* 56(2): 257–289.

Jupille, Joseph. 2004. *Procedural Politics: Issues, influence, and institutional choice in the European Union*. Cambridge: Cambridge University Press.

Jupille, Joseph, Mattli, Walter, and Snidal, Duncan. 2013. *Institutional Choice and Global Commerce*. Cambridge: Cambridge University Press.

Kahler, Miles. 2000. "Legalization as Strategy: The Asia-Pacific Case," *International Organization* 54(3): 549–571.

Keohane, Robert O., Moravcsik, Andrew, and Slaughter, Anne-Marie. 2000. "Legalized Dispute Resolution: Interstate and Transnational," *International Organization* 54(3): 457–488.

King, David C. 1997. *Turf Wars: How Congressional Committees Claim Jurisdiction*. Chicago: University of Chicago Press.

Koremenos, Barbara and Betz, Timm. 2013. "The Design of Dispute Settlement Procedures in International Agreements," in Dunoff, Jeffrey L. and Pollack, Mark A. (eds.), *Interdisciplinary Perspectives on International Law and International Relations: The State of the Art*. Cambridge: Cambridge University Press, pp. 371–393.

Krapohl, Sebastian, Faude, Benjamin, and Dinkel, Julia. 2010. "Judicial Integration in the Americas?: A Comparison of Dispute Settlement in NAFTA and Mercosur," in Laursen, Finn (ed.), *Comparative Regional Integration: Europe and Beyond*. Abingdon: Ashgate, pp. 169–192.

Kwak, Kyung and Marceau, Gabrielle. 2006. "Overlaps and Conflicts of Jurisdiction between the World Trade Organization and Regional Trade Agreements," in Bartels, Lorand and Ortino, Federico (eds.), *Regional Trade Agreements and the WTO Legal System*. Oxford: Oxford University Press, pp. 465–524.

Lavranos, Nikolaos. 2008. "Regulating Competing Jurisdictions among International Courts and Tribunals," *Zeitschrift für ausländisches öffentliches Recht und Völkerrecht* 68: 575–621.

Lavranos, Nikolaos and Vielliard, Nicolas. 2008. "Competing Jurisdictions between MERCOSUR and WTO," *The Law and Practice of International Courts and Tribunals* 7(2): 205–234.

Mansfield, Edward D. and Milner, Helen V. 1999. "The New Wave of Regionalism," *International Organization* 53(3): 589–627.

Marceau, Gabrielle and Wyatt, Julian. 2010. "Dispute Settlement Regimes Intermingled. Regional Trade Agreements and the WTO," *Journal of International Dispute Settlement* 1(1): 67–95.

Mayntz, Renate. 2004. "Mechanisms in the Analysis of Social Macro-Phenomena," *Philosophy of the Social Sciences* 34(2): 237–259.

McCall Smith, James. 2000. "The Politics of Dispute Settlement Design: Explaining Legalism in Regional Trade Pacts," *International Organization* 54(1): 137–180.

Mestral, Armand de. 2006. "NAFTA Dispute Settlement: Creative Experiment or Confusion?," in Bartels, Lorand and Ortino, Federico (eds.), *Regional Trade Agreements and the WTO Legal System*. Oxford, New York: Oxford University Press, pp. 359–381.

Morse, Julia C. and Keohane, Robert O. 2014. "Contested Multilateralism," *The Review of International Organizations* 9(4): 385–412.

Pauwelyn, Joost. 2004. "Going Global, Regional, or Both? Dispute Settlement in the Southern African Development Community (SADC) and Overlaps with the WTO and Other Jurisdictions," *Minnesota Journal of Global Trade* 13(1): 231–304.

2006. "Adding Sweeteners to Softwood Lumber: The WTO-NAFTA 'Spaghetti Bowl' is Cooking," *Journal of International Economic Law* 9(1): 197–206.

Pelc, Krzysztof J. 2014. "The Politics of Precedent in International Law: A Social Network Application," *American Political Science Review* 108(03): 547–564.

Powers, Kathy and Goertz, Gary. 2011. "The Economic-institutional Construction of Regions: Conceptualisation and Operationalisation," *Review of International Studies* 37(5): 2387–2416.

Raustiala, Kal. 2013. "Institutional Proliferation and the International Legal Order," in Dunoff, Jeffrey L. and Pollack, Mark A. (eds.), *Interdisciplinary Perspectives on International Law and International Relations*. Cambridge: Cambridge University Press, pp. 293–320.

Raustiala, Kal and Victor, David G. 2004. "The Regime Complex for Plant Genetic Resources," *International Organization* 58(2): 277–309.

Rittberger, Volker, Zangl, Bernhard, and Kruck, Andreas. 2012. *International Organization, 2nd edn.*, Basingstoke: Palgrave Macmillan.

Romano, Cesare P. R. 2011. "A Taxonomy of International Rule of Law Institutions," *Journal of International Dispute Settlement* 2(1): 241–277.

Safrin, Sabrina. 2002. "Treaties in Collision? The Biosafety Protocol and the World Trade Organization Agreements," *American Journal of International Law* 96 (3): 606–628.

Shany, Yuval. 2003. *The Competing Jurisdictions of International Courts and Tribunals*. Oxford: Oxford University Press.

Simmons, Beth and Guzman, Andrew. 2002. "To Settle or Empanel? An Empirical Analysis of Litigation and Settlement at the World Trade Organization," *Journal of Legal Studies* 31(1): 205–S236.

Snidal, Duncan. 1985. "Coordination Versus Prisoners' Dilemma: Implications for International Cooperation and Regimes," *American Political Science Review* 79(4): 923–942.

Squatrito, Theresa, Young, Oran R., Follesdal, Andreas, and Ulfstein, Geir. 2018. "*A Framework for Evaluating the Performance of International Courts and Tribunals*," Chapter 1 in this volume.

Steinberg, Richard H. 2002. "In the Shadow of Law or Power? Consensus-Based Bargaining and Outcomes in the GATT/WTO," *International Organization* 56(2): 339–374.

Stone Sweet, Alec. 1997. "The New GATT. Dispute Resolution and the Judicialization of the Trade Regime," in Volcansek, Mary L. (ed.), *Law above Nations: Supranational Courts and the Legalization of Politics*. Gainesville, Florida: University Press of Florida, pp. 118–141.

Tallberg, Jonas and McCall Smith, James. 2014. "Dispute Settlement in World Politics: States, Supranational Prosecutors, and Compliance," *European Journal of International Relations* 20(1): 118–144.

Trachtman, Joel P. 2014. *The Future of International Law: Global Government*. Cambridge: Cambridge University Press.

Voeten, Erik. 2010. "Borrowing and Nonborrowing among International Courts," *The Journal of Legal Studies* 39(2): 547–576.

Williams, Russell A. 2010. "Assessing the Success of the WTO DSM. Lessons from Softwood Lumber IV," *Canadian Foreign Policy Journal* 16(1): 17–34.

WTO Economic Research and Statistics Division. 2013. Mapping of Dispute Settlement Mechanisms in Regional Trade Agreements – Innovative or Variations on a Theme? Staff Working Paper ERSD-2013–07.

Yearbook of International Organizations. 2013. *Yearbook of International Organizations*. New York: Union of International Associations.

Zangl, Bernhard. 2008. "Judicialization Matters! A Comparison of Dispute Settlement under GATT and the WTO," *International Studies Quarterly* 52(4): 825–854.

Zangl, Bernhard, Helmedach, Achim, Mondre, Aletta, Kocks, Alexander, Neubauer, Gerald, and Blome, Kerstin. 2012. "Between Law and Politics: Explaining International Dispute Settlement Behavior," *European Journal of International Relations* 18(2): 369–401.

8

International Judicial Performances and the Performance of International Courts

JEFFREY L. DUNOFF AND MARK A. POLLACK

Introduction

How should we conceptualize and measure the performance of international courts? By what criteria could one determine whether the European Court of Human Rights (ECtHR) is performing well – or how its performance compares to that of, say, the World Trade Organization's (WTO) Appellate Body (AB)? The Introduction to this volume emphasizes that any evaluation of performance is a function of the underlying criteria against which performance is evaluated, and urges the adoption of "realistic criteria based on common understandings of the functions of international courts."[1]

This deceptively simple-sounding advice masks a series of difficult conceptual and methodological issues. The functions of international courts are multiple and contested, criteria are rarely identified neutrally or uncontroversially, and different courts fulfill different functions. Hence, "performance" is a term that admits of more than one definition, is measured against more than one criterion, and can be analyzed via more than one approach. Given the multi-dimensionality of "performance," the embrace of theoretical and methodological pluralism is one of the most attractive features of the framing paper that introduces this volume.

Building on the editors' call for pluralism, this chapter complements and extends the insights of other contributions to this volume along at least two dimensions. First, as a matter of *substantive focus*, virtually all of the other chapters focus on *outcome performance*. In contrast, this chapter highlights *process performance*. Process, for these purposes, refers to

[1] T. Squatrito, O. R. Young, A. Follesdal, and G. Ulfstein, "A Framework for Evaluating the Performance of International Courts and Tribunals," Chapter 1, in this volume.

the rules, principles and practices applicable to dispute-settling procedures. Process lies at the heart of the judicial undertaking, and occupies such a fundamental place in legal proceedings that tribunals lacking appropriate procedures are criticized for holding "sham proceedings" and said to be unworthy of being called courts.

Second, this chapter also seeks to enlarge the *theoretical and methodological approaches* on offer for evaluating court performance. In particular, this paper introduces an approach, "practice theory," that can be used to illuminate many otherwise hidden aspects of process performance – and at the same time offers an innovative and fruitful way to approach international court performance more generally. In this context, we start with the observation that the term "performance" can connote not only the pursuit or achievement of a task or goal, but also the notion of "competent performance" as that phrase is used in practice theory. Adopting a practice-oriented perspective, our central claim is that to fully understand and evaluate the *performance of international courts*, it is necessary to understand and appraise the *performances of international judges*. Thus, our aim in this contribution is less to pronounce definitively on the performance of any particular tribunal than it is to enrich the study of international court performance by introducing an innovative approach to identifying, understanding and evaluating judicial performances.

To do so, this chapter proceeds in three parts. In Part I, we provide a necessarily brief introduction to some of the key ideas associated with "practice theory" and explain why many judicial behaviors can usefully be analyzed through the lens of this approach. In Part II, we focus on a cluster of international judicial practices that are directly relevant to a court's process performance, namely those associated with evidence and fact-finding. In particular, we show that judicial practices in this area cannot simply be read off of court statutes or rules, but rather are created by the judges themselves, and that international courts demonstrate substantial variation in the practices they adopt. In Part III, we discuss several well-known instances where controversial evidentiary practices have directly impacted the structure and content of judicial opinions. In the language of this volume, we link a particular aspect of *process performance* – namely evidentiary and fact-finding practices – to the *outcome performance* of international courts as found in their core work product, judicial opinions. A brief conclusion follows.

What are International Judicial Practices?

"Practice theory" is an umbrella term that captures a variety of approaches and methods that have been widely employed across the social sciences. In the early 2000s, Emanuel Adler and Vincent Pouliot popularized the use of practice theory in the study of international relations.[2] In their conceptualization, "[p]ractices are competent performances. More precisely, practices are socially meaningful patterns of action which, in being performed more or less competently, simultaneously embody, act out, and possibly reify background knowledge and discourse in and on the material world."[3]

Adler and Pouliot highlight five dimensions of practice. First, and most basically, "a practice is a *performance*, that is, a process of doing."[4] Second, they continue, "practice tends to be *patterned*, in that it generally exhibits certain regularities over time and space. . . . These patterns . . . are part of a socially organized context, which not only gives them meaning, but also structures interaction. This is not to say that practice is strictly iterative, however, as there is always wiggle room for agency even in repetition."[5] Third, practices are performed more or less competently, as determined by an audience capable of appraising the performance.[6] Fourth, "practice[s] rest[] on *background knowledge*," which is intersubjective and practice-oriented. Fifth and finally, a "practice weaves together the *discursive* and *material* worlds," featuring a linguistic element that gives practices their meaning, as well as a material element acting in and upon the world.[7]

While practice theory has rarely been applied to international courts,[8] many activities of international judges exhibit the five features of practice that Adler and Pouliot highlight. Specifically, judges engage in multiple *performances*. Some are private, such as deliberating with judicial colleagues. Others are public, such as questioning counsel or witnesses at oral hearings. Still others involve off-the-bench activities, such as delivering speeches or publishing scholarly writings. Second, these performances are highly *patterned*. Many of them take place within the highly structured context of international litigation. Even those that take place

[2] See, e.g., E. Adler and V. Pouliot, "International Practices," *International Theory*, 3, no. 1 (2011); E. Adler and V. Pouliot (eds.), *International Practices* (Cambridge: Cambridge University Press, 2011).

[3] Adler and Pouliot (eds.), *International Practices*, 6. [4] Ibid. [5] Ibid. [6] Ibid., 6–7.

[7] Ibid., 7–8.

[8] For a notable exception see J. Meierhenrich, "The Practices of the International Criminal Court," *Law and Contemporary Problems*, 76, no. 3–4 (2013), 1.

outside the courthouse display common patterns across time and space. Third, the performance of these judicial practices can be more or less *competent* as measured by a particular audience – whether litigants, member states, "the invisible college of international lawyers," or larger publics – against some set of intersubjective standards. Fourth, judicial activities presuppose and draw on various forms of *background knowledge*. These practices are informed by a deep knowledge of international legal doctrine and, no less importantly, widely shared and taken-for-granted understandings of how international judges are "supposed" to act. Finally, judicial practices weave together and implicate both the discursive and material worlds, taking the form of legal discourse but drawing upon material resources and having material implications for the litigants in any given case. For example, the court's judgment takes a discursive form, but has material, real-world implications for the litigants and other parties.

Judicial practices include those that determine certain "background" or "institutional" features of litigation, such as linguistic and translation practices, as well as those applicable to the conduct of written and oral pleadings, and the drafting of the court's judgment. Thus, judicial practices exist throughout a dispute's life cycle, from the moment a complaint is filed to the choreographed release of a final judgment. Moreover, judicial practices are interdependent; a court's practices regarding oral proceedings will be, in part, a function of its practices regarding written proceedings. Finally, while there is a broad overlap among international courts in the areas where practices take place, there is considerable variation across tribunals in the specific content of their practices, inviting inquiry into the causes and consequences of this variation on court performance.[9]

Judicial Practices Concerning Evidence and Fact-finding

Having briefly introduced practice theory and the concept of international judicial practices, we now turn to an analysis of several practices associated with evidence and fact-finding. We foreground evidentiary practices for several separate but related reasons. First, the appraisal of

[9] Elsewhere, we provide a synoptic overview of international judicial practices intended to illustrate the range and diversity of these practices. See J. L. Dunoff and M. A. Pollack, "A Typology of International Judicial Practices" in G. Ulfstein and A. Follesdal (eds.), *The Judicialization of International Law – A Mixed Blessing?* (Cambridge: Cambridge University Press, 2017).

evidence and finding of facts lie at the center of a court's work; "adjudication, at its core, is a process by which information is generated and assessed for the purpose of obtaining an appropriate legal outcome."[10] Accurate and impartial fact-finding is essential to a proper determination of whether a legal norm has been violated. Moreover, international tribunals are frequently expected to generate authoritative historical records of contested events. Thus, many contemporary legal disputes are less about the existence or interpretation of legal rules than the existence or nonexistence of legally significant facts. For these reasons, "the role and place of evidence in international legal proceedings are of fundamental importance for international justice and the rule of law."[11]

It is not possible in this short chapter to comprehensively to address all of the issues related to fact-finding in international courts.[12] Instead, we will provide a brief introduction of the topic, followed by examination of judicial practices associated with the admissibility of evidence, construction of the relevant "standard of proof," and the judges' role in the production of evidence. In each case, we will foreground the practices of the International Court of Justice (ICJ), although in several instances, we shall compare and contrast practices at the ICJ with those at other prominent international tribunals.

Fact-finding as a Practice

The starting point for understanding fact-finding as a practice is the relative silence of most treaties creating international courts on evidentiary matters. The ICJ Statute, for example, states that all "papers and documents in support" shall be submitted as part of the written proceedings; and that the oral proceedings "shall consist of the hearing by the Court of witnesses, experts, agents, counsel, and advocates." It also

[10] L. Kaplow, "Information and the Aim of Adjudication: Truth or Consequences?," *Stanford Law Review*, 67, no. 6 (2015), 1304.

[11] P. Tomka and V. Proulx, "The Evidentiary Practice of the World Court" in J. C. Sainz-Borgo (ed.), *Liber Amicorum Gudmundur Eiriksson* (San José: University for Peace Press, 2017).

[12] For fuller treatments, see, e.g., C. Foster, *Science and the Precautionary Principle at International Courts and Tribunals* (Cambridge: Cambridge University Press, 2013); A. Riddell and B. Plant, *Evidence Before the International Court of Justice* (London: British Institute of International and Comparative Law, 2009); M. Grando, *Evidence, Proof, and Fact-Finding in WTO Dispute Settlement* (Oxford: Oxford University Press, 2010).

provides that "even before the hearing begins," the Court may call upon the parties' agents to "produce any document or supply any explanations."

In addition to these relatively terse provisions, Article 30 of the ICJ Statute empowers the Court to "frame rules for carrying out its functions," including rules of procedure. ICJ judges have adopted Rules of Court as well as Practice Directions. Even a cursory review of these texts reveals, however, that they are silent, or nearly so, on a number of key evidentiary issues, prominently including the admissibility, role, scope, weight, and effect of evidence. In short, despite the promulgation of various rules, the Court has notably "refrained from developing a formal set of detailed standards governing the character or weight of the evidence."[13]

Provisions on evidence in the constitutive instruments of other tribunals follow a similar pattern. WTO dispute settlement is based on the Understanding on Rules and Procedures Governing the Settlement of Disputes (DSU). DSU Article 11 provides that "a panel shall make an objective assessment of the matter before it, including an objective assessment of the facts of the case and the applicability of and conformity with the relevant [WTO law]." Paragraph 4 of Appendix 3 to the DSU provides that "the parties to the dispute shall transmit to the panel written submissions in which they present the facts of the case and their arguments." Article 13 of the DSU provides that WTO members "should respond promptly and fully to any request by a panel for such information as the panel considers necessary and appropriate," and authorizes panels "to seek information and technical advice from any individual or body it deems appropriate." An Appendix to the DSU sets out "working procedures" for panels, but they say little about evidentiary matters.

Thus at the WTO, as at the ICJ, the relevant treaty texts say remarkably little about procedural and evidentiary issues. In particular, the relevant legal instruments are silent concerning the admissibility, weight and scope of evidence, as well as burdens of proof and persuasion. Like their brethren at the ICJ, WTO panelists "are generally free to admit and evaluate evidence of every kind, and to ascribe to it the weight they see fit."[14]

[13] Riddell and Plant, *Evidence before the International Court*, 14.

[14] Appellate Body Report, European Communities – Anti-Dumping Duties on Imports of Bed Linen from India, WT/DS141/AB/R (March 1, 2001), para. 6.34.

Much the same is true at the human rights courts. For example, judges at the European Court of Human Rights are not bound by strict rules of evidence, and may consider any form of evidence. The ECtHR has noted that "there are no procedural barriers to the admissibility of evidence or pre-determined formulae for its assessment. It adopts the conclusions that are . . . supported by free evaluation of all evidence, including such inferences as may flow from the facts and the parties' submissions."[15] The Statue of the Inter-American Court of Human Rights (IACtHR) says little regarding evidentiary matters, and the treaty creating the African Court on Human and Peoples' Rights provides only that the court "may receive written and oral evidence including expert testimony" and shall "make its decision on the basis of such evidence." At each of these international human rights courts, the relevant statutes and rules of court are silent regarding the admissibility and weight of evidence, burdens of proof, standards of proof, etc.

The basic instruments of international criminal courts, in contrast, contain detailed provisions regarding the presentation and evaluation of evidence. The International Criminal Court (ICC) Statute, for example, contains a number of procedural norms, which are supplemented by ICC Rules of Procedure and Evidence which encompass more than 220 provisions and some additional 120 Regulations of the Court. Similarly, the Rules of Procedure and Evidence of the International Criminal Tribunal for Yugoslavia (ICTY) and the International Criminal Tribunal for Rwanda (ICTR) each contain more than 120 provisions, supplemented by several Practice Directions. Nonetheless, international criminal judges retain considerable discretion on evidentiary matters. For example, ICC trial judges have authority to determine the proper method for organizing the production of evidence. More broadly, criminal procedure at ICC trials can assume more of a common law or more of a civil law form, depending on the judges and the case.

In practice, then, there are very few limits on the evidence that can be submitted to most international tribunals.[16] Some argue that international courts' evidentiary procedures and practices reflect the structural

[15] See, e.g., *Nachova* v. *Bulgaria* [2005] ECtHR App. Nos. 43577/98 and 43579/98, para. 147.

[16] Thus, Permanent Court of International Justice (PCIJ) Judge Huber's observation that "[t]he Parties may present any proof that they judge useful and the Court is entirely free to make the evidence into account to the extent that it deems it pertinent" is as accurate today as when it was made in 1925. See Acts and Documents Concerning the Organization of the Court (Addendum to No. 2 Revision of the Rules of Court) [1926] PCIJ Series D, 250.

reality that that the litigants appearing before most international tribunals are sovereign states.[17] Relatedly, many agree with Lauterpacht's observation that "the importance of the interests at stake [in international litigations] precludes excessive or decisive reliance upon formal and technical rules."[18] Still others link the lack of evidentiary rules to the absence of appeal, the lack of "discovery" rules at many international tribunals, and the difficulties of obtaining "best" evidence in many international litigations.[19] An alternative explanation looks less at the structural constraints of international litigations than at the judges themselves. From this perspective, the lack of detailed evidentiary rules and standards can be seen as a means of maximizing judicial discretion, and flexibility.

Practice theory is well suited to analysis of the collection and assessment of evidence by international tribunals, and complements alternative theoretical approaches. A structural approach to evidentiary practices, for example, might focus on a court's statutes or rules of procedure. While these do establish broad parameters of judicial behavior, as we have seen these structural constraints are often abstract and open-ended, and therefore in most cases underdetermining. Agentic approaches to judging, which focus on "rational" decision-making by utility-maximizing judges, can be productive in revealing voting patterns of individual judges. But these approaches are much less useful in illuminating evidentiary practices at and across international tribunals. In particular, they fail to account for the strong influence exercised by informal norms and standards, and the collective background knowledge embedded in evidentiary practices. The approach we urge, in contrast, views evidentiary practices as existing between agency and structure, but not reducible to either. Practice-oriented approaches suggest that, within the more or less precise provisions of relevant treaties, statutes, and rules of court, international judges confront and make real choices about how to treat and evaluate evidence – and in doing so establish a broad, patterned set of practices.

[17] R. Higgins, "Respecting Sovereign States and Running a Tight Courtroom," *International and Comparative Law Quarterly*, 50, no. 1 (2001), 124.

[18] H. Lauterpacht (ed.), *The Development of International Law by the International Court* (Cambridge: Cambridge University Press, 1958), 366.

[19] C. N. Brower, "Evidence before International Tribunals: The Need for Some Standard Rules," *International Lawyer* 28, no. 1 (1994), 47.

Standards of Proof

As discussed more fully below, the primary responsibility for producing and introducing evidence in international litigations falls on the parties to the dispute. Judges, in contrast, must "determine which facts must be considered relevant, . . . assess their probative value, and . . . draw conclusions from them as appropriate."[20] In undertaking this task, a judge will – in principle at least – apply a "standard of proof," that is, determine a level of confidence (or type of evidence) required to decide an issue in favor of one party or another.

Domestic courts vary widely in their treatment of the standard of proof. In many common law jurisdictions, a plaintiff must prove her case by "a preponderance of the evidence." On certain issues, however, a court might require "clear and convincing" evidence, and in criminal proceedings the prosecution must establish guilt "beyond a reasonable doubt." Civil law systems, in contrast, typically do not distinguish between standards of proof in civil and criminal matters. Many civil law systems use a standard of *intime conviction* or *conviction raisonnée*. The German Federal Supreme Court has described this standard as a "personal conviction [. . .] in doubtful cases, the judge may and must be content with a degree of certainty useful for practical life that silences doubt without completely excluding it."

With the exception of the international criminal courts, the statutes and rules of procedure of international tribunals typically do not address the standard of proof. Thus, it falls to the judges themselves to decide upon and apply a standard. But judges at many international courts have been unwilling – or unable – to articulate the relevant standard of proof in a consistent manner. For example, in various cases, ICJ judges have invoked the "preponderance of the evidence" standard widely used in common law systems,[21] as well as of proof "beyond a reasonable doubt."[22] At other times, ICJ judges have characterized evidence as being "convincing" or "conclusive."[23] In yet other cases, ICJ judges have invoked a variety of other standards, and rendered determinations "on the basis of a balance of evidence," "on a balance of probabilities," "in all probability," and "consistent with the

[20] Pulp Mills on the River Uruguay (*Argentina* v. *Uruguay*), 2010 ICJ Rep. 14, 72.

[21] E.g., Kasikili/Seduku Island (*Botswana/Namibia*), 1999 ICJ Rep. 1045, 1233.

[22] E.g., Land and Maritime Boundary (*Cameroon* v. *Nigeria*), 2002 ICJ Rep. 303, 599.

[23] E.g., Armed Activities on the Territory of the Congo (*Democratic Republic of the Congo* v. *Uganda*), 2005 ICJ Rep. 168, 268.

probabilities."[24] In other cases, judges have noted that evidence established facts or claims "to the Court's satisfaction," and "with the necessary degree of precision and certainty."[25]

The standard of proof at other tribunals is similarly murky. The DSU does not explicitly address the standard of proof, and neither the AB nor panels have articulated precisely how much and precisely what kind of evidence will be required. Instead members of the Appellate Body have repeatedly emphasized that the nature and scope of evidence required "will necessarily vary from measure to measure, provision to provision, and case to case."[26]

The European Convention and the ECtHR's rules are silent regarding the standard of proof. The ECtHR frequently states that a complainant must establish "proof beyond a reasonable doubt" to show a violation of the Convention.[27] This might appear to be a familiar criminal law standard of proof. Yet the court has expressly stated that its invocation of this standard "should not be interpreted as requiring such a high degree of probability as in criminal trials"[28] – without being entirely clear on what specific degree of "probability" is required.

The standard of proof at the IACtHR is similarly protean. The IACtHR has noted that "international case law has upheld the power of international tribunals to freely evaluate evidence, without adopting a strict assessment of the quantum necessary to provide the grounds for a judgment, and it is essential for the [IACtHR] to pay attention to the circumstances of the specific case and to take into account the limits imposed by respect of legal certainty and procedural balance between the parties."[29] IACtHR judges have emphasized that the standard of proof "is less formal in an international legal proceeding than in a domestic one,"[30] and self-consciously avoided "making a rigid determination of the amount of evidence required to support a judgment."[31]

[24] K. Del Mar, "The International Court of Justice and Standards of Proof" in K. Bannelier et al. (eds.), *The ICJ and the Evolution of International Law: The Enduring Impact of the Corfu Channel Case* (New York: Routledge, 2012), 99.

[25] Ibid.

[26] See, e.g., Appellate Body Report, Chile – Price Band System and Safeguard Measures Relating to Certain Agricultural Products, WT/DS207/AB/RW (September 22, 2002), para. 134.

[27] *Veznedaroglu* v. *Turkey* (2000) ECtHR App. No. 32357/96, para. 30; *Kilic* v. *Turkey* (2000) ECtHR App. No. 22492/93, para. 64.

[28] *Nachova* v. *Bulgaria*, para. 147.

[29] *Kawas-Fernandez* v. *Honduras* (2009) IACtHR (ser. C) No. 196, para. 82.

[30] *Velasquez Rodriguez* v. *Honduras* (1988) IACtHR (ser. C) No. 4, paras. 127, 128.

[31] *Cesti Hurtado* v. *Peru* (Reparations and Costs) (May 31, 2001) IACtHR (ser. C), No. 78, para. 21.

In short, there is a "general lack of consensus on the appropriate standard of proof in international adjudication. International courts apply different tests depending on the facts and circumstances of each case."[32] The lack of a clear and consistent standard of proof at specific courts, and the use of different standards of proof across courts, underscores that the determination of a standard of proof and the evaluation of evidence in international proceedings can properly be understood as judicial practices. A judicial application of a standard of proof, that is, a judicial pronouncement that certain evidence is or is not "convincing," or "sufficient," or "clear and compelling," is performative. Such statements do not simply report on or describe reality, but actually do something, namely, determine an actor's legal liability (or nonliability). Thus, a declaration that evidence has or has not satisfied a standard of proof reframes and reorganizes the evidence that it purports to describe, in ways that bring the facts into line with legal categorizations. Moreover, these performances are highly patterned. They occur within the genre of the judicial opinion, which draws on the tonal, methodological and rhetorical modes associated with this form of writing. Evidentiary pronouncements weave together the discursive and material worlds. The pronouncements of the relevant standard of proof are made in written judicial decisions. However, the finding that a party has or has not met the standard of proof on various issues has material implications for the litigants.

Finally, judicial performances regarding the standard of proof can be undertaken more of less competently. In *DRC* v. *Congo*, the ICJ considered variously whether a claim was "proved to its satisfaction,"[33] sometimes whether it received "convincing evidence,"[34] and sometimes found that a claim failed because the evidence was "unreliable,"[35] "not persuasive,"[36] "not weighty and convincing,"[37] or "not satisfactory."[38] The treatment of evidence in this case, and in others, raises the question of whether similar fact patterns and similar legal issues can be judged under different standards at different tribunals, as discussed in Part III.

The Power of International Courts to Obtain Evidence

The responsibility for identifying and producing the information that informs judicial decisions lies in the first instance with the litigants. There

[32] C. Brown, *A Common Law of International Adjudication* (Oxford: Oxford University Press, 2007), 101.

[33] Armed Activities on the Territory of the Congo (*Democratic Republic of the Congo (DRC)* v. *Uganda*), 2005 ICJ Rep. 1, 77.

[34] Ibid., 93. [35] Ibid., 114. [36] Ibid. [37] Ibid., 118. [38] Ibid., 121.

is a certain logic to this approach. Litigants in international disputes have powerful incentives and, generally, sufficient resources to produce relevant evidence. Moreover, the parties are considered "masters of the evidence . . . because the purpose of the judgment is to decide as between the parties, and [the ICJ's decision] has no binding force except between the parties and in respect of that particular case."[39] Finally, as a practical matter, "[n]o other system would be workable as the [ICJ] has neither the financial means nor the resources to carry out far-reaching investigations in order to ascertain the facts independently."[40] Nonetheless, litigants may not always produce a full and accurate record of the underlying facts, and, as a result, international courts have been granted wide-ranging powers to intervene in the evidentiary process.

The judges at different international tribunals have, however, reached different conclusions regarding their power to order parties, or other actors, to produce evidence. The ICJ Statute provides that the Court may "call upon the [parties] to produce any evidence or to supply any explanations." ICJ judges have read this language as authorizing the Court to *request* parties to produce further evidence, but not as granting the power to *compel* the production of evidence.

Judges at other courts have read similar treaty language as conferring authority to compel the production of evidence. DSU Article 13(1) states that a "member *should* respond promptly and fully to any request for . . . information." In interpreting this provision, the Appellate Body noted that "[a]lthough the word 'should' is often used colloquially to imply an exhortation . . . it is not always used in those ways. It can also be used to express a duty [or] obligation . . . . We are of the view that the word 'should' in [article 13(1)] is used in a normative, rather than a merely exhortative sense. Members are, in other words, under a duty and an obligation to 'respond promptly and fully' to requests made by panels for information . . . "[41]

The international criminal tribunals have the authority, in principle, to order the production of evidence and compel the attendance of witnesses. However, the extent to which these tribunals can, in fact, order states to assist in securing evidence and the attendance of witnesses is less certain.

[39] *Western Sahara*, Advisory opinion, 1975 ICJ Rep. 12, 138 (Separate Opinion of Judge de Castro).

[40] R. Kolb, *The Elgar Companion to the International Court of Justice* (Cheltenham, UK: Edward Elgar Publishers, 2014), 78.

[41] Appellate Body Report, Canada – Measures Affecting the Export of Civilian Aircraft, WT/DS70/AB/R (August 20, 1999), para. 185.

In a recent decision, the ICC Appeals Chamber held that a state is obligated to assist with obtaining the testimony of witnesses found within the state's territory; the Court was careful to note, however, that this principle did not extend to the forcible international transfer of witnesses from one state to another to testify.[42]

Another area involving judges' role in the production of evidence where the practices of international tribunals diverge involves the use of independent technical or scientific experts. The ICJ Statute provides that "[t]he Court may, at any time, entrust any individual, body, bureau, commission, or other organization . . . with the task of carrying out an enquiry or giving an expert opinion." Other international tribunals possess similar authority. The DSU empowers WTO panels to "seek information and technical advice from any individual or body which it deems appropriate."[43] The United Nations Convention on the Law of the Sea (UNCLOS) and the Statute of the Court of Justice of the European Union (CJEU) Statute likewise provide for the appointment of experts.

Despite the similarities in the relevant legal texts, international tribunals differ widely in their use of this power, with some making frequent use of this authority, and others seldom doing so. The ICJ (and its predecessor, the Permanent Court of International Justice), in particular, have been notably reluctant to appoint experts, having done so just a handful of times. On two occasions, for example, the ICJ has appointed experts to assist in the determination of damages. Experts have likewise twice been appointed in cases involving boundary disputes to assist with the process of demarcating the boundary. Only once – in the Court's very first decision in a contentious case – has the ICJ appointed experts to assist with determination of facts relevant to the merits of a dispute. In *Corfu Channel*, appointed experts made a site inspection, conducted practical tests, filed written reports, and responded to questions put by individual members of the Court.[44] Much more frequently, however, the Court has declined to appoint experts, notwithstanding requests by one or both parties to the dispute, or the suggestion of individual judges.[45]

42 *Prosecutor* v. *Ruto and Sang*, No ICC-01/09-01/11 OA 7 OA 8, Decision on Prosecutor's Application for Witness Summonses and resulting Request for State Party Cooperation, October 9, 2014.

43 Understanding on Rules and Procedures Governing the Settlement of Disputes, 1869 UNTS 401 (1994) Art. 13.1.

44 C. E. Foster, "New Clothes for the Emperor? Consultation of Experts by the International Court of Justice," *Journal of International Dispute Settlement*, 5, no. 1 (2014), 143.

45 See, e.g., Oscar Chinn case (*U.K.* v. *Belgium*), PCIJ Rep Series A/B No 63, 107–09 (individual opinion of Judge Anzilotti); Temple of Preah Vihear (*Cambodia*

Thus, within the broad parameters of the Court's statute, the decision to appoint (or not to appoint) experts is a matter of judicial practice, as is the weight to be given to any opinions that are submitted. As discussed more fully below, the Court's practice of only rarely engaging experts has proved problematic in some cases, and prompted widespread scholarly criticism as well as complaints by a number of judges.

Judges at some other international tribunals have been more open to the appointment of experts, with the WTO providing perhaps the most notable counter-example. The DSU provides for the appointment of an "expert review group" (ERG). Appendix 4 to the DSU sets out detailed modalities for such ERGs. Significantly, however, "[i]nstead of appointing ERGs under the detailed provisions of Article 13.2 and Appendix 4 . . ., and notwithstanding the requests of some disputing Members to do so," panels have developed a practice of seeking expert advice from individual experts.[46] As of 2012, WTO panelists had consulted with scientific or technical experts in at least thirteen disputes. Moreover, WTO panelists had sought input from other international organizations due to their specialization or expertise in at least nineteen additional disputes.[47] Thus, of the first 163 WTO panels that were established, no less than thirty-two panels consulted with experts, a rate of nearly 20 percent.

Over time, WTO panelists have developed a set of practices regarding the identification of relevant experts, the actual consultation with experts, and the interpretation of expert reports. Thus, for example, panelists engage in extensive consultations with parties with respect to the need for expert advice, the specific technical areas in which advice is needed, and the names of individual experts who might serve.[48] Moreover, panelists

v. *Thailand*), 1962 ICJ Rep. 6, 100 (dissenting opinion of Judge Koo); Military and Paramilitary Activities in and Against Nicaragua (*Nicaragua* v. *US*), 1986 ICJ Rep. 6, 321–23 (dissenting opinion of Judge Schwebel); Kasikili/Seduku Island (*Botswana v Namibia*), 1999 ICJ Rep. 1045, 1118–19 (separate opinion of Judge Oda); Maritime Delimitation and Territorial Questions (*Qatar* v. *Bahrain*), 2001 ICJ Rep. 40, 275 (dissenting opinion of Judge Torres Bernardez).

46 G. Z. Marceau and J. K. Hawkins, "Experts in WTO Dispute Settlement," *Journal of International Dispute Settlement*, 6, no. 1 (2012), 5. See also Appellate Body Report, Argentina – Measures Affecting Imports of Footwear, Textiles, Apparel and Other Items, WT/DS556/AB/R and Corr.1 (April 11, 1998) (affirming panels' wide discretion to develop practices regarding experts).

47 Marceau and Hawkins, "Experts in WTO Dispute Settlement."

48 D. Baker, M. Goldstein, M. J. Pereyra, and C. Wakoli, "When Science Meets Law: The Rule of Law in the Development of the Panel's Expert Consultation Process" in G. Marceau (ed.), *A History of Law and Lawyers in the GATT/WTO: The Development of*

have developed a set of practices whereby the parties can engage with the experts. Thus, parties are sometimes permitted to comment on the questions panelists pose to the experts; to send their own written questions to the experts, via the panel; and to respond to expert reports.[49] Despite substantial efforts to ensure transparency and fairness in the process, however, panel practices regarding the use of experts can sometimes cause difficulties, as discussed below.

These thumbnail discussions do no more than scratch the surface of international tribunals' evidentiary practices. They are intended to illustrate, by way of example, the wide variety of evidentiary and fact-finding practices that international courts engage in. We now turn to an exploration of the impact of evidentiary practices on the performance of international tribunals.

Evidentiary Practices and Court Performance

The evidentiary practices of international tribunals have a substantial impact on the decisions these courts render. Given the large number and diverse nature of these practices, no universal and unequivocal evaluation of evidentiary practices on tribunal performance is possible; rather, the different practices sometimes serve, and sometimes disserve, systemic interests in developing a full factual record, reaching accurate legal conclusions, and providing fairness and due process to the litigants. In this section, we provide a few examples, primarily involving the ICJ, intended to illustrate the complex and diverse ways that judicial evidentiary practices impact judicial decisions.

Deference to State Sensibilities in the Admissibility of Evidence and the Power to Compel Introduction of Evidence

Part 2 examined the ICJ's unwillingness to impose meaningful restrictions on the introduction of evidence and the Court's conclusion that it lacks power to compel the production of evidence. Both positions are frequently justified by reference to the authority of sovereign states to freely decide what evidence they wish to produce – or *not* produce – in international litigations. Taken together, however, evidentiary practices

the Rule of Law in the Multilateral Trading System (Cambridge: Cambridge University Press, 2015), 439–440.

49 Ibid.

in this area sometimes result in the introduction of excessive or less than fully relevant evidence, and/or the failure to introduce relevant and pertinent evidence.

The Introduction of Evidence

It is not unusual for parties to submit between 5,000 and 7,000 pages of documentation to the Court,[50] and the written record is often substantially more voluminous. In *Barcelona Traction*, for example, the parties submitted some 60,776 pages – or 25 kilograms (55 pounds) of documentation – to the Court, and several other cases have featured evidentiary records of comparable size.[51] Over time, litigants developed the practice of submitting, in the words of one ICJ judge, "every possible scrap of paper, however marginal to the outcome."[52] The tendency to submit any and all evidence, even that of doubtful relevance, imposes enormous burdens on the Court and its staff. It "reduces the efficacy, not to mention the speed, of the treatment given to cases. It complicates the problem of identifying the key issues, and imposes strains on the translation services, not to mention considerable other associated costs."[53] For these reasons, in recent years the judges have begun to show less deference to litigants and undertaken substantial efforts to streamline evidentiary submissions. These efforts have enjoyed some success, and have helped the Court to dispose of a backlog of older cases and to dispose of newer cases more efficiently.[54]

This is not to say that the Court's traditional deference to sovereign sensibilities in evidentiary matters has entirely disappeared. Consider *Qatar* v. *Bahrain*, which involved, *inter alia*, the question of which state had sovereignty over the Hawar Islands. In support of its claim, Qatar submitted eighty-two letters, affidavits, maps, and other documents. Having not seen any of this evidence previously, Bahrain engaged forensic experts and historians to examine these documents. The forensic experts found a large number of "paper distortions and splices, handwriting disguises, stamp irregularities, and other

[50] S. Talmon, "Article 43" in A. Zimmermann et al. (eds.), *The Statute of the International Court of Justice: A Commentary* (Oxford: Oxford University Press, 2006), 998.

[51] E.g., M. Bedjaoui, "The 'Manufacture' of Judgments at the International Court of Justice," *Pace Yearbook of International Law*, 3, no. 29 (1991), 36–37.

[52] Higgins, "Respecting Sovereign States," 129.

[53] R. Kolb, *The International Court of Justice*, 962.

[54] See, Talmon, "Article 43."

flaws."[55] The historians found a different set of flaws, including documents "riddled with historical anachronisms, letters written to and from persons dead at the time of the alleged writing, letters written to and from officials whose positions did not exist, [and] letters written in Arabic between two English speakers."[56] As one expert concluded:

> there are so many incongruities, inconsistencies, false information, anachronisms, inappropriate sheets of recycled paper, and suspect seals that permeate this collection of documents that they cumulatively add up to a massive fraud. My overall conclusion, in addition to my document by document conclusions, is that absolutely no confidence may be placed that any of these suspect documents are genuine. They should be ignored and no credence placed on the veracity of any substantive matters purporting to arise from their content.[57]

Upon receiving these reports, Bahrain formally challenged Qatar's evidence. After retaining its own set of experts, several of whom found the documents to contain numerous "flaws," Qatar declared that "it will disregard all the challenged documents for the purposes of the present case so as to enable to the Court to address the merits of the case without further procedural complications."[58] Qatar also expressed "regret at the situation that [had] arisen and the inconvenience that this [had] caused the Court and Bahrain."[59]

The Court's judgment provides a skeletal narrative of the submission and withdrawal of the documents. Remarkably, however, the judgment offers absolutely no criticism – or even commentary – regarding this episode. Thus, the Court refers to documents whose "authenticity had been challenged" but carefully – and surely deliberately – avoids using the words forgery, fraud, counterfeit, fabrication, fake, or related terms. Writing separately, Judge ad hoc Fortier chastised the Court for "chos[ing] not to address the issue," instead "simply disregard[ing] and fail[ing] to take into consideration this

[55] W. M. Reisman and C. Skinner, *Fraudulent Evidence before Public International Tribunals* (Cambridge: Cambridge University Press, 2014), 180.

[56] Ibid. [57] Ibid. 185, quoting J. C. Wilkenson, Historical Report (September 3, 1997).

[58] Interim Report on the Question of the Authenticity of the 82 Documents Annexed to the Memorial and Counter-Memorial of the State of Qatar and Challenged by Bahrain, para. 7, submitted in Maritime Delimitation and Territorial Questions Between Qatar and Bahrain, 2001 ICJ Rep. 40.

[59] Letter from Agent of the State of Qatar to Registrar of the International Court of Justice, December 15, 1998, submitted in Ibid.

unprecedented incident."[60] Judge Fortier recounted how the submission and withdrawal of the documents had "a direct bearing on the substance of various important aspects of the case,"[61] and concluded that this "extraordinary incident" had "polluted" and "infected" the entirety of Qatar's case. Fortier was the only judge to raise "the damage that would have been done to the administration of international justice, indeed to the very position of this Court, if the challenge by Bahrain of the authenticity of these documents had not led Qatar, eventually, [to disclaim reliance on the challenged documents.]"[62]

It is difficult to understand the Court's treatment of Qatar's forged evidence as rooted in anything other than a traditional view of the deference due to sovereign litigants. To be sure, the Court's heightened respect for state sensibilities may well be rooted in powerful structural realities of international litigation, including that the Court has jurisdiction only by consent of the parties, and lacks any direct means to compel compliance. Indeed, the Court's deference to sovereign sensibilities in evidentiary matters may contribute to its ever-increasing caseload and the relatively high rates of compliance with its judgments. Nevertheless, it is not difficult to conclude that the Court's reticence to comment upon, let alone condemn, this massive effort at fraud hardly reflects well upon the ICJ. Any use of fraudulent evidence – let alone massive forgery – is antithetical to the Court's efforts to discern the truth and threatens to undermine the legitimacy of any judgment that follows. Given that the challenged evidence in this action would have constituted a major fraud upon the Court, and could have called into question the Court's ability to fairly adjudicate any fact-intensive dispute, the judges' failure to condemn Qatar's actions is striking. This (in) action may have helped Qatar to save face, particularly in a context where their claims to sovereignty over the islands were rejected. As a systemic matter, however, the Court's silence runs a serious risk of incentivizing future litigants to undertake similar efforts to introduce fraudulent evidence, as they could reasonably conclude that if they are not caught, they can reap enormous benefits, and if they are caught they will suffer minimal consequences.

[60] Maritime Delimitation and Territorial Questions between Qatar and Bahrain, 2001 ICJ Rep. 40, 452.
[61] Ibid. [62] Ibid.

The Nonintroduction of Evidence

As noted, the ICJ can request, but not compel, the production of evidence. The Court has authority to draw adverse inferences when parties refuse to produce evidence, but it has developed a practice of not doing so. Taken together, these evidentiary practices can likewise compromise the Court's ability to render judgment based upon a full and accurate factual record.

This problem is not new; it arose, for example, in *Corfu Channel*, the ICJ's first contentious case, which involved British allegations that Albania was responsible for damage caused by mines to UK warships engaged in innocent passage thru the channel. When Britain's lawyers filed this action, they were unaware of a naval operation order ("XCU") that contained a number of statements difficult to reconcile with Britain's theory of innocent passage.[63] "XCU" was, however, referenced in a different document Britain submitted to the Court. Upon Albania's request, the President of the Court asked Britain to produce the document. This request prompted to numerous contentious exchanges involving the British Attorney General, Solicitor General, First Lord of the Admiralty, Lord Chancellor and Prime Minister, and eventually resulted in a decision by the Prime Minister *not* to disclose the document.[64] The Court's judgment stated:

> [T]he Court requested the United Kingdom Agent to produce the document referred to as XCU for the use of the Court. These documents were not produced, the Agent pleading naval secrecy; and the United Kingdom witnesses declined to answer questions relating to them. It is not therefore possible to know the real content of these naval orders. The Court cannot, however, draw from this refusal to produce the orders any conclusions differing from those to which the actual events gave rise [namely, that the British warships were engaged in innocent passage].[65]

Thus, Britain deliberately suppressed a highly relevant and probative document, but as the Court declined to draw any adverse inference, the

[63] For example, when Sir Hartley Shawcross, the Attorney General, learned of the document, he advised the Prime Minister its disclosure could "result in a judgment very adverse to ourselves." Reisman and Skinner, *Fraudulent Evidence*, 63 (quoting PREM 8/1312, Letter from Hartley Shawcross, Attorney General, to Clement R. Attlee, Prime Minister (October 19, 1946).

[64] A. Carty, "The Corfu Channel Case – and the Missing Admiralty Orders," *Law and Practice of International Courts and Tribunals*, 3, no. 1 (2004) pincite, page 1.

[65] Corfu Channel (*United Kingdom of Great Britain and Northern Ireland* v. *Albania*), 1949 ICJ Rep. 4, 32.

UK suffered no adverse consequences. It is less certain the same can be said of the Court's performance. Document XCU was eventually declassified. After review of the document – and of the exchanges over production of the document – a broad scholarly consensus has developed that Britain's motivations for nondisclosure had very little to do with naval secrecy. Rather, the decision not to produce the document was instead motivated by Britain's concern that the document's contents would cause political embarrassment and harm its position in the pending litigation.

British officials, and some scholars, have debated whether the blame for what happened lies with the navy or with Britain's lawyers. An alternative approach might suggest that if blame is to be attributed, it should be assigned to the Court for its failure to draw any negative inferences from Britain's refusal to produce the document. It is difficult to avoid the conclusion that, in its landmark first decision, the Court's evidentiary practices resulted in a substantially incomplete, if not misleading, understanding of the underlying facts.

Similar issues arose in the *Genocide Convention* case, involving allegations by Bosnia and Herzegovina that Serbia and Montenegro was responsible for acts of genocide. In the course of litigation, a dispute arose over transcripts of certain meetings involving the Presidents of the Federal Republic of Yugoslavia and the Republics of Serbia and Montenegro, and high-ranking military officials. Serbia had disclosed the documents to the ICTY in the *Milosevic* case, but the transcripts were publicly available only in a heavily redacted form. Bosnia requested that Serbia produce an unredacted version of the transcript, believing that they would show Serbia's participation in the Srebrenica massacre. In the alternative, Bosnia asked the Court to draw appropriate inferences from any failure to produce the transcripts. Serbia indicated that it would not produce the documents on the grounds that they had been classified as a "military secret" and their contents a matter of "national security interest."[66] The Court declined to ask Serbia to produce the documents, stating that Bosnia had "extensive documentation and other evidence available to it," particularly from the ICTY.[67] The Court "note[d]" Bosnia's "suggestion that the Court may be free to draw its own conclusions" from Serbia's failure to produce this evidence, but declined to draw any adverse inference.[68]

[66] Application of the Convention on the Prevention and Punishment of the Crime of Genocide (*Bosnia and Herzegovina* v. *Serbia and Montenegro*), 2007 ICJ Rep. 43, 128.

[67] Ibid., 129. [68] Ibid.

From the perspective of the Court's interests in a full and accurate factual record, and in doing justice as between the litigants, the Court's evidentiary practice appears problematic. As Vice President Khasawneh noted in his dissenting opinion, it was "a reasonable expectation that those documents would have shed light on the central questions of intent and attributability. The reasoning given by the Court [that Bosnia had access to extensive documentation and ICTY records] is worse than its failure to [request that Serbia produce the documents]."[69] Judge Khasawneh also criticized the Court's failure to draw any inferences from Serbia's failure to produce documents: "It would normally be expected that the consequences of the note taken by the Court would be to shift the *onus probandi* or to allow a more liberal recourse to inference as the Court's past practice and considerations of common sense and fairness would all demand."[70] Judge Khasawneh's critique has particular force, given that Serbia had already disclosed the documents in full to another international tribunal.

Significantly, the Court's practice in these cases is not compelled by its Statute or rules. Indeed, the Statute not only empowers the Court to "call upon" litigants to produce evidence, but also directs that "[f]ormal note shall be taken of any refusal." Some judges have urged the Court to draw adverse inferences in cases where "a party fails to produce on demand a relevant document which is in its possession."[71] Notably, other international tribunals have adopted different practices regarding adverse inferences for nonproduction of evidence. For example, notwithstanding the lack of explicit textual authority in the DSU, the Appellate Body has made clear that panels have authority to draw adverse inferences in response to the nonproduction of evidence,[72] and subsequent panels have at times exercised this authority,[73] and at other times declined to do so.[74]

In *Corfu Channel* and the *Genocide Convention* cases, the Court confronted a tension between its need (and the parties' need) for a full and complete factual record, and a pragmatic concern with respecting

[69] Ibid., 254. [70] Ibid., 255.

[71] Barcelona Traction, Light and Power Company, Ltd. (*Belgium* v. *Spain*), 1970 ICJ Rep. 3, 217 (Separate Opinion of Judge Jessup).

[72] Appellate Body Report, Canada—Measures Affecting the Export of Civilian Aircraft, WT/DS70/AB/R (August 2, 1999), paras. 200, 202, 205.

[73] Panel Report, Turkey – Measures Affecting the Importation of Rice, WT/DS334/R (September 21, 2007), paras. 7.106–7.

[74] Panel Report, Korea – Measures Affecting Trade in Commercial Vessels, WT/DS273/R (March 7, 2005), para. 7.401.

a sovereign state's right to withhold evidence in certain circumstances. To be sure, there is no guarantee that the drawing of an adverse inference would have resulted in a more accurate decision in these or any other particular cases. Demonstrating the willingness to draw adverse inferences in appropriate cases may, however, have important systemic implications. In particular, doing so might ensure that that states are more likely to cooperate in future litigations, which would further the search for truth and would lead to more accurate application of the law in future cases. The Court's contrary practice can be understood as incentivizing states not to produce relevant evidence that is harmful to that state's litigation position.

Standards of Proof

As noted above, the ICJ and many other international tribunals have not clearly articulated the applicable standard of proof, and have applied different standards in different cases. The uncertainty that follows necessarily complicates the parties' litigation strategies and can undermine predictability and certainly in the law. It has also sparked substantial debate and critique in the relevant community of practice, including among international judges themselves.

One prominent example of this dialogue can be found in the multiple opinions issued in the *Oil Platforms* case, involving Iranian claims that the United States had unlawfully destroyed three offshore Iranian oil production complexes. The United States argued that these acts were taken in self-defense, following armed attacks on US vessels for which Iran was responsible. The Court stated that it "has examined with great care the evidence and arguments presented on each side, and finds that the evidence indicative of Iranian responsibility for the attack on [the US vessels] is not sufficient to support" the US contentions. The Court concluded that the United States had therefore "not ... discharged" its burden of proof on this issue.[75]

Several judges were highly critical of this analysis. In his separate opinion, Judge Owada stated that "I should have liked to see the Court engage in a much more in-depth examination of this difficult problem of ascertaining the facts of the case ... including those relating to the questions of the burden of proof and the standard of proof, in the

[75] Oil Platforms (*Islamic Republic of Iran* v. *United States of America*), 2003 ICJ Rep. 161.

concrete context of the present case."[76] Judge Burgenthal's separate opinion was more pointed:

> One might ask . . . where the test of "insufficient" evidence comes from . . . and by reference to what standards the Court applies it? What is meant by "insufficient" evidence? Does the evidence have to be "convincing," "preponderant," "overwhelming" or "beyond a reasonable doubt" to be sufficient? The Court never spells out what the here relevant standard of proof is.[77]

Judge Higgins took up this theme in her separate opinion, writing:

> [I]t may immediately be noted that neither here nor elsewhere does the Court explain the *standard* of proof to be met. . . . [I]n a case in which so very much turns on evidence, it was to be expected that the Court would clearly have stated the standard of evidence that was necessary for a party to have discharged its burden of proof . . . Beyond a general agreement that the graver the charge the more confidence there must be in the evidence relied on, there is thus little to help parties . . . as to what is likely to satisfy the Court. Other judicial and arbitral tribunals have of necessity recognized the need to engage in this legal task themselves, in some considerable detail. The principal judicial organ of the United Nations should likewise make clear what standards of proof it requires to establish what sorts of facts. Even if the Court does not wish to enunciate a general standard . . . it should in my view have decided, and been transparent about, the standard of proof required in this particular case.[78]

Inconsistent or unclear standards produce confusion and uncertainty for judges, litigants, and other actors. They also permit similar fact patterns and similar issues to be judged under different standards, potentially producing different outcomes. For example, in several cases the ICTY has considered whether genocide and other serious violations of international humanitarian law were committed in the former Yugoslavia, including particularly at Srebrenica. ICTY judges, using the "proof beyond a reasonable doubt" standard, convicted individuals of genocide.[79] In the *Bosnia* v. *Serbia* case, the ICJ considered whether genocide was committed in the former Yugoslavia, including particularly at Srebrenica. The ICJ used a different standard of proof, requiring "evidence fully conclusive" of the commission of genocide and attribution of those acts to the state.

76 Ibid., 306, 323 (Separate Opinion of Judge Owada).

77 Ibid., 270 (Separate Opinion of Judge Burgenthal).

78 Ibid., 233–234 (Separate Opinion of Judge Higgins).

79 See, e.g., *Prosecutor* v. *Krstić, Judgment, Appeals Chamber*, No. IT-98–33 (2004), para. 81; *Prosecutor* v. *Blagojević, Appeals Chamber*, No. IT-02–60-A (2007), para. 226.

Applying this standard, the ICJ found that genocide had been committed in Srebrenica, but that Serbia-Montenegro did not commit, conspire to commit, or incite to commit genocide, and had not been complicit in the commission of genocide.[80]

It is not *per se* troubling that the tribunals would use different standards of proof – the ICTY has jurisdiction over *individuals* and adjudges *criminal* responsibility while the ICJ has jurisdiction over *states*, which are subject to *noncriminal* liability. Nonetheless, it is somewhat anomalous that that the ICTY judges, using an apparently higher standard of proof, are handing down convictions while the ICJ judges, ostensibly applying a lower standard of proof to the same or related fact patterns, is disinclined to find a state directly responsible for genocide.[81]

Like other evidentiary practices, the standard of proof is not reducible to the Court's statute or rules. The inconsistencies among judges within a single case, and across cases (and courts), may reflect unresolved differences between judges trained in common law systems, who are familiar with clear and consistent standards of proof, and judges trained in civil law systems, where standards of proof are much less formalized.[82] But even if the causes are unclear, the effects are less so. First, as a practical matter, the lack of clarity substantially complicates the parties' litigation strategy, for they often do not know precisely what level of proof they must establish in order to prevail in their dispute. Second, as a normative matter, the lack of clarity and consistency in standards of proof disserves the interest in transparency and seems incompatible with notions of procedural fairness. Third, as a political matter, the lack of clarity and consistency in standards of proof empowers the judges by maximizing their flexibility. This consequence has led some to go so far as to suggest that "[t] he Court's prime objective as to standard of proof appears to have been to retain a freedom in evaluating the evidence, relying on the facts and circumstances in each case."[83] Whether or not this political judgment is entirely accurate, it seems clear that these

[80] Application of the Convention on the Prevention and Punishment of the Crime of Genocide (*Bosnia-Herzegovina* v. *Serbia-Montenegro*), 2007 ICJ Rep. 17.

[81] See, e.g., A. C. Asuncion, "Pulling the Stops on Genocide: The State or the Individual?," *European Journal of International Law*, 20, no. 4 (2010), 1195.

[82] E.g., R. Higgins, President of the ICJ, Speech to the Sixth Committee of the General Assembly – Judicial determination of facts (November 2, 2007) (suggesting that the failure to establish a clear and consistent standard of proof "is caused by the gap between the explicitly standard-setting approach of the common law and the 'intime conviction du judge' familiar under civil law").

[83] Ibid.

actors' sensitization and the development of a judicial culture supporting the Court's performance would be a long-term process, African Court officials have made this program a fixture of the Court's work.

The African Court's activities, and the similar activities among other ICs, invite us to reconsider how ICs try to influence their own performance. Generally, the scholarship on ICs focuses on their core mandate of adjudication, where international judges interpret and apply international law, and settle international disputes. This chapter, however, shows that ICs can move beyond adjudication and their mandated activities to adopt policies and practices aimed at socializing actors in their legal regimes. Through strategies such as diplomacy, training, and outreach, ICs attempt to socialize relevant actors in their legal regimes (e.g., IC officials, government officials, national judges, and civil society organizations) into ICs' norms, rules, and procedures – and thus influence various dimensions of ICs' performance.

After reviewing existing accounts of socialization, including the concept's limited application to ICs, the chapter presents a framework for conceptualizing ICs' socialization strategies and their intended influence on IC performance. The framework draws distinctions between ICs' strategies for influencing actors internal or external to a court, and for affecting ICs' actual or perceived performance. The chapter elucidates ICs' three core strategies, as well as the challenges to IC performance they address. An analysis of reports from all twenty-three permanent, operational ICs shows the prevalence of and variation in ICs' internal and external socialization strategies. The chapter thus reveals how ICs view socialization as a key means of influencing various dimensions of their performance.

Socialization and ICs

Socialization is a concept that has been taken up by constructivist scholars of international relations (IR) and, more recently, by some scholars of international law (IL).[1] It is the process through which principled ideas become norms in the sense of collective understandings of appropriate

[1] This IR literature generally does not study socialization specifically vis-à-vis legal norms. Though relatively few IL scholars have drawn on the insights offered by constructivist IR theory (Brunnée and Toope 2013: 138), IL scholars are increasingly making connection between socialization and IL, including Koh's (1996; 1997) transnational legal process theory, Brunnée and Toope's (2010) interactional account of IL, and Goodman and Jinks's (2004; 2013) work on states' socialization in the area of human rights.

conduct, which lead to changes in identities, interests, and behavior. Socialization can affect individuals within organizations, states and nonstate actors within international society, and actors within states. Particular international actors can drive socialization processes. These agents of socialization, often referred to as "norm entrepreneurs," can be virtually any international actor, including states, international organizations (IOs), and transnational advocacy networks.[2] IOs are not only "social environments" in which socialization can occur (Johnston 2001), but they also can be "teachers of norms" (Finnemore 1993). ICs are no exception.

These agents of socialization can influence actors' beliefs and behavior by promoting two key processes of persuasion and social influence (Johnston 2001).[3] Agents of socialization can persuade actors by exposing them to counter-attitudinal information, which can change actors' beliefs and behavior (Johnston 2001: 496–499). Agents of socialization can also affect actors through social influence, which promotes actors' conformity with norms of their community based on the distribution of social punishments and rewards. They can, for example, shame actors for not behaving in accordance with their role and identity through shunning, excluding, and demeaning these actors, but they can also praise and reward behavior for conforming to role expectations (Johnston 2001: 299). These socializing processes can culminate in internalization, where norms are so deeply embedded that actors take them for granted (Finnemore and Sikkink 1998; Risse and Sikkink 1999; Checkel 2005; Bearce and Bondanella 2007). But they can also be influential through "weaker" socialization, where actors conform to community norms without internalizing them (e.g., Johnston 2001; Goodman and Jinks 2004; Checkel 2005). Socialization, however, is not a linear process; it often proceeds in fits and starts, and may or may not progress (e.g., Risse and Sikkink 1999).

[2] There is a broad literature on how states and elites (e.g., Ikenberry and Kupchan 1990; Wang 2003; Wiener 2008), and nonstate actors, such as NGOs and transnational advocacy networks (e.g., Finnemore and Sikkink 1998; Checkel 1999; Risse, Ropp, and Sikkink 1999), promote socialization processes.

[3] Scholars posit numerous socialization mechanisms (see e.g., Park 2014), including coercion, persuasion, social influence, and acculturation. Socialization through coercion is largely irrelevant to ICs, which lack the material capacity for coercion. Acculturation (Goodman and Jinks 2004; 2013) is similar to social influence (Johnston 2001) but does not require that actors conform because they recognize the legitimacy of the reference group's norms. This distinction is irrelevant to understanding socialization strategies specifically.

The scholarship on ICs has only minimally engaged with socialization and its role in ICs' performance. Scholars, for instance, have recognized the crucial role of transnational norm advocacy in the emergence and development of the International Criminal Court (e.g., Deitelhoff 2009). In addition, scholars have shown that European legal communities' socialization has played a critical role in European legal integration (e.g., Vauchez 2014). The interaction of the Court of Justice of the European Union's (CJEU's) jurisprudence with national courts and litigation communities created a "virtuous cycle" where more actors were socialized into the system (Stone Sweet 2010: 17). These accounts, while important beginnings for the socialization research agenda on ICs, are limited in their scope. The agents of socialization are generally legal elites, transnational advocacy networks, and states. IC agency, when it is considered, is largely through adjudication and rulings. These accounts also tend to use single case studies and lack comparative analysis across different ICs.

Essentially, the literature has yet to fully recognize ICs' agency vis-à-vis socialization and how this can relate to their performance. This chapter aims to fill this gap by showing how ICs formulate and implement socialization strategies targeting various actors in their legal regimes and aiming to influence their performance.[4] It therefore captures a realm of ICs' decision-making and activity that has received little attention.

ICs, Socialization, and Performance: A Framework

From a constructivist perspective, any organization's performance depends on the degree to which relevant actors are socialized into its standards of legitimate, appropriate behavior. Each IC has its associated collection of norms, rules, and procedures that should guide actors' beliefs and behavior. These norms, rules, and procedures can be evident from ICs' founding treaties, but they can also develop over time based on ICs' judgments, legal doctrines, institutional reforms, and so on. ICs' norms, rules, and procedures are intended to influence not only IC officials' behavior, but also how various actors, including states, national judges, and civil society groups, engage with an IC. There are, for instance, norms and rules of judicial conduct in ICs, procedures for

[4] The chapter builds on De Silva's (2016) study of how ICs develop strategies beyond adjudication and can act as agents of socialization.

national judges to refer cases to ICs, and rules obligating states to cooperate and comply with ICs. The degree to which these relevant actors internalize ICs' norms, rules, and procedures influences their behavior and, by extension, ICs' performance.

ICs' core activity of adjudication can socialize actors in ICs' legal regimes. For example, the process of adjudication is inherently based on legal argumentation and persuasion. In addition, ICs' rulings praise compliance and shame noncompliance with international law, which can exert social pressure for actors to conform to legal rules. These adjudicatory processes, however, may not be sufficient to socialize actors and effectively tackle ICs' performance challenges. They may not address the full range of the norms, rules, and procedures that underpin ICs' performance, and may not reach all the relevant actors in ICs' legal regimes. Socialization through adjudication would highly depend on ICs' caseloads and the extent to which IC decisions are disseminated, for example.

IC officials, as strategic actors who are conscious that IC performance matters, can therefore turn to alternative means of socializing actors and influencing IC performance. While an IC's primary mandate is adjudication and rendering judicial decisions, IC judges and administrative officials also collectively decide on the organizational policies and practices that guide an IC's diverse activities. Many ICs conduct strategic planning exercises, and judges at the International Tribunal for the Law of the Sea (ITLOS), for instance, have committees dedicated to particular issues, such as finances and public relations. Through this broader decision-making, ICs can assess and respond to their performance challenges, and thus can develop strategies specifically oriented towards socializing actors in their legal regimes. An IC's judges and administrative officials can identify actors that apparently have not been socialized into ICs' norms, rules, and procedures, and formulate strategies involving new forms of communication and interaction that could promote persuasion and social influence. Through these strategies, ICs can try to guide actors' beliefs and behavior, and thus influence IC performance. The AfCHPR judges' evaluation of the Court's challenges, and development of strategies to sensitize actors and develop a judicial culture, is a clear example. ICs' strategies generally use IC officials (typically judges and other senior officials, such as the registrar) as the agents of socialization who, acting on behalf of the IC, interact with and attempt to socialize ICs' targets. Still, ICs may also decide to use other agents (e.g., international legal experts, NGOs) to socialize actors. The ICC, for example, actively encourages NGOs to persuade states to increase their support for the Court (De Silva 2017).

As Squatrito et al. highlight in Chapter 1, IC performance can be conceptualized based on both process and outcomes, and IC officials' and other actors' socialization underpins both dimensions of performance. ICs' process performance – the degree to which IC practices conform to procedural standards – highly depends on the socialization of IC officials and other relevant actors (e.g., litigants) into ICs' norms, rules, and procedures. ICs' outcome performance – the degree to which ICs attain substantive goals, such as dispute settlement and compliance – also depends on actors both within and beyond ICs being socialized into and behaving in accordance with ICs' norms, rules, and procedures. Thus, if these various actors are not socialized into ICs' norms, rules, and procedures, ICs can face performance challenges.

ICs' socialization strategies, therefore, can target actors both *internal* and *external* to the court (Table 9.1), as both sets of actors' adherence to ICs' norms, rules, and procedures can influence ICs' performance. ICs can aim to socialize judges and administrative officials, so they learn the appropriate norms, rules, and procedures associated with their respective roles that underpin the IC's overall performance. Recognizing that ICs' performance is contingent on other actors, ICs can target their socialization strategies to states and other relevant actors in their legal regimes, so they fulfill their appropriate roles and contribute to ICs' performance.

Furthermore, as ICs perform their activities to serve particular objectives and stakeholders, these external actors' perceptions of ICs'

Table 9.1 *IC socialization strategies*

	Internal Strategy	External Strategy
Actual Performance	Socializing IC judges & administrators into their appropriate roles	Socializing relevant actors in ICs' legal regimes into their appropriate roles
Perceived Performance		Socializing ICs' stakeholders into norms for evaluating ICs' performance

performance matter.[5] Multiple disciplines draw the distinction between actual and perceived performance, including management studies (for organizations), marketing studies (for consumer satisfaction), and computer engineering (for human satisfaction with websites, software, and apps). The central idea is that factors beyond how an entity actually performs can influence users' or observers' perceptions of and satisfaction with that performance. The distinction between actual and perceived performance is equally applicable to ICs. ICs' stakeholders may receive information concerning ICs' performance (e.g., the number of cases they adjudicate, or compliance with their rulings), but their perceptions of ICs' performance are shaped by normative standards against which they evaluate this information. Stakeholders' assessments of IC performance thus depend on their normative preferences vis-à-vis ICs' roles, behavior, and influence. If these actors' norms of evaluation are not aligned with how ICs believe they should be evaluated, ICs will face challenges to their perceived performance among their stakeholders – those for whom IC performance matters most.

ICs' external socialization strategies therefore can target both their *actual* and *perceived* performance (Table 9.1). To influence their actual performance, ICs' strategies can aim to socialize relevant actors into the norms, rules, and procedures associated with their appropriate roles within ICs' legal regimes. But to change their perceived performance, ICs can direct their strategies towards socializing their stakeholders into appropriate norms for evaluating ICs' performance. The two forms of performance are obviously intrinsically linked: Higher performance in real terms can also improve perceived performance. But drawing this distinction recognizes that, independent of any actual change in performance, shaping norms of evaluation can increase (or decrease) perceived performance among ICs' users and observers. ICs' socialization strategies are therefore complementary. ICs can socialize actors to change their behavior in ways that support ICs' performance in real terms, but then also socialize actors to ensure they appropriately perceive this performance. While these strategies are analytically distinct, ICs may pursue both within the same policy or practice vis-à-vis external actors in their legal regimes.

[5] The distinction between perceived and actual performance is irrelevant for ICs' internal socialization strategies. First, the same norms that define IC officials' appropriate roles would also guide their perceptions of their own performance. In addition, ICs' strategies would target the perceptions of the stakeholders they are intended to serve, which are external, not internal, to the court.

Thus, as Table 9.1 shows, to improve their performance in real terms, ICs can focus their socialization strategies internally or externally. ICs' socialization strategies can also aim to influence their performance in real terms or shape their stakeholders' and observers' perceptions of it. The following sections elucidate how ICs formulate these three core socialization strategies in response to their performance challenges.

Internal Strategies

Socialization within an organization can improve its performance, as the study of "organizational socialization" in the discipline of management studies attests (e.g., Wanberg 2012). ICs' performance significantly depends on the behavior of its judges and administrative officials, and whether they are socialized into their respective roles within an IC. ICs' founding treaties and rules of procedure often explicitly set the norms, rules, and procedures that define IC officials' appropriate roles. For example, they include provisions regarding a judge's legal expertise, independence, and grounds for removal from office. Many aspects of IC officials' roles, however, are not specified and left open to the discretion of ICs, such as officials' freedom of expression and extrajudicial activities (BIIJ 2009: 25–30). ICs can fill these gaps through informal norms or, occasionally, formal policy documents.

There is an expanding body of evidence to support the link between socialization, IC officials' behavior, and, therefore, IC performance. Studies of domestic judges, such as state and federal judges in the US,[6] find that judicial socialization "produces a subculture of justice and encourages judges to adhere to prevailing norms, practices, and precedents."[7] Other studies directly connect socialization to how judges exercise discretion, saying judicial socialization contributes to "a perimeter beyond which judicial decisions are unlikely to stray" (Garrison 1995: 413), and can affect judges' fairness, impartiality, and efficiency in processing cases (Goldberg 1985; Gavison 1987; Geyh 1993). Scholars are increasingly applying sociological or constructivist approaches to studying international judicial behavior as well (Voeten 2014: 561–566), though these accounts generally consider "prebench" rather

[6] For an overview of the seminal studies of judicial socialization at the domestic level, see Maveety (2003, 175–186). Cook (1971) was among the first to recognize socialization's importance for understanding judicial behavior.

[7] Spohn (1990: 1212) makes this argument to support her finding that sentencing decisions reached by judges of different races are less dissimilar than some would expect.

than "on-the-job" socialization.[8] For example, one key study of international judges suggests that previous experience and professional background can be "almost more important" than their nationality (Terris et al. 2007: 64). Another study of European Court of Human Rights (ECtHR) judges indicates the importance of prebench socialization, as judges who were former diplomats were more likely to accept *raison d'état* and a higher margin of appreciation for member states than judges from other professional backgrounds (Voeten 2008). Courts' administrative officials have been overlooked in this work, but socialization could be equally consequential for their behavior and contributions to ICs' performance.

Challenges to IC Officials' Socialization and ICs' Actual Performance

The degree to which IC officials are socialized into their appropriate roles can vary. One area of variation is the degree to which IC officials are socialized into ICs' norms, rules, and procedures when they are selected for their roles within ICs. Of course, the IC officials whom states appoint or ICs hire will inevitably have a basic level of socialization that qualifies them for their positions. Judges, for example, must be socialized into the professional and reputational norms associated with their position in order to perform their duties, and they are largely appointed based on their demonstrable experience adhering to these standards. The same can be said for administrative officials. But judicial appointments can be highly politicized, rather than a mere search for expertise, so states can appoint less than ideally qualified judges (Mackenzie et al. 2010). International judges can be career judges, academics, former diplomats, and private practitioners, but they can also be politicians with barely any legal experience (Voeten 2014: 565–566).

Part of the challenge is that ICs demand officials with rare combinations of experiences and skills, and the most qualified officials who are appointed or hired still may not be fully qualified. Often, particularly in developing countries or regions, few candidates have the full range of expertise required for fulfilling many judicial and administrative roles at ICs. A registrar might have experience with international law but not in administration, or a judge might have expertise in some areas of an IC's law but not others. The procedures for electing judges for the

[8] This distinction is commonly used in the literature on the judicial socialization of domestic judges (e.g., Carp and Wheeler 1972).

International Criminal Court (ICC), for instance, acknowledge that few judges possess all the various skills required and thus a combination of judges with particular sets of skills is necessary. ICC judges are elected from two distinct lists of candidates, one of which has candidates with competence in criminal law and procedure, while the other has candidates with competence in relevant areas of international law (Art. 36, Rome Statute). Essentially, each IC has its own unique set of norms, rules, and procedures, which even highly experienced officials need to learn. Moreover, ICs' norms, rules, and procedures can evolve over time, and states occasionally amend ICs' mandates (e.g., access rules, jurisdictions). For example, when states formally expanded the jurisdiction of the Economic Community of West African States (ECOWAS) Court of Justice (ECCJ) to cover human rights, the existing group of judges lacked human rights expertise (Alter et al. 2013).

At the collective level, significant variation in officials' levels of socialization can have negative implications for cooperation and performance. ICs, as regional or international organizations, attract officials with diverse backgrounds. Judicial and administrative officials come to ICs from different states, regions, and legal systems. But this diversity can potentially inhibit their collaboration and collective performance, as different backgrounds can contribute to distinctive and potentially conflicting ways of performing professional roles. For example, judges from civil law systems are more investigative than common law judges, which function more as arbiters between parties that present their arguments. In the realm of international commercial arbitration, there were clashes between different forms of expertise (European academic law vs. American-style Wall Street law) (Dezalay and Garth 1998). In international adjudication, judges with different professional backgrounds have exhibited different approaches to judicial reasoning, case management, and solving institutional issues (Terris et al. 2007: 64).

ICs' Internal Socialization Strategies for Influencing Their Actual Performance

To address these challenges, ICs can design strategies for socializing their officials and improving ICs' performance. With these strategies, ICs do not merely rely on officials' previous socialization or officials' socialization through their day-to-day activities on-the-job. For instance, judges' on-the-job socialization would depend heavily on the breadth of their dockets, so these effects could be limited in ICs with small caseloads or with judges serving only part-time. Rather, ICs' internal socialization strategies are targeted to particular areas of IC officials' behavior and IC performance. For internal socialization strategies, ICs can arrange for experts in these areas to socialize their officials into their appropriate roles, and IC officials can also socialize other officials within an IC. These internal strategies increase IC officials' interactions through training and dialogue, which can facilitate processes of persuasion and social influence.

ICs can organize training for judges and administrative officials through specialized courses (e.g., on a particular area of law they are required to interpret and apply, or a form of judgment writing). ICs may bring in a qualified individual or organization, such as a jurist or management consultant, or IC officials may travel for training elsewhere. The training is inherently normative, oriented towards disseminating "best" practices to IC officials, and improving their ability to conduct judicial proceedings and effectively administrate the IC. Thus, IC officials can encounter counter-attitudinal information and be persuaded to adopt particular norms, rules, and procedures associated with their roles within an IC. Training can also clarify appropriate and inappropriate behavior for IC officials.

The East African Court of Justice (EACJ), for example, arranged for its judges to attend a training course on arbitration – an area of the EACJ's jurisdiction that had barely been used and the judges lacked experience. A "leading figure within, and pioneer of, the field of international arbitration" (EACJ 2015: para. 9) facilitated the sessions, which emphasized that "arbitration is popular in the business community as well as the investors" and that the EACJ can play "a big role in enforcing arbitration awards" (EACJ 2015: para. 5). The session also aimed to "moderniz[e] the Court's existing rules of Arbitration in order to optimize the Court's efficiency as an arbitration institution" (EACJ 2015: para. 5). The training was thus aimed at persuading judges to perform their appropriate role in arbitration, according to particular, "modern" normative standards. The training also seemed to involve a degree of shaming EACJ judges for their existing arbitration rules (EACJ 2012) that failed to conform to the norms of the wider international legal community.

In addition to specific training, judges and administrative officials can also undertake "study visits" at other ICs as a means of professional socialization. For example, judges and other officials from the European Court of Human Rights (ECtHR) and the Inter-American Court of Human Rights (IACtHR) regularly visit each other (e.g.,

ECtHR 2014: 28; IACtHR 2015: 93), and the AfCHPR has an "exchange programme" with other ICs, where judges and the deputy registrar have visited the ECtHR, ICC, and International Court of Justice (ICJ) (AfCHPR 2012: 7). An ICJ judge, for instance, gave a presentation on "the role of an international judge" to AfCHPR Judges (AfCHPR 2007: 37). Through these exchanges, officials from newer ICs, who are still clarifying their appropriate roles, visit more established ICs to learn best practices and professional standards. While not a study visit per se, the Caribbean Court of Justice (CCJ) hired a consultant, an experienced judge from the region, to guide its development of a Legal Unit in response to its increasing caseload. The consultant, based on his knowledge of "best practices," defined the unit in terms of its "structure, composition, role and responsibilities" to ensure it could "provide the full measure of judicial assistance to the President and to the other judges of the Court so as to enable them to deliver reasoned judgments, reflective of the most thorough research of all relevant issues, in the shortest possible time" (CCJ 2013: 25). In so doing, CCJ officials within the Legal Unit were socialized into their appropriate roles in the interest of improving the CCJ's performance.

In addition to training, ICs can prioritize dialogue on the norms, rules, and procedures IC officials should follow. This can be through officials' discussion and debate, or ICs' development and dissemination of professional standards to their officials, which help promote shared understandings of officials' appropriate behavior. For example, the CCJ, CJEU, ECtHR, ICC, and Appellate Body (AB) of the World Trade Organization (WTO) have all developed codes of judicial conduct or ethics for their officials (WTO 1996; CCJ 1998; ICC 2005; EU 2007; ECtHR 2008). Similarly, many ICs formulate and adopt strategic plans, which delineate an IC's plans for future operations and shared understandings of officials' roles in contributing to achieving agreed upon performance objectives. ICs may also have policy documents on particular areas of their activity, which clarify IC officials' standards for appropriate conduct. For example, the ICC's Office of the Prosecutor has developed and disseminated various policies regarding its interpretation of the Rome Statute, such as its interpretation of specific crimes, and operational issues, such as its guidelines for using intermediaries. These codes, strategic plans, and policy documents are the products of processes of argumentation and persuasion among IC officials (often with input from legal experts or their stakeholders) regarding these officials' appropriate roles. In addition, ICs disseminate these standards of appropriate behavior to their various officials, persuading them to adopt them. ICs may also hold retreats for their officials, facilitating dialogue on how officials should perform. The EACJ, for example, held retreats for both judges and administrative officials, where it evaluated "staff performance as individuals and as a team towards the achievement of the Court's goals" (EACJ 2011: 20). Through praising good performance and criticizing bad performance within its organization, the EACJ was clearly using social influence to improve its performance. Thus, these forms of dialogue within ICs contribute to socializing IC officials and influence how they perform their roles.

Engaging in these forms of dissemination, dialogue, and training can socialize IC officials into ICs' norms, rules, and procedures. When IC officials learn how to appropriately perform their roles, they contribute to ICs' overall performance in its various dimensions. This sort of organizational socialization aimed at optimizing performance is largely to be expected, and the targets of these internal strategies are highly receptive to them given their professional commitments to IC performance. This contrasts with ICs' external strategies targeting other relevant actors in ICs' legal regimes, which will be discussed in the next two sections.

External Strategies

The behavior of IC officials is not the only determinant of IC performance. ICs' performance is also significantly contingent on the behavior of other actors in ICs' legal regimes, including states, national judiciaries, lawyers, academics, NGOs, and individuals. Depending on ICs' institutional designs, these actors play various roles in ICs' performance, including supplying ICs with operational resources, litigating in ICs, and choosing to comply with ICs' decisions. These actors' socialization into ICs' norms, rules, and procedures, which define their appropriate roles within ICs' regimes, contributes to many dimensions of IC performance.

States are always crucial to ICs' performance, as they are the actors that create ICs, accept their jurisdiction, and supply courts with their operational resources. Many scholars have noted ICs' inherent dependence on states when studying ICs' autonomy,[9] and states therefore can

[9] E.g., Helfer and Slaughter (2005) argue that ICs' dependence on states means that they only have "constrained independence," while Ginsburg (2004) similarly refers to ICs' "bounded discretion." Shany (2014) also notes that states are ICs' core constituency.

considerably shape ICs' performance. States, for example, can amend ICs' founding treaties to reform their norms, rules, and procedures, influencing virtually every dimension of ICs' operations. States can also subtly shape an IC's performance through resource restrictions, compromising activities such as caseload management and legal aid provision. In terms of ICs' outcomes, states can influence compliance with ICs by choosing, for instance, to invoke diplomatic pressure or political enforcement procedures (e.g., sanctions) for IC judgments. Beyond this overarching influence, states also substantially affect IC performance based on whether they adhere to ICs' norms, rules, and procedures as applicants and respondents in ICs' cases. States can undermine the efficiency of adjudicatory process through noncooperation (e.g., nonappearance, withholding documentation, etc.). States, as the typical respondents in ICs' cases, crucially choose whether to comply with ICs' judgments or, even if they are not brought to court, refrain from violations of international law.

Beyond states, however, the actors contributing to ICs' performance can vary depending on ICs' institutional designs. The actors that have standing in adjudication are particularly relevant for process performance, while those involved with implementing IC decisions are especially important for outcome performance. Some ICs are more "interstate" in nature, as they only directly involve states in adjudication, while other ICs are more "transnational," as they involve a range of actors (e.g., national courts, NGOs, individuals) (Keohane et al. 2000). In general, the more transnational the IC's institutional design, the wider the constellation of actors that potentially influence the IC's performance. National courts, for example, are significant actors for regional integration courts, where their requests for preliminary rulings can account for a considerable portion of regional integration courts' activity. For ICs that only hear cases after the exhaustion of local remedies (e.g., the ECtHR and ICC), national courts, which are litigants' first port of call, can also influence ICs' caseloads. In other legal regimes, such as the Inter-American and African human rights systems, commissions refer cases to their respective courts and can function as gatekeepers. The legal professionals that litigate cases at ICs also matter, as they can provide an IC a steady stream of cases and opportunities to develop jurisprudence (Vauchez 2014).

Nonstate actors, however, can also influence IC performance in subtler ways. Academics, through their legal scholarship, and NGOs, through their legal arguments supplied in *amicus curiae* briefs, can contribute to

ICs' judicial reasoning. In addition, many scholars have noted the importance of "compliance constituencies" for pressuring states to comply with international law (e.g., Dai 2005; Alter 2014). In the context of ICs, these can include national courts, parliamentarians, academics, bar associations, civil society organizations, and the general public. Scholars have noted how jurist advocacy movements and litigation communities have facilitated the CJEU's performance in terms of its development of legal doctrines, its academic legitimation, and states' compliance with CJEU judgments (Alter 2009; Bernier 2012; Vauchez 2014). Conversely, as a comparison between lawmaking at the CJEU and Andean Tribunal of Justice (ATJ) shows, lower substate support (from national judges and administrators, and advocacy networks) can undermine IC lawmaking (Alter and Helfer 2010). This points to the importance of what could broadly be termed "legal culture," among a variety of actors, in promoting ICs' performance.

Challenges to External Actors' Socialization and ICs' Actual Performance

Among these diverse actors that can contribute to ICs' performance, there can be significant challenges to their adoption of ICs' norms, rules, and procedures as their standards of legitimate, appropriate behavior. Actors may lack exposure to ICs' norms, rules, and procedures, or they may be aware of them but still contest ICs' legal authority. With states, the challenges are largely to be expected. As the ECCJ observed, for instance, filing a "direct suit" against another state at an IC "is often seen as confrontational and an inimical act," especially compared to traditional diplomatic means of dispute resolution (ECCJ 2006: 6). Statehood is predicated on norms of sovereignty and nonintervention, which ICs' supranational authority may seem to challenge. Misunderstanding ICs' institutional designs and laws can compound the problem and promote fears of judicial activism, for example. States can have ambivalent relationships with ICs: IC decisions in their favor can provide a useful tool for legitimizing states' policies, but when decisions are unfavorable and require domestic policy change, for instance, states often oppose ICs. These factors can challenge states' willingness to join ICs, supply them with adequate support for their operations, and accept and enforce their judgments – all of which influence ICs' performance.

Nonstate actors can also lack understanding of, or actively resist, ICs' norms, rules, and procedures. IOs with the capacity to refer cases to ICs – such as commissions in regional integration regimes and regional human rights systems, or the United Nations (UN) Security Council for the ICC – may resist "judicializing" issues, perhaps to maintain their control over the issue, and thus undermine ICs' performance. National courts similarly may not accept ICs' norms, rules, and procedures pertaining to national courts referring cases to ICs and implementing ICs' laws and decisions at the national level. The European Free Trade Area (EFTA) Court has grappled with this issue, where the Norwegian Supreme Court refrained from referring cases for many years (Fredriksen 2014). Lawyers may lack the expertise to litigate in ICs, particularly in new or highly technical areas of law, or in developing country contexts. Individuals may lack understanding of ICs' mandates and the legitimacy of seeking redress for violations of international law through ICs.

If these actors, however, do not fulfill their appropriate roles in ICs' legal regimes, they undermine ICs' performance both in terms of adjudicatory processes and outcomes. For example, national courts' failure to adopt key referral procedures can compromise ICs' process performance, and the resultant lack of cases can compromise ICs' outcome performance, given their limited opportunities to settle disputes, clarify law, and influence compliance with international law. Conversely, in regimes based on subsidiarity or complementarity, the failure of national courts to implement international law domestically can place a significant burden on ICs that can exceed their capacities and reduce their efficiency. Litigants' inability to access legal representation can undermine IC performance in terms of the ideals of equality before the law, where some parties may have unfair advantages in litigation, and of access to justice, where actors whose rights have been violated may not be able to obtain legal counsel and cases therefore may never reach court. In addition, if actors do not generally accept ICs' authority, ICs will lack compliance constituencies, and public opinion could support states' defiance of and withdrawal from ICs, undermining their performance.[10]

ICs' External Socialization Strategies for Influencing Their Actual Performance

To address these performance challenges, ICs can formulate strategies specifically oriented towards socializing relevant actors into their appropriate roles within ICs' legal regimes. ICs can adopt particular policies

[10] For example, the British public opinion has favored openly defying ECtHR decisions and even withdrawing from its jurisdiction. Bolivia's, Ecuador's, and Venezuela's withdrawals from ICSID have all coincided with public outcries over decisions that awarded significant damages to multinational corporations (Voeten 2013: 412).

and practices aimed at increasing actors' interactions with agents of socialization, which promote processes of persuasion and social influence. ICs can create opportunities for agents of socialization, typically IC officials themselves, to persuade actors to adopt ICs' norms, rules, and procedures as their standard of appropriate behavior. ICs can also facilitate interactions supporting processes of social influence, where IC officials can praise actors who conform to and condemn actors who violate ICs' norms, rules, and procedures.

ICs can actively disseminate their norms, rules, and procedures to actors in ICs' legal regimes. These activities are often referred to as "dissemination," "outreach," and among several African ICs, "sensitization." ICs, of course, often have reporting requirements, but they can exceed these requirements and direct dissemination activities towards socializing actors that may otherwise be unaware of the IC's existence or misunderstand the IC's mandate and their roles in contributing to it. This dissemination can occur through the media (e.g., press releases, social media); reports and other publications directed at stakeholders (e.g., case law summaries, court user guides, and practice directions); and direct engagement with actors, either by drawing them to ICs or engaging with actors in their own locales (e.g., conferences, seminars, workshops, meetings). The ECCJ, for instance, organized conferences and seminars whose "central objective" was "to re-awaken the awareness of the stakeholders of the Community, and consequently, enhance a true legal culture in West Africa" (ECCJ 2007: 9). In these forms of communication and interaction, ICs and their officials can use persuasive arguments regarding the legitimacy of ICs' norms, rules, and procedures, or can praise or shame actors for fulfilling or failing to fulfill, respectively, their appropriate roles. For example, with states, IC officials can use persuasion and pressure in diplomatic settings, such as meetings of IOs or private meetings, to increase states' sense of obligation to support ICs through supplying adequate operational resources for ICs, using ICs for dispute settlement, complying with ICs' decisions, and so on.

ICs can also conduct specialized training as a means of professional socialization for relevant legal professionals, such as national judges and lawyers, who contribute to ICs' performance. ICs can train national judges on their roles within ICs' legal regimes, including how they should use preliminary reference procedures or implement international law domestically. For example, the ECtHR, which operates based on the principle of subsidiarity, has a Training Unit that focuses on educating national judiciaries in European states on their obligations under the

European Convention on Human Rights and the ECtHR's regime. Other training programs focus on potential litigators in ICs' cases. The IACtHR's Latin American defender program, the ITLOS's Summer Academy, and the CCJ's Caribbean Academy for Law and Court Administration provide training where IC officials essentially persuade legal professionals to adopt their norms, rules, and procedures – and thus contribute to litigation in ICs, access to justice, and so on. ICs' socialization strategies, therefore, can be diverse, but they are all oriented towards ensuring that the various actors who contribute to IC performance have a strong sense of obligation to fulfill their appropriate roles in ICs' legal regimes.

Challenges to External Actors' Socialization and ICs' Perceived Performance

Various state and nonstate actors are also relevant to ICs' performance as they are the stakeholders for which ICs perform their mandates. The general public, NGOs, lawyers, national judiciaries, and, of course, states all observe and develop distinct perceptions of ICs' performance. Gutner and Thompson (2010: 233) call this the "eye of the beholder" problem, where analyses of performance vary significantly depending on the analyst. Actors' perceptions of performance can depend on the information available to them (e.g., Elsig 2010: 357–359), but different actors' interpretations of the same information can diverge based on their distinct norms of evaluation. Challenges to ICs' perceived performance, therefore, relate to the absence of a stable normative framework for evaluating ICs' performance.

ICs are a relatively new phenomenon, and for lack of other bases for comparison, ICs can be subjected to the domestic analogy. ICs' observers, particularly those lacking legal expertise, tend to use the role that domestic courts play in national legal systems as a frame of reference for ICs. Even much of the scholarship on ICs "implicitly assumes that the role of these tribunals is essentially the same as that of domestic courts" (Guzman 2008: 178). While it is important not to overstate the difference between international and domestic courts (Staton and Moore 2011), ICs lack many features that underpin the performance of domestic courts. For example, the international level lacks an enforcement authority for compelling compliance with ICs, so the domestic analogy could make noncompliance with even a few IC judgments seem like mediocre performance. Observers might also draw comparisons across different ICs and skew their perceptions of IC performance. ICs' institutional designs can be quite dissimilar, and ICs operate in different political, social, and economic contexts. Generally, European courts have been seen as the most "successful" ICs (Helfer and Slaughter 1997: 276) and have been emulated in other regions (Alter 2012). But, returning to the comparison between the CJEU and ATJ, these two courts with similar institutional designs have performed remarkably differently because of contextual factors largely beyond ICs' control (Alter and Helfer 2010). Holding an IC to the performance standards of a domestic court or another IC skews perceptions of their performance.

Relatedly, the complexity of ICs' mandates makes assessing their performance a challenge. Understanding many aspects of IC performance (e.g., quality of judicial reasoning and judgments, adherence to due process standards, etc.) are contingent on legal expertise, which many stakeholders lack. In addition, though ICs' core mandate is adjudication, ICs can have multiple and potentially conflicting objectives associated with this mandate. The Statute of the ICJ, for example, focuses on adjudication and its role as the UN's judicial organ, but the ICC's Rome Statute sets out various requirements for prosecuting international crimes, contributing to the prevention of those crimes, victims' assistance, and so on. The more vague and/or expansive an IC's mandate, the more challenging it is to determine appropriate standards for evaluating its performance.

Given this complexity, stakeholders with divergent preferences for ICs' performance can impose different expectations on ICs, prioritize some aspects of performance over others, and therefore develop disparate perceptions of ICs' performance. For ICs' adjudicatory processes, civil society may favor transparency and openness to various actors (e.g., *amicus curiae*), while states may value confidentiality and confining proceedings to the parties to the dispute. Legal professionals may believe strongly in the "equality of arms" between the prosecution and defense sides of international criminal trials, while affected communities might merely be concerned with individuals being indicted, convicted, and sentenced. For outcome performance, states, as the funders of ICs, may be concerned primarily with the number of cases adjudicated and getting "value for money." Legal communities may prioritize the clarification and development of different international legal fields, and the promotion of an international rule of law. Satisfying these various stakeholders with differing normative preferences can be challenging for ICs.

These differing preferences among various stakeholders is not uncommon for IOs, but contrary to many other IOs, ICs generally have not attracted demands for independent evaluations based on agreed upon standards.[11] IOs, such as the United Nations, World Bank, International Monetary Fund, and WTO, are subjected to far greater scrutiny and external evaluation regarding their performance.[12] Most ICs undergo external financial audits, which evaluate their expenditure in terms of their budget allocations, but systematic assessments of their overall performance based on normative standards are lacking. There have been a couple attempts to develop general standards and codes of conduct for international judges,[13] but these are not widely implemented and are focused merely on judicial independence – just one facet of ICs' process performance. The lack of normative consensus on how ICs should perform can lead to endlessly subjective, and potentially conflicting, evaluations of IC performance.

ICs' External Socialization Strategies for Influencing Their Perceived Performance

In the absence of consensus regarding the appropriate standards for IC behavior, ICs can shape perceptions of their performance by acting as norm entrepreneurs, and socializing actors into particular norms of evaluation based on ICs' founding treaties, broader interpretations of their mandates, and standards within the wider international legal community. ICs' strategies can aim to persuade actors to adopt these normative standards for evaluating ICs' performance. But they also can use social influence to praise the use of norms of evaluation that ICs deem appropriate and criticize the use of norms of evaluation they consider inappropriate. External socialization strategies can thus serve to mitigate the eye of the beholder problem, and help to develop shared understandings and perceptions of ICs' performance.

ICs can promulgate particular standards of evaluation for both instrumental and normative reasons. In their self-interest, ICs may want to wish to align norms of evaluation with what they actually do or what is reasonably achievable, given their various constraints. In other words, ICs may wish to manage expectations, so they improve their perceived performance relative to their actual performance. For example, ICs may

11 The ICC may be considered an exception, as its Assembly of States Parties established an "independent oversight mechanism" (ICC 2009).

12 The Independent Evaluation Group, for instance, exists purely to objectively evaluate the World Bank's performance. See http://ieg.worldbankgroup.org/about-us.

13 The Bangalore Principles of Judicial Conduct (UN 2002) and the Burgh House Principles on the Independence of the International Judiciary (ILA 2004).

want to focus on procedural aspects of performance, which they can more easily control, and steer actors away from evaluating performance based on outcomes such as compliance with rulings.[14] Equally, ICs may wish to set high performance standards and lower their perceived performance to flag their weaknesses and mobilize support among their stakeholders. Still, IC officials generally have their own normative beliefs, most commonly derived from their founding treaties, regarding their appropriate roles and how actors should evaluate them. Thus, ICs may choose to spread "high" standards of evaluation, which could reduce ICs' perceived performance.

These norms of evaluation can appeal to universal standards for ICs, which usually focus on judges and adjudication. Judicial integrity, for example, is typically thought to be foundational to the process of judging, so ICs can emphasize norms of fairness and impartiality, as well as norms against certain behavior, such as *ex parte* communications, expressed political bias, and prejudging issues or cases. With administration, efficiency is often the normative standard, typically relating to the speed with which cases are handled and the optimal use of limited resources. ICs also tend to argue that they should contribute to an international rule of law. The CCJ's annual report, for example, even includes a section titled, "Promoting the Rule of Law," which clarifies that normative standard and how the court adheres to it (CCJ 2013: 16–20). Similarly, the ICC President, addressing the general public, has noted that the prosecution of international crimes "must make a contribution to the international rule of law" (Fernández de Gurmendi 2015: 6).

Universal standards, however, are inadequate for evaluating the various dimensions of ICs' performance. Each IC is unique in either its institutional design or context, so ICs can also shape their stakeholders' perceptions of their performance through regime-specific norms. Some ICs disseminate to their stakeholders their formalized judicial codes of conduct or ethics, with normative criteria for evaluating their judges' performance. Many ICs write strategic plans and reports on their activities, which allude to norms for evaluating their performance. Strategic plans necessarily prioritize some objectives and means of implementation over others, and often set targets against which performance can be measured. ICs' reports are more evaluative and often contextualize quantitative and qualitative indicators of performance within particular

[14] E.g., White (2001: 1073–1074) argues that "outcome-based evaluations" of American domestic court judges, though common among politicians, are illegitimate.

normative standards. For example, the IACtHR's rulings, which tend to impose remedial measures beyond mere compensation (as in the ECtHR), have often received delayed compliance from states (Hawkins and Jacoby 2010: 35); the Court, therefore, has emphasized the normative desirability of even partial compliance in its reporting.

ICs can widely disseminate these documents, containing appropriate norms of evaluation, to their various stakeholders to shape their perceptions of ICs' performance. IC officials can also use various forms of interaction (e.g., diplomatic meetings, training, workshops with stakeholders, press conferences), as discussed in the previous section, to disseminate norms of evaluation and influence their perceived performance. The AfCHPR, for example, has recognized "the critical role of the media to promote human rights" (AfCHPR 2015b: para. 12) and has conducted media training for journalists to essentially teach them how to report on the Court's activities. In addition, the inaugural ICC Prosecutor Luis Moreno-Ocampo, in interactions ranging from stakeholder workshops to press conferences, frequently argued that the ICC's lack of cases should be seen as evidence of its effectiveness at deterring crimes and catalyzing national proceedings (Moreno Ocampo 2003). Thus, through these external socialization strategies, ICs can shape actors' norms of evaluation and, therefore, ICs' perceived performance.

The Prevalence of Socialization Strategies across ICs

The foregoing analysis elucidated how ICs can use internal and external socialization strategies to respond to challenges to their actual and perceived performance (Table 9.2). Based on this framework, this section evaluates the prevalence of ICs' internal and external socialization strategies through a content analysis of all twenty-three permanent, operational ICs' recent formal reports on their activities.[15] These reports, which are most commonly annual reports, are the main means by which ICs report on their activities and performance to their member states and other stakeholders. For example, in its annual reports, the CCJ "accounts to the Caribbean people for its performance" (CCJ 2006: 2).

[15] ICs are considered "operational" if they have appointed judges and the capacity to adjudicate cases. This includes ICs that do not receive cases but have appointed judges that can hear cases, such as the European Nuclear Energy Tribunal, but it excludes ICs like the Association of Southeast Asian Nations' Appellate Body and the Southern African Development Community Tribunal, which ostensibly lack appointed judges and are inoperative.

Table 9.2 *ICs' performance challenges and socialization strategies*

	Internal	External	
	Actual Performance		Perceived Performance
Performance Challenges	• Officials' diversity and expertise • ICs' unique norms, rules, procedures	• Relevant actors' lack of understanding and contestation of ICs' norms, rules, procedures • Legal professionals' lack of expertise vis-à-vis ICs	• Lack of normative consensus for evaluating ICs' performance • Stakeholders misunderstanding ICs' performance objectives
Socialization Strategies	• Training IC officials • Facilitating officials' interactions with international legal experts • Developing and disseminating norms to IC officials	• Disseminating ICs' norms, rules, procedures to relevant actors • Training legal professionals	• Developing and disseminating norms for evaluating ICs' appropriate behavior

ICs' founding treaties often require ICs produce these reports, and generally, an IC's registry, with input from officials throughout the court, prepares them. These reports are the best systematic record of ICs' various activities and their justifications for those activities available. Still, they may not capture the full scope of ICs' activities, as ICs have considerable discretion over the activities they report, and they may be biased towards reporting formal rather than informal activities, for example. Despite this underreporting bias, ICs' reports include the

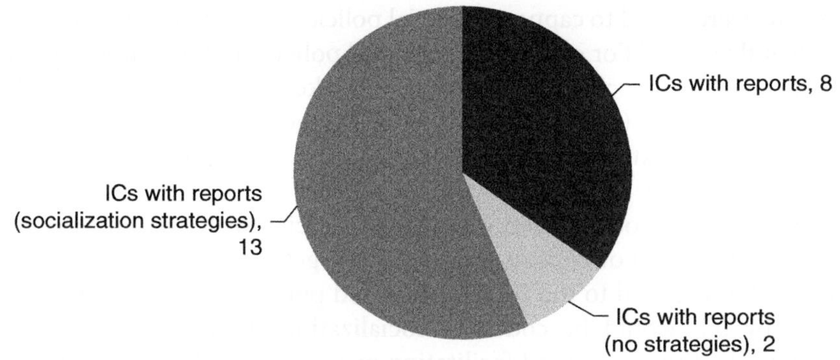

Figure 9.1 IC reporting on socialization strategies

activities they deem significant enough to document and form part of their overall account of their performance.

As Figure 9.1 shows, of the twenty-three ICs surveyed, eight did not provide formal reports on their activities and fifteen did.[16] This itself is a striking finding, as essentially a third (35 percent) of permanent ICs do not systematically report on their performance. Some may publish records of their judicial decisions (e.g., in gazettes or bulletins), and IC officials, acting as representatives of their court, may occasionally give speeches in various forums, but these ICs do not provide a regular, systematic assessments of their activities. The absence of reporting does not necessarily mean that these ICs do not use socialization strategies.[17] In this study, these cases are left aside and their socialization strategies simply considered unknown, rather than absent. Thus, the scope of the content analysis is limited to the fifteen reporting ICs and is a conservative account of the prevalence of socialization strategies in ICs.

To obtain a "snapshot" of ICs' use of socialization strategies, recent reports from the fifteen reporting ICs' were coded for policies and practices reflecting internal and external socialization strategies.[18] Two reports from

[16] The eight ICs are: Benelux Court of Justice, Central American Court of Justice, Court of Justice of the Central African Economic & Monetary Community, European Nuclear Energy Tribunal, Judicial Tribunal of the Organization of Arab Petroleum-Exporting Countries, Mercosur Permanent Review Court, Common Court of Justice and Arbitration of the Organization for the Harmonization of Corporate Law in Africa, Court of Justice of the West African Economic Monetary Union.

[17] ICs' lack of reporting could be linked to their broader lack of external engagement, making external socialization strategies less likely in this subset of ICs.

[18] With coding latent content (meanings of texts), using multiple coders can increase reliability, but one coder was used for this analysis.

each IC were coded to capture potential policies and practices that ICs less frequently used.[19] For coding ICs' reported policies and practices as internal and external socialization strategies, the key considerations were the actors interacting (the agents and targets of socialization), as well as the normative context (targeted actors' beliefs) and the normative content of their interactions.

The agents of socialization would be IC officials or IC-selected experts (e.g., a legal expert or consultant), and the targeted actors would be either internal or external to the IC. The reported policies and practices developed by ICs would be coded as socialization strategies if they were specifically directed toward facilitating processes of either persuasion or social influence.[20] For strategies based on persuasion, ICs' policies and practices would involve agents of socialization disseminating ICs' norms, rules, and procedures to actors whose beliefs, as implicitly or explicitly identified by ICs, did not conform to these norms, rules, and procedures. For strategies based on social influence, ICs would assume a degree of normative consensus existed with the targeted actors' community, and enact policies and practices for praising adherence to and shaming violations of ICs' norms, rules, and procedures within that community. These socialization strategies could relate to the norms, rules, and procedures associated with actors' roles in ICs' legal regimes (for actual performance) or could involve the norms for evaluating ICs (for perceived performance).

Within the fifteen reporting ICs, only two – the ICJ and CJEU – did not report any significant policies and practices that could be categorized as internal or external socialization strategies. The CJEU's reports entirely focus on its judicial activities and therefore do not report on many aspects of its work, including, potentially, socialization activities. The ICJ's reports are more comprehensive but do not articulate socialization strategies.[21] The remaining thirteen ICs reported policies or

[19] For most ICs, reports from 2013 to 2014 were coded, but occasionally, if reporting was less frequent, reports from 2011–12 were coded. This, however, would not substantively impact the analysis. Of course, one could analyze all of ICs' reports to capture potential temporal variation in ICs' socialization strategies. I leave that to future researchers.

[20] Policies and practices would be considered as developed by ICs when they exceeded ICs' mandated activities in their founding treaties. This distinction captures ICs' agency and decision-making in developing socialization strategies (see also De Silva 2016).

[21] The ICJ reported receiving visits from government officials and an internship program, but did not frame these activities in ways that resonated with processes of persuasion or social influence.

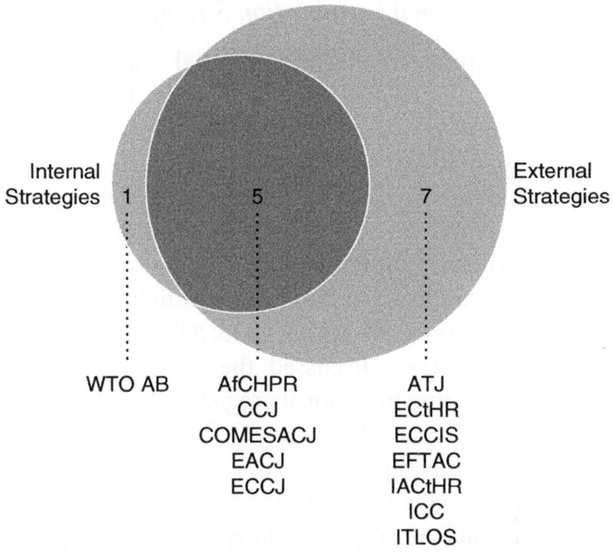

Figure 9.2 IC reporting on internal and/or external socialization strategies

practices that were categorized as internal and/or external socialization strategies (Figure 9.2).

ICs' reported policies and practices, which were identified as socialization strategies, emphasized persuasion far more than social influence. They tended to aim to increase actors' exposure to ICs' various norms, rules, and procedures, which would help develop shared understandings of appropriateness and potentially alter actors' behavior. The general assumption behind the policies and practices was that actors lacked understanding of ICs' norms, rules, and procedures, and different forms of communication and interaction could address this deficit.

In general, ICs did not report on their policies and practices in ways that resonated with processes of social influence. Occasionally, ICs would allude to using social influence with their own officials, but particularly their external socialization strategies relied on persuasion. As previously discussed, however, experts and IC officials often make statements praising adherence and shaming divergence from ICs' norms, rules, and procedures in their interactions with actors in their legal regimes. Social influence, therefore, is not irrelevant to ICs' activities, but capturing it likely requires a finer-grained analysis (e.g., analyzing particular statements). Still, it is significant that ICs did not frame their overarching policies and practices in these terms.

Internal Socialization Strategies

Six ICs reported activities reflecting internal socialization strategies. The WTO AB, ECCJ, and CCJ all reported disseminating new guidelines, codes of conduct, and strategic plans, and attempting to persuade their officials to adopt them to improve the their IC's performance. The WTO AB – the only court reporting merely internal socialization strategies – disseminated Post-Employment Guidelines for AB members, Secretariat staff, and interns to clarify how their obligations of conduct (regarding independence, impartiality, and avoiding conflicts of interests) extend beyond their term of service (WTO AB 2015: 84). The ECCJ held a retreat for its officials, where they discussed the Court's strategic plan and debated draft practice directions for its registry (ECCJ 2012: 4).

The CCJ reported a remarkable range of policies and practices aimed at developing and disseminating norms among its officials. The Court formulated and disseminated a Code of Judicial Ethics for its officials, which "deals with matters such as propriety, independence, integrity, impartiality, equality, competence and diligence and accountability" (CCJ 2013: 29). The CCJ's newly appointed Social Networking Committee also held a workshop with court officials to show "why it is important for the CCJ to have a Code of Ethics and Social Networking Policy" (CCJ 2013: 29). For its strategic planning exercise, the CCJ reported bringing in an external consultant, with "decades of court administration and court strategic planning experience," to lead the process and persuade CCJ officials to plan their activities according to particular norms such as "inclusiveness" (CCJ 2013: 12–13). The CCJ described this process as a "team-building stratagem" (CCJ 2013: 12), which would improve officials' understanding of the Court's goals and their value – clearly resonating with the logic of socialization.

All six ICs that reported internal socialization strategies (Figure 9.2) included training judicial and/or administrative officials among them. Especially for ICs in developing regions, donor funding was often crucial for training (or "capacity-building").[22] These various training programs involved presenting officials with counter-attitudinal information and persuading them to adopt particular norms, rules, and procedures for improving their IC's performance. Training and socializing officials could be a lengthy process, as the AB reported, for example, that it "takes at least a year to 18 months for them to develop specialized skills

[22] Major donors include the Konrad-Adenauer-Stiftung Foundation and the German agency for international development cooperation (GIZ).

and experience necessary to lead a panel or an appeal team" (WTO AB 2015: 90). The training's scope also could be quite broad, as the EACJ's "tailored training programs" sought to familiarize judges with the "regional justice system" in various areas (EACJ 2011: xi), including arbitration, human rights, environmental law, and the East African Community's (EAC's) Common Market Protocol that would soon be operationalized (EACJ 2011: 20).

External Socialization Strategies

External socialization strategies were relatively more common: Twelve ICs – the vast majority of the fifteen reporting ICs – described policies and practices related to training and dissemination, which ostensibly aimed at socializing external actors in their legal regimes. Despite the analytical distinction between actual and perceived performance, in practice, a given external socialization policy or practice could be oriented towards both. For example, in interacting with potential litigants, IC officials may not only persuade them of the appropriateness of adjudication for regional integration, but also persuade them that the IC's performance should be judged based on how it drives regional integration. Given this potential overlap, this overview of ICs' external socialization strategies does not systematically differentiate between those aimed at actual versus perceived performance.

Strategies aimed at dissemination and dialogue (e.g., meetings, reports, policy documents, case law publications, lectures, sharing on social media, streaming video, etc.) were relatively more common than training. Many ICs reported strategically expanding their means of disseminating their norms, rules, and procedures to their stakeholders. The ECtHR conducted "general outreach" through its website, social media, and public relations materials (e.g., ECtHR 2014: 70–72). When the ECtHR modified its rules on the conditions for lodging an application, for instance, it produced a video tutorial in multiple languages and launched a "campaign to make the target group aware of these new conditions" (ECtHR 2015: 75). The IACtHR increased its presence of social networks "to connect with people in a more dynamic and innovative way, and to disseminate its case law more efficiently" (IACtHR 2015: 2), while the ECCJ used radio and television programs and press conferences (ECCJ 2012).

Many ICs used strategies emphasizing direct interactions and dialogue between IC officials and targeted actors in their legal regimes. The ICC, for example, noted its Outreach Unit's interactions with victims' communities, where registry officials would persuade communities to adopt the ICC's norms of individual criminal accountability, fair trial standards, and so on. Several African ICs (e.g., the AfCHPR, Common Market for Eastern and Southern Africa Court of Justice [COMESACJ], ECCJ, and EACJ) held "sensitization" or "publicity" seminars and workshops throughout their regions and sub-regions. ICs framed such forms of socialization as crucial for their performance; the ECCJ, for instance, reported that its sensitization missions "are so significant that the long-term interests of the Court will depend on them" (ECCJ 2012: 2). These programs convened a range of actors relevant to ICs' mandates, which included members of government, national judiciaries, bar associations, the private sector, academia, civil society, and the media. The AfCHPR included the full range of relevant actors in its legal regime in its sensitization program, but also held a "continental judicial dialogue" to "strengthen relations" between the Court, national and subregional judiciaries, and human rights stakeholders, and to "facilitate the dissemination and application of the judgments of the Court" (AfCHPR 2015a: 32). Through these interactions, ICs envisioned that IC officials would improve relevant actors' understanding and appreciation of their mandates and associated norms, rules, and procedures. Given the open-ended nature of these dialogues between IC officials and actors in their legal regimes, these interactions could have involved both persuasion and social influence and been oriented towards influencing ICs' actual and perceived performance. The EACJ, for instance, seemed to specifically aim to shape perceptions of its performance by holding a conference "with a view to touching base with its stakeholders and reviewing its performance" (EAC 2013: 99).

Several ICs, such as the CCJ, ECtHR, IACtHR, and ITLOS, reported legal training programs aimed at professional socialization. Through these programs, IC officials could persuade legal professionals (generally national judges and lawyers) to adopt particular norms, rules, and procedures, and these legal professionals could fulfill their appropriate roles and contribute to ICs' performance. The IACtHR clearly linked training and professional socialization to its performance: "An essential element of the strengthening of the regional system is training all the human capital that, in future, will be working in the area of human rights, such as: future human rights defenders, public servants, members of the legislature, agents of justice, academics, members of civil society, etc." (IACtHR 2015: 95). While most ICs focused training on judges and lawyers, the

Geyh, Charles. 1993. "Informal Methods of Judicial Discipline," *University of Pennsylvania Law Review* 142(1): 243–331.

Ginsburg, Tom. 2004. "Bounded Discretion in International Judicial Lawmaking," *Virginia Journal of International Law* 45(3): 631–673.

Goldberg, Susan. 1985. "Judicial Socialization: An Empirical Study," *Journal of Contemporary Law* 11(2): 423–451.

Goodman, Ryan and Jinks, Derek. 2004. "How to Influence States: Socialization and International Human Rights Law," *Duke Law Journal* 54(3): 621–703.

2013. *Socializing States: Promoting Human Rights through International Law.* Oxford: Oxford University Press.

Gutner, Tamar and Thompson, Alexander. 2010. "The Politics of IO Performance: A Framework," *Review of International Organizations* 5(3): 227–248.

Guzman, Andrew. 2008. "International Tribunals: A Rational Choice Analysis," *University of Pennsylvania Law Review* 157(1): 171–235.

Hawkins, Darren and Jacoby, Wade. 2010. "Partial Compliance: A Comparison of the European and Inter-American Courts of Human Rights," *Journal of International Law and International Relations* 6(1): 35–85.

Helfer, Laurence and Slaughter, Anne-Marie. 1997. "Toward a Theory of Effective Supranational Adjudication," *Yale Law Journal* 107(2): 273–391.

2005. "Why States Create International Tribunals: A Response to Professors Posner and Yoo," *California Law Review* 93(3): 899–956.

Ikenberry, G. John and Kupchan, Charles A. 1990. "Socialization and Hegemonic Power," *International Organization* 44(3): 283–315.

IACtHR. 2015. *Annual Report 2014.* Available at: www.corteidh.or.cr/tablas/informe2015/ingles.pdf (accessed February 21, 2016).

ICJ. 2014. *Report of the International Court of Justice August 1, 2013–July 31, 2014.* United Nations. Available at: digitallibrary.un.org/record/780476/files/A_69_4-EN.pdf (accessed February 21, 2016).

ICC. 2005. *Code of Judicial Ethics.* ICC-BD/02-01-05. March 9, 2005. Available at: www.icc-cpi.int/NR/rdonlyres/A62EBC0F-D534-438F-A128-D3AC4CFDD644/140141/ICCBD020105_En.pdf (accessed February 21, 2016).

"Establishment of an Independent Oversight Mechanism." ICC-ASP/8/Res.1. November 26, 2009. Available at: asp.icc-cpi.int/iccdocs/asp_docs/Publications/Compendium/Resolution-IOM-ENG.pdf (accessed February 21, 2016).

International Law Association (ILA). 2004. *The Burgh House Principles on the Independence of the International Judiciary.* Study Group on the Practice and Procedure of International Courts and Tribunals.

Johnston, Alastair Iain. 2001. "Treating International Institutions as Social Environments," *International Studies Quarterly* 45(4): 487–515.

Keohane, Robert, Moravcsik, Andrew, and Slaughter, Anne-Marie. 2000. "Legalized Dispute Resolution: Interstate and Transnational," *International Organization* 54(3): 457–488.

Koh, Harold. 1996. "Transnational Legal Process," *Nebraska Law Review* 75(1): 181–208.

1997. "Why Do Nations Obey International Law?," *Yale Law Journal* 106(8): 2599–2659.

Mackenzie, Ruth, Malleson, Kate, Martin, Penny, and Sands, Philippe. 2010. *Selecting International Judges: Principle, Process, and Politics*. Oxford: Oxford University Press.

Maveety, Nancy (ed.). 2003. *The Pioneers of Judicial Behavior*. Ann Arbor: University of Michigan Press.

Moreno Ocampo, Luis. 2003. "Statement Made at the Ceremony for the Solemn Undertaking of the Chief Prosecutor of the ICC," June 16, 2003. Available at: www.icc-cpi.int/NR/rdonlyres/D7572226-264A-4B6B-85E3-2673648B4896/143585/030616_moreno_ocampo_english.pdf (accessed February 21, 2016).

Park, Susan. 2014. "Socialisation and the Liberal Order," *International Politics* 51 (3): 334–349.

Risse, Thomas, Ropp, Stephen, and Sikkink, Kathryn (eds.). 1999. *The Power of Human Rights: International Norms and Domestic Change*. Cambridge: Cambridge University Press.

Risse, Thomas and Sikkink, Kathryn. 1999. "The Socialization of International Human Rights Norms into Domestic Practices: Introduction," in Risse, Thomas, Ropp, Stephen, and Sikkink, Kathryn (eds.), *The Power of Human Rights: International Norms and Domestic Change*. Cambridge: Cambridge University Press. pp. 1–38.

Rome Statute of the International Criminal Court. 1998. July 17, 1998, 2187 UNTS 3.

Shany, Yuval. 2014. *Assessing the Effectiveness of International Courts*. Oxford: Oxford University Press.

Spohn, Cassia. 1990. "The Sentencing Decisions of Black and White Judges: Expected and Unexpected Similarities," *Law and Society Review* 24(5): 1197–1216.

Staton, Jeffrey and Moore, Will. 2011. "Judicial Power in Domestic and International Politics," *International Organization* 65(3): 553–587.

Statute of the International Court of Justice. 1945. June 26, 1945, 33 UNTS 993.

Stone Sweet, Alec. 2010. "The European Court of Justice and the Judicialization of EU Governance," *Living Reviews in European Governance* 5(2). Available at: europeangovernance-livingreviews.org/Articles/lreg-2010-2 (accessed February 21, 2016).

Terris, Daniel, Romano, Cesare, and Swigart, Leigh. 2007. *The International Judge: An Introduction to the Men and Women Who Decide the World's Cases.* Oxford: Oxford University Press.

UN. 2001. *The Bangalore Principles of Judicial Conduct.* E/CN.4/2003/65. Available at: www.unodc.org/pdf/corruption/bangalore_e.pdf (accessed February 21, 2016).

Vauchez, Antoine. 2014. "Communities of International Litigators," in Romano, Cesare, Alter, Karen, and Avgerou, Chrisanthi (eds.), *The Oxford Handbook of International Adjudication.* Oxford: Oxford University Press, pp. 655–668.

Voeten, Erik. 2008. "The Impartiality of International Judges: Evidence from the European Court of Human Rights," *American Political Science Review* 102 (4): 417–433.

2013. "Public Opinion and the Legitimacy of International Courts," *Theoretical Inquiries in Law* 14(2): 411–436.

2014. "International Judicial Behavior," in Romano, Cesare, Alter, Karen, and Avgerou, Chrisanthi (eds.), *The Oxford Handbook of International Adjudication.* Oxford: Oxford University Press, pp. 550–567.

Wanberg, Connie (ed.). 2012. *The Oxford Handbook of Organizational Socialization.* Oxford: Oxford University Press.

Wang, Qingxin Ken. 2003. "Hegemony and Socialisation of the Mass Public: The Case of Postwar Japan's Cooperation with the United States on China Policy," *Review of International Studies* 29(1): 99–119.

White, Penny. 2001. "Judging Judges: Securing Judicial Independence by Use of Judicial Performance Evaluations," *Fordham Urban Law Journal* 29(3): 1053–1077.

Wiener, Antje. 2008. *The Invisible Constitution of Politics.* Cambridge: Cambridge University Press.

WTO. 1996. *Rules of Conduct for the Understanding on Rules and Procedures Governing the Settlement of Disputes.* WT/DSB/RC/1. December 11, 1996. Available at: www.wto.org/english/tratop_e/dispu_e/rc_e.htm (accessed February 21, 2016).

WTO AB 2015. *Appellate Body Annual Report for 2014.* Appellate Body Secretariat, World Trade Organization. Available at: docs.wto.org/dol2fe/pages/ss/directdoc.aspx?filename=q:/wt/ab/24.pdf (accessed February 21, 2016).

10

What Happens after a Judgment is Given? Judgment Compliance and the Performance of International Courts and Tribunals

CHIARA GIORGETTI

Introduction

Analyses of the work of international courts and tribunals often stop when the judgment is issued, and focus on the rules and procedures that made that resolution possible.[1] But the issuance of the decision does not tell the whole story of a judicial proceeding. In truth, judgment compliance is an essential component of any thorough assessment of the working of international courts and tribunals, and one that is often connected to the performance of these forums.

Cognizant of the importance of the link between performance and compliance, this chapter proceeds as follows: it analyzes first the meaning(s) of compliance and highlights the relevance of compliance in the assessment of international judicial forums. It then examines compliance mechanisms adopted by important and diverse international dispute resolution mechanisms (the International Court of Justice, the European Court of Human Rights, the International Convention on Settlement of Investment Disputes and the United Nations Compensation Commission) and examines their success in generating compliance. Finally, it assesses what internal and external factors may encourage or discourage judgment compliance.

[1] Sir Jennings noted that it was "ironic that the Court's business up to the delivery of judgment is lavish in detail, but it is not at all easy to find out what happened afterwards." Sir R. Jennings, "Presentation" in C. Peck and R. S. Lee (eds.), *Increasing the Effectiveness of the International Court of Justice: Proceedings of the ICJ/UNITAR Colloquium to Celebrate the 50th Anniversary of the Court* (The Hague: Kluwer, 1997), 81.

The Complexity of Compliance

In *How Nations Behave*, Louis Henkin famously asserted that "almost all nations observe almost all principles of international law and almost all of their obligations almost all of the time."[2] This section explores whether this observation applies to international judicial decisions also. In particular, it focuses on what compliance means in the context of international decisions and the complexities surrounding the definition.

Surprisingly, defining compliance with a judgment is not as easy as one could expect. Compliance is not a simple on/off button, but is a complex question that requires multiple considerations. As Alexandra Huneeus observed "compliance is not always a straightforward or likely outcome."[3]

While questions of the compliance with judgments of international courts relate mostly to the outcome of the judicial process, analyzing compliance requires a deep understanding of the dispute at issue, the remedies available, and the choices available and made by courts and parties in any given instance. An analysis of compliance also needs to take into consideration when compliance occurred in relation to the date of the judgment and whether full or partial compliance was achieved.[4]

Compliance with a judgment requires some change in behavior as mandated by the Court.[5] Shany defines compliance as "a change in the post-judgment conduct of a party to adjudication brought about by the judgment and resulting in norm-practice convergence."[6] In other words, compliance with a judgment occurs when the obligated party (i.e., the losing party, the judgment debtor) – which in international proceedings is either a state or another recognized international actor – acts accordingly to the ruling of a court, by either doing what the court asked to be done, or by refraining from doing what the court prohibited it to do.[7]

2 Louis Henkin, *How Nations Behave* (New York: Columbia University Press, 1979), 47.

3 A. V. Huneeus, "*Compliance with Judgments and Decisions*" in C. Romano, K. Alter, and Y. Shany (eds.), *The Oxford Handbook of International Adjudication* (Oxford: Oxford University Press, 2014), 437.

4 See for example D. Hawkins and W. Jacoby, "Partial Compliance: A Comparison of the European and Inter-American Courts for Human Rights," *Journal of International Law and International Relations*, 6, no. 1 (2010), 59.

5 D. Kapiszewski and M. Taylor, "Compliance: Conceptualizing, Measuring, and Explaining Adherence to Judicial Rulings," *Law and Social Inquiry*, 38, no. 4 (2012).

6 Y. Shany, *Assessing the Effectiveness of International Courts* (Oxford: Oxford University Press, 2014), 119.

7 Huneeus, "Compliance with Judgments and Decisions," 442.

This definition is particularly useful because it highlights the inter-relational nature of compliance, the need for clear understanding of the pre- and post-judgment conduct and how this dynamic plays out in the international legal system.[8] This also goes to the core of the judicial function. Indeed, measuring the compliance with an international judicial decision requires the understanding, analysis and comparison of the behavior demanded in a judgment from the losing party, as well as the behavior of all other parties after the judgment is given.

Compliance is important for many reasons. First and foremost, it is an essential tenant of the legal system. The rule of law derives its core legitimacy from the uniform application of rules to all.[9] It is important for the existence, stability, and strength of the international legal system that judgments are complied with, even more so when they are directed to a sovereign or other internationally recognized person.[10]

Moreover, the legitimacy of courts and tribunals is linked to compliance with their judgments. On one hand, legitimacy promotes compliance, as parties are more likely to comply with a judgment of a court they find legitimate. On the other hand, compliance may also promote legitimacy because when parties take seriously the decision of a court and comply with it, the work of a court is validated and strengthen.[11]

Similarly, compliance is linked to performance. Indeed, Shany observes that scholars have considered compliance as a "'litmus test' of judicial effectiveness."[12] He remarks that compliance with judgments and other decisions of international courts is central to the discussions about the performance of international adjudicatory bodies.[13] Thus, compliance with judgments could ultimately demonstrate that a court is effective and performs as expected.

Legal realists emphasize the link between performance and the ability to compel compliance and assert that "a tribunal is effective if states comply with its judgment."[14] Helfer and Slaughter also recognize that a tribunal's ability to generate compliance with its own rulings can be a measure of performance, but they advance a more nuanced analysis and caution that the question is more complex. For example, a high rate of compliance could also result from a court

[8] Ibid., 442. [9] Ibid., 440. [10] Kapiszewski and Taylor, "Compliance," 2.
[11] Huneeus, "Compliance with Judgments and Decisions," 453, 459.
[12] Shany, Assessing the Effectiveness of International Courts, 117. [13] Ibid., 117–118.
[14] E. Posner and J. Yoo, "Judicial Independence in International Tribunals," *California Law Review*, 93, no. 1 (2005), 28.

always finding in favor of the defendant or in favor of the more powerful party. Also, a tribunal could ignore the relevant legal questions and just try to decide in the way it thinks the parties would have done through politics.[15]

Guzman points out that the performance of an international tribunal should be assessed through the ability of the forum to improve compliance with the underlying substantive obligation.[16] Hence, an analysis of compliance must also take into consideration the enforcement mechanisms chosen by states, and thus given to the court, in any given judicial forum.

Considering the reasons that triggered the establishment of a court or tribunal is also important when analyzing compliance. States create international courts and tribunals for a variety of reasons. One of the most important reasons is to create a mechanism to support certain legal obligations and ensure that these obligations are respected. It may be that the priorities of the parties lay outside maximizing compliance. Indeed, it is always for the parties to establish agreements that contain robust enforcement mechanisms. If those mechanisms are not there, compliance performance will be affected. As Guzman notes, states sometimes prefer "to stop short of the strongest possible enforcement scheme."[17]

In sum, an analysis limited to measuring compliance only, may tell us little about the judicial impact of the decision, without also taking into consideration the nature, content and history of the judgment, the remedies used and any preexisting practice.[18] Indeed, as Shany points out "the significance of judgment-compliance ought to be understood in light of its contribution to attainment of international courts' goals, such as changing the practices of third parties, resolving disputes, and advancing regime goals."[19]

In the section below, I appraise four international dispute resolutions forums, focusing on their compliance mechanisms and assessing compliance of their judgments.

[15] L. R. Helfer and A-M. Slaughter, "Toward a Theory of Effective Supranational Adjudication," *Yale Law Journal*, 107, no. 2 (1997), 283.

[16] A. T. Guzman, "International Tribunals: A Rational Choice Analysis," *University of Pennsylvania Law Review*, 157, no. 1 (2008), 188.

[17] Guzman, "International Tribunals," 188.

[18] Shany, *Assessing the Effectiveness of International Courts*, 123, see more generally 117–123.

[19] Ibid., 117.

Procedural Mechanisms to Ensure Compliance

The constitutive acts of courts and tribunals typically provide for specific mechanisms to ensure compliance with their decisions. These mechanisms vary quite substantially, from the creation of a fund to ensure payments of judgment, to monitoring and reporting requirements after the judgment is issued and to a direct reference of the United Nations (UN) Security Council powers to enforce a judgment.

The section below reviews the compliance mechanisms of four diverse dispute resolution forums: the International Court of Justice, which relies on the external support of the UN Security Council; the European Court of Human Rights (ECtHR), which benefits from a unique review mechanism constituted by the Ministers of Foreign Affairs of all contracting parties; arbitral tribunals constituted under the Convention for the Settlement of Investment Disputes, for which awards are immediately enforceable as domestic judgments; and the United Nations Claims Commission, where a special fund was created to ensure the payment of all awards made. In conjunction with a review of these mechanisms, this section also assesses the compliance records of these forums. The aim is to offer an appraisal of a variety of mechanisms that mirror the full panoply of existing compliance mechanisms, as well as to evaluate their operability in "real life."

The International Court of Justice: Ensuring Compliance through the UN Security Council

The International Court of Justice (ICJ), the principle judicial organ of the United Nations, hears contentious cases between states on a variety of delicate issues, including border and maritime disputes, use of force and the violation of specific international treaty provisions.

The procedural framework of the Court, including for compliance, is found in the Charter of the United Nations and the Statute of the International Court of Justice. Article 94 of the UN Charter states that UN Members must comply with the decisions of the ICJ "in any case to which it is a party."[20] As it is common for international courts, who lack their own police force, the Statute of the Court does not give any

[20] UN Charter, June 26, 1945, 1 UNTS XVI, Art. 94(1); see also ICJ Statute, June 26, 1945, 33 UNTS 993, Art. 59 (proving that "The decision of the Court has no binding force except between the parties and in respect of that particular case."). Available at: www.icj-cij.org/en/statute (accessed July 2017).

instruments to the Court itself to guarantee compliance.[21] Instead, it is for the Security Council – the political organ of the United Nations tasked with the responsibility of maintaining peace and security – to provide an enforcement mechanism for judgments of the Court. Art. 94(2) mandates that if a party fails to comply with a judgment of the ICJ, the other party "may have recourse to the Security Council, which may, if it deems necessary make recommendations or decide upon measures to be taken to give effect to the judgment."[22]

Compliance with judgments of the ICJ has been the object of a fair amount of academic interest and scrutiny.[23] Scholars agree that, overall, parties have mostly complied with judgments of the ICJ.[24] Examining all the judgments issued between 1946 and 2003, Schulte concluded that the record showed "generally satisfactory compliance."[25] Moreover, even in cases where there may have been issues with compliance, parties have made significant efforts to achieve compliance.[26] Paulson observes that "overall compliance has probably increased or, at least, stayed roughly the same."[27] Writing in 2006, then ICJ President Rosalyn Higgins asserted that very few of the almost 100 contentious cases presented problems of compliance, and even those were mostly temporary.[28] She noted that while at times compliance requires time, it may also be achieved promptly. For example, in the decade-long and intensely fought case of *Qatar* v. *Bahrain*, the parties readily accepted the judgment when it was issued and saw that the decision would provide a new framework for peace in the Gulf.[29]

21 Factory at Chorzow (*Germ.* v. *Pol.*). 1927 PCIJ (ser. A) No. 9 (July 26).

22 UN Charter, Art. 94(2).

23 See C. Schulte, *Compliance with Decisions of the International Court of Justice* (Oxford: Oxford University Press Publisher, 2004); C. Paulson, "Compliance with Final Judgments of the International Court of Justice Since 1987," *American Journal of International Law*, 98, no. 3 (2000); A. P. Llamzon, "Jurisdiction and Compliance in Recent Decisions of the International Court of Justice," *The European Journal of International Law*, 18, no. 5 (2007); H. L. Jones, "Why Comply? An Analysis of trends in Compliance with Judgments of the International Court of Justice since Nicaragua," *Chicago-Kent International & Comparative Law*, 12, no. 1 (2010).

24 See, for example, Paulson, "Compliance with Final Judgments," 434.

25 Schulte, *Compliance with Decisions*, 403.

26 Paulson, "Compliance with Final Judgments," 456–457.

27 Ibid., 460.

28 Speech by H. E. Judge Rosalyn Higgins, President of The International Court of Justice, at The United Nations Security Council's Thematic Debate on Strengthening International Law, June 22, 2006.

29 Jones notes "In the case of the boundary issue between Qatar and Bahrain, for instance, the boundary dispute had soured the relations between the countries for decades. Rather than promoting noncompliance, the Court's decision offered a solution to the rift,

A telling example of compliance is the *Kasikili/Sedudu Island*, a case that was brought by special agreement between Botswana and Namibia over the sovereignty of an island in the Caprivi Strip, which separates the two countries.[30] The Court awarded Botswana sovereignty over the (uninhabited) island in December 1999 and also (importantly) said that nationals and vessels of both countries were to enjoy equal treatment in both channels around the island. The Ministry of Justice of Namibia admitted to being disappointed, but said he "had no other choice" but to respect the Court's decision. The two states set up a technical commission to demarcate the boundary which concluded its work in 2003.[31]

In other cases, a judgment served as a starting point for parties to work out a mutual agreement. For example, in *Maritime Delimitation in the Area Between Greenland and Jan Mayen*[32] the Court was asked by Denmark and Norway to decide on a fishery zone and continental shelf in the area between Greenland and the island of Jan Mayen. The Court issued its decision, and the parties then agreed to a boundary line that was different from the line in the Judgment – and that apparently resulted from a negotiation over possibly oil and gas reserves in the disputed area.[33]

The boundary case brought by Cameroon against Nigeria faced more complex compliance problems. In its 2002 judgment, the Court awarded the important territorial areas of the Bakassi peninsula to Cameroon.[34] These territories had been administered by Nigeria, and Nigerian minorities lived there. Nigeria at first rejected the judgment. Former UN Secretary-General Kofi Annan mediated between the two countries and a commission to facilitate the peaceful implementation of the judgment was then created.[35] Though the Nigerian Senate rejected the transfer of Bakassi as unconstitutional in 2007, the territory was finally transferred

ushered in a new era of cooperation between the two states, and strengthened ties throughout the region." Jones, "Why Comply?," 70.

[30] Kasikili/Sedudu Island (*Bostwana/Namibia*), 1999 ICJ Rep. 1045.

[31] Jones, "Why Comply?," 68.

[32] Maritime Delimitation in the Area Between Greenland and Jan Mayen (*Denmark* v. *Norway*), 1993 ICJ Rep. 38.

[33] Paulson, "Compliance with Final Judgments," 452.

[34] The Land and Maritime Boundary Between Cameroon and Nigeria (*Cameroon* v. *Nigeria: Equatorial Guinea Intervening*), 2002, ICJ Rep. 303. See generally Higgins, "Debate on Strengthening International Law."

[35] Jones, "Why Comply?," 63. (Stating that "through mediation efforts, the United Nations played a pivotal role in the easing of tension and renewing cordiality between Cameroon and Nigeria.")

to Cameroon in 2008.[36] Compliance in this case happened, but required additional time and additional negotiations between the parties.

Parties have only rarely selected to request the assistance of the Security Council to secure the implementation of an ICJ decision. When they have done so, their success has been mixed. For example, in the case brought by Chad against Libya over the sovereignty of the Aouzou Strip, both parties requested the assistance of the UN Aouzou Strip Observer Group, established by the Security Council, to oversee the implementation of the Court's Judgment. The withdrawal of the Libyan forces from the territory declared by the Court to belong to Chad followed very soon after.[37]

In other cases, actions of the Security Council succumbed to power politics. Famously, in *Military and Paramilitary Activities in and against Nicaragua*, a case brought by Nicaragua against the US, the Court found that the US had violated international law by supporting rebel antigovernment groups and by mining the harbors.[38] After the Court found it had jurisdiction, the US refused to participate in the proceedings on the merits and rejected the final judgment. In its judgment on the Merits of April 9, 1984, the Court found that the US was under an obligation to make reparation to Nicaragua for the injury caused by its violation of international law. The Court also decided that the form and amount of the reparation would be decided by the Court only if the parties could not reach an agreement themselves. Nicaragua requested the intervention of the Security Council to enforce the decision of the Court. However, the United States blocked any action by the Security Council using its power of veto, clearly demonstrating the limit of an enforcement mechanism that relies on a political body designed as the Security Council. Indeed, Schulte remarks that cases of defiance of ICJ judgments "regularly involve a permanent member either on the applicant or the respondent side, reinforcing the institution's Cold War stasis."[39] In the instant case, in 1991, after a political change in the Nicaraguan government, Nicaragua requested the Court to remove the judgment from its docket.[40]

[36] T. Gill (ed.), *Rosenne's the World Court: What It Is and How It Works* (Leiden: Brill, 2003), 212.

[37] Territorial Dispute (*Libyan Arab Jamahiriya/Chad*), 1994, ICJ Rep. 6; see also generally Higgins, "Debate on Strengthening International Law."

[38] Military and Paramilitary Activities in and against Nicaragua (*Nicaragua* v. *United States of America*), 1986 ICJ Rep. 392.

[39] Schulte, Compliance with Decisions, 417.

[40] Military and Paramilitary Activities in and against Nicaragua (*Nicaragua* v. *United States of America*), Order of September 26, 1991, 1991 ICJ Rep. 47.

The Court enjoys a good record of judgment compliance. However, there are limitations. The framework for compliance constrains the Court and the parties, and the final enforcement is left to the political organ of the United Nations. When political power is at play, compliance cannot be guaranteed. Still, in most cases, judgments of the Court provide a satisfactory closure and are generally enforced, albeit at times not immediately and/or after further negotiations between the parties are conducted.

The statutes of other international courts created links with the UN Security Council as a mechanism to encourage compliance. The Statute of the International Criminal Tribunal for the former Yugoslavia (ICTY) allows the Court to report states' noncompliance with orders to assist with the investigation to the Security Council. Similarly, the Rome Statute that created the International Criminal Court (ICC) also established an official, and complex, relation with the Security Council.

The European Court of Human Rights: Providing Semiexternal Review by the Committee of Ministers

The European Court of Human Rights hears cases related to the violation of a large number of human rights detailed in the European Convention on Human Rights (ECHR) by any of the forty-seven members states of the Council of Europe, provided certain requirements, such as the exhaustion of local remedies, are fulfilled.[41] For example, individuals can ask for redress for violations of the right to a fair hearing, the protection of property, the respect for private and family life, freedom of expression, and freedom of thought, conscience, and religion.

The ECtHR can decide on a variety of remedies if it finds that the respondent state has violated a right of the individual. First, it can provide for the payment of a just satisfaction, which included compensation for moral or material damages and for cost incurred during the proceeding. The Court can also mandate specific measures aimed at erasing the consequences of the violations for the individual, such as reopening court proceedings that were found to be unfair or repealing the conviction of a journalist who was wrongfully accused of defamation. More generally, the Court can also request the respondent state to enact measures to ensure that similar violations do not occur, for example, amend certain legislation or improve conditions of detention.[42]

[41] ECHR, November 4, 1950, ETS 5, as amended.

[42] See generally: Council of Europe, Department for the Execution of Judgments of the European Court of Human Rights, available at: www.coe.int/en/web/execution/home

Since 1998, when the jurisdiction and procedures of the ECtHR received a major overhaul,[43] the compliance mechanism of the judgments of the ECtHR is monitored by the Committee of Ministers (CoM) composed of all the foreign ministers of the member states of the Council of Europe.[44] The CoM meets four times a year to review compliance and the status of judgments that have not been complied with. Since 2007, the CoM produces an annual report that highlights the status of execution of the main judgments and provides statistics and information on cases that are still pending or were closed during the year.[45]

The ECtHR is therefore (and similarly to the ICJ) not directly responsible for the execution of its judgments, yet a specific mechanism linked to it is established as a compliance review organ. When a judgment becomes final, it is transmitted to the Committee of Ministers, which is assisted in its work by the Department for the Execution of Judgments of the European Court of Human Rights of the Council of Europe. Importantly, the CoM decides by majority, and no member enjoys a veto power. Respondent states transmit an action plan to the CoM to describe how they plan to execute the judgment, which will then be followed by an action report. The CoM reviews the plan and the report, and decides whether to accept it or not. During the time leading to the supervision process, applicants can inform the CoM of any problems they encounter in securing the execution of the judgments. Interested NGOs and civil society representatives can also communicate with the CoM in relation to the execution of a particular judgment.[46]

Further, the Council of Europe allows the CoM to suspend membership of a state for failure to implement judgments. Although the Council of Europe has never formally suspended a noncompliant member, it voted to suspend Russia's voting rights due to noncompliance with ECtHR decisions.[47]

(accessed July 27, 2017). For the mandate of the Department, see https://rm.coe.int/16805a997c (accessed July 27, 2017).

43 With the entry into force of Protocol 11, restructuring the control power of the human rights protection system under the Council of Europe and providing direct access to individuals. See Protocol 11, available at: https://rm.coe.int/168007cda9 (accessed July 27, 2017).

44 ECHR, November 4, 1950, ETS 5, as amended by Protocols Nos. 11 and 14, Art 46.

45 The Annual Reports for 2007–2014 are available at: www.coe.int/en/web/execution/annual-reports (accessed June 12, 2017).

46 See generally, Council of Europe, "The Supervision Process." Available at: www.coe.int/en/web/execution/the-supervision-process (accessed July 27, 2017).

47 C. Hillbrecht, "The rocky relationship between Russia and the European Court of Human Rights," *The Washington Post*, April 23, 2014. Available at: www.washingtonpost.com/news/monkey-cage/wp/2014/04/23/the-rocky-relationship-between-russia-and-the-european-court-of-human-rights/ (accessed July 27, 2017).

The ECtHR is a success story amidst international courts. It has become enormously active and influential in Europe, so much so that its docket has ballooned almost to its stretching point. Its judgments have been largely complied with by member states, and indeed the ECtHR has "long boasted perfect or near perfect compliance."[48]

On one side, this case can be explained by the strong commitment to human rights protection in Europe, especially after WWII. In fact, domestic actors – like the legislature, the executive, an independent judiciary, and civil society – play a key role in the execution of ECtHR's judgments. The record of compliance is therefore enhanced as those domestic actors become stronger.[49]

On the other side, some commentators have also pointed out that the ECtHR has often chosen low cost judgments, making it relatively easy for member states to comply.[50] For example, the ECtHR has traditionally provided the individual with a modest compensation of a few thousands euros, so that paying the sum would not be too burdensome for the respondent state.[51] More recently, however, the ECtHR has signaled a change of course in a judgment in favor of Yukos, a former oil giant company, in case Yukos brought against Russia.[52]

In this 2011 decision, the ECtHR found that Yukos' rights had been violated by Russia and held that its right to fairness in legal proceedings in relation to a tax reassessment for 2000 had been breached. The Court also found that Russia had violated Yukos' right to protection of property through enforcement proceedings carried out over tax assessments from 2000 to 2003. In the compensation proceedings, concluded in July 2014, the ECtHR awarded US$ 1.86 billion in just compensation, by far the largest amount it has ever awarded.

The judgment remains unpaid. Russia failed to submit a comprehensive plan, including a binding time frame, for the payment of the judgment by the initial deadline set by the CoM of June 2015. Russia also advised the CoM that it had submitted a request to Russia's Constitutional Court on the matter, which was issued in January 2017.

48 Shany, *Assessing the Effectiveness of International Courts*, 125.

49 C. Hillbrecht, "The Power of Human Rights Tribunals: Compliance with the European Court of Human Rights and Domestic Policy Change," *European Journal of International Relations*, 20, no. 4 (2014), 1117.

50 Shany, *Assessing the Effectiveness of International Courts*, 125.

51 See D. Shelton, "Performance of Regional Human Rights Courts," this volume.

52 *Case of OAO Neftyanaya Kompaniya Yukos* v. *Russia* (Just Satisfaction) [2014] ECtHR App No. 14902/04.

In its meeting of March 2017, the CoM expressed serious concern at the nonimplementation of the judgment of July 31, 2014, and reiterated the unconditional obligation assumed by Russia to abide to the judgment of the European Court, and resumed consideration of this case in September 2017.[53] At the moment of writing, it seems unlikely that the sum will ever be paid. If that remains the case, it will undermine the record of the Court and weaken its stature as one of the most effective courts among international courts.[54]

Another reason that may explain the low cost of compliance with judgments of the ECtHR may be the adoption by the ECtHR of a doctrine of "margin of appreciation" that allows member states a significant individual leeway when making decisions in relation to the application of ECHR provisions. By allowing states a margin of appreciation, one can argue, the ECtHR does not enter into some of the most contested issues, and allows the state to decide the most appropriate method to apply a provision into its domestic system. For example, in *Şahin* v. *Turkey*, a case that went all the way to the Grand Chamber, the ECtHR upheld a Turkish law that banned wearing the Islamic headscarf in state institutions, including public universities, and found that having regard to Turkey's margin of appreciation, the ban could be considered necessary in a democratic society and proportioned with the aim of secularism and equality pursued by Turkey.[55]

More specifically, the case was brought by Leyla Şahin a practicing Muslim who considered her religious duty to wear the Islamic headscarf. At the relevant time in 1998, she was studying medicine at the University of Istanbul, a public university. In the same year, the University issued a circular advising students with beards and wearing the Islamic headscarf that they would be refused admission to lectures, courses, and tutorials. Later in the year, Ms. Şahin was indeed denied access to a written examination because she was wearing the Islamic headscarf. She was also subsequently refused enrollment in university courses. Ms. Şahin brought a case to the ECtHR claiming, inter alia, that those measures violated her right to freedom of thought, conscience and

[53] *OAO Neftyanaya Komaniya Yukos* v. *Russia* (Enhanced Procedure), 14902/04, Last Exam of the Committee of Ministers, Note of March 7–10, 2017.

[54] Note that under Art. 46 of the ECHR, the CoM could serve a formal notice on the Party that has not complied with the decision and then refer to the Court the question whether that Party has failed to fulfill its obligation. If the Court finds a violation it can refer the case to the Committee of Ministers for consideration of the measures to be taken.

[55] *Leyla Şahin* v. *Turkey* [2005] ECtHR App. No. 44774/98.

religion, and the prohibition of discrimination – as protected by Articles 9 and 14 of the ECHR respectively. The ECtHR found that the measures did interfere with those provisions, but that there was a legal basis for the interference, which was grounded on the principles of secularism and equality that the Court found to be consistent with the values underpinning the ECHR. The ECtHR thus found that the restrictions, duly enacted by law, were necessary to protect the rights and freedom of others and to protect the public order, and held that their enactment was within the margin of appreciation of Turkey.[56]

The case may seem surprising, but it epitomizes the deference that the ECtHR provides to member states in the application of the doctrine of margin of appreciation. It also means that many possibly contested issues are left out of the purview of the Court, possibly making other remaining judgments "low-cost," and thus more easily compliable.

The same margin of appreciation doctrine can be used by states to comply with general measures ordered by the ECtHR. Indeed, while states have a legal obligation to remedy a violation, they enjoy a margin of appreciation as to how to do so. So, general measures necessary to prevent violations in possible future situations are identified by the state itself and presented to the CoM in an action plan. Depending on the judgment, such measures can include adoption of remedies to prevent excessive length of court proceedings or to limit restrictions on the freedom of expression of journalists or to ensure that telephone tapping is not arbitrary.[57]

The record of compliance with judgments of the ECtHR is a positive one. Though the CoM is, as the Security Council, a political organ, its power of supervision is more equalitarian, and (differently from the Security Council) no member state enjoys a veto power.[58] Member states can use political pressure to ensure compliance, but not to undermine it.

It is worth noting that the American Convention on Human rights also allows the Inter-American Court of Human rights (IACtHR) to refer noncompliance to the Organization of American States' (OAS) General

[56] For an overview of the case, see ECtHR, Press Release Issued by the Registrar, Grand Chamber Judgment *Leyla Şahin* v. *Turkey*, November 10, 2005. Available at: http://hudoc.echr.coe.int/eng-press?i=003-1503367-1572572 (accessed July 27, 2017).

[57] Council of Europe, "The Supervision Process."

[58] See CoM, Rules of the Committee of Ministers for the supervision of the execution of judgments and of the terms of friendly settlements (Adopted by the Committee of Ministers on May 10, 2006 at the 964th meeting of the Ministers' Deputies), doc no. CM/Del/Dec(2006)964/4.4-app4 12/05/2006, available at: https://search.coe.int/cm/Pages/result_details.aspx?ObjectId=09000016805d7e18 (accessed June 12, 2017).

Assembly. However, as one judge observed, "there exists no mechanism for the OAS General Assembly to regularly discuss the court's compliance reports."[59] In the context of the IACtHR, compliance is largely left to the Court itself.[60]

The International Convention on the Settlement of Investment Dispute: Immediate Effect of Awards in Domestic Courts

The International Convention for the Settlement of Investment Disputes (ICSID Convention) provides a framework to resolve international investment disputes by binding arbitration.

Investors bring cases against contracting states on the basis of applicable legal instruments (typically bilateral investment agreements, contracts, or domestic laws) that guarantee certain rights to the investor, such as the rights of nondiscrimination, fair and equitable treatment, and the provision of full protection and security to the investment.

Typically, ICSID tribunals' awards order the payment for damages, interests and costs. The ICSID Convention mandates contracting states to recognize an award rendered pursuant under ICSID "as binding and enforce the pecuniary obligations imposed by that award within its territories as if it were a final judgment of a court in that state."[61] This provision gives ICSID awards the same stature as that of a final domestic judgment which are to "be governed by the laws concerning the execution of judgments in force in the state in whose territories such execution is sought."[62] Thus, an ICSID award does not have to be recognized by a domestic court to be executed, rather, it can be immediately enforced. One restriction, however, remains. ICSID awards do not derogate from domestic provisions related to immunity of the state for certain state assets in a foreign country. Given that awards are generally issued against a state, this may become problematic.[63]

[59] As reported in Huneeus, "Compliance with Judgments and Decisions," 450.
[60] See Shelton, "Performance of Regional Human Rights Courts."
[61] ICSID Convention, March 18, 1965, 575 UNTS 159, Art. 54.
[62] ICSID Convention, Art. 54(3).
[63] See A. Bjorklund, "Sovereign Immunity as a Barrier to the Enforcement of Investor-State Arbitral Awards: The Re-Politicization of International Investment Disputes," *American Review of International Arbitration*, 21, nos. 1–4 (2010), 219; I. Uchkunova and O. Temnikov, "Enforcement of Awards under the ICSID Convention: What Solutions to the Problem of State Immunity?," *ICSID Review—Foreign Investment Law Journal*, 29, no. 1 (2014); D. Behn, "The Performance of Investment Treaty Arbitration," Chapter 3.

Still, the great majority of ICSID awards have been respected and awards have usually been paid.[64] Indeed, investors have an expectation that states will enforce the pecuniary obligations of awards.[65] There are several reasons that give support to this expectation. States rely on foreign investors and are reluctant to act in a way that would damage their credibility in the international investment community or their appeal to foreign investors.[66] Should it become known that a state does not comply with an ICSID award, a similarly situated foreign investor may decide not to invest or to postpone its investment until the situation is resolved.[67]

More recently, however, certain states, including Venezuela and Argentina, have refused to comply with ICSID awards, contesting the jurisdiction of ICSID or citing additional procedural requirements.[68]

Under the letter of the ICSID Convention, enforcement mechanisms are limited. Article 53 only provides that "the award shall be binding on the parties and shall not be subject to any appeal or to any other remedy except those provided for in this Convention. Each party shall abide by and comply with the terms of the award except to the extent that enforcement shall have been stayed pursuant to the relevant provisions of [the] Convention."[69] However, claimants have resorted to important diplomatic and trade-related mechanisms to encourage compliance.

Argentina is an interesting example. Argentina faced a severe economic and political crisis in early 2000s, and took several actions that impacted the rights of the many foreign investors active in that country. Many foreign investors claimed that these actions violated their internationally recognized rights and filed claims at ICSID. Soon, Argentina was confronted with forty-three claims at ICSID, the largest number of cases ever brought against an ICSID member.[70] As a matter of course,

[64] C. Rosenberg, "The Intersection of International Trade and International Arbitration: Suspending Trade Benefits to 'Encourage' Compliance with ICSID Awards," *Transnational Dispute Management*, 3 (2014).

[65] A. S. Alexandroff and I. A. Laird, "Compliance and Enforcement," in P. Muchlinski, F. Ortino, and C. Shreuer (eds.), *The Oxford Handbook of International Investment Law* (Oxford: Oxford University Press, 2008).

[66] Rosenberg, "The Intersection of International Trade and International Arbitration," 4.

[67] Bjorklund, "Sovereign Immunity as a Barrier," 219.

[68] Rosenberg, "The Intersection of International Trade and International Arbitration," 3–8. For an analysis of Argentina and ICSID, see O. Lopez, "Smart Move: Argentina to Leave the ICSID," *Cornell Journal of International Law Online*, 1 (2014).

[69] ICSID Convention, Art.53.

[70] L. Reed, "Scorecard of Investment Treaty Cases Against Argentina since 2001," *Kluwer Arbitration Blog*, March 2, 2009. Available at: http://kluwerarbitrationblog.com/2009/03/

Argentina resisted those procedures and tried to prolong them as much as possible, frequently challenging arbitrators and requesting annulments of most awards. Argentina was also one of the few countries that resisted enforcement of ICISD awards.

For example, in *Azurix* v. *Argentina*, the claimant, a US water service company, was awarded US$ 65 million in compensation because the tribunal found that Argentina had acted arbitrarily and in violation of its obligation to provide fair and equitable treatment and full protection and security to Azurix investment.[71] Argentina refused to pay the award, even after its request for annulment was rejected.[72]

Azurix took some unusual steps to persuade Argentina to comply with the award, which became final in September 2009. In May 2009, the US Trade Representative (USTR) had initiated the 2009 Annual Review of its Generalized System of Preferences (GSP) program "to modify the GSP status of certain GSP beneficiary developing countries because of country practices." In December 2009, Azurix filed a petition with the USTR office requesting the US withdraw Argentina's designation as beneficiary because of her failure to enforce the Azurix award.[73] A similar request was also filed in June 2010 by Blue Ridge Investment for Argentina's failure to enforce *CSM Gas* v. *Argentina*, another ICSID award worth more than US$ 132 million, to which it was the beneficiary.[74] The petitions were accepted for review, and in 2012 US President Obama declared that it was appropriate to suspend Argentina's trade preferential status because Argentina's failure to "act in good faith in recognizing as binding or in enforcing arbitral awards in favor of US citizens or a corporation."[75] Argentina was, in 2011, the ninth-largest beneficiary of GSP, which allowed her to export goods valued at more than US$ 470 million duty free. Argentina's suspension of GSP status had immediate repercussion. In November 2013, Argentina announced that it had settled five

02/scorecard-of-investment-treaty-cases-against-argentina-since-2001/ (accessed June 12, 2017).

71 *Azurix Corp.* v. *The Argentine Republic*, (ICSID Case No. ARB/01/12). 72 Ibid.

73 See, generally, Rosenberg, "The Intersection of International Trade and International Arbitration," 12–13.

74 *CMS Gas Transmission Company* v. *The Republic of Argentina* (ICSID Case No. ARB/01/8).

75 President Obama suspended aid to Argentina on the basis of their noncompliance with ICSID. See Proclamation 8788 of March 26, 2012. Available at: www.gpo.gov/fdsys/pkg/CFR-2013-title3-vol1/pdf/CFR-2013-title3-vol1-proc8788.pdf (accessed July 27, 2017).

outstanding ICSID awards, including Azurix and CSM.[76] More recently, Argentina also settled other high-stake cases relating to the sale of sovereign bonds, mostly to Italian investors.[77]

ICSID awards are most often complied with: states readily pay up the damages investors are awarded. When this is not done, parties have found an effective political way to ensure compliance, as the example of Argentina shows.

The United Nations Claims Commission: Creation of a Special Fund to Ensure Compliance

The United Nations Compensation Commission (UNCC) was created as a subsidiary organ of the United Nations Security Council under Security Council resolution 687 (1991) to process claims and pay compensation for losses and damage suffered as a direct result of Iraq's unlawful invasion and occupation of Kuwait in 1990–1991.

The UNCC was a unique structure, and was organized as a claims commission able to hear claims from individuals, international organizations and states that had suffered losses as a result of Iraq's invasion of Kuwait. Also uniquely, the UN Security Council Resolution 692 (1991) created a United Nations Compensation Fund to pay compensation for successful claims at the UNCC and the Commission administered the Fund. Financing for the fund were received from a percentage of the sale of oil from Iraq.[78]

Under the UNCC, claims were divided in six categories. Category "A" claims were for departure from Iraq and Kuwait during the period of August 2, 1990 to March 2, 1991. Category "B" claims were claims for or the payment of fixed amounts to any person who, as a result of Iraq's unlawful invasion and occupation of Kuwait, suffered serious

[76] Allan & Overy, "Argentina Settles Five Investment Treaty Awards," November 7, 2013. Available at: www.allenovery.com/publications/en-gb/Pages/Argentina-settles-five-investment-treaty-awards.aspx (accessed June 12, 2017).

[77] Herbert Smith Freehills, "Argentina Settles Five Outstanding Investment Treaty Arbitration Claims in Historic Break with its Anti-Enforcement Stance," October 14, 2013. Available at: http://hsfnotes.com/arbitration/2013/10/14/argentina-settles-five-outstanding-investment-treaty-arbitration-claims-in-historic-break-with-its-anti-enforcement-stance/ (accessed June 12, 2017).

[78] See generally, V. Heiskanen, "The United Nations Compensation Commission," *Recueil des Cours: Collected Courses of The Hague Academy of International Law*, 296, (2002), 393. L. Brilmayer, C. Giorgetti, and L. Charlton, *International Claims Commissions: Righting Wrongs After Conflict* (Cheltenham: Edward Elgar Publishing, 2017)

personal injury, or whose spouse, child, or parent died. Claims "C" were individual claims for damages up to US$100,000 and "D" were individual claims for damages in excess of US$100,000. Category "E" claims: claims by corporations, other private legal entities, and public sector enterprises and Category "F" were claims of governments and international organizations. Individual claims were processed and decided first, using mass claims techniques and data processing. Claims from governments, international organizations and private and public enterprises were considered large and complex claims and were considered at a later stage. These claims were processed more similarly to arbitration claims, whereby both parties argued and presented their evidence.[79]

The UNCC, which has now completed its work, processed more than 2.5 million claims and awarded compensation for over 1.5 million claims for a total of US$52 billion. Thanks to the creation of the fund mechanism, most of the claims have been paid. The Commission paid out about US$ 47.8 billion in compensation awards to successful claimants. The existing balance of US$ 4.6 billion relate to one category of claims only ("E1") for outstanding production and sales losses as a result of damages to Kuwait's oil-field assets.[80]

Overall, the UNCC has been a success in terms of compliance with judgments. This is certainly, even if not completely, due to the fact that the UNCC is the product of very unique circumstances that made it possible to create a fund for payment of all awards. These circumstances include a (rare) concerted action of the UN Security Council, a clear losing party (Iraq) and the possibility to get funds from oil-for-food sanctions directly into a separate account to be used to pay awards.

Other reasons also explain the perceived success of the UNCC. First, the UNCC adopted an expedited procedure to process small claims of individuals who were forced to leave Kuwait after Iraq's invasion. These claims, the most numerous by far, were considered a priority and were processed first and through a mass claims process that ensured expeditious resolution. In that way, the UNCC also assured immediate results.

Second, the UNCC also had sufficient funds to create a web of legal and technical personnel who quickly became experts in claims. The UNCC

[79] See generally, T. J. Feighery, "The United Nations Compensation Commission" in C. Giorgetti (ed.), *The Rules, Practice, and Jurisprudence of International Courts and Tribunals* (Leiden: Nijhoff, 2012), 515.

[80] See generally, L. Brilmayer, C. Giorgetti, and L. Charlton, *International Claims Commissions: Righting Wrongs after Conflict* (Cheltenham, UK: Edward Elgar 2017), chapter 4.

became an efficient body, and a rare example of a UN organ that dissolved when its operations had been completed. The Secretariat of the UNCC, sitting in Geneva, acted as a neutral body who was able to coordinate and mediate among the many parties involved.[81]

Finally, one should also note that the UNCC decisions were balanced. Overall, claimants got only about 14.86 percent of the amount claimed. This is important for two reasons: first because, given the historical background related to the creation of the UNCC, it is important that the UNCC was seen as fair and neutral and not just awarding compensation to all claimants. Second, because the UNCC showed that it was discerning between real claims and overblown claims by states in the region. For example, while about 91 percent of the compensation sought for category A (small and individual) claims was awarded, only 6.2 percent of amount claimed in category F4 (large and complex) claims was accepted.

The UNCC certainly was a unique institution with a unique mandate. However, important lessons can be drawn from its success.

Factors Influencing Compliance

The overview above assessed some of the mechanisms in place that support courts and parties to reach successful compliance of judgments. It is striking to note that, by and large, these mechanisms are not particularly strong. Yet, judgment compliance remains the norm. Indeed, parties seem to mostly comply with international judicial decisions despite generally fable enforcement measures. Thus, in addition to analyzing mechanisms in place to ensure compliance, it is also important to appraise factors that affect compliance. These factors emanate both from internal features proper of the judgment, as well as relate to external characteristics that are typical of the dispute.

Internal Factors Affecting Compliance

Several factors deriving from the structure of the court may affect compliance. The section below analyses five such factors, and namely: the types of remedies awarded, the available compliance mechanisms, the low/high cost of compliance, the kind of case and the composition of the

81 A. Spain, "Using International Dispute Resolution to Address the Compliance Question in International Law," *Georgetown Journal of International Law*, 40, no. 3 (2009), 847.

court. Some scholars have also noted that compliance is more likely when parties have given specific consent to the proceedings before the court.[82] However, Paulson observes that at the ICJ there was "no link between submission by special agreement and compliance"[83] and Llamzon also confirms that "the mode by which the ICJ was seized of jurisdiction thus appears to be a rather poor predictor of subsequent compliance."[84]

What Remedies Were Awarded?

Successful compliance is also a function of the kind of remedies that are available to courts. In general, the less onerous the remedies issued are, the more likely it is for the losing party to comply with the judgment.

As explained earlier, certain international courts and tribunals, like the tribunals instituted under the International Convention for the Settlement of Investment Disputes, usually only issue remedies in the form of monetary compensation or damages. Awards issued by ICSID tribunals are generally expeditiously complied with. Other courts and tribunals have more complex remedies systems. In judgments of the ECtHR, for example, a usually modest monetary compensation for "just satisfaction" is often coupled with a request to reform some facets of the legal system that resulted in the human rights violation. Similarly, judgments of the IACtHR have called for the establishment of a remembrance day or other nonmonetary remedies.

Compliance with monetary judgments is generally easier that complying with other forms of remedies. For example, the record of human rights tribunals shows that judgments ordering the payment of monetary compensation are more likely to be complied with than those awarding other kinds of remedy.[85] Huneeus observes that equitable relief orders, such as those ordering an investigation of a crime, receive lower compliance.[86] The record of the IACtHR is emblematic in this respect. One study shows that only 6 percent of the IACtHR's decisions receive full compliance.[87] Shany asserts that this is because the IACtHR's

82 Schulte, *Compliance with Decisions.*
83 Paulson, "Compliance with Final Judgments," 457.
84 Llamzon, "Jurisdiction and Compliance in Recent Decisions of the International Court of Justice," 852.
85 Huneeus, "Compliance with Judgments and Decisions," 448.
86 Huneeus, "Compliance with Judgments and Decisions," 448. For additional information on the court's judgment-compliance, see A. Huneeus, "Courts Resisting Courts: Lessons from the Inter-American Court's Struggle to Enforce Human Rights," *Cornell International Law Journal*, 44, no. 3 (2011), 493.
87 Hawkins and Jacoby, "Partial Compliance," 59.

remedies often "specify onerous individual and general measures that bear significant financial and political implications" unlike those of the ECtHR.[88] The ECtHR has also until recently refrained from issuing very large compensation, making it easy for states found in violation to issue the payment. Whether this will remain the same in the post-Yukos world remains to be seen.[89]

Compliance in monetary judgments may also be linked not only to the total amount awarded by the tribunal (the larger the sum the less likely it is to be paid), but also to how the sum awarded compares with the amount initially requested by the parties.

What Compliance Mechanisms Exist?

Compliance is also affected by the type of and the existence of compliance procedures within each forum. As explained earlier, different forums are endowed with different compliance mechanisms.

In certain forums, for example, compliance with judgments is verified periodically. If a party is not in compliance with a judgment of the ECtHR, for example, a specific procedure is followed to develop a plan with the CoM to bring the state into compliance. The plan for compliance is then reviewed and followed up, and parties can communicate any problems they may have during the execution. Interested NGOs and civil society can also be in contact with the CoM in relation to the execution of a particular judgment. These kinds of ex-post follow-ups both encourage and ensure compliance.

External or semi-external bodies tasked with ensuring compliance, however, are quite rare. Even in the case of the Security Council, its role in ensuring compliance is not a principal function and is seldom used by the parties.

Automatic mechanisms for compliance also make a difference. The existence of specific, dedicated funds to comply with monetary judgments also affect compliance and makes it easier. In the case of the UNCC, for example, the existence of specific funds controlled by the UNCC to pay awards made it simpler to pay all awards. The Iran-US Claims Tribunal (IUSCT) also adopted a similar mechanism that also simplified the enforcement of awards. Under the Algiers Accord which created the IUSCT, Iran agreed to place US$ 1 billion in an account as security for payment of IUSCT awards against Iran, and to keep that

[88] Shany, *Assessing the Effectiveness of International Courts*, 126.

[89] See above discussion on the ECtHR and review by the Committee of Ministers.

account at US$ 500 million until all awards against Iran were satisfied.[90]

Cost of Compliance: Low and High Cost Decisions

Another element that could promote compliance is the kind of decision that the court produces. Indeed, courts may adopt several means to make a substantive judgment a low-cost decision for the losing party.

If the losing party finds that the substantive part of the judgment is understandable and that the court listened to its arguments, it will make it easier to comply. For example, a court can induce low resistance in a judgment by including language that support or accept some of the positions expressed by the losing party, thus showing a sympathetic eye. The WTO Appellate Body (AB) did so magisterially in the *US-Shrimp* case, where it took pains to show how the US position was understandable, though it could not agree to it from a legal prospective under WTO rules.[91] When the AB explained why it ruled against the US in a case brought by India, Malaysia, Pakistan, and Thailand over certain US measures prohibiting the import of shrimp and shrimp products from noncertified countries that had not used a certain net to catch the shrimp, it stated:

> In reaching these conclusions, we wish to underscore what we have *not* decided in this appeal. We have *not* decided that the protection and preservation of the environment is of no significance to the Members of the WTO. Clearly, it is. We have *not* decided that the sovereign nations that are Members of the WTO cannot adopt effective measures to protect endangered species, such as sea turtles. Clearly, they can and should. And we have *not* decided that sovereign states should not act together bilaterally, plurilaterally or multilaterally, either within the WTO or in other international fora, to protect endangered species or to otherwise protect the environment. Clearly, they should and do.
>
> What we *have* decided in this appeal is simply this: although the measure of the United States in dispute in this appeal serves an environmental objective that is recognized as legitimate under paragraph (g) of Article XX of the GATT 1994, this measure has been applied by the United States in a manner which constitutes arbitrary and unjustifiable discrimination between Members of the WTO, contrary to the requirements of the chapeau of Article XX.[92]

[90] For more information, see the website of the Tribunal at: www.iusct.net/Pages/Public/A-About.aspx.

[91] Appellate Body Report, *United States – Import Prohibition of Certain Shrimp and Shrimp Products*, WT/DS58/AB/R (October 12, 1998).

[92] Ibid., paras. 185–186 (emphasis in original).

It is hard to think of a better way to soothe the hurt ego of a losing party than to say that their position was completely understandable, but that the court was constrained by the letter of the law to decide as it did.

On the other hand, courts may also be too inclined to aim low and neutralize adverse consequences and possible resistance. In this sense, the ICJ Kosovo Advisory Opinion is telling. In this decision, the Court was requested by the UN General Assembly to decide whether Kosovo's unilateral declaration of independence in respect of Kosovo was in accordance with international law.[93] By ten votes to four, the Court found that the declaration of independence of Kosovo adopted on February 17, 2008 did not violate international law. By doing so, however, the ICJ decided on very narrow grounds and avoided opining on the underlying question of the existence of a right to succession in international law, which was at the heart of the matter.[94]

A judgment of a court may also affect sensitive political issues, though it is not always easy for a court to predict how the judgment will be received. For example, in *Greens* v. *UK*, the ECtHR ordered the UK in 2010 to revoke within six months from the judgment its blanket prohibition on prisoners' voting. The judgment touched a hugely sensitive issue in British politics. It has still not been complied with, and it has been cited as one of the causes of British dissatisfaction with the ECtHR and European politics.[95]

Type of Cases

The type of cases may also affect compliance. Indeed, cases that involve land boundary disputes, have a history of armed conflict and involve a high number of people or large areas generally receive the lowest level of compliance.[96] Further, boundary decisions also involve complex technical issues and parties may require outside support to finalize the demarcation on the ground.[97]

Further, highly controversial or politically sensitive cases are less likely to receive compliance. For example, the 2002 decision of the

93 Accordance with International Law of the Unilateral Declaration of Independence in Respect of Kosovo, Advisory Opinion, 2010 ICJ Rep. 403.

94 Ibid.

95 *Greens and MT* v. *UK* [2010] ECtHR App. Nos. 60041/08 and 60054/08. (The case concerned two British prisoners serving determined sentences in the UK. Applying its pilot judgment procedure, the Court gave the UK Government six months to introduce legislative measures to bring the UK into judgment compliance.)

96 Paulson, "Compliance with Final Judgments," 457.

97 Ibid., 437.

Eritrea-Ethiopia Boundary Commission on the location and demarcation of the boundary between the two countries has still not been complied with by Ethiopia, which has refused to leave the territory awarded to Eritrea, and which was one of the main reasons for the Eritrea – Ethiopia War. [98]

The extent to which the law has been developed in a particular field also matters. Deciding situations where the law is very much in development may be particularly challenging for international courts.[99]

An important element that affects compliance is also the determinacy of the decision.[100] In fact, research shows that "vague judicial opinions are less likely to be implemented than clear opinions."[101] Parties may find it difficult to decipherer what the judgments say, or they may use the vagueness of the opinion as an excuse to delay or refuse compliance.[102]

Composition of the Court

Some research also suggests that the composition of the court itself may affect compliance. For example, in an empirical study, Erik Voeten found that "judgments written by benches with a relatively high proportion of career judges are more likely to be implemented quickly than judgments that come from a bench with high proportions of former academics, legal diplomats, politicians, or private practitioners."[103] The study analyzed judgments of the ECtHR, which is composed of judges from each of the member states with great variance in background. Voeten suggested that one of the reasons for this may be that professional judges "have practice in how to write judgments that appeal to domestic compliance constituencies."[104]

Given the varied background of judges in international courts and tribunals, this is certainly an interesting issue to consider.

[98] Fikrejesus Amahazion, Justice Deferred: The 15th Anniversary of the Eritrea-Ethiopia Boundary Commission Verdict, Foreign Policy Journal, April 14, 2017 Available at: www.foreignpolicyjournal.com/2017/04/14/justice-deferred-the-15th-anniversary-of-the-eritrea-ethiopia-boundary-commission-verdict/.

[99] Schulte, *Compliance with Decisions*, 414. [100] Jones, "Why Comply?," 72.

[101] J. Staton and G. Vanberg, "The Value of Vagueness: Delegation, Defiance, and Judicial Opinions," *American Journal of Political Science*, 52, no. 3 (2008), 504.

[102] Jones, "Why Comply?," 72.

[103] E. Voeten, "Does a Professional Judiciary Induce More Compliance?: Evidence from the European Court of Human Rights." Working Paper, March 2012. Available at: https://ssrn.com/abstract=2029786 (cited with permission).

[104] Ibid., 2.

External Factors

There are also external factors, proper of the dispute and not the judgment, that may affect compliance. These include external pressure and internal features of the state.

External Pressure

Outside pressure is another important element that encourages judgment compliance. This pressure can come both from the international community generally, or from specific actors in the region. The presence, as well as the assistance, of international organizations in the area where the judgment is to be complied with also encourages compliance.[105] For example, Peskin argues that the fact the ICTY and the International Criminal Tribunal for Rwanda (ICTR) got favorable press coverage and were able to convince third states to support their order were important factors of their success.[106] On the other hand, pressure (or lack thereof) may also ostracize compliance. For example, in the case brought to the ICJ by Chad against Libya over the sovereignty of the Aouzou (discussed above), Libya's initial acceptance of the judgment was disregarded. However, had the international community more readily acknowledged Libya's predicament, Libya would have most likely felt more pressure to enforce the judgment rather than delaying.[107]

In addition to international pressure it is also important to consider internal pressure to comply by the relevant constituencies, as well as pressure from the other party and its allies. The relative power relations between the two parties can also play an important role.[108] Moreover, when the parties in the dispute have a close relationship, because of cultural, historical, or economic ties, parties are generally more inclined to comply with the judgment they receive.[109]

Further, the reputational costs of noncompliance also provide an important incentive to comply.[110] In fact, when an international judgment is issued, it becomes important to states to be seen as being in compliance with it to maintain their international status and thus access to future bargaining situations, including those relating to trade and

[105] K. Alter, *The New Terrain of International Law* (Princeton: Princeton University Press, 2014).

[106] V. Peskin, *International Justice in Rwanda and the Balkans: Virtual Trials and the Struggle for State Cooperation* (Cambridge: Cambridge University Press, 2008), 7.

[107] Paulson, "Compliance with Final Judgments," 441. [108] Jones, "Why Comply?," 72.

[109] Ibid., 70. [110] Ibid., 58.

investment.[111] The case of Argentina at the ICSID, discussed above, is a telling example of the reputational costs that disregard of international decisions can incur and the consequences, for example, to Argentina's access to foreign capital.

Features of the Implementing State

Another factor that could affect compliance with a judgment relates to the domestic legal system. In fact, it is important to consider how international judgments are adopted domestically and whether they can be immediately executed or have to be first formally accepted in a domestic system.

The complex case of the attempt to implement the ICJ *Avena* judgment in the US is telling. *Avena* was the last of a series of cases brought against the US for violation of the Vienna Convention on Consular Relations. In its 2004 judgment, the ICJ found that the US had breached its treaties obligations by not informing fifty-one Mexican nationals arrested and imprisoned for crimes in the US of their right to access the Mexican consulate.[112] The Court found, by fourteen votes to one, that the appropriate reparation in the case consisted of the obligation of the US to provide, by means of its own choosing, review and reconsideration of the convictions and sentences of the Mexican nationals.

José Medellín, who was given the death penalty in 1997, was one of the named Mexicans in the *Avena* case. His case went all the way to the US Supreme Court, who accepted a *writ of certoriari* in 2008. Before the Supreme Court heard the case, then President George W. Bush issued a Memorandum to the United States Attorney General, in which he asserted that he had the authority under the US Constitution and laws to order states to review the convictions and sentences of foreign nationals who had not been advised of their Vienna Convention rights.

The Supreme Court, however, disagreed. In *Medellín* v. *Texas*, the Supreme Court held that the *Avena* judgment could not be enforced as domestic law.[113] It held that the relevant treaties (the Optional Protocol of the Vienna Convention on Consular Rights, the UN Charter, and the ICJ Statute) were not self-executing, and therefore could not be enforced until Congress's enacting legislation.

[111] Ibid., 65.

[112] Avena and Other Mexican Nationals (*Mexico* v. *United States of America*), 2004 ICJ Rep. 12.

[113] *Medellin* v. *Texas*, 552, US 491 (2008).

In contrast, supreme courts of several Latin American countries recently held that orders of the Inter-American Court of Human Rights are automatically binding and become immediately justiciable domestically.[114]

Conclusion

Compliance with judgments is a complex enterprise. It involves both legal and political factors. This chapter offers a *tour d'horizon* that discuss both existing mechanisms to ensure compliance as well as political, sociological, and other factors that affect compliance.

Ultimately, it is for states to make sure that sufficient judgment compliance mechanisms are included in the rules of procedures of international courts and tribunals. Thus, international courts also need political bodies and political will to enforce decisions. If compliance mechanisms are not included in the statutes of international courts, states cannot then complain courts do not succeed.

[114] Huneeus, "Compliance with Judgments and Decisions," 545.

11

Problem-Solving Structure and International Courts and Tribunals: Lessons from the Study of International Regimes

STEINAR ANDRESEN

Introduction: Purpose and Scope

In studying international courts and tribunals (ICs), what can we learn from how international regimes have been studied in the international relations literature? In my view, such an approach has much to offer for explaining the performance of international courts at the broader issue area level. In this exploratory chapter, I illustrate the value of the international regimes approach, without examining any specific court in detail. My main empirical focus is on international human rights and international courts within this issue area.

The first step in regime analysis is to define the regime. It may make a difference for the performance of ICs whether they are operating within the confines of an international regime or not. Also important in regime studies is the focus on why and how international regimes are established in some areas while they never emerge in others. This is relevant for international courts and tribunals as well, since there are distinct variations along this dimension. For example, in some regions there are several courts for human rights, but none in others. However, there is no universal human rights court – in contrast to the field of world trade, where the Dispute Settlement Mechanism of the World Trade Organization (WTO) represents an almost-universal judicial mechanism. How can we explain these profound differences, and what are the consequences for the significance of international courts in different issue areas?

Probably the most important contribution of international regime studies is their analysis of the effectiveness of international regimes. How, then, can effectiveness be measured and explained? Measuring effectiveness links up with one of the main goals of this book, as outlined in Chapter 1: to study the variance in the role of international courts in contributing to global governance. Against this backdrop, an important focus is on the performance of specific courts in different issue areas, making individual courts the chief unit of analysis. This makes sense – but the focus needs to be broadened to analyze their general significance within a given issue area when "(the) objective is to make judgments regarding the *proportion* of the variance in outcome that we can attribute to the activities of specific courts" emphasis added, as stated in the introductory chapter. This entails huge methodological challenges, but the main point here is that in order to decide the proportion of variation, two qualifications need to be made. First, we must control for other agents of influence, as international courts are not the only actors in various areas of global governance. This links up with the challenge of complex causality as outlined in Chapter 1. Next, an overview of the "state of affairs" or the evaluation criteria is required in order to determine the significance of ICs. For example, in some regions, international human right courts are nonexistent – but we still need to give an account of the state of affairs in these regions, to determine their overall significance within this issue area. International courts may be the main unit of analysis, but when operating at the broader issue area level we will need to cast the net wider. Admittedly there are pragmatic reasons for this broader focus, as my own knowledge of international courts is limited. However, this approach is also legitimate from a methodological point of view. My chapter therefore deals mainly with the "meso-level," and not the functions performed by individual courts in specific cases, or the micro-level. The macro-level will not be dealt with. Regime analysis is well equipped to deal with the meso-level as it focuses on the linkage between the institution at hand and behavioral change in a specific issue area.

In the introduction, the editors use some of the same factors to explain performance as are used to explain the effectiveness of international regimes. They note that various traditions in international relations may shed light on this issue. Here special emphasis will be paid to the problem structure, which is traditionally placed within the realist school of thought. In line with Underdal (2002), I find it pertinent to focus on the extent to which these international institutions are able to deal effectively with difficult or "malign" issues. Other explanatory factors from the liberal and constructivist schools of thought are also relevant, considering my focus on human rights courts. For example, the prominence assigned to "the rule of law" in a geographic area may affect both the establishment and performance of such courts. Another explanatory perspective borrowed from the international regime approach will be applied as well: the significance of the problem-solving ability of the institution in question. How well equipped are these international institutions to handle the problem at hand (Miles et al. 2002)?

The Study of International Regimes: Definition, Establishment, and Effectiveness

Opinion differs as to how many "grand theories" there are in international relations, but there is agreement there is no such thing as a "regime theory." It is more of a perspective in the study of international relations, and most scholars place it within the liberal institutional approach. However, it may also have links to realism and the social constructivist approach, as power and ideas are relevant in regime studies as well (Underdal 2002). The international regimes concept has gained increasing recognition and is widely applied in international political economy and even more so in the study of international environmental regimes.

The crux of the debate on international regimes concerns the significance of social institutions as determinants of the course of interaction among actors in international society, linked to the discussion on governance without government. *Institutions* are assemblages of rights, rules, and decision-making procedures that give rise to social practices, assign roles to the participants in these practices, and regulate interactions among them. *Regimes* are institutions specialized in a particular issue area or a spatially defined area. International regimes differ from international organizations, as the latter are material entities with offices, personnel, budgets, and legal personality. Thus, international courts are similar to international organizations often operating within broader international regimes. The relationship between regimes and organizations is therefore an important focus for study (Biermann and Siebenhuner 2009).

Opinion differs on the significance of regimes and organizations and thereby also on the significance of international courts. Those of the realist school claim that they are mere epiphenomena that echo the interests of powerful members (Strange 1983). There are those who claim that international institutions have a strong and independent effect. A middle ground has been taken by Steven Krasner (1983) in his classic definition of an international regime, where they are considered as intermediate variables. He defines international regimes as sets of implicit or explicit principles, rules and norms, and decision-making procedures around which actors' expectation converge in a given area of international relations. This definition consists of three elements: 1) an interrelated array of principles, norms, rules, and decision-making procedures; 2) a group of actors using this array to guide their expectations regarding their own behavior and that of others; and 3) an issue area where that array and those expectations will be engaged. Thus, to qualify as an international regime, actor expectations must converge because they all expect and follow a certain array of normative and procedural guidelines. If they converge for some other reason, for example due to individual utility maximization or by mere accident, there is no "regime" at work.

To qualify as a regime is rather demanding, and considerable research effort has been invested in identifying and specifying international regimes. The importance of the regime-study approach is that it stresses the significance of a regime's effect on behavior, demonstrating that quite a few agreements are "paper tigers" or "dead-letter agreements" that do not qualify as regimes (Levy et al. 1995). A major achievement of regime analysis lies in its helping to escape from the traditional formalistic description of international organizations focusing instead on the significance of international institutions from a behavioral point of view. Many micro-level studies of international courts come close to these more formalistic studies. That is why the regime study approach has something to offer when we operate at the meso-level.

Krasner (1983) introduced the idea of regimes as intervening variables, and this approach squares well with findings from subsequent research. Neither international regimes nor international courts are usually the main drivers in international politics. Other forces – such as geopolitics, economic development, technology, population growth – tend to be far more important. However, through their roles as intermediate variables, regimes and courts can channel and guide human interaction within this broader framework. As international courts are usually elements within broader regimes, their role will normally be more moderate than that of the regime as a whole. But there are instances where international institutions are independent variables – for example, the international trade regime through WTO, some argue, has had significant consequences for the development of the world economy, and its Dispute Settlement

Mechanism has become crucial in settling disputes worldwide (see Chapter 2).

So far we have discussed international regimes mainly as intervening variables. However, the first studies of international regimes focused primarily on regimes as dependent variables: What were the conditions needed for regimes – or the institutions or organizations embedded within them, such as international courts – to be established? Realists contend that the anarchy in the international system causes states to focus on relative gains, their position vis-à-vis other states in the system. Consequently, states will be reluctant to enter into cooperation that leaves them in a worse position relative to others. As regimes do in fact exist, realists have to account for their existence, and the most frequent explanation involves the hegemonic stability approach. A hegemon has the resources to support – and bear the costs of – establishing the regime even if others act as free riders. Moreover, the hegemon has enough power to compel others to participate. The regime will exist as long as the hegemon sees it in his interest; the regime will disappear when this is no longer the case. This approach certainly has some merit and can contribute to explaining, for example, the establishment of NATO as well as the Bretton Woods system. However, detailed empirical research has documented that other factors are often more important than hegemons, and regimes do not always die even if powerful actors fade away (Young and Osherenko 1993). Even though this approach has its limitations, that is not to say that power may not be important when regimes are established. As international courts can be intrusive on national sovereignty, realists would argue that ICs are established only if they are in line with the interests of the most powerful actors. Otherwise, they will be "paper tigers" without practical significance.

Adherents of the (neo)liberal school of thought accept the anarchy assumption, but, unlike realists, they claim that states are primarily preoccupied with absolute gains. When deciding whether to cooperate or not, states will reflect on what can be gained from cooperation and not on how their cost-benefit calculations compare to those of others. International regimes are regarded as mechanisms that may facilitate cooperation by providing information, reducing transaction costs, and forging useful linkages (Keohane 1984). While the interests of relevant state actors are key in this tradition, the growing role of nonstate actors is also emphasized. The gist of the argument is that international regimes can serve as useful vehicles for facilitating international cooperation, understood as mutual adjustment of behavior among the parties. And here, it would be argued, international courts could have an important role in contributing to this development.

A key feature of the social constructivist approach is that individuals and groups are shaped by their worlds, and can in turn affect changes in how international society works. This perspective views politics as a process of social learning where cooperation may change actor perceptions. Here the emphasis on learning, ideas, and knowledge in regime establishment is particularly relevant, especially the concept of expert networks or epistemic communities (Haas 1992). Such networks tend to share values and beliefs about the causes and solutions of problems identified. Ever since the late 1980s, various academics and expert networks have been active in efforts to establish an international environmental court, but without success (Zengerling 2013). This does not mean that this explanatory perspective is not relevant. However, the fact that no single state has supported this idea is a strong indication that some state leadership is needed for international courts to be established.

Unless we know that international regimes can have some effect, it does not make sense to establish them. This is why we should study their effectiveness. By far most emphasis has been on effectiveness in terms of problem solving, whether a regime has been able to make a positive difference for the problems it was established to address. Three criteria for measuring the dependent variable have been introduced: output, outcome, and impact. As these are fairly similar to the three analytical levels (micro-, meso-, and macro-level) presented in the introduction, I will not dwell on these here. However, there is one challenge – and controversy – among scholars regarding the measurement of the dependent variable that has a direct bearing on the perspective introduced in the introduction: Precisely how can we measure the proportional difference made by the relevant international court?

Underdal (2002) has introduced two measurements of effectiveness. The one compares the actual performance of the regime against a nonregime counterfactual; the other compares the state of affairs to the best solution that could be established, or the "collective optimum." The first was used as a tool to investigate whether and to what extent regimes do matter, in terms of the relative improvement brought about by the regime. The second was designed to show whether and to what extent a particular problem is in fact solved by the regime. Through a step-wise procedure, Helm and Sprinz (2000) combine these components into one comprehensive measure, arriving at a simple coefficient of regime effectiveness that falls into a standardized interval (0–1). Briefly put: It is argued that effectiveness – and performance – can be measured very precisely. However, there is no agreement among scholars that this is the case.

It has been argued that neither the nonregime counterfactual nor the collective optimum can be precisely measured. "How can we separate the signal of regime effects from the noise arising from the impacts of a wide range of other sources that operate simultaneously in our efforts to understand regime effectiveness?" (Young 2001: 100). This "noise" was identified as issuing from the basic drivers identified earlier in this chapter. They interact with each other in complex ways, producing far-reaching impacts on the problem quite apart from the dynamics of the regime. Consequently, the question becomes: "[H]ow can we determine the proportion of observed change in the target variables?" (100). This point is important for analysts of international regimes as well as for policymakers, and gives rise to serious methodological challenges. Further discussion of these is not needed for the purpose of this chapter, but I will present an empirical example to indicate my view on this question.

A recent study of the international environmental regime on acid rain (Wettestad 2011) shows how difficult it is to decide exactly how much of the change in behavior can be attributed to the regime, compared to other factors. Wettestad finds that achievements made have been the result of better scientific knowledge, an advanced regime design, changed attitudes on the part of key players, the fall of Communism, as well as an increased role of the EU. He concludes: "It is hence clearly challenging to measure the exact impact of the multilateral mechanism on these achievements" (Wettestad 2011: 35). His more general conclusion is easier: "We are reasonably sure that emissions in Europe would be considerably higher in such a counterfactual regime situation" (35). In my opinion, the same logic applies when assigning a "score" to the performance of international courts. This relates back to the question of complex causality: To single out the significance of one causal agent is exceedingly difficult. However, in some instances it may be simple to assign a score: When there are no international courts present in a given region, their significance is necessarily zero.

Turning to independent variables, how can effectiveness and performance of various international institutions be explained? This too is a complex issue; here only a few key points will be presented. This question is frequently discussed in relation to collective action problems, calling for joint solutions. As voluntary cooperation is often hard to establish, it is important to understand the conditions for success or failure. At the general level, this question has two possible answers. The first lies in the character of the problem itself. Some problems are intellectually less challenging and politically more benign than others and thereby easier to solve. The second possibility focuses on problem-solving ability. Some efforts are more successful than others because more powerful institutional tools are used or because more skill and energy is employed. These are analytical devices with complex interlinkages. While the former approach may be most important in explaining effectiveness, the latter is more interesting in the sense that it can be more easily manipulated. Due to its application in game theory we have more knowledge of what makes problems malign. The political malignancy of a problem can be conceived as a function of the configuration of actor interests and preferences that is generated. Accordingly, a "perfectly" benign problem is one that is characterized by identical preferences; the further we get from this state of harmony, the more malign the problem will become (Underdal 2002).

Most issue areas have both malign and benign characteristics. A detailed empirical analysis of the effectiveness of international environmental regimes showed that most of them had a medium score as to degree of malignancy (Miles et al. 2002). Given our focus on human rights, we are not concerned about the significance of the intellectual dimension; and human rights do not represent a collective action problem. But political conflicts and the value dimension loom large in international human rights. Research has shown that the prospects for regime creation as well as regime effectiveness are greatly reduced when there are deep conflicts over values (Andresen 2000; Underdal 2002). It is difficult to reach agreement when bargaining over values: by contrast, material national interests can be more easily quantified. Take, for instance, the International Whaling Commission where the contending parties say either "yes" or "no" to whaling – leaving no room for compromise (Andresen 2000). Although values play a significant role in human rights, that of course does not turn it into an intrinsically malign issue area. As will be shown, this varies considerably from one geographical region to another. In regions where the rule of law features prominently, the chances for the establishment of international courts and for good performance increase significantly. Where these values are less prominent, the score points in the opposite direction.

Finally, how are we to deal with the problem-solving ability of these courts? In regime studies this is often conceived of as a function of power, leadership, and institutions (Underdal 2002). To illustrate, when there is a powerful actor who exerts leadership within a strong institutional setting, the chances of higher effectiveness increase considerably. Regarding the role of international courts, I do not take up the role of power or leadership, but focus on one institutional aspect: the scope of participation in relation to the underlying problem structure. This dimension has two aspects. The better the match between the states of the respective region and participation in the relevant court, the greater will be the chances for good performance. If we want to know the overall effect of an international court in a specific area, its scope needs to be as extensive as possible. This aspect is not relevant at the micro-level, where courts may do an excellent job in individual cases, irrespective of how many states are members. The second dimension relates to the significance of including the states with the most negative scores on human rights. The overall effect of the relevant court will be much more modest if only states with fairly good scores are members. This also has bearing upon our interest in the ability of international courts to deal with malign problems.

From this it follows that I will not be able to assign any precise scores to the performance of the international courts examined here. However, for illustrative purposes, and following the approach in Miles et al. (2002), a five-point scale is used.

Human Rights and the Performance of International Courts

As my focus is on courts at the meso-level, I will not examine individual court cases or the process aspects of the relevant international courts. I proceed in the following steps: First, the evaluation criteria or the state of affairs of human rights internationally must be established. This will indicate what the challenges are on the ground – essential when dealing with the meso-level. The next step is to give a brief account of relevant ICs, identifying the regions where they are present and where they are absent.[1] At this general level I can offer only a very crude overview of their significance, but one that is sufficient to demonstrate the considerable regional variance. In order to discuss the relative influence they will be compared with other relevant candidates like states and relevant

[1] I will not deal with the International Criminal Court or similar specialized tribunals.

international organizations as regards making a difference for human rights internationally. To determine the influence of international courts more precisely, an in-depth analysis is needed so one can link the micro-level with the meso-level – but that is beyond the scope of this illustrative chapter.

Several overviews and indexes can give a general indication of the state of affairs of human rights internationally. One of my two main sources is the Human Rights Watch's World Report 2015 (HRWR) a highly comprehensive document, 600 pages in all (Human Rights Watch 2015). The bulk of the report concerns detailed human rights challenges and violations in ninety-three countries along a number of indicators, varying somewhat according to the most relevant issues in these countries. No country rankings are provided. The HRWR is particularly valuable from the perspective of this chapter, as it contains a separate point on the presence and role of international actors in the countries. This gives an indication of the significance of various actors, which is necessary if we are to place the international courts in a broader perspective. One specific year will not necessarily provide a representative picture of the significance of various actors, but, since the aim of this chapter is to demonstrate the value of the regime approach, it will be sufficient here.

Another relevant source for identifying a baseline for human rights internationally is the World Justice Project (WJP), an independent interdisciplinary organization working to advance the rule of law around the world. WJP has a Rule of Law Index (WJP 2015). The index provides new data on eight rule of law rankings, with scores based on 400 variables from general population polls and a qualified respondent questionnaire. The index draws on a survey of more than 100,000 households and 2,400 experts in ninety-nine countries. Given this elaborate and ambitious approach, many countries where human rights violations are particularly severe are not included, but again it provides illustrative results for our purpose.

Turning then to the various geographical regions, the region where the fewest countries are listed in the HRWR is Europe. Perhaps somewhat surprisingly the EU is listed, but this is due to challenges caused by the huge recent influx of new immigrants. Under the EU heading, ten member states are listed, seven of which are in Western Europe and three in Eastern Europe, due mainly to the same challenges. In general, violations are minor, when viewed in a comparative perspective. The negative human rights "hot-spots" in Europe are relatively few, but severe violations are identified in Russia and Turkey, with a negative trend in both places. Here, however, we should recall that these two countries are geographically and culturally more distant from the core of "Europe" than other European states even though they are members of the Council of Europe. Five other countries with less serious violations are all located in Eastern Europe and are members of the Council of Europe. Turning to the 2015 WJP Rule of Law Index, we find that nineteen of the thirty countries with the highest scores are European, most of them from Western Europe; four Nordic countries top the list. This indicates that, although there are significant differences among countries, Europe is the geographical region that comes closest to the ideal of "rule of law."

Almost half of the countries in Africa are listed (twenty-four) in the HRWR Report, including all the major countries with large populations – like Kenya, Egypt, Nigeria, Ethiopia, and South Africa. Some of the worst cases of human rights violations in Africa are Sudan, South Sudan, and Somalia. In the overwhelming majority of the countries listed there has been no discernible progress on the many indicators listed. Here the main exception is Tunisia, the only North African country to "survive" the Arab Spring. Tellingly, there are no African countries on the top thirty list of the Rule of Law. Among the twenty African countries listed on the Rule of Law Index, the great majority have low or very low scores, with Zimbabwe at the bottom. The most positive exception listed is Botswana, which is close to the top thirty list. Other African countries with fairly acceptable scores are Ghana, South Africa, and Senegal.

Regarding Asia, the HRWR includes all major Asian countries: China, India, Indonesia, Pakistan, Cambodia, Bangladesh, Vietnam, Myanmar, and Afghanistan. Despite significant variations in their human rights records, in all cases the violations listed are serious, showing the weak rule of law in this most populous section of the world. Overall, little or no progress in human rights records is noted in these states. According to the WJP Rule of Law Index, the only countries from Asia on the top thirty list are Singapore (nine), South Korea (eleven), Japan (thirteen), and Hong Kong (seventeen). Of the fourteen other Asian countries listed on this index, Afghanistan, Cambodia, and Pakistan have the lowest scores, but all others also have low scores, with partial exceptions for Nepal, Thailand, and the Philippines. A separate group of countries are the "-stans" of Central Asia: Kazakhstan, Kyrgyzstan, Tajikistan, Turkmenistan, and Uzbekistan. The HRWR notes very low scores in all of them, strongly supported by the Rule of Law Index, which, however, has data for only three of them.

The picture is less bleak when we move to the Americas. The overall human rights situation in North America is good, with strong protection regarding most of the classic human rights indicators, but some serious violations are noted in the HRWR regarding the death penalty in many US states as well as the extremely large prison population. The picture is more negative in Latin America, where twelve countries are listed in the report, including the major and most populous states of Brazil, Argentina, Chile, and Peru. It should be noted, however, that in a comparative perspective, violations of human rights in these countries are rather mild. The situation is much more negative in Cuba, Venezuela, Honduras, Bolivia, and Ecuador. One rare instance where considerable progress is noted is in Guatemala, but its score on the Rule of Law Index is still very low. While both the USA (nineteen) and Canada (fourteen) are on the top thirty list, in Central and South America this applies only to Uruguay (twenty-two), Costa Rica (twenty-five), and Chile (twenty-six), all low on this list. The ranking lists sixteen other Latin American countries, with Venezuela at the very bottom.

Finally, a brief note on the region with the most severe violations of human rights: the Middle East. The following countries are listed in the HRWR: Bahrain, Iran, Iraq, Jordan, Kuwait, Lebanon, Israel/Palestine, Oman, Qatar, Saudi Arabia, Syria, United Arab Republic, and Yemen – just about the whole Middle East. The only Arab country on the top thirty list of the Rule of Law Index is the United Arab Emirates (twenty-seven). Illustrative of the poor state of human rights in this region, the index has data for only two other countries here: Iran with a very low score, whereas Jordan has a fairly acceptable score.

Let us now turn to the international courts of human rights in various geographical regions. Our account is based on information from the International Justice Resource Center, providing advocates, civil society organizations, and victims of human rights abuse with information and resources. As mentioned, such courts have been established in some regions but not in others (see Chapter 4). Where they exist, they are embedded in previous political and legal processes, and were subsequently established to strengthen the enforcement dimension of human rights in their regions. Sometimes these approaches are regimes; in other cases, I would hold, they are not. We focus on the three main international courts in the three geographical regions where they exist according to our source. However, we also deal briefly with institutions and actors promoting human rights in regions where no international courts exist.

The oldest court is the European Court of Human Rights (ECtHR), established in 1959 on the basis of the European Convention of Human Rights. It was adopted within the context of the Council of Europe, and its members are elected by the Parliamentary Assembly (previously the Consultative Assembly) of the Council of Europe. The ten founding nations were Western European countries, all with high regard for human rights. In the course of the next few decades, some fifteen other Western states – with basically the same values – joined. With the fall of the Iron Curtain, all Eastern European countries have now joined and all forty-seven members of the Council of Europe are members of the ECtHR.

In terms of our analytical perspective here, the European Court of Human Rights should be in a good position to perform well, as it now has jurisdiction over all the states in the geographical area which it covers. The initial problem structure was benign, as its members were all Western European countries, holding similar human rights values. But its potential for contributing to improved human rights in European states which were not members was obviously very limited. This changed with the entry of the Eastern European states in the Council of Europe. On the one hand, this made the challenge for the Court more malign, as these states had little or no experience in upholding the virtues of human rights. On the other hand, it increased the Court's potential for making a positive difference for the whole region within the context of the broader European human rights regime.

From the account given above, Europe stands out as the region with the best human rights track record at present. No doubt, the general situation regarding human rights is much better for the great majority of Eastern European countries than it used to be, although considerable challenges remain in some of them. The crucial question is then: what has caused this positive development – and how much has the ECtHR contributed? Interestingly, the HRWR mentions some cases from the Court, indicating that it may have some positive influence in some states. However, I will assume that explanation for the positive development is the change towards democracies in many of these countries has also made a difference. The human rights requirements for achieving EU membership have also been instrumental here. However, these are offered as assumptions only. Detailed empirical analysis focusing on the role and significance of the wider regime as well as the role of the

Court in bringing behavioral change is needed to answer this question more conclusively.

In line with the importance of focusing on efforts to make a positive difference regarding "malign" problems, it would be particularly relevant to direct attention to the role played in *negative* human rights hot spots like Turkey and Russia. The human rights situation here has worsened recently. What role has the ECtHR played, and what is its potential to improve the situation? Other and less malign cases could also be chosen to investigate under what conditions the Court can make a difference.

As compared with the other courts in our sample (see below), the ECtHR probably deserves a rather high score as regards performance, due to its inclusive membership and relatively benign challenge, due to the fairly high regard paid to human rights in the majority of its member states. For illustrative purposes I give it a score of three on a five-point scale.

The Inter-American Court on Human Rights (IACtHR) has been in operation since 1979, twenty years after its European predecessor, the ECtHR. It was based on the American Convention on Human Rights and linked to the Inter-American Commission on Human Rights (IACHR). While all thirty-five members of the Organization of American States are participants in the Commission, there are only twenty states that have accepted the jurisdiction of the Court. Thus we see that it takes more to become a member of a body with more judicial bite compared to the broader political body, indicating it has a higher potential for having a real behavioral effect compared to the Commission. However, two of the states with the worst human rights records, Venezuela and Cuba, are not members of the Court. The same goes for the USA, which has traditionally been wary of letting supranational institutions have any influence on its national sovereignty. Thus, compared to the ECtHR there is a greater mismatch between the members of the Inter-American Court and the number of states in the region, indicating less likelihood of contributing to improvements in human rights compared to its European counterpart. One would also expect that those with least interest in improving human rights would not join, thereby reducing the Court's potential for influence. Here it is indeed interesting to note that some of the worst violators of human rights in the region – Bolivia, Ecuador, and Honduras – have all joined the Court. Why this is the case, how it should be interpreted, and whether the Court has had any influence in these countries is worthy of study, focusing on "malign" cases.

Various UN human rights mechanisms are present in the region, as are key actors like the USA and the EU using various means to improve the human rights situation in the region. Again, detailed empirical on-the-ground analysis is necessary to determine the significance of these actors for the state of human rights compared with the role of the Court. Given the rather low institutional capacity of the IACtHR due to limited membership, its potential for achieving its goals is lower than that of the ECtHR. The nature of the problem is also considerably more malign because of strong and active resistance to human rights in several countries. This indicates that performance in terms of goal achievement is probably considerably lower than in their European counterpart. On a more positive note, the score in terms of human rights would have been significantly lower a few decades earlier, before the significant transitions from dictatorship to democracy in major Latin American countries. If this trend continues it may create more fertile ground for IACtHR in the future. Recall also that its history is much shorter than that of the ECtHR. I assign a score of two to the Inter-American Court on Human Rights.

The African human rights system is the youngest of the three. Like the two it consists of a Commission and a Court. The African Commission on Human and Peoples Rights was established in 1987 to protect human rights in the fifty-four member states of the African Union. With the exception of South Sudan, all have ratified the African Charter on Human and Peoples Rights. The African Court on Human and Peoples Rights has been in operation since 2006; its first case was decided three years later. Also here, two decades passed between the establishment of the Commission and the establishment of the Court. Thirty countries are members of the Court; this includes most major African states – but not the major violators of human rights, like Sudan and Somalia. Thus, the score in terms of membership is fairly low. Even more importantly, human rights violations are far more severe here than in the American region. Considering its short history, limited membership, and the extremely malign challenges, it is not realistic to expect too much from the African Court in terms of goal achievement.

According to the Human Rights Watch Report, several international actors are also involved in the African region, but the role of the Court is only mentioned in one instance. Also here, mention is made of the role of the USA, the EU and key European states, and of traditional diplomacy as well as sanctions applied in some cases to improve human rights records. Various UN human rights mechanisms are also engaged, conducting inspections and publishing reports, but it is up to the individual states to decide whether to allow them into their territories. On the basis of this source and realities on the ground, it appears that the relative positive difference made by the Court is probably modest. I assign it a score of one.

Although according to our sources no courts exist in Asia or the Middle East, international human rights institutions have been established recently. The Association of Southeast Asian Nations' (ASEAN) Intergovernmental Commission on Human Rights began operating in 2009 under the auspices of the ASEAN. It is composed of ten states, and China is not a member. Several meetings and conferences on human rights have since been arranged, and in 2012 the ASEAN Human Rights Declaration was established. This may be interpreted as a first positive step. UN human rights mechanisms are also relevant for some countries, but at the discretion of the states. As to the "-stans" countries, they belong to Central Asia, but probably due to its geographic proximity they have several partnership agreements with various European institutions. These have been active in writing human rights reports and arranging various dialogue meetings as well as exerting political pressure, but the effects so far appear very modest, judging from the facts presented above.

The status is fairly similar regarding the Middle East. The Arab Human Rights Committee was established in 2009 to oversee compliance with the Arab Charter on Human Rights, which entered into force in 2008. The great majority of Middle Eastern states are members, one exception being Iran. We do not know whether these institutions have made a positive difference for the state of human rights, but that would also be worth studying. As all the other regions that now have international courts of human rights started up with political commissions, this may be an indication that courts will eventually be established for these regions as well. However, the commissions are not mentioned in the Human Rights Watch Report, but key states have again voiced their concern in some cases. However, when states that are powerful or have strategic significance they tend to refrain from criticizing them, for reasons of political expediency.

Brief Concluding Discussion

What lessons and conclusions can be drawn from this overview? Starting out with the evaluation criteria of the state of human rights internationally, we note as a first observation that the rule of law regarding human rights is more the exception than the rule when the focus is on actual practices – always assuming that the sources we have used are reliable.

Despite isolated instances of improvements, the overall situation has worsened recently. We find severe violations of human rights in the most populous regions of the world – Asia, Africa, and the Middle East. The situation is somewhat better on the American continent, but Europe is the only region where the rule of law is more the rule than the exception. Considering there are now (as of early 2016) some 7.4 billion people on our planet, a rough estimate would be that at most perhaps 1 to 1.5 billion are living under conditions characterized by the rule of law. Protecting human rights may be a universal value on paper, but this is not so in practice. This observation is one advantage of the international regime approach, due to its focus on practice and behavior on the ground, and not only on the formal aspects of international organizations.

As to the role of international courts at the aggregate level, their overall significance regarding improvement of human rights is modest, again based on the sources used here. Indeed, such institutions are simply nonexistent in regions where they are most needed, Asia and the Middle East – in line with the logic of focusing on achievements made toward reducing problems where they are most malign. Where courts do exist, we can note major variations in their performance, but to answer this question more conclusively, far more detailed empirical analysis is needed, linking the micro-level to the meso-level. According to the illustrative approach employed here, the European Court of Human Rights scores highest, trailed by the Inter-American Court and the African Court. This difference can be explained by how long they have existed and their participatory scope, but primarily by the severity in the challenges facing them. All these international courts have been established after previous relevant political and legal frameworks. The fact that a similar process is now under way in Asia and the Middle East may indicate that international courts may subsequently be established in these regions as well.

These international courts are intervening variables working within broader driving forces. Here perhaps the most important of these drivers is domestic regime type, in the comparative sense of the term. From the findings presented in this chapter, there is a very high correlation between democracies and the human rights situation – not surprisingly. Probably the most important reason for the improvements achieved in Eastern Europe and Latin America is the turn to more democratic regimes in significant parts of these regions, illustrating the significance of the political pathway. Economic development may also be an important driver in some cases, but not always – as the example of China reminds us. Democratic states are generally more positive toward human rights courts than are autocratic regimes and are thereby inclined to establish them. These can then contribute to strengthening the role of human rights further, creating positive feedback. Further study is needed of why such institutions have been established also in predominantly nondemocratic areas, and of their role there.

What significance have international courts had in promoting human rights, compared to other agents like states and international organizations working towards the same goal? Again, more detailed empirical research is needed to answer this question. Here my main point has been to illustrate the importance of controlling for these other agents, if we are to determine the actual influence of international human rights courts. That being said, the crude empirical findings indicate that other actors may often be quite significant. According to our sources they have a broader presence than international courts and some of them have a variety of political and economic means at their disposal to promote human rights. Under what conditions the various actors – including international courts – can make a positive difference for human rights represents a highly relevant avenue for future research. Here I have only been able to scratch the surface.

References

Andresen, Steinar. 2000. "The International Whaling Regime," in Andresen, Steinar, Skodvin, Tora, Underdal, Arild, and Wettestad, Jørgen (eds.), *Science and Politics in International Environmental Regimes: Between Integrity and Involvement*. Manchester: Manchester University Press, pp. 35–70.

2015. "Effectiveness," in Pattberg, Philipp H. and Zelli, Fariborz (eds.), *Encyclopedia of Global Environmental Governance and Politics*. Cheltenham: Edward Elgar, pp. 441–447.

Biermann, Frank and Siebenhuner, Berndt (eds.). 2009. *Managers of Global Change: The Influence of International Environmental Bureaucracies*. Cambridge, MA: MIT Press.

Creamer, Cosette D. and Strezhnev, Anton. 2018. "Court Performance within the Multilateral Trade Regime," Chapter 2 in this volume.

Haas, Peter. 1992. "Introduction: Epistemic Communities and International Policy Coordination," *International Organization* 46(1): 1–37.

Helm, Carsten and Sprinz, Detlef. 2000. "Measuring the Effectiveness of International Environmental Regimes," *Journal of Conflict Resolution* 44 (5): 630–652.

Human Rights Watch. 2015. "World Report 2015." Available at: www.hrw.org/world-report/2015 (accessed March 2016).

International Justice Resource Center. "Courts and Monitoring Bodies." Available at: www.ijrcenter.org/courts-monitoring-bodies/ (accessed March 2016).

Keohane, Robert O. 1984. *After Hegemony: Cooperation and Discord in the World Political Economy*. Princeton, NJ: Princeton University Press.

Krasner, Stephen D. 1983. "Structural Causes and Regime Consequences: Regimes as Intervening Variables," in Krasner, Stephen D. (ed.), *International Regimes*. Ithaca, NY: Cornell University Press, pp. 1–22.

Levy, Marc, Young, Oran, and Zurn, Michael. 1995. "The Study of International Regimes," *European Journal of International Relations* 1(3): 267–330.

Miles, Edward L., Underdal, Arild, Andresen, Steinar, Wettestad, Jørgen, Skjærseth, Jon B., and Carlin, Elaine M. 2002. *Environmental Regime Effectiveness: Confronting Theory with Evidence*. Cambridge, MA: MIT Press.

Strange, Susan. 1983. "Cave: Big Dragones! A Critique of Regime Analysis," in Krasner, Stephen D. (ed.), *International Regimes*. Ithaca, NY: Cornell University Press, pp. 337–354.

Underdal, Arild. 2002. "One Question Two Answers," in Miles, Edward L., Underdal, Arild, Andresen, Steinar, Wettestad, Jørgen, Skjærseth, Jon B., and Carlin, Elaine M. (eds.), *Environmental Regime Effectiveness: Confronting Theory with Evidence*. Cambridge, MA: MIT Press, pp. 3–46.

Wettestad, Jørgen. 2011. "Reducing Long-range Air-pollutants in Europe," in Andresen, Steinar, Boasson, Elin Lerum, and Hønneland, Geir (eds.), *International Environmental Agreements: An Introduction*. London: Routledge, pp. 23–37.

WJP. 2015. "Rule of Law Index 2015." Available at: https://worldjusticeproject.org/sites/default/files/documents/roli_2015_0.pdf (accessed March 2016).

Young, Oran R. 2001. "Inferences and Indices: Evaluating the Effectiveness of International Environmental Regimes," *Global Environmental Politics* 1(1): 99–121.

Young, Oran R. and Osherenko, Gail. 1993. "Testing Theories of Regime Formation: Findings from a Large Collaborative Research Project," in Rittberger, Volker (ed.), *Regime Theory and International Relations*. Oxford: Clarendon Press, pp. 223–250.

Zengerling, Cathrin. 2013. *Greening International Jurisprudence Environmental NGOs before International Courts, Tribunals and Compliance Committees*. Leiden: Martinus Nijhoff.

PART III

12

Measurement and Methods: Opportunities for Future Research

THERESA SQUATRITO

Introduction

The chapters in this volume have strived to evaluate the performance of international courts (ICs) across several courts and tribunals and in the context of different issue areas.[1] The authors of these chapters have relied upon a variety of measurements of performance and methods of analysis. This diversity raises crucial questions for future research. How can performance be observed and measured? How do we go about examining and testing the role of various determinants of performance? Do we use qualitative comparisons, multivariate statistical analyses, or some other method of analysis?

With these questions in mind, this chapter has two main objectives. First, the chapter aims to map how prior research operationalizes and measures aspects of IC performance. I understand operationalization as the process of defining a theoretical concept such that it can be observed and measured. In reviewing the operational definitions and measurement strategies found in existing research and the contributions in this volume, I highlight key methodological concerns that arise from efforts to evaluate the performance of ICs. Second, the chapter aims to identify methods of analysis that hold promise for future research on international courts and tribunals. For this purpose, I emphasize methods that are less typical in international court research. While qualitative case studies and quantitative analyses based on observational data will continue to be valuable methods, my goal is to highlight lesser known methodological options. This is not to say that qualitative case studies or conventional statistical analysis should be left out of the researcher's

[1] I thank Nicole De Silva, Anton Strezhnev, and Oran R. Young for very helpful comments on earlier drafts of this chapter.

toolbox of methods. The goal is rather to suggest that additional tools provide opportunities for future research.

This chapter proceeds in five sections. In the first section, I review how researchers have operationalized outcome performance in relation to dispute settlement, compliance, and legal clarification. The second section considers the operationalization of process performance based on the criteria of procedural fairness, efficiency, and legal reasoning. In the third section, I discuss operationalization of performance at the meso- and macro-level, focusing on problem-solving. Fourth, I introduce five methods for analysis that hold promise for the study of IC performance. These five are: experimental designs, meta-analysis, qualitative comparative analysis, counterfactuals, and multimethod designs. Last, I conclude the chapter with a brief summary of the main points.

Operationalizing and Measuring Outcome Performance

The outcome performance of international courts refers to the outcomes or the results that ICs produce. Three criteria for evaluating outcome performance were identified in Chapter 1: dispute settlement, compliance, and clarification of the law. Each of these outcome criteria raises unique methodological challenges. In this section, I discuss various approaches to operationalizing outcome performance along each criterion, highlighting a range of challenges and considerations.

Dispute Settlement

A review of empirical research on international courts and tribunals reveals that researchers take varying approaches to operationalizing dispute settlement. I identify five generic operational definitions for dispute settlement performance that have been used in previous research. This discussion briefly summaries these different approaches to operationalizing dispute settlement performance and considers their merits and demerits.

One generic operationalization of dispute settlement performance is based on how much a court or tribunal is used. For example, one could measure dispute settlement performance as the number of petitions a court receives or registers. This approach to operationalizing dispute settlement performance is advantageous because information on petitions to international courts is relatively easy to acquire. Most courts produce lists of the petitions they receive, if not statistical reports on received petitions. Even with basic information on the petitions received by a court, a researcher can usually identify variation across time, space and the content of petitions to investigate the determinants of performance. This operational definition of performance assumes that for every petition a court receives, the court settles the dispute, or at least plays a role in its settlement. However, not all petitions that are filed result in a court judgment. Some petitions are deemed inadmissible, and others may be settled out of court. Additionally, even if a court were to issue a judgment for every petition it receives, the underlying political disputes is not per se settled even though the legal dispute is. Also, court usage can reflect a variety of other phenomena, such as litigiousness or the absence of alternatives for redress or dispute resolution. For these reasons, court usage may have weak validity and thus be a poor measure.[2]

A second operational definition of a court's dispute settlement performance relates to whether the court reaches decisions in the disputes brought before it. Accordingly, researchers use judgments to observe dispute settlement. For example, dispute settlement performance can be operationalized as the yearly number of judgments a court issues. In comparison to a measure based on court usage, this approach better reflects whether a court actually is involved in the settlement of disputes. Yet, several challenges can arise with this operationalization. Not all types of judgments may similarly reflect dispute settlement. For example, does a decision in which the court dismisses a dispute on grounds that it does not have jurisdiction – irrespective of the merits of the dispute – indicate the settlement of a dispute or not? Similarly, does a friendly settlement is the shadow of a court count as court-generated dispute settlement? The answers to these questions are not obvious. Researchers have used different strategies, and measurement error can arise as a result of these choices. For example, if there is good reason to think that friendly settlements do not actually reflect any actions on the part of a court, including them would undermine the validity of the measure. Another disadvantage of operationalizing performance as the judgments adopted by a court is that it assumes every time a court issues a judgment the dispute is settled. Yet, we can imagine that some disputes persist despite a court's judgment. If disputes typically persist after a court intervenes, this operationalization would result in systematic measurement error.

[2] Validity refers to whether a measure is measuring what it is supposed to measure. In other words, it speaks to how closely the operational definition corresponds to the theoretical definition or concept.

Despite these challenges, operationalizing dispute settlement performance in terms of court judgments may be suitable, especially if the measure focuses on judgments that are most reflective of settlement arising from a court's involvement.

A third operationalization of dispute settlement performance used by some scholars is dispute duration – the amount of time it takes for a court to conclude a case. This operationalization assumes that shorter dispute durations correspond with good performance and longer durations with poor performance. To use dispute duration, researchers determine the time elapsed between the beginning and conclusion of a dispute. Typically, researchers identify the beginning of a dispute as the official date on which a petition is registered and the conclusion as the date a final judgment is delivered. For example, previous studies on the World Trade Organization (WTO) have adopted this approach (Grinols and Perrelli 2006; Davis 2012: chapter 6). This approach however assumes a legal dispute begins when it is formally filed with a court and does not necessarily capture the point at which any legal action between the parties begins, let alone when the political dispute starts. Instead of highlighting the distance in time between the start and the end of the legal dispute, some researchers therefore use a categorical indicator that reflects the various stages of the legal processes. Performance is then measured as the stage at which a dispute is settled (e.g., Busch and Reinhardt 2000; Börzel et al. 2012). Generally, operationalizing dispute settlement performance in terms of dispute duration appears to have validity because it concentrates on the legal dispute and court intervention. In other words, it would appear to reflect court performance while excluding other aspects affecting dispute settlement. However, the validity of this type of measure might be weakened if the duration of disputes are significantly affected by other factors. For example, the complexity of the legal issues, the number of parties, the legal capacity of the disputing parties, or whether there are formal deadlines structuring the timing of the legal process can all impact dispute duration, irrespective of a court's capacity and willingness to produce dispute settlement. If these other factors can be controlled and accounted for, dispute duration offers a good option for operationalizing dispute settlement performance.

Fourth, dispute settlement performance has been studied in terms of a court's ability to generate out of court, negotiated settlement prior to judgment – which might be called early or friendly settlement. This operationalization would aim to capture an international court or tribunal's capacity to bring parties to settle a dispute after filing a complaint but prior to a judicial decision. Early settlements could be indicative of a well-functioning court that incentivizes parties to find a negotiated agreement in its shadow. Existing literature has studied early settlement in international adjudication, using indicators like the proportion of disputes that conclude in early settlement. Examples of such research include a study by Busch and Reinhardt (2006) on early settlements in the Dispute Settlement Mechanism (DSM) of the WTO and a study on friendly settlement at the European Court of Human Rights (ECtHR) by Keller et al. (2011). In both studies, authors are careful to identify actual settlement, distinguishing settlement from withdrawal of a dispute. A similar approach would be to measure performance according to what stage of the judicial process disputes are settled, where early settlement is understood as one possible stage (Busch and Reinhardt 2000; Börzel et al. 2012). When courts do not have a formal procedure for registering early settlement or readily available information of settlements, this strategy for measuring dispute settlement performance may not be possible, especially for a large-N analysis. Moreover, this operationalization runs the risk of overestimating a court's role in early settlement. Indeed, early settlement of disputes can reflect dynamics that have little to do with a court's performance, such as the bargaining leverage of the disputing parties, the strength of the legal claims, or the intention and capacity of disputing parties to proceed with litigation. As a result, a measure of dispute settlement performance based on early settlement may not capture performance in general, but it could be useful for research aiming to study the capacity of an IC to produce dispute settlement outside the courtroom.

Last, some research operationalizes dispute settlement performance as whether disputes recur. This operational definition of performance makes no assumption that a court judgment brings an end to the underlying political dispute. Instead, this operationalization assumes one possible outcome of judicial intervention is the continuation of a political dispute and the renewal of a legal dispute. As a result, dispute recurrence is treated as an indicator of unsuccessful dispute settlement. Dispute recurrence can be used in both large-N and small-n analyses. For example, Kim (2015) developed an indicator of dispute recurrence for a large-N study on the WTO DSM based on whether a WTO dispute was followed by another dispute involving like products and policies. Qualitative case studies could also operate with a measurement based on dispute recurrence. Dispute recurrence appears to have strong face validity because it reflects whether a dispute is truly settled and if court intervention played a role. However, we need to have confidence that the procedure for identifying dispute recurrence avoids false negatives and false positives. For example, sometimes a dispute could recur but in a different venue, or with different legal content even through it is a reiteration of the same underlying dispute. As Dunoff (2007) illustrates in an analysis of US-Canada disputes related to softwood lumber, the growing density of international adjudicative processes suggest that several legal disputes concerning the same issue can arise in different forums (see also Faude 2018). Thus, casting the net either too broadly or too narrowly as to what constitutes a recurrence can introduce measurement error. Nevertheless, when these concerns are taken into consideration, dispute recurrence offers a strong option for operationalizing dispute settlement performance.

Generally, this discussion suggests a few issues should be considered when deciding how to operationalize dispute settlement. Some ways to operationalize dispute settlement will be limited by data availability. Beyond this, not all approaches provide equally valid measures. We should aim to identify an approach that maximizes validity and controls for confounding factors.

Compliance

Compliance generally is defined as the correspondence of behavior to a rule. First-order compliance concerns compliance with the rule itself, while second-order compliance is the correspondence of behavior with a judicial decision about the rule. This discussion focuses primarily on second-order compliance. Operationalizing compliance with international courts generally entails identifying whether an actor's behavior corresponds to the demands of a court's ruling (Kapiszewski and Taylor 2012). In the abstract, "measuring compliance with a judicial ruling entails three steps: (1) identifying, analyzing, and scoring the specific behavioral mandate(s) in the court's ruling; (2) identifying, analyzing and scoring the action(s) authorities appeared to take in response, and (3) comparing the two" (Kapiszewski and Taylor 2012: 809). In practice, each of these steps can be fraught with problems. Determining what a court mandates is not always straightforward and can in fact be subject to various interpretations (Huneeus 2013). Also, what actions are taken by states in response to a court decision may not be readily known and acquiring such information might be difficult. For example, when states self-report on compliance with decisions, they may have incentives to misrepresent compliance.

Literature on compliance with the rulings of international human rights courts exemplifies some approaches to operationalizing compliance performance. Where scholars have analyzed state compliance with human rights judgments, they often operationally define compliance performance as the extent to which respondent states have implemented the judgments of the court, based on assessments from an intergovernmental organ or by the court itself.[3] Using this definition, compliance is measured either as a binary (compliance or no compliance) or ordinal outcome (no compliance, partial, full). This approach, especially the former, can overestimate noncompliance by not capturing partial compliance. A better measurement strategy has been adopted by several scholars who study the European Court of Human Rights and the Inter-American Court of Human Rights (Basch et al. 2010; Hawkins and Jacoby 2010; Hillebrecht 2014). These authors measure compliance at the level of the discrete obligations or remedial measures of a judgment, rather than the judgment as a whole and include partial compliance.

Another option is to operationalize compliance performance as the time it takes states to comply with judgments (Grewal and Voeten 2015). Still another approach has been to operationalize compliance as whether states that are not legally bound to do so implement a judgment, which is known as *erga omnes* compliance.[4] For example, Helfer and Voeten (2014) measure compliance in terms of whether states generally adapt their policies on LGBT rights to accord with the jurisprudence of the ECtHR, even when they are not legally required to do so.

Research on the European Court of Justice (ECJ), now known as the Court of Justice of the European Union (CJEU), has operationalized compliance in a few ways (Conant 2002; Panke 2010; Börzel et al. 2012). For example, Conant (2002) operationalizes compliance performance as *erga omnes* compliance, or the general policy response to ECJ decisions even when a state is not legally obligated. She then triangulates

3 For example, for compliance with ECtHR decisions, scholars have developed compliance data based on monitoring by the Council of Europe's Committee of Ministers. The Inter-American Court of Human Rights issues reports on compliance, which have been used by several researchers to extract data. For more on these compliance monitoring processes see Giorgetti (2018) and Shelton (2018).

4 *Erga omnes* compliance can resemble first-order compliance, especially when ICs' judgments have high precedential value.

various data (e.g., court citations, preliminary references, infringements) to illustrate how and when states implement the Court's decisions through policy, even though they may not be bound to do so. Recent scholarship offers alternatives, assessing *erga omnes* compliance performance by looking at how legislators adapt their behavior and legislation with "Luxembourg in mind," that is, how national parliaments behave in the shadow of the CJEU (Stone Sweet 2000: chapter 6; Blauberger 2012; see also Squatrito 2016). Others operationalize compliance performance in terms of when infringement proceedings are completed (Börzel et al. 2012).[5] The earlier stages of infringement however do not measure the direct impact of the CJEU because infringements begin with interactions between the state and the EU Commission. Nevertheless, one could argue that compliance in the early stages of infringement proceedings indirectly reflects the CJEU's performance because states often comply at these stages in order to avert review by the Court. In other words, compliance in the early stages of infringement is indicative of compliance in the shadow of the Court.

Scholars operationalize compliance with the WTO DSM differently, taking into account that the system allows for countermeasures.[6] For example, Busch and Reinhardt (2000) operationalize compliance as the stage of the dispute settlement process at which a panel or the Appellate Body's decision is satisfied. This approach factors in instances where countermeasures are endorsed and imposed by the DSM – compliance occurs in the absence of behavioral change on the part of the offending party because legal satisfaction is achieved through countermeasures. Similarly, compliance performance in international investment arbitration does not focus on policy response or behavioral change but the monetary satisfaction of arbitral awards. In this context, compliance might be measured as: (1) the extent to which the award is satisfied through payment of monetary compensation according to the dictates of the award; (2) what type of action generated satisfaction by distinguishing between no satisfaction, payment, and court enforced seizure of assets; or (3) the time it takes for the award to be satisfied.

Finally, compliance performance in international criminal law presents some unique challenges for operationalization and measurement.

[5] In the EU, infringement proceedings are legal proceedings initiated by the European Commission against a member state for failure to correctly apply a legal rule or transpose EU directives.

[6] In this volume, see Creamer and Strezhnev (2018) for an illustration and discussion of the approaches to measuring compliance with the WTO DSM.

In international criminal law, two key questions must be answered: (a) compliance by whom, and (b) what constitutes court intervention? In this area of law, compliance might be operationalized in terms of three different behaviors in response to a court. First, it could be operationalized as the change in criminal behavior of the actors involved in specific situation following court interventions into that situation, such as whether behavior changes after an IC initiates an investigation or there is a proximate threat of prosecution. This would translate into examining whether the court has a specific deterrence effect. This is the approach taken by Jo, Radtke, and Simmons (2018). Alternatively, one could look at whether there is compliance with international criminal law by any actor, not just those involved in a specific situation, following the intervention of an international criminal tribunal in some conflict. This would translate into a general deterrence effect (e.g., Escribà-Folch and Wright 2015). This second approach is closer to first-order compliance because it aims to see if the threat of punishment leads to compliance with the law itself. Of course, both approaches to measuring compliance performance are exceedingly difficult to develop on one's own, not to mention the challenges of attributing causality to the actions of a court. A third operational definition of compliance performance with international criminal tribunals relates to how states meet their legal obligations to cooperate and assist the court in criminal prosecutions. For example, once a warrant of arrest is issued, the member states of the International Criminal Court (ICC) have a legal obligation to arrest and surrender the accused. Failure to do so is a form of noncompliance. This form of compliance could also be a potential avenue of research and operationalization of compliance performance.

All approaches to operationalizing and measuring compliance have pros and cons. Compliance performance that highlights *erga omnes* compliance may reflect not only compliance with ICs judgments but also compliance with the law more broadly (or first-order compliance) and distinguishing the role of an IC in that compliance can be extremely difficult. Measurement based on the temporal dimension of compliance – how long it takes for compliance to transpire – might underestimate compliance if there is no consideration of partial compliance. Similarly, a measure that captures only whether compliance has occurred in substance, irrespective of time, may become so temporally removed from a court's intervention that it can no longer realistically be attributed to that court. In the end, this type of measure might overestimate performance compliance. Thus, in any operationalization of compliance performance, researchers should ask how confident we can be in measurement validity (whether the measure truly speaks to performance of the court) and whether systematic measurement error is minimized as well as whether confounding factors are adequately accounted for.

Clarification of Law

Existing literature operationalizes clarification of law in different ways. First, clarification of law is operationalized in terms of the mode of clarification. As Goldstein and Steinberg argue, there are two modes of legal clarification: "filling gaps and clarifying ambiguities. Gap-filling refers to judicial lawmaking on a question for which there is no legal text directly on point, whereas ambiguity clarification refers to judicial lawmaking on a question for which there is legal text that needs clarification" (Goldstein and Steinberg 2008: 268). Thus, this conceptual division can be used to identify whether a judicial decision fills a gap or clarifies an ambiguity. Goldstein and Steinberg (2008) illustrate this operationalization in the WTO context.

A second operationalization focuses on the directionality of legal clarification, such that one measures whether judicial decisions move the law towards position A (e.g., trade liberalization, rights expansion) or position B (e.g., trade restriction, rights contraction). For example, an indicator in the WTO context could treat a win for the complainant as trade liberalization and a win for the respondent state as trade restrictive. A similar approach has been adopted in the EU context (Cichowski 2007; Gabel et al. 2012). For example, Cichowski (2007) codes whether the ECJ's decisions uphold EU interests or member state positions (by looking at observations in preliminary rulings). Her coding scheme helps to elucidate whether the ECJ's decisions move the law towards more or less institutionalization of EU law. Van Harten (2012) uses a similar measure to study how investment arbitration performs in terms of clarifying the law. He codes arbitration decisions according to whether they are expansive or restrictive in favor of a state-respondent. This approach reveals patterns in how arbitrators' discrete decisions develop the law in the aggregate. Simmons (2014) further illustrates how this approach to measuring legal clarification could be used to analyze performance.

These two ways of operationalizing legal clarification have merits and shortcomings. Operationalizing legal clarification in terms of the mode of clarification offers the possibility of measuring clarification for each discrete legal claim as opposed to the judgment as a whole. However, this approach often results in subjective assessments. What one person views as gap-filling another could view as resolving ambiguities. This measurement can thus be unreliable – recurrent measurement would most likely yield different results – and prone to systematic measurement error. Operationalizing legal clarification in terms of directionality seems to be less prone to measurement error, but treating judicial decisions as single outcomes of legal clarification can oversimplify very complex legal decisions. For example, some aspects of a WTO decision could be viewed as trade liberalizing and others as trade restrictive. Consequently, measurements based on directionality may subsume assumptions about the relative importance of discrete aspects of a decision when specifying the nature of legal clarification. Additionally, while measuring the directionality of legal change can be telling, it may stretch the concept of legal clarification since it does not necessarily capture whether law is more or less ambiguous.

Operationalizing and Measuring Process Performance

Process performance can relate to various aspects of a court's procedures, ranging from the production of evidence, participation of experts, witnesses and victims, deliberation and judgment writing, among others. Evaluating process performance requires an examination of how these procedures compare against criteria such as procedural fairness, efficiency, and legal methods and reasoning. In this section, I review how scholarship operationalizes these three criteria in court procedures.

Procedural Fairness

Procedural fairness is the extent to which values, such as impartiality, independence, transparency, consistency (like cases are treated alike), equal access and participation, and accuracy, are supported by court procedures. These values can be incorporated into procedures through formal rules or the practices of ICs. Thus, assessing procedural fairness requires the operationalization of court procedures. Existing research generally operationalizes procedure in one of two ways.

The first is by the codified, formal rules governing a court (e.g., treaties, protocols, rules of procedures, etc.). Procedural performance is then measured by if and the extent to which a court's rules espouse the values of fairness. Formal rules are probably the most accessible way to observe procedural fairness – most ICs' formal rules can be easily accessed – and measurement based on formal rules is more reliable and replicable than the alternatives. Moreover, one can also observe changes in formal rules, and thus look at temporal variations in procedural fairness. We can also be reasonably confident that this approach will measure the same thing for court B that it does with court A. This allows for cross-sectional comparisons. On the other hand, operationalizing procedural fairness in terms of formal rules has limitations. It assumes actual practice corresponds to the codified rules. Yet practices do not always reflect the rules, generating some degree of measurement error. As Dunoff and Pollack (2018) illustrate, formal rules often leave a variety of issues unresolved on the production of evidence and courts develop their own evidentiary practices. Operationalizing the procedural fairness at ICs on the basis of formal rules could lead to weak measurement validity when practice diverges significantly from the formal rules.

The second or alternative operationalization of procedural fairness of ICs is thus based on the actual practice, or the informal rules or norms by which a court operates. Measuring actual practice often requires measurement instruments like participant observation, expert surveys, or elite interviews. Terris et al. (2007) exemplify this last approach. They operationalize procedures in terms of actual practice, interviewing thirty-two international court judges to assess procedures relating to recusal, deliberation, judgment writings, and more. While operationalizing process performance as practice may better reflect actual procedures, it has a few disadvantages. First, studying actual practices depends on good access to interviewees who can provide reliable information on practices. Second, some aspects of judicial process can be shielded by obligations of secrecy and lack of transparency, especially deliberations among judges. Observing how judges deliberate in practice, either directly or indirectly through interviews, may be intractable for researchers. Similarly, in most instances, research on practices will be restricted to cross-sectional observations, that is, longitudinal studies on procedures are impracticable with this operationalization. Ultimately, this limits our ability to address questions related to if, how, and why process performance changes over time and evolves. Finally, this operationalization is not easily replicated: We may not have repeated access to the same interviewees and their perceptions may change and differ amongst themselves.

Efficiency

While not extensive, some existing scholarship examines the efficiency of international courts and tribunals. In this literature, efficiency is operationalized as the monetary costs of: (a) operating a court in general or per case or (b) the cost of litigating a case before a court (Ingadottir 2004; Romano 2005). Operationalizing efficiency in terms of money, however, has some limitations. The budgets for some courts can be difficult to come by, and even then, these budgets may reflect more than their capacity to process cases. For example, budgets may reflect funders' capacities or willingness to provide funds or funders' priorities. An alternative way to operationalize judicial efficiency might be the time it takes to process cases. Operationalizing efficiency as the time it takes to process cases offers an option for empirically observing court performance but one must bear in mind that other factors, like the capacities of parties to litigate or the complexity of the legal issues, can also affect processing time. In the end, operationalizing and measuring efficiency demands attention to these sort of confounding factors which can affect the validity of either time-oriented or monetary indicators of efficiency.

Legal Method and Reasoning

Process performance might also be evaluated against modes of legal method and reasoning. For example, previous literature suggests that the quality of legal reasoning is a significant aspect of an IC's performance (Helfer and Slaughter 1997: 273–274). To assess such claims, legal reasoning has been operationalized as the degree of deference ICs give to states. Deference is typically observed through the standard of review used by a court, the application of doctrines such as the "margin of appreciation" or subsidiarity, as well as the methods of treaty interpretation used by a court. Others operationalize legal reasoning in terms of whether courts exercise judicial economy. This operationalization focuses on whether a court responds to all legal claims in a dispute or if it reserves judgment on those that are not essential to resolving the dispute. One way judicial economy has been measured is based on whether it is present within a judgment, using the judgment (as a whole) as the unit of analysis. Brutger and Morse (2015) use this type of measure, coding whether judicial economy was exercised at all in a judgment. Another way to measure judicial economy is to determine whether each discrete legal claim in a dispute is decided upon by the court (Busch and Pelc 2010) – in other words, the unit of analysis is the legal claim and not the entire judgment. A third operationalization of legal reasoning pertains to how a court's legal argumentation is grounded on prior jurisprudence, as shown by citations to past judicial decisions. Despite the fact that the decisions of most international courts are not binding beyond the original dispute, references to past opinions are central to legal reasoning (Pauwelyn and Elsig 2014: 456). For this reason, some researchers have begun to study how decisions are grounded in existing case law (Lupu and Voeten 2012; Pelc 2014; Larsson et al. 2017).

Each of these options has advantages and disadvantages. For example, identifying case citations in judgments is not likely to require specialized knowledge or subjective assessments, both of which improve measurement reliability. On the other hand, operationalizing legal reasoning as deference may entail more subjective assessments, making measurement less reliable or replicable. At the same time, counting citations or identifying patterns in usage of precedent may not correspond as closely to the concept of legal reasoning as does mapping the exercise of deference. For example, citations are standard practice for courts and as such may not shed as much light on how a decision is actually reached as it does the core sources of legal authority for a body of law. In the end, measurement validity and reliability are affected by which operationalization is used.

Operationalizing Meso- and Macro-level Performance

Meso- and macro-level analyzes of the performance of international courts, as discussed in Chapter 1, pose additional methodological challenges. The causal chain that links the actions and behaviors of an IC to some broader outcome or process can be difficult to establish because causality is typically complex at these levels. Despite these challenges, studying the meso- and macro-level performance of ICs can be done, and recent scholarship suggests that innovative methodological approaches advance our ability to work with long causal chains. Even with the most sophisticated of methods, a researcher must still give careful consideration to the operationalization and measurement of the outcome or process to which ICs might contribute. While the possible outcomes or processes at the meso- and macro-levels that one might be interested in are numerous, this discussion focuses on one possible meso- or macro-level outcome of interest. In particular, a perennial question in existing research is if, how and when do ICs contribute to the capacity of governance systems to achieve substantive goals, such as peace, security, development, regional integration, or trade liberalization. Does the ICC contribute to a reduction in violence or increase criminal accountability?

Has the ECtHR contributed to the improvement of human rights across Europe? Does the WTO's Dispute Settlement Mechanism lead to trade liberalization? Given widespread interest in ICs' contribution to global problem-solving, I consider the various ways extant research operationalizes problem-solving.

Researchers have identified several ways to empirically observe and measure the prevalence of different governance problems. In the area of human rights, researchers have developed data on the incidences of human rights violations. The most widely used data source in this area is the database by Cingranelli and Richards (2015). This database, referred to as the CIRI database, is built on information from Amnesty International and US State Department reports, and includes data on extrajudicial killings, torture, political imprisonment, freedom of speech, movement and association, workers' rights, and women's rights. Hathaway (2002) offers an alternative dataset on human rights that covers genocide, torture, civil liberty, fair and public trials, and political representation of women and draws from a variety of sources to develop its measures along each of these rights.[7] Even though these data are frequently used by scholars, they are not immune to criticism, especially because the data are constructed using sources that some people believe are politically biased.

Another way researchers examine the prevalence of human rights protections is to look, not at actual practice, but at the codified law. Helfer and Voeten (2014) exemplify this approach, identifying whether national policies conform to ECtHR jurisprudence on LGBT rights. Operationalizing problem-solving as "law on the books" can at times be a good alternative to measuring human rights "on the ground." If the law has low implementation costs, we can generally assume the codified law will closely correspond to actual implementation. On the other hand, if implementation costs are high or if there is reason to believe that there is insufficient will to implement the law, operationalizing human rights in terms of legal provisions will not provide a valid measure of the actual prevalence of human rights violations.

The effects of international criminal tribunals (ICTs) have been explored by recent scholarship. This literature looks at criminal prosecutions and ICTs' performance against a few different criteria, including the protection of human rights, the end of conflict and violence,

[7] This data is not ideal for research that seeks to capture human rights patterns in more recent years.

democratic transition, and the rule of law. To measure performance against these criteria, scholars often rely upon a range of different existing databases on political violence, political regimes, and human rights, including the Political Terror Scale (PTS) (Gibney et al. 2015), the CIRI database, Freedom House, and Polity IV. One way to conceive of the problem-solving performance of ICTs is as their capacity to deter crime or decrease repression. To measure this operational definition of performance, scholars have looked to human rights indices on torture, summary execution, disappearances, and political imprisonment, frequently using the CIRI database's index on physical integrity rights and the PTS data. The Political Terror Scale, for example, is used by Sikkink and Walling (2007). Kim and Sikkink (2010) ask if "human rights prosecutions" decrease repression and rely on the CIRI physical integrity rights index and the PTS data for robustness checks. Likewise, Olsen et al. (2010) assess the impact of "transitional justice mechanisms" – amnesty, truth and reconciliation commissions, and criminal prosecutions – on both CIRI's physical integrity rights and terror according to the PTS data.[8]

The PTS data and human rights data include incidences of terror or human rights violations that are unrelated to armed conflict. As a result, relying on these data for measuring the problem-solving performance of ICTs can be problematic. Alternative data, however, measures violence associated more directly with armed conflict and is more appropriate for researchers interested in measuring the immediate problem-solving performance of an ICT. Such an attempt has been offered by Jo and Simmons (2016), who assess if the ICC contributes to a de-escalation of killings in conflict zones. Their dependent variable measures intentional civilian killings, based on data from the Uppsala Conflict Data Project on One-sided Violence Dataset (Eck and Hultman 2007). Using this data, they are able to focus on civilian killings that are most likely related to the conflict and thus crimes that probably fall within the jurisdiction of the ICC. If a researcher is interested in the long-term impacts of ICTs or their broader societal impacts, as opposed to the more immediate effects of the ICC on war crimes in a conflict zone, the PTS and human rights data may be less problematic. For example, Meernick et al. (2010) explore the impact of international and domestic trials in terms of the sustained absence of conflict and respect for human rights. To measure the

[8] These examples include prosecutions at domestic courts, hybrid courts, and international courts.

presence or absence of conflict they rely on the Armed Conflict dataset (Gleditsch et al. 2002) and the PTS data.

Researchers have also operationalized problem-solving by ICTs as their democratizing impact. Freedom House and Polity IV data are often used to measure democracy. For example, Olsen et al. (2010) look at the effect of transitional justice mechanisms on democracy, and for this purpose they use data from Freedom House and Polity IV. Another approach to studying the democratizing effects of ICTs is to look at their effect on regime transitions in neighboring states. For example, Escribà-Folch and Wright (2015) examine whether prosecutions influence a neighboring state's transition to democracy, relying on data on autocratic regimes. Nettelfield (2013) examines the impact of the International Criminal Tribunal for the former Yugoslavia (ICTY) on democratic attitudes and institutions in Bosnia and Herzegovina. She uses a multimethod approach to assess the impact of the ICTY on political identities, drawing from survey and interview data and case illustrations. Other work that has tried to establish the link between international criminal tribunals and democratization has also relied heavily on interview data, governmental reports, and official documentation to measure performance. For example, Burke-White's (2008) in-depth case study employs a variety of empirical material including interviews to illustrate how the ICTY had a positive impact on domestic judicial institutions in Bosnia and Herzegovina.

In the area of trade, existing scholarship explores the effects of litigation on international trade and trade liberalization. Trade liberalization is often operationalized as the flow of trade, measured using import and export statistics. For example, Bown (2004) assesses the effects of General Agreement on Tariffs and Trade/WTO dispute settlement decisions on trade liberalization using data from UN Conference on Trade Development (UNCTAD) on trade imports. Bechtel and Sattler (2015) also use UNCTAD data to measure the effects of litigation on exports. An alternative operationalization of trade liberalization is based on trade policy, and not trade flow statistics. For example, Busch and Reinhardt (2003) develop an indicator of whether substantial, partial or no trade concessions are made by a respondent state. Davis (2012), in an analysis of the impact of WTO litigation, develops a measure that looks at the adoption of policy that removes trade barriers. She uses a dichotomous indicator for whether a trade barrier is removed based upon the National Trade Estimate

Reports (Davis 2012: 248). Similar work on the effects of the CJEU has examined how trade-liberalizing court decisions impact intra-EU trade, drawing from data from the Organization for Economic Co-operation and Development (Gabel et al. 2012; Carrubba and Gabbel 2014).

Beyond problem-solving, researchers might be interested in a vast array of broader impacts resulting from ICs. Indeed, existing literature has tried to illustrate the relationship between international courts and broader political processes and outcomes. What role has the CJEU played in the institutionalization of the European Union and regional integration? Has international investment arbitration lead to a depoliticization of investment disputes? Is the ECtHR responsible for the expansion of rights across Europe? Have international courts raised legal consciousness among the public or led to an empowerment of civil society? The range of questions one could ask about ICs' meso- and macro-level performance is quite extensive. As a result, it is not feasible to identify all the possible criteria against which to evaluate IC performance or how they might be operationalized. Nevertheless, the above discussion makes clear that broader impacts are typically operationalized as either formal laws and policy or dynamics "on the ground." Formal laws and policies can at times be useful for empirical research. Its advantages are accessibility, comparability, and reliability. However, as laws and policies may not be implemented, a focus on formal law and policy can generate invalid measurement; that is, we may not be observing the impacts which interest us. On the other hand, "on the ground" impacts may have greater face validity but be less reliably measured across time and space. Any time measurements are based on subjective assessments, it is possible that replication would not yield the same results. In the end, operationalizing and measuring the broader impacts of ICs requires careful attention to validity and reliability.

Methods for Evaluating the Performance of ICs

To evaluate the performance of ICs a range of methods are employed by researchers. Existing research has primarily drawn on observational data and used conventional qualitative or quantitative methods. An array of other methods offers possibilities for future research on international courts. In this section, I discuss five potentially fruitful methods for evaluating the performance of ICs. I point to these methods because they diverge from standard large-N multivariate statistical analysis based on observational data and small-n qualitative case studies. The five methods are: experimental design, meta-analysis, Qualitative Comparative Analysis (QCA), counterfactuals, and multimethods. This discussion aims to briefly introduce these methods and how they might be useful for research on the performance of international courts.

Experimental Designs

Experimental designs have become increasingly common in the social sciences (Druckman et al. 2011a: 4–5). Typically, researchers assess causal impact by comparing:

> between two states of the world: one in which some sort of intervention is administered (a treated state, i.e., exposing a subject to a stimulus) and another in which it is not (an untreated state) . . . *Observational research* involves a comparison between people or entities subjected to different treatments (at least, in part, of their own choosing) . . . *Experimental research* differs from observational research in that the entities under study are randomly assigned to different treatments (Druckman et al. 2011b: 16).

Thus, in experimental studies, subjects are randomly assigned to two groups: a treatment group and a control group. The researcher then compares the outcomes for the two groups to estimate the effect of the treatment. Experiments are typically classified according to the setting in which the randomization occurs:

> a *lab experiment* involves an intervention in a setting created and controlled by the researcher;[9] a *field experiment* takes place in a naturally occurring setting; and a *survey experiment* involves an intervention in the course of an opinion survey (which might be conducted in person, over the phone, or via the web) (Druckman et al. 2011b: 17).

Another category of experiments is called a *natural experiment*, where random assignments occur naturally in the world. "The term natural experiment is sometimes defined more expansively to include events that happen to some people and not others, but the happenstance is not random" (Druckman et al. 2011b: 22).[10]

[9] These types of experiments are widely used in the natural sciences – in a controlled laboratory environment.

[10] Others might call the broader type of natural experiments where the treatment does not occur at random as a "quasi-experiment." Others argue that these cannot be called "experiments."

To my knowledge, there has not yet been extensive use of experimental designs in research on international courts. One notable exception is the chapter by Jo, Radtke, and Simmons in Chapter 6.[11] Two types of experimental designs could most probably be applied to international courts. First, survey experiments could be used to assess the performance of international courts. A survey experiment relies on a survey instrument for measurement, where the survey is manipulated to assess the impact of a causal factor. The researcher randomly assigns respondents into control and treatment groups. The treatment group is "primed" by the provision of alternative information or questions in the survey to highlight the determinants of opinions. The differences in responses across the groups are then compared to find if they are statistically significant. A central concern with the use of survey experiments is their external validity, or whether or not they produce results that would transpire in the real world (Barabas and Jerit 2010).

Survey experiments on the performance of international courts would most likely focus on *perceived performance*. Researchers have previously used survey experiments when studying national courts. For instance, Gibson et al. (2011) have examined the effects of judicial campaign ads on the legitimacy of American courts based on a survey experiment. Clark and Kastellec (2015) employ a survey experiment to examine if and how elite endorsements of the US Supreme Court affect public views of the Court. Similarly, Hume (2013) examined whether the US Supreme Court confers more legitimacy on public policy than other branches of government. All of these studies suggest there is opportunity to utilize survey experiments in research on international courts, especially for understanding what factors shape how ICs' performance is perceived. However, researchers need to be careful in designing survey experiments and interpreting their results to maximize their usefulness.[12]

Second, natural experiments might also hold promise for future research on the performance of ICs. A natural experiment would be based on observational data from a naturally occurring phenomenon, and examine the effect of some treatment that "naturally" occurs outside the researcher's control. Jo et al. (2018) offers an example. To understand how the ICC performed at deterring mass atrocities, they compare civilian killings before and after the ICC's interventions in Uganda.

[11] By some definitions, their analysis does not qualify as an experiment because the treatment was not random. See previous footnote.

[12] For a general discussion of these considerations, see Barabas and Jerit (2010) and Gaines et al. (2017).

Thus, the ICC's interventions can be construed as a "randomly assigned treatment."[13] Natural experiments, similar to theirs, could be used in other instances. For instance, one could look at how the Permanent Court of Arbitration's (PCA) judgment changed the dispute between the Philippines and China over the South China Sea by looking at the state of the dispute before and after the intervention of the PCA. Such studies would examine the causal impact of an IC's intervention into a dispute or a particular problem. At a large-N level, for example, one could look at territorial disputes to see how international arbitration or legal intervention affects these disputes.[14] Other strategies resembling natural experiments might examine the impact of particular judgments, the appointment of certain judges, or changes in rules governing a court or its jurisdiction to see what causal impact these factors might have on the performance of an IC. In essence, such research designs would isolate the effect of a causal factor by comparing the state of the world when it does not exist to when it does.

Meta-Analysis

The study of ICs may benefit from the use of meta-analysis. Meta-analysis is defined as the "analysis of analyses" (Glass 1976: 3), and it aims to identify general patterns from a variety of empirical studies. More specifically, it is the " . . . analysis of a large collection of test results coming from individual studies for the purpose of integrating the findings . . . " (Imbeau et al. 2001: 3). Meta-analysis can apply to primary analyses that are either qualitative or quantitative. While differences exist between the qualitative and quantitative versions of meta-analysis, I will refer to them collectively as meta-analysis in this discussion.[15]

[13] This is not to say that the intervention by the ICC was truly random. Rather, speaking of this research design as a natural experiment places less emphasis on the randomization of the treatment and highlights the comparison of outcomes across discrete groups when the treatment does not apply to all of the groups. Consequently, one can determine the causal effect of the treatment by comparing the outcomes across the groups.

[14] Goertz et al. (2016: chapter 8) makes steps towards this type of inquiry by looking at legal intervention in the resolution of territorial disputes, compared to other types of mediation.

[15] Some researchers use the labels of qualitative meta-analysis, qualitative data synthesis, or systemic review to refer to meta-analysis that is based on qualitative analyses (Dacombe 2017).

Despite appearances, meta-analysis (MA) is a method and not a literature review (LR). As Imbeau et al. (2001: 4) explain, LRs examine how:

> a particular phenomenon has been studied by scholars in published works with the objective of justifying the need for further research. MAs deal with specific empirical hypotheses and try to tell something about them with the objective of assessing, on the basis of the empirical work so far published, whether there is an impact of some independent variable upon some dependent variable, and, if so, what the magnitude of this impact is . . .. Furthermore LRs limit themselves to the most important studies in a given field whereas MAs tend towards comprehensiveness.

Meta-analysis entails three broad steps: (1) problem formulation and defining the types of research findings to be analyzed; (2) systematic data collection of previous studies; and (3) translating findings into a common metric and comparison across analyses (Lau et al. 2007: 1178; Dacombe 2017: 3).

Meta-analysis has been used in political science to address a range of topics, such as the effectiveness of negative campaign ads (Lau et al. 1999; Lau et al. 2007), voter turnout (Geys 2006; Smets and Van Ham 2013; Stockemer 2016), and the policy impact of political parties (Imbeau et al. 2001). It is also used in several studies in criminology (e.g., Pratt 1998; Cottle et al. 2001). Meta-analysis has been not been applied to law and courts research (for one notable exception, see Pinello 1999), and to my knowledge, it has not been used in any study on international law or courts. The lack of meta-analysis in law and courts scholarship is most likely because it requires a sizeable number of roughly comparable studies to form the basis of aggregation.

The increased quantification of data among international relations and legal scholars would appear to make IC research in some areas fertile ground for meta-analysis to address questions such as whether there is a bias in international investment arbitration (e.g., Van Harten 2012; Franck 2014; Behn 2018), whether the CJEU is constrained by the threat of an override (e.g., Carrubba et al. 2008; Stone Sweet and Brunell 2012; Larsson and Naurin 2016), or whether there is bias in the WTO DSM (for instance, Horn et al. 1999; Guzman and Simmons 2005; Busch et al. 2009; Fattore 2013). These are only some of the topics related to international courts and tribunals that have been subject to numerous quantitative assessments. There are also topics that have received repeated analysis using qualitative data. For instance, scholarship on compliance with International Court of Justice (ICJ) decisions is ample, often arriving at similar yet different conclusions. A synthesis of this research could advance our understanding of what lies at the heart of (non)compliance with the ICJ. Overall, there seems to be room for the integration of meta-analysis into the researcher's toolbox of methods for studying performance of ICs.

Qualitative Comparative Analysis

Another method that might hold promise for exploring the determinants of IC performance is QCA. Developed by Charles Ragin (1987; 2000), QCA focuses on explaining social phenomenon through set relations by identifying whether key explanatory variables are consistently present across a medium number of cases that have a similar outcome. For example, if all (or almost all) states with independent judiciaries are stable democracies, then we can say that states with independent judiciaries are a subset of stable democracies. As independent judiciaries constitute a consistent subset of stable democracies, we will most likely consider independent judiciaries to be a key factor explaining democratic stability. Using this basic understanding of relationships, Ragin (1987) introduced a form of analysis, based on Boolean logic, which identifies causal relationships from the construction of truth tables of comparative qualitative data. Truth tables capture whether explanatory factors and outcomes are present. By comparing the presence or absence of explanatory factors across cases we can identify which factors are necessary and/or sufficient for an outcome to occur. In this first version of QCA, explanatory factors (or the elements of sets) are "crisp," meaning they are binary (present or absent/true or false). Ragin (2000) then incorporated fuzzy sets, such that explanatory factors and outcomes may not be fully present or absent, into QCA.

QCA differs from regression-oriented logic. The latter focuses on the "effects of causes" and its research designs aim to estimate the average effects of determinants, while QCA focuses on the "causes of effects" (Mahoney 2010: 132). QCA assumes that there can be multiple paths to an outcome and "conjunctural causation" is possible; it makes no assumption of linearity or probabilities. Nevertheless, Ragin (2008) argues that QCA bridges qualitative case study analysis and quantitative methods because it requires in-depth assessment of particular cases while also pointing to cross-case patterns as in quantitative analysis.

While QCA is not common in previous scholarship on international relations or international law (Bennett and Elman 2007: 182), the tide may be turning. Recent scholarship on international arbitration (Grynaviski and Hsieh 2015) and litigation at the WTO (Yildirim 2016) has used QCA.

QCA could be a useful methodological strategy for the study of international courts and tribunals for three reasons. First, QCA is helpful for understanding complex causality and when outcomes are the product of a conjunction of causal conditions. In several instances, we can easily imagine that ICs' contributions to outcomes are only partial explanations, or that their performance is contingent on a combination of conditions. Second, it is also well suited for research dealing with a medium-N (the number of cases is somewhere between a few and fifty). Several new ICs still have few judicial decisions, and the number of international courts in existence is also limited. Studying these new courts, either individually or comparatively, will therefore typically lead to a medium-N, for which QCA is well suited. Third, sitting at the crossroads of qualitative and quantitative research, QCA is useful for data that is qualitative. Several aspects of court procedures and outcomes are qualitative in their natural form and may not be easily translated into quantitative data. QCA may offer an alternative to researchers. QCA however has limitations. The generalizability of its results are modest (Berg-Schlosser et al. 2009). Also, while it may be able to identify the combination of factors that lead to an outcome, it cannot tell us about the relative importance of any one factor and important factors may be excluded from the analysis.

Counterfactuals

Counterfactual analysis also provides opportunity for research on the performance of international courts. Counterfactuals are what-if statements, that is, they consider what would have occurred if a hypothesized causal factor had been absent. Counterfactual analysis is a thought experiment that asks: if A had (or had not) been the case, then would C have (or have not) been the case. Counterfactuals can be useful for trying to understand how a certain factor, such as a court or its judgment, contributed to an outcome.

For example, one could hypothesize that the ECtHR has been a critical causal factor leading to the advancement of minority rights in Europe. To address this question, a researcher could take two methodological approaches. One could compare the status of minority rights protections in states where the ECtHR has jurisdiction to one of two possible comparative cases: (a) a case of similarly situated countries where a similar court does not have jurisdiction (e.g., US, Canada, Australia, New Zealand, etc.), or (b) an imagined case where the ECtHR did not exist in Europe.[16] This latter approach would be a counterfactual case.[17] The hypothetical case in some instances may be the only possible approach, as there may not be any actual cases that are sufficiently similar.

It is important to note, however, that counterfactual analysis is not freeform. Counterfactuals are grounded in facts; "counterfactual arguments, like any historical argument, are only as compelling as the logic and 'evidence' offered by the researcher to substantiate the links between the hypothesized antecedent and its expected consequences. Every good counterfactual thus rests on multiple factuals . . . " (Lebow 2000: 556). Also, while it is not settled what makes a good counterfactual, they should be theoretically and historically consistent – also knowns as the "minimal-rewrite rule" (Capoccia and Kelemen 2007: 356).[18] While I know of no extensive use of counterfactuals in existing research on international courts and tribunals, counterfactual analysis that adheres to these standards could be a beneficial tool for researchers who aim to understand the determinants of IC performance and how they contribute to broader effects.

Multimethod Research Designs

Multimethod research designs have become quite popular in international relations and other social sciences. Multimethod designs can be defined as the combining of qualitative and quantitative tools or data in a single research design. When done well, a multimethod research design entails combining these tools in a targeted fashion to benefit from the comparative advantage of qualitative and quantitative evidence. Specifically, quantitative methods are valuable for establishing aggregate patterns of correlation, while qualitative analysis is useful for exploring causal mechanisms.

Multimethod research may use qualitative case studies to supplement quantitative results (Mahoney 2010: 139–141). A multivariate analysis might reveal a statistically significant correlation exists between two

[16] For a discussion of these two different methodological strategies, see Fearon (1991).

[17] Option (a) would constitute a natural experiment by some definitions. See discussion on experimental designs.

[18] Lebow (2000) offers a thorough discussion of the criteria for good counterfactuals.

factors, however this analysis may leave several questions unresolved: Is the relationship spurious; does causality operate in the opposite direction to what is hypothesized; is a missing variable unaccounted for; and through what causal mechanisms are variables related? A case study can help to resolve these uncertainties. To supplement quantitative analysis, the case selection process should be informed by what purpose it serves. For example, an outlier is ideal if the case study is intended to identify possible missing variables, but a typical case is suitable for elucidating causal mechanisms (Lieberman 2005).

Quantitative research can also be used to supplement qualitative research (Mahoney 2010: 141–143). A qualitative study may be used to identify how plausible a causal account is – acting as a "plausibility probe" – but a supplemental quantitative analysis might test the generalizability of that account. It might also suggest how the account should be modified.

Well-structured multimethod research designs are beneficial because they improve the specification of causal models. For this reason, multimethod designs can be a powerful tool for understanding the performance of ICs. As we move towards understanding why ICs are able to perform well or not and the conditions under which international courts have broader impacts, scholars should consider how qualitative and quantitative methods can be combined. Nevertheless, one needs to be careful that case selection is principled.[19] Also, one should be careful to avoid conceptual stretching in the efforts to find both qualitative and quantitative measurements.[20]

Conclusion

The aim of this chapter has been to identify possible ways to operationalize and measure the performance of ICs. It has argued that performance should be operationalized with special consideration given to the validity and reliability of measures. Validity entails ensuring that we measure what we really intend to measure so that our empirical observations capture our theoretical concepts. Canvasing alternative options and considering ways to control for confounding factors can improve our measurement validity. Measurement reliability is also important. Avoiding subjective assessments and looking for measurement strategies

[19] For guidance on case selection techniques, see Gerring (2007: chapter 5).

[20] Ahram (2013) discusses the issue of conceptual stretching in multimethod research.

that transcend time and space ensure greater reliability. Jointly, taking these considerations seriously will minimize systematic measurement error as we move forward in the study of IC performance.

In addition, this chapter aimed to identify methods of analysis that might be fruitful for researchers. I have argued that five methods in particular hold promise for research on the performance of international courts. My purpose has been to increase familiarity with these methods and to hint at how they might be used for those interested in international courts and tribunals. They however need not replace more conventional qualitative case studies or quantitative analysis based on observational data. Rather, the five methods I discussed should in addition be considered among the possible tools available to researchers. In this sense, this is a call for bringing a wider set of methods to future research.

References

Ahram, Ariel I. 2013. "Concepts and Measurement in Multimethod Research," *Political Research Quarterly* 66(2): 280–291.

Barabas, Jason and Jerit, Jennifer. 2010. "Are Survey Experiments Externally Valid?," *American Political Science Review* 104(2): 226–242.

Basch, Fernando, Filippini, Leonardo, Laya, Ana, Nino, Mariano, Rossi, Felicitas, and Schreiber, Bárbara. 2010. "The Effectiveness of the Inter-American System of Human Rights Protection: A Quantitative Approach to Its Functioning and Compliance with Its Decisions," *Sur International Journal of Human Rights* 12(7): 9–25.

Bechtel, Michael M. and Sattler, Thomas. 2015. "What Is Litigation in the World Trade Organization Worth?," 69(2): 375–403.

Behn, Daniel. 2018. "The Performance of Investment Treaty Arbitration," this volume.

Bennett, Andrew and Elman, Colin. 2007. "Case Study Methods in the International Relations Subfield," *Comparative Political Studies* 40(2): 170–195.

Berg-Schlosser, Dirk, De Meur, Gisèle, Rihoux, Benoît, and Ragin, Charles C. 2009. "Qualitative Comparative Analysis (QCA) as an Approach," in Rihoux, Benoît and Ragin, Charles (eds.), *Configurational Comparative Methods: Qualitative Comparative Analysis (QCA) and Related Techniques*. Thousand Oaks, CA: SAGE Publications, pp. 1–18.

Blauberger, Michael. 2012. "With Luxembourg in Mind … The Remaking of National Policies in the Face of ECJ Jurisprudence," *Journal of European Public Policy* 19(1): 109–126.

Bown, Chad P. 2004. "On the Economic Success of GATT/WTO Dispute Settlement," *Review of Economics and Statistics* 86(3): 811–823.

Brutger, Ryan and Morse, Julia. 2015. "Balancing Law and Politics: Judicial Incentives in WTO Dispute Settlement," *Review of International Organizations* 10(2): 179–205.

Burke-White, William W. 2008. "The Domestic Influence of International Criminal Tribunals: The International Criminal Tribunal for the Former Yugoslavia and the Creation of the State Court of Bosnia & Herzegovina," *Columbia Journal of Transnational Law* 46(2): 279–350.

Busch, Marc L. and Pelc, Krzysztof J. 2010. "The Politics of Judicial Economy at the World Trade Organization," *International Organization* 64(2): 257–279.

Busch, Marc L. and Reinhardt, Eric. 2000. "Bargaining in the Shadow of the Law: Early Settlement in GATT/WTO Disputes," *Fordham International Law Journal* 24(1): 158–172.

2003. "Developing Countries and General Agreement on Tariffs and Trade World Trade Organization Dispute Settlement," *Journal of World Trade* 37 (4): 719–735.

2006. "Three's a Crowd: Third Parties and WTO Dispute Settlement," *World Politics* 58(3): 446–477.

Busch, Marc L., Reinhardt, Eric, and Shaffer, Gregory. 2009. "Does Legal Capacity Matter? A Survey of WTO Members," *World Trade Review* 8(4): 559–577.

Börzel, Tanja A., Hofmann, Tobias, and Panke, Diana. 2012. "Caving in or Sitting It Out? Longitudinal Patterns of Non-Compliance in the European Union," *Journal of European Public Policy* 19(4): 454–471.

Capoccia, Giovanni and Kelemen, R. Daniel. 2007. "The Study of Critical Junctures: Theory, Narrative, and Counterfactuals in Historical Institutionalism," *World Politics* 59(3): 341–369.

Carrubba, Clifford J. and Gabbel, Matthew J. 2014. *International Courts and the Performance of International Agreements: A General Theory with Evidence from the European Union.* Cambridge: Cambridge University Press.

Carrubba, Clifford J., Gabel, Matthew, and Hankla, Charles. 2008. "Judicial Behavior under Political Constraints: Evidence from the European Court of Justice," *American Political Science Review* 102(4): 435–452.

Cichowski, Rachel A. 2007. *The European Court and Civil Society: Litigation, Mobilization and Governance.* Cambridge: Cambridge University Press.

Cingranelli, David and Richards, David 2015. "The Cingranelli-Richards (Ciri) Human Rights Dataset." Available at: www.humanrightsdata.org (accessed June 2017).

Clark, Tom S. and Kastellec, Jonathan P. 2015. "Source Cues and Public Support for the Supreme Court," *American Politics Research* 43(3): 504–535.

Conant, Lisa. 2002. *Justice Contained: Law and Politics in the European Union.* Ithaca, NY: Cornell University Press.

Cottle, Cindy C., Lee, Ria J., and Heilbrun, Kirk. 2001. "The Prediction of Criminal Recidivism in Juveniles," *Criminal Justice and Behavior* 28(3): 367–394.

Creamer, Cosette D. and Strezhnev, Anton. 2018. "Court Performance within the Multilateral Trade Regime," Chapter 2 in this volume.

Dacombe, Rod. 2017. "Systematic Reviews in Political Science: What Can the Approach Contribute to Political Research?," *Political Studies Review*. Online first, DOI: https://doi.org/10.1177/1478929916680641.

Davis, Christina. 2012. *Why Adjudicate?: Enforcing Trade Rules in the WTO*. Princeton, NJ: Princeton University Press.

Druckman, James N., Green, Donald P., Kuklinski, James H., and Lupia, Arthur. 2011a. "Experimentation in Political Science," in Druckman, James N., Green, Donald P., Kuklinski, James H., and Lupia, Arthur (eds.), *Cambridge Handbook of Experimental Political Science*. Cambridge: Cambridge University Press, pp. 3–12.

2011b. "Experiments: An Introduction to Core Concepts," in Druckman, James N., Green, Donald P., Kuklinski, James H., and Lupia, Arthur (eds.), *Cambridge Handbook of Experimental Political Science*. Cambridge: Cambridge University Press, pp. 15–26.

Dunoff, Jeffrey L. 2007. "The Many Dimensions of Softwood Lumber," *Alberta Law Review* 45(2): 319–356.

Dunoff, Jeffrey L. and Pollack Mark A. 2018. "International Judicial Performances and the Performance of International Courts," Chapter 8 in this volume.

Eck, Kristine and Hultman, Lisa 2007. "One-Sided Violence against Civilians in War: Insights from New Fatality Data," *Journal of Peace Research* 44(2): 233–246.

Escribà-Folch, Abel and Wright, Joseph. 2015. "Human Rights Prosecutions and Autocratic Survival," *International Organization* 69(02): 343–373.

Fattore, Christina. 2013. "The Influence of Legal Capacity on WTO Dispute Duration," *International Trade Journal* 27(5): 450–464.

Faude, Benjamin. 2018. "How the Fragmentation of the International Judiciary Affects the Performance of International Judicial Bodies," Chapter 7 in this volume.

Fearon, James D. 1991. "Counterfactuals and Hypothesis Testing in Political Science," *World Politics* 43(2): 169–195.

Franck, Susan D. 2014. "Conflating Politics and Development? Examining Investment Treaty Arbitration Outcomes," *Virginia Journal of International Law* 55(1): 13–71.

Gabel, Matthew J., Carrubba, Clifford J., Ainsley, Caitlin, and Beaudette, Donald M. 2012. "Of Courts and Commerce," *Journal of Politics* 74(4): 1125–1137.

Gaines, Brian J., Kuklinski, James H., and Quirk, Paul J. 2017. "The Logic of the Survey Experiment Reexamined," *Political Analysis* 15(1): 1–20.

Gerring, John. 2007. *Case Study Research: Principles and Practices*. Cambridge: Cambridge University Press.

Geys, Benny. 2006. "Explaining Voter Turnout: A Review of Aggregate-Level Research," *Electoral Studies* 25(4): 637–663.

Gibney, Mark, Cornett, Linda, Wood, Reed, Haschke, Peter, and Arnon, Daniel. 2015. "The Political Terror Scale 1976–2015." Available at: www.politicalterrorscale.org (accessed July 2017).

Gibson, James L., Gottfried, Jeffrey A., Delli Carpini, Michael X., and Jamieson, Kathleen Hall. 2011. "The Effects of Judicial Campaign Activity on the Legitimacy of Courts," *Political Research Quarterly* 64(3): 545–558.

Giorgetti, Chiara. 2018. "What Happens after a Judgment is Given? Judgment Compliance and the Performance of International Courts and Tribunals," Chapter 10 in this volume.

Glass, Gene V. 1976. "Primary, Secondary, and Meta-Analysis of Research," *Educational Researcher* 5(10): 3–8.

Gleditsch, Nils Petter, Wallensteen, Peter, Eriksson, Mikael, Sollenberg, Margareta, and Strand, Håvard. 2002. "Armed Conflict 1946–2001: A New Dataset," *Journal of Peace Research* 39(5): 615–637.

Goertz, Gary, Diehl, Paul F., and Balas, Alexandru Balas. 2016. *The Puzzle of Peace: The Evolution of Peace in the International System*. Oxford: Oxford University Press.

Goldstein, Judith L. and Steinberg, Richard H. 2008. "Negotiate or Litigate? Effects of Wto Judicial Delegation on U.S. Trade Politics," *Law and Contemporary Problems* 71(1): 257–282.

Grewal, Sharanbir and Voeten, Erik. 2015. "Are New Democracies Better Human Rights Compliers?," 69(2): 497–518.

Grinols, Earl L. and Perrelli, Roberto. 2006. "The WTO Impact on International Trade Disputes: An Event History Analysis," *Review of Economics and Statistics* 88(4): 613–624.

Grynaviski, Eric and Hsieh, Amy. 2015. "Hierarchy and Judicial Institutions: Arbitration and Ideology in the Hellenistic World," 69(3): 697–729.

Guzman, Andrew and Simmons, Beth A. 2005. "Power Plays and Capacity Constraints: The Selection of Defendants in World Trade Organization Disputes," *Journal of Legal Studies* 34(2): 557–598.

Hathaway, Oona. 2002. "Do Human Rights Treaties Make a Difference?," *Yale Law Journal* 111(8): 1934–2042.

Hawkins, Darren and Jacoby, Wade. 2010. "Partial Compliance: A Comparison of the European and Inter-American Courts of Human Rights," *Journal of International Law & International Relations* 6(1): 35.

Helfer, Laurence R. and Voeten, Erik. 2014. "International Courts as Agents of Legal Change: Evidence from Lgbt Rights in Europe," *International Organization* 68(1): 77–110.

Helfer, Laurence and Slaughter, Anne-Marie. 1997. "Towards a Theory of Effective Supranational Adjudication," *Yale Law Journal* 107(2): 273–391.

Hillebrecht, Courtney. 2014. *Domestic Politics and International Human Rights Tribunals: The Problem of Compliance, Cambridge Studies in International and Comparative Law*. Cambridge: Cambridge University Press.

Horn, Henrik, Nordström, Håkan, and Mavroidis, Petros C. 1999. "Is the Use of the WTO Dispute Settlement System Biased?," *CEPR Discussion Paper 2340*.

Hume, Robert J. 2013. *Courthouse Democracy and Minority Rights: Same-Sex Marriage in the States*. Oxford: Oxford University Press.

Huneeus, Alexandra. 2013. "Compliance with Judgments and Decisions," in Romano, Cesare, Alter, Karen, and Shany, Yuval (eds.), *The Oxford Handbook of International Adjudication*. Oxford: Oxford University Press, pp. 437–463.

Imbeau, Louis, Pétry, François, and Lamari, Moktar. 2001. "Left-Right Party Ideology and Government Policies: A Meta-Analysis," *European Journal of Political Research* 40(1): 1–29.

Ingadottir, Thordis. 2004. "The Financing of Internationalized Criminal Courts and Tribunals," in Romano, Cesare P. R., Nollkaemper, André, and Kleffner, Jann K. (eds.), *Internationalized Criminal Courts: Sierra Leone, East Timor, Kosovo, and Cambodia*. Oxford: Oxford University Press, pp. 271–289.

Jo, Hyeran, Radtke, Mitchell, and Simmons, Beth A. 2018. "Assessing the International Criminal Court," Chapter 6 in this volume.

Jo, Hyeran and Simmons, Beth A. 2016. "Can the International Criminal Court Deter Atrocity?," *International Organization* 70(3): 443–475.

Kapiszewski, D. and Taylor, M. M. 2012. "Compliance: Conceptualizing, Measuring, and Explaining Adherence to Judicial Rulings," *Law and Social Inquiry* 38(4): 803–835.

Keller, Helen, Forowicz, Magdalena, and Engi, Lorenz. 2011. *Friendly Settlements before the European Court of Human Rights: Theory and Practice*. Oxford: Oxford University Press.

Kim, Hunjoon and Sikkink, Kathryn. 2010. "Explaining the Deterrence Effect of Human Rights Prosecutions for Transitional Countries," *International Studies Quarterly* 54(4): 939–963.

Kim, Moonhawk. 2015. "Enduring Trade Disputes: Disguised Protectionism and Duration and Recurrence of International Trade Disputes," *Review of International Organizations* 11(3): 283–310.

Larsson, Olof and Naurin, Daniel. 2016. "Judicial Independence and Political Uncertainty: How the Risk of Override Affects the Court of Justice of the EU," *International Organization* 70(2): 377–408.

Larsson, Olof, Naurin, Daniel, Derlén, Mattias, and Lindholm, Johan. 2017. "Speaking Law to Power. The Strategic Use of Precedent of the Court of

Justice of the European Union," *Comparative Political Studies* 50(7): 879–907.

Lau, Richard R., Sigelman, Lee, Heldman, Caroline, and Babbitt, Paul. 1999. "The Effects of Negative Political Advertisements: A Meta-Analytic Assessment," *American Political Science Review* 93(4): 851.

Lau, Richard R., Sigelman, Lee, and Rovner, Ivy Brown. 2007. "The Effects of Negative Political Campaigns: A Meta-Analytic Reassessment," *Journal of Politics* 69(4): 1176–1209.

Lebow, Richard Ned. 2000. "What's So Different About a Counterfactual?," *World Politics* 52(4): 550–585.

Lieberman, Evan S. 2005. "Nested Analysis as a Mixed-Method Strategy for Comparative Research," *American Political Science Review* 99(3): 435–452.

Lupu, Yonatan and Voeten, Erik. 2012. "Precedent in International Courts: A Network Analysis of Case Citations by the European Court of Human Rights," *British Journal of Political Science* 42(2): 413–439.

Mahoney, J. 2010. "After KKV: The New Methodology of Qualitative Research," *World Politics* 62(1): 120–147.

Meernik, James D., Nichols, Angela, and King, Kimi L. 2010. "The Impact of International Tribunals and Domestic Trials on Peace and Human Rights after Civil War," *International Studies Perspectives* 11(4): 309–334.

Nettelfield, Lara J. 2013. *Courting Democracy in Bosnia and Herzegovina. The Hague Tribunal's Impact in a Postwar State*. Cambridge: Cambridge University Press.

Olsen, Tricia D., Payne, Leigh A., and Reiter, Andrew G. 2010. "The Justice Balance: When Transitional Justice Improves Human Rights and Democracy," *Human Rights Quarterly* 32(4): 980–1007.

Panke, Diana. 2010. *The Effectiveness of the European Court of Justice: Why Reluctant States Comply*. Manchester: Manchester University Press.

Pauwelyn, Joost and Elsig, Manfred. 2014. "The Politics of Treaty Interpretation: Variations and Explanations across International Tribunals," in Dunoff, Jeffrey and Pollack, Mark (eds.), *Interdisciplinary Perspectives on International Law and International Relations*. Cambridge: Cambridge University Press, pp. 445–474.

Pelc, Krzysztof J. 2014. "The Politics of Precedent in International Law: A Social Network Application," *American Political Science Review* 108(03): 547–564.

Pinello, Daniel R. 1999. "Linking Party to Judicial Ideology in American Courts: A Meta-Analysis," *The Justice System Journal* 20(3): 219–254.

Pratt, Travis C. 1998. "Race and Sentencing: A Meta-Analysis of Conflicting Empirical Research Results," *Journal of Criminal Justice* 26(6): 513–523.

Ragin, Charles C. 1987. *The Comparative Method: Moving Byeond Qaulitative and Quantitative Strategies*. Berkeley: University of California Press.

2000. *Fuzzy-Set Social Science*. Chicago: University of Chicago Press.

2008. *Redesigning Social Inquiry: Fuzzy Sets and Beyond.* Chicago: University of Chicago Press.

Romano, Cesare. 2005. "The Price of International Justice," *Law & Practice of International Courts and Tribunals* 4(2): 281–328.

Shelton, Dinah. 2018. "Performance of Regional Human Rights Courts," this volume.

Sikkink, Kathryn and Walling, Carrie. 2007. "The Impact of Human Rights Trials in Latin America," *Journal of Peace Research* 44(4): 427–445.

Simmons, Beth A. 2014. "Bargaining over Bits, Arbitrating Awards: The Regime for Protection and Promotion of International Investment," *World Politics* 66(1): 12–46.

Smets, Kaat and Van Ham, Carolien. 2013. "The Embarrassment of Riches? A Meta-Analysis of Individual-Level Research on Voter Turnout," *Electoral Studies* 32(2): 344.

Squatrito, Theresa. 2016. "Domestic Legislatures and International Human Rights Law: Legislating on Religious Symbols in Europe," *Journal of Human Rights* 15(4): 550–570.

Stockemer, Daniel. 2016. "What Affects Voter Turnout? A Review Article/Meta-Analysis of Aggregate Research," Government and Opposition: 1–25.

Stone Sweet, Alec. 2000. *Governing with Judges: Constitutional Politics in Europe.* Oxford: Oxford University Press.

Stone Sweet, Alec and Brunell, Thomas L. 2012. "The European Court of Justice, State Noncompliance, and the Politics of Override," *American Political Science Review* 106(1): 204–213.

Terris, Daniel, Romano, Cesare P. R., and Swigart, Leigh. 2007. *The International Judge: An Introduction to the Men and Women Who Decide the World's Cases.* Oxford: Oxford University Press.

Van Harten, Gus. 2012. "Arbitrator Behaviour in Asymmetrical Adjudication: An Empirical Study of Investment Treaty Arbitration," *Osgoode Hall Law Journal* 50(1): 211–268.

Yildirim, Aydin B. 2016. "Domestic Political Implications of Global Value Chains: Explaining EU Responses to Litigation at the World Trade Organization," *Comparative European Politics.* Online first, DOI: https//doi:10.1057/s41295-016–0085-3.

13

What We Know So Far

ORAN R. YOUNG, THERESA SQUATRITO, ANDREAS FOLLESDAL, AND GEIR ULFSTEIN

Introduction

We return now to the issues regarding the performance of international courts and tribunals (ICs) identified in Chapter 1 in the light of the accounts set forth in the chapters that make up the two substantive sections of this book. How well have international courts performed across a variety of indicators, ranging from the treatment of specific cases that come before them to the initiation of chains of events affecting the character of international society as a whole? Have they succeeded in meeting relevant normative standards relating to the processes through which they have played their roles? Are there significant variations in these terms either across time with regard to the performance of individual courts or with regard to the performance of a number of courts operating in different issue domains? What are the prospects for the future with respect to the performance of these judicial bodies?

In the substantive chapters of the book, we have tackled these questions in two distinct but related ways. The chapters included in Part I approach these issues through a broad examination of judicial performance, mostly aiming to evaluate the state of IC performance against several criteria in four key issue domains: trade, investment, human rights, and international criminal law. Here, we compare and contrast the findings of these analyses dealing with individual issue domains. The chapters included in Part II, by contrast, concentrate on examining specific aspects of IC performance in a variety of contexts, offering in-depth accounts based on original research. Here, we compare and contrast the accounts from these chapters to explore the relative importance of factors relating to the practices of the courts themselves and factors dealing with characteristics of the settings within which they operate. Combining the two sets of observations, we seek both to generate insights regarding the performance of international courts and tribunals that go beyond previous research on this topic and to identify cutting-edge questions to guide the efforts of those who take an interest in this topic in the future.

To address these matters, we proceed in this chapter as follows. The first substantive section provides what we think of as a box score regarding the performance of international courts. This is in essence a descriptive effort; it seeks to characterize the performance of courts in various ways rather than to explain these findings. The next section then takes up the question of the determinants of the performance of international courts based on our findings. As in most areas of interest to students of law and politics, we are dealing here with a world of complex causality, especially as we move beyond what Chapter 1 characterizes as the micro-level. Many factors are relevant in developing satisfactory explanations of the phenomena we are considering. Although we cannot offer definitive answers regarding the determinants of performance, we can offer a critical assessment of the evidence relating to the relative importance of a variety of specific factors. The penultimate section turns to future prospects. What can we say about changes in the broader setting during the foreseeable future and the performance of international courts in this setting, and what factors are likely to emerge as the major determinants of performance in this context? Then, in the final section, we turn to the issue of research opportunities, asking about topics our analysis has turned up that seem particularly promising as themes for the next stage of research in this field and commenting on the methods and models needed to make progress in addressing these topics.

The Record So Far

One thing that stands out in any comparison of the roles that courts and tribunals play in the four issue domains we have examined is the diversity of the relevant universe of cases. All the entities we have considered are recognizably judicial institutions. But they differ dramatically in a number of important respects. In terms of numbers, they range from the absence of any dedicated court or similar mechanism addressing international environmental issues to the thousands of investor-state dispute settlement mechanisms established under the terms of bilateral international investment agreements. As this observation suggests, international courts and tribunals vary also regarding both their institutional character and the scope of their jurisdiction. While the investment agreements call for arbitral tribunals established on a case-by-case basis and the World Trade Organization (WTO) treaty establishes a unique system of dispute settlement panels and an Appellate Body, the regional human rights treaties and the Rome Statute set up more conventional courts. Whereas each international investment agreement is open only to litigants associated with two parties, both the WTO treaty and the Rome Statute have well over 100 members who are entitled to make use of the judicial mechanisms they establish.

Nor are these the only important types of variation among the universe of international courts and tribunals. While most of these courts are limited to civil matters, the International Criminal Court (ICC) has jurisdiction over actions involving criminal behavior on the part of individuals. Some courts are open only to states as litigants; others allow individuals to bring cases. The European Court of Human Rights (ECtHR), for example, deals with applications from individuals who feel victimized by the actions of states. International courts also vary greatly with regard to the rules they have developed regarding who has standing and the procedures they use for determining admissibility and jurisdiction. Not surprisingly, this means that there is great variation among these courts with regard to their caseloads. Some courts (e.g., the ECtHR) are besieged with prospective litigants, forced to resort to (often controversial) procedures to determine which cases to accept, and still struggle with a large backlog. Others deal with no more than a handful of cases; they are waiting for opportunities to come their way in order to demonstrate that they are effective mechanisms for dealing with issues at the international level.

The micro-level. This extreme diversity makes it difficult to engage in systematic comparisons regarding the performance of international courts and tribunals in our four issue domains. Nevertheless, the business of every court is to address those specific cases that appear on its docket. It follows that any assessment of the performance of international courts must start at the micro-level with a consideration of the cases these courts have handled and the judgments they have rendered. In this regard, it seems helpful to consider three distinct (though obviously related) aspects of performance at the micro-level: (i) a court's caseload, (ii) the judgments a court renders regarding cases appearing on its docket, and (iii) the immediate reactions to a court's decisions by interested parties. Among other things, focusing first on performance at the micro-level will provide a point of departure for our subsequent consideration of the impacts of ICs at the meso-level and the macro-level.

Characterizing a court's caseload may seem like a straightforward matter. But this is not the case for several reasons. It is difficult to tell whether the cases on a court's docket represent a large or a small proportion of the potential cases in the relevant issue domain. Potential litigants may be deterred from initiating legal action for various reasons. A court may determine that some complaints are inadmissible; it may refuse to accept jurisdiction over others on a number of grounds. The rules regarding standing may make it difficult to find a way to present a dispute in a manner that is justiciable. In criminal cases, the court may not have access to prospective defendants. All these factors make it difficult to characterize precisely the "caseload" of any given IC.

The chapters in Part I of this book do not provide statistics on courts' caseloads in a uniform and easily comparable manner. Still, some interesting observations about caseloads do emerge. The International Criminal Court has dealt with twenty-three cases since the Rome Statute entered into force in 2002; the ICC prosecutor is currently investigating ten situations and monitoring eight. In twenty-plus years, the WTO Dispute Settlement Mechanism (DSM) has dealt with 125 disputes requiring implementation. Taken together, the arbitral mechanisms established under the international investment agreements have handled 760 disputes. The European Court of Human Rights has dealt with hundreds of cases and is struggling to find ways to dispose properly of a large backlog of applications. By contrast, the caseloads of the Inter-American Court of Human Rights (IACtHR) and the African Court of Human and Peoples Rights are modest, though these courts are now receiving more cases.

For the most part, the caseloads of these courts and tribunals have grown over time. This is particularly dramatic in the cases of the European Court of Human Rights and the arbitral mechanisms established under the international investment agreements. The ECtHR is flooded with applications. At the end of 2014, it had 7,386 applications listed in its priority categories alone. As a result, the Court has resorted to drastic measures to limit its caseload, such as allowing a single judge to reject an application after reviewing a one or two sentence summary of the complaint prepared by a court employee. In the case of international investment arbitration, only forty-three arbitrations had been initiated by 2000, but 383 have been initiated just in the period from 2010 to the present.

There are also some striking patterns in the cases that have appeared on the dockets of various courts. For instance, Shelton notes in Chapter 4 that a high proportion of the cases handled by the ECtHR have involved Italy, Russia, Turkey, and the Ukraine (143). With regard to investment arbitration, the top ten respondent states have been involved in nearly 50 percent of the claims addressed under the terms of international investment agreements. In the WTO, the most common users of the DSM are the wealthiest member states. So far, the ICC has prosecuted crimes in situations arising in African states only.

Like all courts, the international courts we have analyzed hand down a stream of judgments pertaining to the individual cases that appear on their dockets. The International Criminal Court reaches decisions to convict or acquit individuals charged with serious war crimes. So far, the ICC has convicted three individuals and acquitted one in the twenty-four cases it has heard. The arbitral arrangements operating under international investment agreements, by contrast, normally make judgments regarding the validity of claimants' cases and award compensation in cases where these claims are judged to be persuasive. To date, awards have ranged from under US$1 million to over US$1 billion, with an average of around US$ 74.5 million. The judgments rendered by the WTO DSM and the various human rights courts are not as easy to describe. Trade disputes normally center on claims that the actions of a party violate one or more provisions of international trade law. As a result, they vary widely in terms of their specific content, even though all claims concern whether a party's trade restrictions are permissible or incompatible under some specific provisions of the international trade regime (e.g., Article 20 of the WTO treaty dealing with admissible restrictions relating to environmental protection and other similar interests). The complexity regarding the judgments of the human rights courts stems not only from the fact that there are several courts that belong to this category whose practices are not identical, but also from the reality that human rights contexts vary considerably across regions. While rights pertaining to fair trials predominate in cases before the ECtHR, for example, cases before the IACtHR often concern rights to life, personal liberty, and humane treatment.

There are various ways to characterize the judgments that international courts render, none of them obviously more fundamental or revealing than the others. Judgments may be narrow or expansive, depending upon the extent to which the court relies on minimal considerations in reaching a conclusion or seizes the opportunity afforded by a specific case to interpret prevailing rules of law broadly. Judgments may rely more or less on applications of the idea of judicial economy, reaching decisions based on a limited range of considerations. Judgments may reflect differing views with regard to the scope of judicial review, according more or less deference or, as some put it, a broader or narrower margin of appreciation to the actions of domestic legislatures, government officials or municipal courts. Judgments also vary regarding the standards of proof they use and the evidence they consider (see Chapter 8 by Dunoff and Pollack). All these factors may vary over time with regard to the performance of the same court or even from case to case when judges whose judicial philosophies differ regarding such matters take the lead in drafting the judgments of the court. As a result, it is not easy to discern clear developmental patterns in the judgments that international courts have rendered over time.

Beyond this, there is the matter of outcomes arising from the judgments of courts. How have the judgments of international courts been received and what effects have they produced? The chapters in this book suggest that there are two distinct, albeit related, ways to respond to this question. Perhaps the classic response focuses on compliance, asking whether the parties accept a court's judgments and implement them as a matter of practice. An alternative approach directs attention to the content of the disputes leading to litigation and asks whether the judgments of courts settle or resolve the issues at stake in some lasting manner. Both approaches have merit; each involves complications that can make it difficult to arrive at simple or straightforward conclusions.

With regard to compliance, the judgments of the international criminal tribunals again constitute a distinct category. While they do not address compliance with specific decisions, Jo, Radtke, and Simmons in Chapter 6 suggest that the ICC can facilitate compliance with international criminal law in the future through the operation of a deterrent effect. In the case of judgments rendered by investment tribunals, on the other hand, the issue of compliance turns on the payment of monetary awards rendered against respondent states. If the respondent state wins, no further action is required, and the case is regarded as closed. But if the investor wins, the issue becomes a matter of the respondent state paying the compensation awarded. Although compliance has been relatively good in these terms, especially since the ICSID Convention provides for the direct enforceability of awards, recent notable exceptions make clear that some states (e.g., Argentina) have refused to satisfy the terms of awards and in non-ICSID cases some states have actively pursued domestic litigation to have an award set aside (e.g., Russia in the Yukos affair) or to contest its enforceability (see Chapter 3 by Behn and Chapter 10 by Giorgetti in this volume).

Compliance with judgments in the areas of trade and human rights is more complex. While a losing state in cases involving such matters may accept a decision on a pro forma basis, this does not mean that it will actually change its behavior in such a way as to conform to the requirements of a judgment or, in any case, do so in a prompt and lasting manner. Not only are there matters of domestic politics that may impede implementation of the prescribed behavioral changes, there may also be difficulties in finding effective ways to influence the behavior of those responsible for the actions giving rise to cases in the first place. High-level policymakers may have difficulty in shifting the standard operating procedures of entrenched domestic agencies that deal with matters of international trade. Special interest groups may make it politically costly for officials to abandon protectionist trade regulations. In the area of human rights, governments may have difficulty reforming deeply embedded policies or institutions that lead to systematic violations. For example, correcting protracted delays in judicial proceedings, which lead to violations of the right to a speedy trial, may require extensive judicial reforms that are resistant to policy interventions (e.g., lengthy judicial proceedings in Italy). In other cases, issues of compliance are highly contentious domestically; procompliance constituencies may lack the political influence needed to support domestic reform (e.g., granting voting rights to prisoners in the UK). As Shelton argues in Chapter 4, "[d]ecisions that challenge a society's core values and traditions often meet fierce resistance" (142).

Additional complexities arise when we endeavor to produce a systematic assessment of the performance of ICs with regard to compliance. If enforcing a court's judgment requires activating a compliance mechanism, for example, does this count as good IC performance? How should we assess situations in which one IC requires high-cost remedies that are partially satisfied by a state, while another IC requires low-cost remedies that a state can satisfy easily? Does the former case count as an instance of failure regarding compliance and the later as an instance of success? Many factors come into play in determining outcomes with regard to compliance; the judgments that courts render are by no means the only factors in the causal complexes involved in the responses of states. It is pertinent in this connection to consider questions regarding the nature of the problems that give rise to cases appearing on courts' dockets. As is true in domestic systems, controversial issues may be litigated over and over again; ultimate outcomes are likely to be determined by broader social changes as much as or more than by the judgments of courts.

Disentangling the roles that courts play in such situations is exceedingly challenging. Still, the evidence that the contributions to this book present suggests that open refusal to comply with the decisions of international courts is relatively uncommon.

Turning to dispute settlement, the contributions to the book introduce several additional complexities. Compliance with the judgments of ICs is not equivalent to the settlement or resolution of the underlying problems that give rise to litigation. Does a negotiated settlement following a judicial decision, especially if the compromise is one that diverges from the findings of the court, suggest that the court performs well at dispute settlement? How are we to assess IC performance when pre-litigation negotiated settlements occur in the shadow of ICs? Does financial compensation ordered by an arbitral tribunal in an investment case ensure that the underlying problem will go away? What if two ICs produce conflicting rulings, prompting political negotiations? Does this qualify as successful dispute settlement by ICs? If an IC endorses compensatory measures against a state as a means of enforcing its decision, is the dispute settled? All in all, the experience of international courts regarding the settlement or resolution of disputes bears a strong resemblance to the experience of domestic courts regarding such matters. Without doubt, these issues are ripe for further examination.

Turning to matters of process at the micro-level, it is pertinent to begin with the observation that this topic encompasses a multiplicity of considerations. In examining the performance of international courts and tribunals, we think it makes sense to distinguish processes relating to access to the courts on the part of potential litigants, the procedures courts adopt in hearing individual cases, the length of time and resources it takes to reach a judgment once a case is initiated, and the activities ICs engage in outside the judicial process (e.g., outreach). As several chapters suggest, empirical work on international courts has focused more on outcome performance than on process performance. Nonetheless, the findings reported in this book do raise some significant issues regarding process performance.

The issue of access involves (at least) two distinct dimensions. In cases where courts are flooded with applications, there is the challenge of determining which cases to include on a court's docket. The ECtHR has been criticized for the procedures it uses to dismiss large numbers of applications. Even so, it has a huge backlog of cases under consideration. As Shelton notes in Chapter 4, the Court had a list of 7,386 applications in its priority categories alone as of the end of 2014 (127). On the other hand, there are issues relating to the capacity of potential litigants to bring cases to the attention of courts. For example, states that do not accept the jurisdiction of a human rights court or do not recognize the right of individual petition effectively limit access to ICs. Also, absent international investment treaties, not all investors have global access to international investment arbitration. In the WTO, the limited legal capacity of developing states appears to limit their access to the WTO DSM. As Creamer and Strezhnev explain in Chapter 2, the most common users of the WTO DSM are the wealthiest members of the trade regime. These are clearly serious concerns that affect the process performance of international courts.

The issue of procedures for hearing cases encompasses matters relating to admissible evidence, transparency, representation, and the role of third parties. For example, Behn explains in Chapter 3 that critics of investment arbitrations argue " . . . arbitration is a secretive process that is conducted behind closed doors with low levels of transparency" (107). In Chapter 4, Shelton claims that human rights courts face difficulties when there is a need " . . . to engage in extensive fact-finding to determine State responsibility" (129). Those concerned with the performance of the WTO DSM have focused attention on processes that may improve the capacity of developing countries to pursue trade-related issues. Looming over these concerns is the matter of time. According to Behn in Chapter 3, on average " . . . investment treaty arbitrations take over three and a half years to resolve in the first instance" (109). Trade disputes can drag on for years, especially when they involve appeals from initial decisions to the WTO's Appellate Body. Human rights controversies may take even longer to resolve. Such courts may require potential litigants to exhaust local remedies before agreeing to take on a case, a requirement that can slow the pace of dispute settlement substantially. These concerns point to important ways in which the process performance of ICs merits further study.

The meso-level. The contributions to this book suggest that there are two distinct (albeit related) ways to think about the performance of international courts at the meso-level. One centers on the extent to which the judgments of international courts in specific cases play a role in the clarification or development of international law in the relevant area going forward. The other, somewhat more expansive, perspective asks whether the judgments of courts make a significant difference regarding broader trends in major issue domains (e.g., the general status of human rights in a region like Europe or the growth of international trade on a global scale). Both these lines of enquiry involve a lengthening of the causal chain in efforts to evaluate the performance of courts. In fact, there is a continuum regarding the length of the relevant causal chains. There is no question about the responsibility of courts for decisions they make about their own caseloads or about the content of the judgments they render. When it comes to compliance with judgments or the settlement of underlying disputes, factors beyond the control of the courts clearly come into play among the determinants of outcomes. Considering the roles ICs play regarding the development of international law in an issue domain adds another link to the causal chain. Arguments to the effect that courts exert significant influence over the evolution of issue areas more generally lengthen the causal chain still farther. The authors of the chapters included in this book have not developed new methods for making causal inferences regarding these matters, but they do present reasoned arguments regarding the performance of courts at the meso-level.

Arguments regarding the development of international law are sensitive, especially among those schooled in civil law practices in contrast to common law traditions. As a result, many analysts talk about clarifying law, discovering law, or (less often) establishing precedents in order to avoid criticisms regarding what some commentators see as efforts on the part of courts or judges to make law. Nevertheless, as Creamer and Strezhnev observe in this volume, " ... [t]he line between correctly interpreting an existing obligation and introducing a new one is very thin" (53). Their conclusion is that " ... the importance of the DSM's clarification role has only grown in recent years, as multilateral negotiations on new treaties under the WTO's auspices have ground to a halt" (55). Similar remarks are in order regarding the role of the human rights courts. As Shelton observes in Chapter 4, for instance, the actions of the European Court of Human Rights " ... often fill in gaps in the generally-written provisions and allow for the development of new norms, using a variety of sources deemed relevant" (137).

The case of international criminal courts and tribunals (ICTs) is particularly interesting in this regard. Because international humanitarian law and international criminal law are not as highly developed as law in other issue domains, the international criminal tribunals for the former Yugoslavia and Rwanda (ICTY and ICTR) in particular adopted an active role in articulating and interpreting legal principles relating to criminal behavior. As Hayashi argues in Chapter 5, " ... [O]ccasionally, [ICTs] have even acted as if they were not just finders but also creators of law" (178). Understandable as such efforts are in this realm, however, they have provoked opposition in a number of cases. Hayashi concludes that it is difficult to gauge the contributions of international criminal courts in such lawmaking efforts and that the Courts' "outcome performance in this department appears mixed" (178). In the end, he acknowledges the role of ICTs in the development of international law, but he arrives at the cautious conclusion that " ... ICTs have not yet 'supplanted' states in their role as [international humanitarian law and international criminal law] developers" (178).

Our contributors have not shied away from making broader claims regarding the impacts of international courts on the issue domains in which they operate. Creamer and Stezhnev, for instance, open Chapter 2 with the assertion that " ... [I]nternational and regional courts play a growing and critical role in facilitating world trade" (39). Shelton's closing remark in Chapter 4 is that several major reports on the European Court of Human Rights " ... can only lead to the conclusion that the European Court has had a real impact in improving human rights in the member states" (147). Somewhat more cautiously, Behn concludes Chapter 3 stating, " ... investment treaty arbitration does seem to be serving a valuable function" (113). His closing remark is that " ... given the problems that investment treaty arbitration has sought to address in the aggregate ..., ITA does appear to be performing commensurate with its historic purpose" (113). Jo, Radtke, and Simmons, relying on an in-depth study of responses to criminal behavior in Uganda, develop a sustained argument to the effect that the activities of the International Criminal Court have made a significant difference in deterring violations of criminal law (see Chapter 6). As they put it " ... [t]he evidence that the Rome Statute has contributed to strengthening of the laws and institutions to deter international crimes is strong and systematic" (206).

What should we make of these and other related optimistic assertions about the performance of international courts at the meso-level? The contributions to this book do not offer compelling solutions to the methodological challenges involved in teasing out the causal role of international courts from the mix of factors operating in situations featuring complex causality. Even so, we should not dismiss these claims regarding performance at the meso-level lightly. Jo, Radtke, and Simmons provide us with an intriguing natural experiment (see Chapter 6). They formulate a hypothesis about the incidence of criminal behavior before and after intervention on the part of the ICC and then proceed to assemble evidence supporting this hypothesis, at least in the case of civil strife in Uganda. Behn offers a wealth of descriptive statistics regarding the results of a large number of investment treaty arbitrations and presents evidence regarding the rise of the rule of law in this issue area over time (see Chapter 3). Others arrive at their conclusions based on an intensive interrogation of the evidence in their issue domains. Obviously, there is much more work to be done to justify substantive conclusions regarding the performance of international courts at the meso-level. But we feel justified in concluding that the judgments of international courts do make a difference beyond the level of the individual cases that appear on their dockets.

The macro-level. Can we say anything about the performance of courts at the macro-level based on the contributions included in this book? At the outset, it is important to ask what we mean in asking such a question. Our work suggests two distinct lines of thinking in this regard. First, we can enquire whether we are witnessing the growth or spread of something recognizable as the rule of law, or at least legalization, in interactions between and among states. This is a matter of whether international law imposes constraints on the behavior of states or leads to legalized interactions, rather than contributing to a replacement of states as the dominant actors in international society. Second, we can ask whether international courts have become significant players in international society. This is a matter of asking whether courts are contributing to a shift in the composition of international society by empowering nonstate actors or supplanting states in important issue areas.

Our work does not offer any decisive responses to these queries. Accounts of the roles of the regional courts of human rights and of the international criminal courts and tribunals may be read as indicating that we are beginning to see meaningful changes in the nature of interactions between states and other actors in international society (Alter 2014). Yet, as Andresen reminds us, political power remains the ultimate currency of international relations (see Chapter 11). There is no reason to conclude either that states are becoming obsolescent or that the exercise of power on the part of states is no longer crucial in determining outcomes regarding many issues appearing on the international agenda. What we can do in this regard is to point to certain developments that lead to significant changes in the role of law at the international or transnational level and that deserve to be monitored closely by all those who share an interest in the evolving roles of international courts and tribunals. This leads to a shift from efforts to measure the performance of international courts to an analysis of factors that can account for the patterns and trends regarding performance we have documented.

Determinants of Court Performance

We have not sought to construct a theory or model of judicial behavior that would support the development of a comprehensive or integrated explanation of the performance of ICs as described in the preceding section. Rather, we have chosen to supplement the largely descriptive accounts set forth in the chapters in Part I regarding the roles that courts play in four major issue domains with a series of chapters that deal in some depth with a number of otherwise underexplored factors involved in the performance of international courts. In this section, we bring the two components of our work together in an effort to shed light on the forces giving rise to some of the most significant developments we have documented regarding the performance of international judicial mechanisms.

A good place to begin is with a consideration of the overall landscape of international courts and tribunals and, more specifically, with a discussion of variations in the status of these institutions across our four issue domains. Why is there an overarching International Criminal Court and a global dispute settlement mechanism for trade coupled with a collection of regional trade arrangements but no international court dedicated to environmental issues, despite the fact that many analysts of global governance regard the environment as an area in which significant advances have occurred? Why are there regional courts of human rights in some parts of the world but not in others, and why is the ECtHR so much more advanced in terms of performance than its counterparts in the Americas and in Africa? Why has the effort to deal with disputes relating to investment given rise to several thousand distinct international investment agreements with their own mechanisms for settling disputes instead of an integrated dispute settlement mechanism like the one embedded in the global trade regime?

According to Jo, Radtke, and Simmons in this volume, the creation of the ICC appears both to reflect and to intensify the extraordinary rise of a broad-based " . . . culture that refuses to tolerate impunity for violations of international criminal law" (193). As public revulsion in reaction to mass killings in Rwanda and the former Yugoslavia during the 1990s attests, this emerging concern extends to cases involving the killing of innocent civilians in situations featuring civil strife as well as to cases of warfare in the traditional interstate sense. Jo, Radtke, and Simmons note, for example, that " . . . [a] scan of billions of books . . . shows references as a percentage of written words to the ICC exploded in the late 1990s and now surpasses written discussion of the much longer lived ICJ" (199). References to international criminal law have increased in tandem with references to human rights law and now exceed references to international trade and investment law. Whether this heightened public concern about the need to take action at the international level to address the problem of largescale criminal behavior is destined to become even more intense going forward is an open question; the performance of the ICC itself may well play a role in this regard. But it seems clear that recent developments in this realm, including the work of the ICTR and the ICTY as well as the emergence of the ICC, reflect widespread social pressure.

The emergence of human rights courts at the regional level, by contrast, is likely attributable to social, economic, and cultural differences that rule out the prospect of any overarching global consensus regarding normative standards applicable to matters involving human rights. What seems like a violation of human rights in one cultural setting may seem perfectly acceptable in another. Beyond this, it is worth asking why the ECtHR has proven so successful even by comparison with its counterparts in the Americas and in Africa, much less by comparison with developments in other regions in which no such judicial mechanism operates. Speaking of the ECtHR, in Chapter 10 Giorgetti notes that this court " . . . has become enormously active and influential in Europe . . . Its judgments have been largely complied with by member states" (334). Andresen is no doubt correct to point to the role of democratic politics and economic development as factors conducive to the development of a serious concern for human rights (see Chapter 11). Yet, social, economic, and cultural factors do not account fully for the performance of human rights courts. To take a prominent example, these factors cannot explain adequately the contrast between the European case and the case of the United States, a country that has demonstrated little interest in participating in the IACtHR. This suggests that we may need to think about Europe as a special case with regard to the role of international courts concerned with human rights.

The absence of an international environmental court seems puzzling given the striking advances in environmental governance in recent times. Several factors may be at work here. For one thing, more general international courts (including the ICJ) have taken up environmental issues on a fairly regular basis. Even though the jurisdiction of the ICJ is not compulsory, the activities of this court may suffice to address a range of environmental issues so long as they are strictly interstate in nature. The ECtHR, which does respond to applications lodged by individuals, has handed down rulings on a number of issues that touch on environmental concerns. Many multilateral environmental agreements have compliance mechanisms of their own that reduce the need for a judicial mechanism to address problems of compliance. The Montreal Protocol on ozone-depleting substances has been particularly successful in this regard. Then, there is the problem of developing a constitutive foundation for an environmental court. The establishment of an environmental counterpart to the WTO DSM, the International Tribunal on the Law of the Sea, or even the ICC seems unlikely at this stage. Underlying all this may be a relatively low level of public interest, popular demand, and international commitment when it comes to the establishment of an international court to address environmental issues. Some environmental NGOs have espoused the creation of an environmental court vigorously. But the fact remains that even with growing concern regarding the impacts of climate change, it is difficult to rouse public opinion regarding environmental issues in a manner that resembles the emotional intensity of public reactions to widely reported cases of atrocities affecting innocent civilians.

There is a tendency to assume that courts must wait for business to come to them. While this is true in a formalistic legal sense, international courts are not simply passive bodies waiting for others to seek their services. De Silva's account of the socialization strategies of courts is instructive in this context (see Chapter 9). As she observes, ICs can " . . . adopt policies and practices aimed at socializing actors in their legal regimes" (289). The point here is that courts can make use of practices (e.g., diplomacy, training, and outreach) not only to advertise their services but also to encourage both government officials and members of civil society more generally to consider using their services in efforts to settle or resolve disputes of various kinds. ICs can also catalyze future litigation through the judgments they render in specific cases. There is no doubt also that outstanding performance on the part of an international court in dealing with specific cases that come before it can encourage others to avail themselves of the court's services. A court that consistently renders judgments that are well-grounded in the available evidence, show clear respect for the appropriate judicial practices, and are widely seen as fair will earn a reputation for handling disputes in a judicious manner that makes it attractive to potential litigants seeking forums in which to resolve their differences. As a number of our contributors have noted, this can give rise to a widely shared sense of legitimacy regarding the role of an IC that generates business in the form of new cases to address. Of course, as the experience of the ECtHR makes clear, the result can be a surge in applications that challenges the capacity of a court to avoid the development of a debilitating backlog.[1] When it comes to generating business for a court, too much of a good thing can prove almost as challenging as the lack of opportunities to play an influential role stemming from an absence of cases. The ability of an IC to catalyze litigation may contribute to its performance, but only if it has adequate resources to manage its caseload.

Another type of determinant explored in several contributions to this book involves the relationship between process performance and outcome performance. As De Silva explains, socialization processes may contribute to outcome performance (see Chapter 9). This suggests a more general enquiry into the role of judicial practices and procedures as a source of performance. Bringing to bear what they characterize as "practice theory," Dunoff and Pollack in Chapter 8 argue that this way of thinking " . . . offers an innovative and fruitful way to approach international court performance more generally" (262). Without attempting to provide an exhaustive account, they draw attention to the processes a court develops in the areas of factfinding, standards of proof, and procedures for obtaining evidence including the use of experts. The underlying premise of this analysis is that courts that are able to develop rigorous and widely respected practices regarding such matters will produce judgments that not only satisfy demanding criteria with regard to quality but also produce more significant impacts on the behavior of relevant parties. As Dunoff and Pollack state in Chapter 8, " . . . [w]hen these procedural practices are competently performed, they often go unnoticed, yet are essential to satisfactory outcome performance. . . . we believe that to fully understand and evaluate *the performance of international courts*, it is necessary to understand and appraise the *performances of international judges*" (287, emphasis in original).

Compliance, a number of our contributors note, is seldom a straightforward matter. Creamer and Strezhnev in Chapter 2 explain that in the

[1] The surge of applications to the ECtHR is a reflection, in part, of the adoption of Protocol 11 to the European Convention of Human Rights and the expansion of membership of the Council of Europe to include Central and Eastern European states.

WTO DSM disputing parties " . . . can negotiate a settlement or achieve partial – but still acceptable – compliance at any point during [judicial] proceedings" (44). Pro forma acceptance of judgments may not translate into significant behavioral changes, and efforts to achieve full compliance with the judgments of courts may drag on indefinitely. Nevertheless, most international courts have achieved favorable results with regard to compliance. As Giorgetti tells us in Chapter 10, "parties have mostly complied with judgments of the ICJ"; the ECtHR has "long boasted perfect or near perfect compliance"; awards under the International Convention on the Settlement of Investment Disputes " . . . are most often complied with [as] states readily pay up the damages investors are awarded"; and the UN Claims Commission " . . . has been a success in terms of compliance with judgments" (341).

Several factors may come into play in explaining these striking observations regarding compliance. Some states that might well refuse to comply with the rulings of courts are not members of the relevant judicial arrangements. Canada, Cuba, and the United States, for example, are not members of the Inter-American Court of Human Rights. At the same time, states have strong incentives to comply in many cases. Some judgments do not call for costly remedies (see Chapter 10). In terms of the logic of consequences, moreover, states that find themselves on the losing side regarding specific judgments may conclude that the costs of refusing to comply measured in terms of harm to their reputations exceed the costs of compliance. The logic of appropriateness may also play a role in this realm. When the judgments that international courts render are widely regarded as legitimate or fair, for instance, states may feel normative pressure to comply. However we explain the propensity of states to comply with the judgments of international courts, the fact that rates of compliance are generally high raises serious questions about the arguments of those who assert that international law is not "real" law due to the underdeveloped nature of compliance and enforcement mechanisms in international society.

It would be a mistake, however, to equate compliance with a court's judgment in a specific case with the settlement of the underlying issue(s) at stake. This is especially true when we consider the broader consequences of any given judgment. As Creamer and Strezhnev note in Chapter 2 about the realm of trade, " . . . identifying for any given dispute whether it was merely resolved satisfactorily between parties, resulted in implementation of the WTO ruling, or contributed to compliance with WTO rules more generally is not a straightforward endeavor" (44). It is probably fair to argue that the awards rendered by arbitral panels operating under the terms of international investment agreements normally settle the issues at stake. But the legal issues embedded in international judicial proceedings may arise repeatedly in a stream of distinct yet related cases. Repeat violations and the adoption of pilot judgments in the ECtHR suggest that underlying problems are not always resolved by a judgment of the Court. As is true in most judicial systems, interested parties may litigate contentious issues again and again until some collective consensus emerges. Even then, the consensus of one era may be overturned at some later time, reflecting overarching shifts in the character of international society.

When it comes to explaining the role of international courts at the meso-level, complications abound. Partly, this is a matter of unwillingness or reluctance on the part of courts to engage in expansive reasoning about the implications of specific decisions. Judges operating in a civil law tradition are apt to deny that their rulings may prove significant beyond the confines of specific cases. Their job is to apply existing law to the fact patterns of specific cases rather than to set precedents, much less to engage in activities contributing to what may be considered the progressive development of law. Even those schooled in common law traditions may find it expedient to deemphasize the extent to which their rulings contribute to the development of precedents that may prove influential in the reasoning of judges endeavoring to arrive at clear-cut decisions in later cases. The reason for this is straightforward. When ICs are lightly institutionalized and their decisions may trigger a backlash on the part of powerful actors, there is much to be said for exercising judicial economy and avoiding politically controversial pronouncements. One way of putting this point is to argue that judges dealing with international issues will often experience incentives to invoke judicial economy. As Creamer and Strezhnev put it in Chapter 2 when discussing the role of the WTO DSM, in the " . . . absence of a formal mandate for precedent-setting, it may be that what passes for clarification is the maximum that the membership will tolerate" (55). In short, judges are apt to have good reasons to proceed cautiously in exercising the domain of discretion available to them.

Partly, the problem of explaining the significance of the role of international courts at the meso-level is testimony to the impact of complex causality in this realm. Invoking the example of trade, for instance, Faude in Chapter 7 argues that the legalization of international relations " . . . does not necessarily create a judicialized resolution of conflicts"

(235). Faude argues in Chapter 7 that institutional fragmentation resulting from the creation of a multiplicity of regional trade arrangements creates the potential for forum shopping, and the issuance of divergent legal judgments can " ... compromise the ability of ICs to clarify the law ... Thus, the parties will often need to solve their dispute outside either international judicial body" (236). To the extent that this is the case, the forum shopping made possible by institutional fragmentation may lead to " ... a relapse from judicialized to politicized dispute resolution" (236). It is by no means clear that such dynamics lie in store for us during the foreseeable future in the realm of trade regimes. Nevertheless, this line of thinking does suffice to demonstrate the complexity of the systems we are examining. It depicts a dynamic in which the activities of courts themselves could contribute to the politicization of a major issue domain.

Such concerns are no more straightforward in other issue domains. In the case of criminal behavior, as Hayashi notes in Chapter 6, the very success of ICTs in convicting some individuals may trigger pushback on the part of powerful states. As he puts it, the contribution of ICTs " ... to the development of IHL and ICL is difficult to gauge. Forward-looking legal pronouncements are not enough" (178). Whether states ultimately accept the implied modifications of their rights and obligations remains to be seen. This is not to deny the argument of Jo, Radtke, and Simmons (see Chapter 6) that the International Criminal Court has achieved some success in deterring international criminal behavior in specific cases. Yet at this stage, it is probably fair to conclude as Hayashi does in his chapter that states remain the chief makers of IHL and ICL.

A similar story emerges from an examination of the regional human rights courts. The performance of the ECtHR, for example, is often treated as the gold standard when it comes to the development of barriers to the victimization of individuals by European states. But this court is now struggling with a backlog that threatens to produce great delays in its ability to deal with specific cases, even when they are placed into priority categories. What is more, it is hard to tell what the impacts will be of the growing fear of terrorism in Europe and the turmoil associated with the seemingly intractable challenge of finding humane ways to cope with the waves of immigrants arriving from North Africa and the Middle East. The point is not to belittle the impressive achievements of the ECtHR. Rather, these observations remind us that international courts operate in socioeconomic and political settings that are highly dynamic and that changes in these settings can produce dramatic shifts in public concerns likely to have far-reaching consequences for the performance of the courts.

These examples are not intended to downplay the contributions of international courts at the meso-level. Many of the contributors to this book offer compelling evidence that specific courts play influential roles operating as what Andresen in Chapter 11 characterizes as "... intervening variables working within broader driving forces" (367). It is important to take seriously both elements of this observation. The role of intervening variables may prove decisive in determining outcomes in specific situations. On the other hand, there is no denying the role of the broader driving forces. Larger trends in international society will certainly prove critical in determining the meso-level performance of international courts in each of our issue domains going forward.

Future Prospects

Are we witnessing, as some analysts have suggested, a broad-gauged trend toward the legalization of international affairs? Such a trend would have profound consequences for the role of international courts, both highlighting the importance of their contributions to date and calling for the strengthening of these institutions to meet the growing demand for judicial services in a variety of issue domains going forward. We do not see convincing evidence that international society has evolved to the point where the rule of law determines political behavior. In our view, political power, rational calculations, and normative pressures will continue to be leading determinants of outcomes in most issue areas during the foreseeable future, and cultural diversity will continue to spark conflicts that judicial mechanisms are unable to settle. Nevertheless, this does not mean that the roles that international courts and tribunals play are unimportant or that they are destined to lose ground in the future.

So, how should we think about the world order of the future? What opportunities and challenges will the changing character of international society present to those who play important roles in the development and operation of courts in various issue domains? Simple answers to these questions are not possible. Nevertheless, we can identify some major developments that will have important implications for the activities of international courts and that should guide efforts not only to maximize the contributions of existing courts but also to shape the defining features of new judicial mechanisms that come into being during the foreseeable future.

In socioecological terms, we have entered a new era marked by human domination on a global scale, increasingly thought of as the Anthropocene (Davies 2016). Critical features of this era include increased connectedness across both spatial and functional domains, a rise in the centrality of nonlinear processes of change, and the prominence of emergent properties that make surprise a pervasive feature of the global landscape (Young 2017). Even as our knowledge of both biophysical and socioeconomic systems continues to grow, these conditions will highlight the importance of uncertainty, making it difficult to forecast the likely consequences of policy choices at all levels. What is clear is that decision-makers will need to be alert to the impact of seemingly unrelated events and prepared to adjust to changing circumstances in an agile fashion.

At the global level, governance systems will continue to be structured in sectoral terms, with distinct arrangements operating in major issue areas, like trade, human rights, and investment. Within this framework, we may encounter both fragmentation and integration in individual issue areas. It is quite possible, for example, that the era of free trade featuring a continuous process of reducing barriers to trade is coming to an end. The result may be an end to the progression of trade negotiations under the auspices first of the General Agreement on Tariffs and Trade and more recently the WTO or the emergence, as Faude suggests, of a more fragmented system in which a growing number of regional arrangements challenge the dominance of the global system regarding the governance of trade (see Chapter 7). On the other hand, forces of integration may still hold sway in some issue areas. Behn is undoubtedly right to suggest that centrifugal forces may eventuate in the consolidation of the vast array of bilateral investment agreements into a more comprehensive system of rules governing various types of foreign investment (see Chapter 3). What does seem clear is that we are not headed toward some comprehensive system of global governance based either on a reformed United Nations or some wholly new arrangement created to replace the existing United Nations (Biermann 2014).

In this setting, states will remain the most important actors in world affairs. Nevertheless, there are good reasons to believe that we are moving away from a world in which a model based on the premise that we live in a society of states provides a reasonable point of departure. Not only are many states relatively powerless as players in world affairs but also various nonstate actors, including multinational corporations and major nongovernmental organizations, have achieved levels of influence that make it unrealistic to assume that we can deal with an array of major problems purely as matters of intergovernmental relations. At a minimum, this development will heighten the significance of public/private partnerships in areas ranging from the protection of human rights through the stabilization of global economic relations and the protection of the planet's climate system. Under these circumstances, simplistic assumptions about the character of the emerging world order will become a hindrance to our efforts to handle disputes and to devise a system of rules capable of supporting peace and prosperity on a global scale.

What can we say about the role of international courts in a setting of this sort? Many consequences will be specific to courts operating in particular issue domains. But several general implications are discernible. For one thing, we will need to strengthen or create courts that have both the authority and the capacity to deal with issues that do not take the form of classic interstate disputes. To some extent, the courts the contributors to this book have examined reflect significant responses to this challenge. The human rights courts and several regional trade courts, for example, have moved substantially in the direction of recognizing the complaints of individuals regarding the behavior of the states in which they reside. Even more striking is recognition on the part of international criminal tribunals that much of the behavior they seek to control involves problems arising in the context of civil strife. Both the ICTR and the ICTY focused on these internal problems rather than on more conventional crimes associated with international war. The case of Uganda, discussed in some detail in Chapter 6 by Jo, Radtke, and Simmons, exemplifies this development. The problem in this case centered on atrocities committed by members of different ethnic groups located within a single state rather than on illegal killing of innocent civilians by the forces of different states engaged in an international war. Further developments of this sort are likely to be critical in determining the roles that international courts are able to play going forward. For example, many critics of the human rights regime point to its failures to hold nonstate actors to account for wrongs. This is most obvious in the fact that international human rights courts only deal with claims against states. The performance of international human rights courts moving forward may hinge, in part, on their ability to adapt to the rise of nonstate actors in international relations. To put it another way, to achieve and maintain legitimacy, international courts will need to develop practices that grant standing to a variety of nonstate actors, and allow international courts to reach into the domestic affairs of individual states to remedy wrongs suffered from actions of state and nonstate actors.

Another challenge facing international courts going forward will be to find ways to operate on a timescale that matches the pace of world affairs. The problem is easy to describe but difficult to solve. Most courts are deliberative bodies that operate slowly, seeking to arrive at well-informed and considered judgments that reflect a careful weighing of the evidence presented by a range of interested parties. The result is a process that is apt to play out over a period of years. For example, it has taken the ICTY and the ICTR more than two decades to redress the atrocities and hold individuals to account for the war crimes they were established to address. Yet the pace of world affairs has accelerated under the influence of modern means of communication that make it possible to engage in a wide range of transactions on a global basis and in real time. Under the circumstances, international courts will often face the challenge of accelerating their activities to avoid situations in which the course of events makes judgments rendered months or in some cases years later largely irrelevant. With the exception of advisory opinions, international courts play reactive rather than preventative roles. Thus, it will be important for them to find ways to react promptly to changing circumstances to avoid being overtaken by rapid social changes.

While the developments described in this section present international courts with daunting challenges, they also offer striking opportunities to play a significant role in guiding the course of world affairs. In more settled periods, the role of courts is to apply well-defined rules to more or less familiar situations. To be sure, this role is important. But in more turbulent times, featuring nonlinear and often surprising changes, the need for normative leadership becomes more central. Many issues that appear on courts' dockets will take the form of what are often referred to as cases of first impression. Decisions rendered in such cases can serve as important precedents, even in systems that formally reject or deemphasize the role of precedent. The decisions of courts in such situations may follow and largely reflect broad currents of change in social attitudes and values. On the other hand, courts may also play important roles in shaping social attitudes and values or at least in distilling the legal implications of changes in this realm. The international courts we have examined have proceeded cautiously in this realm, sensitive to the dangers arising from charges that they are seeking to move into the realm of judge-made law. Even so, it is hard to avoid the conclusion that the decisions of international courts or even dicta embedded in their